D1452077

ANGLO-INDIA AND THE END OF EMPIRE

UTHER CHARLTON-STEVENS

Anglo-India and the
End of Empire

OXFORD
UNIVERSITY PRESS

OXFORD

UNIVERSITY PRESS

Oxford University Press is a department of the
University of Oxford. It furthers the University's objective
of excellence in research, scholarship, and education
by publishing worldwide.

Oxford   New York

Auckland   Cape Town   Dar es Salaam   Hong Kong   Karachi
Kuala Lumpur   Madrid   Melbourne   Mexico City   Nairobi
New Delhi   Shanghai   Taipei   Toronto

With offices in

Argentina   Austria   Brazil   Chile   Czech Republic   France   Greece
Guatemala   Hungary   Italy   Japan   Poland   Portugal   Singapore
South Korea   Switzerland   Thailand   Turkey   Ukraine   Vietnam

Oxford is a registered trade mark of Oxford University Press
in the UK and certain other countries.

Published in the United States of America by
Oxford University Press
198 Madison Avenue, New York, NY 10016

Library of Congress Cataloging-in-Publication Data is available
Uther Charlton-Stevens.
Anglo-India and the End of Empire.
ISBN: 9780197669983

Printed in the United Kingdom on acid-free paper
by Bell and Bain Ltd, Glasgow

For Virginia and Edward

CONTENTS

ACKNOWLEDGEMENTS

I should first like to thank my publisher and editor Michael Dwyer for his vision in seeking to bring this subject to light and patient determination to see it realised. I am also grateful to Daisy Leitch for overseeing the final stages of the project and Lara Weisweiller-Wu for tracking down the ideal photograph of Merle Oberon for the book's cover; especially appropriate given that family lore insists that my grandmother's brother, George D'Vaz, married one of Merle's cousins. The seeds of this book go back to long nights spent in childhood summer holidays listening to my paternal grandmother's stories of her life in colonial Bangalore, service as an officer in the Women's Auxiliary Corps (India) on the Burma front, and her trip to Kandahar in Afghanistan. An impressive and matriarchal figure, my grandmother, Virginia Mary Stevens (née D'Vaz), arrived in England as a widow with three children and managed to have her Indian teaching qualifications accepted by working for Catholic schools.

She also took immense pride in her late husband's relative, Willoughby Patrick Rosemeyer. As I grew older she repeatedly pressed me to seek out the record of his MBE she was sure must exist at the British Library. Although he had risen to become Engineering Supervisor for the Posts and Telegraphs Department by the time the honour was conferred in 1934, it was nonetheless a rather exceptional achievement for an Anglo-Indian. Not least because, Willoughby was a visibly 'mixed' man of colour, as can be seen from a group photograph in a June 1924 *Geographical Journal* article on the extension of 'The Telegraph to Lhasa'. This write-up of the expedition singles out

ACKNOWLEDGEMENTS

Willoughby as the one who 'was given permission to photograph anything he liked' around the monasteries and the Dalai Lama's Summer Palace, with the exception of 'one image in the Cathedral.' A fair number of photos of Tibet held in the Pitt Rivers Museum in Oxford have accordingly been credited to him, though perhaps fewer than he actually took.

Eager to emphasise this link my grandmother had her husband's headstone inscribed as Edward Aloysious Rosemeyer-Stevens. Having risen to become a Major in the Royal Indian Army Service Corps, Edward died prematurely at the British Military Hospital at Colaba, Bombay in 1948. My father, Stuart Standish Stevens, was then only a year old, having been born at a military station in Ferozepore during the last days of British India. Thus neither he nor I had the chance to get to know my grandfather. Unlike my father, Edward had a European complexion, but (especially considering Willoughby's appearance) Edward's mother, Hilda Stevens (née Rosemeyer), must have been of mixed descent. However they may have identified, the Stevenses too were a domiciled and Catholic family with roots in Madras. Thanks to the efforts of one of my cousins, Elizabeth Stevens, in the British Library, we have Edward's baptism record from St. Francis Xavier's Church, Madras, listing his father, also Edward, as a 'Train Examiner' on the Madras and Southern Mahratta Railway. Thanks should also go to my sister Isabella Charlton-Stevens and my cousin Melanie Hawkins for tracking down and digitising many of our family photos from the Stevens and D'Vaz sides. Many Anglo-Indians and their children have generously furnished me with their own family photographs, including Clayton Roberts, David Brown, Rebecca Calderon, Shirley Gifford-Pritchard, and Susie Longstaff.

Were there space, all of those who I have previously thanked for their help, advice and support from the beginnings of my research into Anglo-Indian history around 2008, through the writing of my doctoral thesis at St Edmund Hall, my fieldwork in India, attendance at the last four triennial International Anglo-Indian Reunions, and the publication of my first academic monograph, could equally be credited here. Of these, there are a few who must be mentioned. Joya Chatterji reassured me as an inexperienced master's student at the LSE that the Constituent Assembly debates alone would contain suf-

ACKNOWLEDGEMENTS

ficient source material for a doctoral dissertation on Anglo-Indians. My principal supervisor, Judith Brown, was endlessly encouraging and has been supportive ever since. Francis Robinson took over upon Judith's retirement, guiding me to further develop the thesis for its first publication as part of the Royal Asiatic Society Books series. Since examining my thesis, Faisal Devji has opened my eyes to the broader implications of my Anglo-Indian research for South Asian History, and provided a bedrock of inspiration for widening its scope.

I was gratified to also receive friendship and encouragement from Barry O'Brien, the President-in-Chief of the All-India Anglo-Indian Association, who is seeking to promote a new generation of Anglo-Indian scholarship. Those whom I have worked most closely with in this effort are Robyn Andrews, Brent Otto, and Merin Simi Raj. My attempts to enlarge upon the hitherto understudied topic of Anglos in Pakistan have benefited greatly from ongoing exchanges with Dorothy McMenamin following my role as international examiner for her doctoral thesis on the subject. My contemporary at Oxford, Yaqoob Bangash, has also recently made a significant foray into this area, supplying me with much-needed material, and leading to many fruitful interactions. It was Otto who furnished the unusual case of the suspected Anglo-Indian Nazi. Morvarid Fernandez's mother Sheila Irani (née Ferguson), formerly Anglo-Indian MLA for Karnataka and Anglo-Indian MP in the Lok Sabha, amassed a treasure trove of press clippings which they happily shared with me.

Kanith Galawaththe deployed his IT expertise to assist me with the ever-expanding array of South Asian digital resources, and during the pandemic, a young legal student, Vishwajeet Deshmukh, most kindly and opportunely offered to research Anglo-Indian legal cases at the High Court of Bombay for me. He has since published his own work on Anglo-Indians, especially their legal and constitutional status and experience of Partition. My lasting gratitude also goes to Abraham Akhter Murad, Alexander Morrison, Anna Elkina, Blair Williams, Brian Hamnett, Elena Russkova, Enrico Emanuele Prodi, Jamal Cassim, Jay Sexton, Jeevan Deol, Keith Butler, Mikhail Anipkin, Newal Osman, Pavel Timachev, Ritesh Kumar Jaiswal, Sally Hadden, Travis Seifman, Victoria Batmanova, and Withbert Payne for mentorship, motivation, and stimulating conversations across a broader array

ACKNOWLEDGEMENTS

of topics over the years. It is obligatory to state at this point, however, that, naturally, I alone am responsible for any errors which may have crept into the pages that follow.

LIST OF ILLUSTRATIONS

Illustration 1: Anglo-Indian women of the Friis Browne Family c. 1920s, showing characteristically differing complexions among sisters, courtesy of Rebecca Calderon.

Illustration 2: First Communion for Mary Philomena Keating (seated fourth from the left in the longest dress, b. 20 November 1936) and other children presumed to be Anglo-Indian at the Sacred Heart Convent in Dalhousie, courtesy of her granddaughter Susie Longstaff.

Illustration 3: Map of the 88 branches of the Anglo-Indian & Domiciled European Association in 1929, still including four affiliated branches in Burma (*AIR*, August 1929, back cover).

Illustration 4: Ethnically caricatured communal cartoon making the case for temporary safeguards for Anglo-Indians and Domiciled Europeans during the Simon Commission (*AIR*, Christmas 1928, p. 17).

Illustration 5: Sir Henry Gidney (left) meeting Sir Stafford Cripps in 1942 (LIFE Magazine, Mansell Collection, © Time Inc.).

Illustration 6: Close-up of Sir John Pratt, Consul-General, Shanghai, attending the Boy Scouts Parade at the British Consulate, Shanghai, on Armistice Day, Tuesday 11 November 1924, courtesy of Special Collections, University of Bristol Library, DM2833 (www.hpcbristol.net).

Illustration 7: Wide-shot version of Sir John Pratt (foreground left), alongside (left to right) an unidentified Royal Navy commander, Sir Skinner Turner (1868–1935), Chief Judge of the British Supreme

LIST OF ILLUSTRATIONS

LIST OF COMMON ABBREVIATIONS

AF(I)	Auxiliary Force (India)
AIF	Anglo-Indian Force (not to be confused with the Australian Imperial Force of the same acronym)
AIR	The Anglo-Indian Review, briefly published as The Anglo-Indian Review and Railway Union Journal, and later simply The Review
BOR(s)	British Other Ranks
IAF	Indian Air Force
ICS	Indian Civil Service
IMS	Indian Medical Service
ISMD/IMD	Indian Subordinate Medical Department/Indian Medical Department
INA	Indian National Army
PAF	Pakistani Air Force
QA(s)	Queen Alexandra nurses
RAF	Royal Air Force
WAC(I)	Women's Auxiliary Corps (India)

INTRODUCTION

In October 2020 British television's Channel 5 announced that it was casting a black actor, Jodie Turner-Smith, in the role of Anne Boleyn, the beguiling and ill-fated second wife of Henry VIII. The first instalment of the three-part miniseries premiered in the spring of the following year. Rooted in an 'identity-conscious' rather than colour-blind approach to casting, the decision prompted widespread criticism for its deliberate ahistoricity. However, as the *Smithsonian Magazine* was quick to highlight, Turner-Smith was not the first 'woman of color' to portray 'the white Tudor queen'.[1] That distinction goes to Estelle Merle O'Brien Thompson (1911–79), better known as Merle Oberon, for her brief yet emotive breakout role in *The Private Life of Henry VIII* (1933), in which she appears in the publicity still on the cover of this book. In pursuit of a film career, she was willing to lather herself in 'highly toxic heavy makeup ... designed to whiten her face'.[2] Yet even with the heightened colour contrast of the black-and-white medium of most of her early films, Oberon's complexion was discernibly mixed, and biographers as late as 1983 described her 'mysterious slanting eyes'.[3] When *Queenie* (1985), a thinly fictionalised account of her life, penned by her nephew-in-law Michael Korda, was adapted for television by the American Broadcasting Company in 1987, the Italian-American Mia Sara was cast to depict Oberon's passing as white. However, Sara was much too fair for the role. The transatlantic film industry of the 1930s doubtless knew better but required a degree of plausible deniability.

1

In the United States, the 'Big Five' film studios (MGM, Paramount, Warner Brothers, Fox and RKO) had routinised the process of creating fake biographies with wildly varying relationships to the truth 'for every actor who was under contract', their publicity departments ensuring that they followed 'the unwritten rule that no star could have a Jewish name'.[4] At London Films, Oberon similarly collaborated in the construction of a new identity and origin story that would conceal her 'Eurasian' or 'mixed-race' Anglo-Indian background and humble Bombay beginnings from the public. This pretence enabled her to become 'one of the biggest movie stars of the 1930s and 1940s'[5] and the first Asian nominated for an Academy Award—for Best Actress in *The Dark Angel* (1935). As the Spanish 'Antonita, a dancer of passionate temperament' in *The Private Life of Don Juan* (1934), she kissed the titular character played by Douglas Fairbanks;[6] in *The Scarlet Pimpernel* she starred as the French-born English high-society Lady Blakeney alongside Leslie Howard—both roles that might have seemed more congruent with her appearance. Yet as Leslie Steele in *The Divorce of Lady X* (1938), co-starring with Laurence Olivier in early three-strip 'Technicolor', her character is the genteel daughter of an English judge. Central to the romantic comedy's plot, however, is a tantalising misrepresentation of who she really is.

Oberon's near contemporary Anna May Wong (1905–61) was less fortunate. Despite Wong's pioneering position as 'one of the most glamorous and memorable female movie stars of color to ever grace the silver screen ... [and] the first Asian-American actress to achieve international stardom',[7] she was typecast in villainous roles to the point of 'mental indigestion'.[8] The crux was that, without the possibility of even a thinly veiled attempt at passing, a non-white actor could not be seen engaging in an explicitly physical romance with a white counterpart. With many American states upholding anti-miscegenation laws until the 1967 Supreme Court ruling in *Loving v. Virginia*,[9] Hollywood had always had a fraught relationship with on-screen depictions of interracial romance. The British Board of Film Censors largely followed suit, issuing 'a mandate forbidding [the English actor] John Longden to kiss ... Wong in the new talkie, *The Road to Dishonour* [1930]. He may sit at her feet; sing her a love song; kiss her hand; clasp her in his arms; but on no account must he kiss her lips.'[10] This despite the fact that the Englishman was playing 'a Russian officer who is madly in love with a Chinese girl'.[11] The Australian *Northern Territory Times* highlighted the 'farcical' nature of the decision to forbid interracial 'love kissing', when it would have been allowed if Wong's part had been 'played by a white girl dressed as a Chinese' girl.[12] Wong herself told the *Sydney Morning Herald*:

> I can't for the life of me understand why a white man couldn't fall in love with me on the screen ... What is the difference between a white girl playing an Oriental and a real Oriental, like myself, playing them? The only difference I can see is that in most cases I would at least look the part ... [Without] this terrible censorship barrier, a new field would open for me ...[13]

Such restrictions went both ways, as demonstrated by a 1935 'Paramount film, *Shanghai*, in which the son of a Russian aristocrat and a Manchu princess renounced happiness with an American girl, because even in that cosmopolitan town 'anything goes but *that*'.'[14] Wong was not mixed, but perhaps owing to her own culturally cosmopolitan experience and liminality, she so 'closely identified with' the soulful lyricism and 'theme of placelessness' of Noël Coward's 1929 song 'Half-Caste Woman' that she 'always sang' the song alongside her standard repertoire of Chinese folksongs when she moved on to the matinee circuit.[15] Notably, Wong opted for the more personalised use of the first person, as in *Cochran's 1931 Revue* version. This creed was supposedly to live for the moment. Offensive as was the song's description of a 'half-caste woman' with 'slanting eyes',[16] it conveyed a hauntingly lyrical poignancy by embodying the stereotypical 'tragic Eurasian', lost between cultures and races, lacking a clear sense of home and identity, and consumed by an unanswerable longing to belong and to find their place in the world.

In North America similar tropes had developed around the 'tragic mulatto', 'mulatta', 'octoroon', and 'mestizo' (depending on gender, degree of admixture, and type of non-white ancestry). The supposed hypersexual availability of women of colour to white men was further amplified in stereotypes of mixed-race women. By contrast, 'oriental' women were often painted as coyly enigmatic, their supposed sensuality and suppressed hypersexual nature only being unleashed reluctantly through masculine conquest. Coward's verses blend these themes, his

3

tragic Eurasian falling easy prey to romantic but ultimately unavailable sailors.[17] Supplying each other's 'need' was assumed to be a temporary exchange, with the loss of 'dreams' to follow 'in its wake'.[18] Even observers with more direct experience, such as Malcolm Muggeridge, assistant editor at the Calcutta *Statesman*, were apt to perceive India's Eurasians—the Anglo-Indians—through the lens of tragedy. Visiting 'a dreary place called the Casanova Bar ... full of Anglo-Indians and lower grade Europeans' towards the end of 1934, Muggeridge and 'Shahid' mused on their 'favourite subject, the strange deadness' or 'unhappiness ... that the British connection with India ... engendered', projecting this onto the Anglo-Indians present, whom Muggeridge called 'quite the unhappiest people in the world. Ghosts haunting the British Raj.'[19] To Oberon's biographers, Charles Higham and Roy Moseley, Anglo-Indians were

> an amusing, delightful, inventive, energetic, religious and forward-looking group ... [who] *never really belonged anywhere*; despite their clinging to British ways they could never escape the misery of being looked down upon, not only by the British ... but by the Indians whose blood ran in their veins and whose rich heritage they could not in their deepest hearts accept. The anguish of the Anglo-Indian was heightened in Merle, not only because of her extreme sensitivity, concealed behind a mask of composure and elegance, but because of her need to have a career. Her early compulsion towards success, money and fame later evolved into a Hinduist rejection of the importance of material possessions, tempered by her powerful Anglo-Indian's need to be accepted at the top of white society.[20]

Despite earnestly sympathetic attempts to dispel 'the many lies that grew up about her',[21] her biographers' portrait remained mired in the problematic language and ideas still prevalent when it was written. Nonetheless, they correctly diagnosed the Anglo-Indian dilemma towards the end of empire—'caught in the middle between Indian nationalism and British imperialism' and facing variable degrees of prejudice from both sides that tended to cast their mixed 'blood' as a source of 'shame'.[22] Oberon was born in late-colonial Bombay in the exact year in which the official designation of the mixed in the Indian census was changed from 'Eurasian' to 'Anglo-Indian'—a term which had hitherto referred to the colonial British population and their institutions. Although Oberon fits the constitutional definition of this community and was certainly brought up within it, her South Asian ancestry was actually from Ceylon (now Sri Lanka). As a result of divergent histories and separate governance, the Sri Lankan mixed-race community, known as Burghers, were generally far less intertwined with Anglo-Indians than the mixed peoples of Burma (now Myanmar). More unusually, Oberon was also 'part-Maori'.[23]

In *Wedding Rehearsal* (1932), her first credited role, Oberon played Miss Hutchinson, the secretary and companion of an ageing aristocratic lady. This marchioness is busy preparing a list of suitable wives for her perpetual bachelor grandson. The (only relatively) young marquis engages in 'Jeeves and Wooster'-type antics to ensure that each suggested bride is quickly affianced to someone else. After finally succumbing to his grandmother's pressure, he selects the humble Hutchinson, whose suitability in class terms is questionable. Perhaps the infatuation of the director of London Films, Alexander Korda, with Oberon began here, for he next elevated her to the role of the young Tudor Queen, following which she was cast in a string of self-assuredly aristocratic roles, whether by birth or marriage. Korda 'was a striking combination of supersalesman and colossal dreamer, and a producer and director of extraordinary gifts, with the romantic tale-spinning ability of Scheherazade'.[24] Beginning with silent films in Austria and Germany before 'ill-fated' attempts to make it in Hollywood and France, Korda finally achieved his greatest success in Britain, flattering the monarchy, schmoozing with aristocrats, and establishing himself as the titan of British wartime propaganda film-making.[25] Oberon herself had become 'very well' acquainted with the future king Edward VIII and Wallis Simpson, the twice-divorced American for whom he abdicated his throne in 1937.[26] Two years later Oberon agreed to become Korda's second wife, so that, with his knighthood in 1942, she was to become Lady Korda. The marriage did not ultimately survive, however, and he was to be but the first of her four husbands. Nonetheless the pair shared much in common; having been born 'in poverty ... [they were both] irresistibly attracted to glamour, to the opulent, extravagant, and exotic'.[27]

Like the immigrant Jewish founders of major American studios—the Mayers, Warners and Goldwyns—Korda 'yearned for assimilation' in this wider anglophone world,[28] and might be expected to have understood the personal sacrifices this could entail better than most. In *Whisper of the Moon Moth* (2017), a fictionalised rendition of Oberon's life, Lindsay Ashford explored how Korda's flight from antisemitic persecution in the Hungarian White Terror of 1919–21 may have given him a unique insight into Oberon's own transformation. Confiding that he 'was lucky' to escape alive, the fictional Korda explains how he has since changed his name and tried to make himself 'less Jewish'.[29] He then enjoins Estelle 'to stop being Estelle Thompson', to 'do whatever it takes to blend in' with this 'tough industry', and 'from this moment on' become 'Merle'.[30]

> 'I will instruct everyone on set to call you Miss Oberon. And you must tell anyone you know outside of London Films to call you by your new name. It's the only way.'
>
> 'What—even my mother?'
>
> '*Especially* your mother. And if anyone else comes to the house, she must remember to call you Miss Oberon.'[31]

Although this dialogue sounds somewhat contrived, it makes for effective story-telling and brings to the fore a tragic point. To commit herself to the fiction that she was wholly European, Oberon felt compelled to present Charlotte Constance Selby, the woman she knew as her mother, to visitors as some kind of servant.

> Charlotte was introduced to some people as *ayah*, the Indian term for a chaperone for young, well-brought-up white women, or as her 'mammy', or her 'nanny', or even as her maid. Charlotte would dress up in a frilly cap and apron and serve tea. Only a very few met Charlotte in her proper role as her mother. Diana Napier says, 'One afternoon, I was having tea with Merle at her flat near Baker Street when for the first time I saw this little, plump Indian woman come into the room dressed in a sari. She stood nervously, hesitantly, as though waiting for orders. Merle was extremely embarrassed. She spoke to her mother in Hindustani. The lady ... was very, very quiet.'[32]

Understandably Charlotte eventually tired of playing this part, and once Oberon's position appeared more secure, she stopped pretending, and spoke of returning home to Bombay. Oberon 'always paid for everything, making sure that her mother was comfortable and free of all responsibilities at all times', often leaving her in the care of sympathetic English friends, the Bensons, 'who surrounded her with love and kindness' while Oberon was away filming.[33] As Charlotte's health began to worsen, Oberon employed a nurse to look after her. After she sadly passed away at the premature age of fifty-four, 'several cemeteries rejected Charlotte on the grounds that she was Indian', and Oberon arranged for a small private funeral with only 'three or four persons ... present' at 'an unmarked grave ... near the Benson home at Shawford Park'.[34] As Oberon's biographers noted:

> Twelve years later, in 1949, Merle, in an intense feeling of nostalgia, had Charlotte's portrait painted from a photograph. The artist lightened ... [her very dark] skin, perhaps in order to sustain the illusion that Merle was not of part-Indian origin ... In other respects, the likeness is perfect; the face is haunting, moving and intriguing. The picture hung in Merle's homes in Los Angeles ... till the end of her life.[35]

It was not until Marée Delofski's documentary *The Trouble with Merle* (2002) that another family secret was unearthed—that Charlotte, the woman who had raised her and whom Oberon knew as her mother, was actually her biological grandmother.[36] It is uncertain how much of the story behind that buried history she herself knew at the time—Charlotte may have taken the burden of this solely upon herself. In her novel Ashford imagines Charlotte as having passed on the revelation as a deathbed confession.[37] In any event, Charlotte's own suppression of truth was ultimately as important as the dramatic steps Oberon herself took to shed her past and reshape her identity. 'Korda's sharp-witted publicist' supplied the details, creating 'an elaborate fantasy version of Merle's life ... [a] fairy tale [which] would disguise her Anglo-Indian origins ... [and] made her memorize certain "facts", which she would have to regurgitate in interviews for the rest of her life'.[38] Crafting a stage name was standard practice, but all the more important for those whose names could signal mixed, non-white or Jewish backgrounds. Though it is a stretch to suggest that converting her Irish name O'Brien into Shakespeare's Oberon was a significant anglicisation, it did marginally assist in her passing as white, by obscuring the name which appeared on her baptism certificate. The discovery of any of her Indian documentation would have given the lie to the invented backstory that she had been born in Tasmania, Australia. Already familiar as the birthplace of Errol Flynn, Tasmania was sufficiently far away from London and Hollywood to play the imaginative role of a never-never land, beyond most people's experience. Given the time requirements of long-distance travel by sea and the difficulties of communication at the time, it would also have been relatively inaccessible to journalistic fact-checkers.

However, the story did come back to haunt Oberon. On a visit to Australia in 1965 she recounted to reporters 'having been born in Hobart, Tasmania's capital, by an accident of geography; her parents, she said, happened to have been passing through that area by ship on a long Pacific voyage'.[39] This 'story did not jibe with previous accounts she had given over the years, of being born to a distinguished army man connected to the Tasmanian government who had died in a hunting accident, or from pneumonia, before she was born'.[40] After being invited 'to appear at a civic reception' by the lord mayor of Hobart, 'she became tense and uneasy. In the next hours, as more pressure was put upon her to visit her alleged birthplace, she became increasingly ill and ... on the second day' decided suddenly and prematurely to board a return flight.[41] Multiple contradictory narratives were explored in Delofski's documentary, revealing how Oberon's manufactured connection with the island persists in 'Tasmania's folklore ... kept alive through memories passed down the generations'.[42] It was widely claimed 'that Merle was the scion of a mining clan named the Chintocks, who were quarter-caste Chinese', as her 1983 biographers phrased it.[43] A woman from the family had 'for a lifetime sincerely believed that Merle was her long-lost aunt, the illegitimate child of a Chintock girl and a hotel keeper'.[44] Given the truth effects of stories we tell about ourselves and the prevalence of false collective memories of things and events that never actually took place, it is perhaps unsurprising therefore that there are 'Tasmanians today who still swear she's one of them'.[45]

The horizons of the vast majority of those born into her mixed-race Anglo-Indian community were far more limited. However, Oberon's transgression of the dividing lines of colour, race and class which the colonial British society in India sought to erect and maintain were by no means unique. Indeed, racial passing, crossing boundaries, and reformulations of identity—usually as a means to elevate the individual or the collective—are persistent themes of the history presented here. They were in constant tension with this book's predominant narrative—the efforts of the political and intellectual leadership of the mixed-race group to foster internal group solidarity and to forge their claimed constituents into a self-consciously confident and politically unified whole. For most of the late-colonial period—our primary focus—the majority of Anglo-Indians were wedded to a pro-British orientation, often extending to identification of Anglo-Indianness with Britishness. This was the one point upon which the imperialist propagandist Beverley Nichols and his Indian nationalist critic, a 'well-known Bombay journalist' named Narayan Gopal Jog,[46] could agree. In his *Verdict on India* (1944), Nichols accused Anglo-Indians of harbouring a 'deep-rooted inferiority complex', being 'fanatically insistent upon their superiority to their Indian cousins', and losing 'no opportunity of setting themselves apart' by 'carry[ing] their protestations of "loyalty" to a ludicrous extreme; they are *plus royaliste que le roi*' (more royalist than the king).[47] Jog's lengthy riposte, *Judge or Judas?* (1945), similarly declared:

The Anglo-Indian's first loyalty is to the British. To them he looks for patronage, for protection. He serves them faithfully—whenever the opportunity is given him to serve! The two great wars have thus naturally proved the golden era of Anglo-India, nearly eighty per cent. of its manhood being employed … While the young men have distinguished themselves on the front, the young and even elderly ladies have joined the Auxiliary Services in their thousands. The W.A.C.(I) [Women's Auxiliary Corps (India)] is mostly a W.A.C.(A.I.). Nevertheless Anglo-Indian leaders have not been misled by the present wave of illusory and short-lived prosperity. They yet bitterly remember the aftermath of the last war and realize too well that they can no longer rely upon the British rulers for safeguarding their interests. Long before they would be compelled to quit India politically … [the British] have quitted Anglo-India morally, and the earlier the Anglo-Indian learns to drop the Anglo and to carry himself as an Indian, the better it will be for his future welfare. Far-sighted leaders like the late Sir Henry Gidney and Mr. Frank Anthony … have been persistently trying to canalize the community into the broad stream of Indian national life …[48]

Attempting to personalise his narrative, Nichols claimed to have known

> an Anglo-Indian nurse ... a nice girl, patient, efficient, and pretty in her dusky way. There could not be a moment's doubt about her origin, which betrayed itself in her hair, her eyes, the palms of her hands. But to hear her talk you would think that she could trace her pedigree back to the Plantagenets. 'These Indians!' she would cry, in contempt, when the bearer brought the wrong medicine or the sweeper was lazy ... 'Really—these *Indians!* One can do *nothing* with such people!' Her father was British, her mother Indian. She used to show me snapshots of herself with her father. The mother was hardly ever in the pictures; only once did I catch a glimpse of her, a dark little figure hovering in the background. The page of the album was turned quickly when that snapshot came into view.[49]

Jog hit back at Nichols's 'astonishing proposition that in nine cases out of ten, the latter's father is British and the mother Indian. This may have been perhaps true of the year 1744, but it was an atrocious lie in 1944.'[50] Relatively few individuals in the late-colonial period were of first-generation mixed-race parentage. The vast majority of Anglo-Indians were of multigenerational mixed descent, arising from a couple of hundred years of the European mercantile and imperial presence in South Asia. Most Anglo-Indians were the product of marriages between already mixed Anglo-Indian parents, with occasional pairings between British private soldiers and Anglo-Indian women. Nonetheless, many Britons and Indians all too often made such simplistic and erroneous generalisations based on their perception of the varying complexions among the mixed. Even Mohandas ('Mahatma') Gandhi claimed to have seen 'a fat man—an Anglo-Indian—[who] ... could not bear the idea that his mother was an Indian woman'.[51]

A better understanding could hardly be expected from Hollywood. When MGM adapted John Masters's 'book of the month best-seller' novel *Bhowani Junction* (1954) for the cinema in 1956,[52] the film's trailer described its main character, 'the half-caste girl Victoria Jones', as 'the most alluring woman'.[53] The pejorative term 'half-caste' was still so widespread that few among the cinema-going American public would even have perceived its offensiveness. Functionally, however, it would have introduced them to the erroneous stereotype that Anglo-Indians were half-Indian. Visually linking the sex appeal of Ava Gardner to the exoticism that India represented to the unfamiliar, the trailer's opening shot featured her character taking a shower, before cutting to the spectacle of Indians bathing in a river. The story was boiled down to how Victoria, 'loved for [her] beauty, rejected for her colour', was caught 'in the turbulence of two conflicting worlds'.[54] The film itself was more complex and contained significant divergences from the book upon which it was based—such creative choices being closely intertwined with the issue of casting.

The story's protagonist is an Anglo-Indian subaltern in the WAC(I) in the years between the Second World War and Indian independence in 1947. In addition to the WAC(I), many Anglo-Indian women had been serving as nurses, either in India or overseas, particularly in North Africa and the Middle East. Even for those not in uniform the war had created many new opportunities for romance with the large numbers of Allied servicemen fresh from Britain, the Commonwealth and the US, giving a significant number hopes of marriage and emigration after the war. Victoria's father, with the typical Anglo-Indian background of a 'very senior driver' on the railway station's 'Number One Roster', earnestly hopes his daughter will follow this path.[55] He is exceedingly proud to host the British Colonel Savage in his home, which is described as having tasteful second-hand mahogany furniture, chairs draped in white embroidery, a black bear fur rug, and portraits of 'the King Emperor, the Queen Empress, and old Sergeant Duck', the family's first British ancestor to come out to India.[56]

Savage is initially somewhat amused with and condescending towards the Joneses, but his social and racial prejudices eventually break down sufficiently for him to declare his intention to marry her. Victoria's father emotionally tries to persuade her to accept his proposal, 'go Home and never see us or think of us again', and 'say you are partly Spanish', as Jimmy D'Souza's daughter did.[57] Her 'Pater' is described as 'three-quarters English' and married to a 'one-quarter' wife; he clings to the idea of Britain as 'home', and speaks with poignant naivety about the possibility of her living in a 'cantonment' in Britain.[58] In 1940 B. Leadon, president of the Delhi branch of the All-India Anglo-Indian Association, and a prominent radio journalist, coincidentally described just such 'a typical Anglo-Indian' as 'the patriotic Mr. Jones'.[59] The desire to downplay the extent to which many colonial-era Anglo-Indians looked upon

Britain as 'home' and as a source of their identity is perhaps owing to the sting of British jibes on the subject. Alison Blunt cites the following anecdote:

> One Eurasian tells how, travelling to England by sea, he became excessively weary ... and turning to the Ship's Mate ... asked: 'How long do you think, Sir, it will be before we get home?' 'Get HOME! Mr Middlerace, get HOME?' the mate returned for an answer, strongly emphasising the word 'home'; 'I reckon we should make land by about midday tomorrow.' When the next day the ship arrived at the island of St Helena, Mr Middlerace's trunks were ready packed, and on being informed that the ship had arrived at Portsmouth he promptly disembarked—to the intense amusement of the English passengers ... and to his own surprise that an English port should employ so many dark-skinned porters on the quay![60]

Blunt observes that 'Anglo-Indian ideas of Britain as home' evoked such 'snide' and 'cruel' mockery, because British 'racialized snobbery' was built upon 'deeper anxieties and prejudices about discrimination ... [and] attempts to maintain clear boundaries between themselves and Anglo-Indians'.[61] Mr. Jones fantasises that, being an officer and a gentleman, Savage will do right by his daughter. In both book and film, Victoria is able to openly court the British officer Savage, and he is ultimately willing to marry her knowing that she is an Anglo-Indian. If this is not wholly implausible, it is at least rather exceptional. More realistically it was ordinary British soldiers, not officers, who would court and occasionally marry Anglo-Indian women. However, 'Neville Blair, the last commanding officer of the 2nd Black Watch',[62] described how even rank-and-file soldiers were pressured against such marriages:

> When the time came for the battalion to leave ... a number ... asked permission to marry Eurasian girls ... There was no point, though, in simply trying to dissuade them ... [from] bring[ing] the girls home to a country they didn't know ... In the event WVS [the Women's Voluntary Service] stepped in to remind the girls about the problems of living in post-war Britain with its rationing and so on. They told them about the culture shock of exchanging India for a two-roomed tenement flat in Glasgow.[63]

Whether it was in fact the women themselves or their fiancés who had been persuaded by the intervention of British women, 'when the battalion left Karachi in February 1948 it took home with it one Indian wife who had been married to a sergeant for twenty years ... [but] none of the relationships' with the Anglo-Indian women 'survived'.[64] This is not to say that such pressure was always effective. One British consular official complained of 'numbers of married women and girls of very dark Anglo-Indian or in some cases Goanese-Indian extraction, who have a daughter or sister who managed to marry some British soldier in Rangoon' and were seeking assisted passages to join their newly-wed relations in the UK even though the couple were 'obviously living in a poor quarter in some big town, or even ... [in] Married Quarters in Army barracks, where they can clearly not guarantee accommodation' for a mother or sister.[65] Nonetheless, many individuals managed to make that journey and followed their relatives to Britain or Australia. One Anglo-Indian nurse who married a Briton and later migrated to the UK reflected the attitudes of a sizeable proportion of her generation:

> Well of course, naturally we thought the British Raj was grand because, we considered we were British, we were brought up in the British way of life, we spoke English from our birth ... Britain was something, it was ou[r] ... home, we talked about it ... as home, though we'd never seen it, it was home to us. The British flag ... meant something to us. I can remember ... a whole group of Ch[ockras] ... little boys ... and one said to the other: Do you see that flag up there? You could just see the Fort in the distance with ... the Union Jack flying ... and this little fellow said: Do you know there are a lot of people who are je[alous and] ... want to see that flag come down ... But that flag will never come down and ... in my foolishness ... I agreed with them, I thought that flag would never come down. None of us ... [in] the anglo[-]indian community ... knew that after ... World War two the British Raj was going to ... come to an end. We were proud of being British, when we heard God Save the King my father ... even away in the distance, in our own home, he stood up and we had to stand with him. This is what we thought of the British Raj and it came as a shock to us when it ended ... It was the end of our world, because now we did not know where we were ... Were we Indians or were we British or what?[66]

It is easy to dismiss the idea of an identity crisis among Anglo-Indians towards the end of empire as a racialised projection of pathology, serving to cast their situational difficulties as innate defects of character. Yet Anglo-Indians faced similar challenges to those of other minorities in various settings, especially in the demand that they should conform to one or other vision of their place in the world, who they should be, and how they 'ought' to behave. However, they too were a product of their own path-dependent history, and no more likely to jettison their existing identities, culture and attitudes than any other group. For the most part the Anglo-India of the late-colonial period was one of persisting empire loyalism. It was a site that existed within the same time and physical space as the rest of India, but could only subsist within its own mental space, an imaginative location in which many Anglo-Indians felt themselves to be 'more British than the British'.[67] *Bhowani Junction* depicts Anglo-Indians as retreating behind the comfortingly familiar walls of their railway colonies and institutes while, outside, the imperial edifice of British India that has sustained their Anglo-India comes crashing down around them. In both book and film, Victoria personifies the Anglo-Indian dilemma of identity through being called upon to choose between Britain, nationalist India and the imperilled and shrinking 'world of Anglo-India',[68] each embodied in her three potential suitors.

Apart from Savage there is the more conventional choice of an Anglo-Indian 'boy next door' named Patrick Taylor whom she had known since childhood. A railwayman like her father, Patrick is as familiar to her as he is frustrating in his inability to jettison his racial, colour and cultural prejudices and adapt to the prospect of Indian independence. In the book Victoria attempts to shake Patrick and her sister out of their complacency in a heated argument in which she warns them that the British are leaving 'India very soon', and the Indian National Congress Party is destined to take power.[69] Internally conflicted, Patrick furiously declares his intention to 'go Home' with the British, to which Victoria replies with the scream, 'Home? Where is your home, man? England? Then you fell into the Black Sea on your way out?'[70] As she storms off, Patrick is left with an internal monologue which rather simplistically caricatures the supposed identity crisis of the Anglo-Indians, who cannot become English because they are 'half Indian' and cannot become Indian, because they are 'half

English. We could only stay where we were and be what we were.'[71] Giving expression to an opposite impulse, Victoria considers whether by donning a sari and marrying a Sikh railwayman named Ranjit Kasel she can become straightforwardly Indian and resolve the issue of her own identity through a radical reconstruction of self; but it is soon made clear to her that such a choice, within the context of Anglo-Indian attitudes of the day, would entail not only the bitter disappointment of her father, but also near-complete ostracism from within her own group. She also discovers that Ranjit expects her to convert to Sikhism and adopt a new first name, as the name of the late Queen-Empress is a particularly unsuitable name for an Indian, both of which prove a bridge too far.

In the film the possibility of marrying her Anglo-Indian boyfriend Patrick is removed when he dies a redemptively heroic death preventing an Indian terrorist from assassinating Gandhi by derailing the train in which he is travelling. This paves the way for a predictable romantic Hollywood ending, in which Victoria finally accedes to Savage's proposal after he declares his intention to quit the army and settle down in India permanently.[72] This altered ending helps to explain, beyond the usual whitewashing tendencies of 1950s Hollywood, why it was essential for Victoria to be played by a woman who appears to be white, such as Ava Gardner. An obviously interracial marriage at the end between people of different colour would have been unacceptable in a country where laws against miscegenation were still widespread. Indeed, even though Gardner later revealed in the 1980s that she had a 'black sister', thus effectively outing herself as being a 'pass white' individual from a mixed background, her skin was paler than her co-star Stewart Granger's outdoorsy action-man tan. *Bhowani Junction*'s film ending fulfilled the box office requirement that the white hero always 'gets the girl' in the end. However, the original story had a completely different resolution.

In the novel Savage tells Victoria that he intends to marry her, but she ultimately rejects him in favour of Patrick. This could be read in one of two ways depending on the positionality of the author. The Anglo-Indian leader at the time of independence, Frank Anthony, asserted that like 'a large number of actors and actresses who migrated to and achieved fame in America and Britain', this 'fairly well-known author of the rather lurid novel, "Bhowani Junction", who described himself as second or third generation European domiciled in India, was, in fact, Anglo-Indian'.[73] If we set aside the novel's derogatory stereotypes of hypersexual Anglo-Indian womanhood, this would certainly account for Masters's unusual level of knowledge of, familiarity with and interest in the Anglo-Indian community. Yet even if Anthony's allegation were true, this might not have had much to do with Masters's upbringing and self-perception. If Masters is regarded as having had the identity and lived experience of a colonial Briton, then Victoria's decision could be read as the 'correct' one, sticking to her own kind, and upholding the boundary between the mixed and the unmixed; but if Masters were self-conscious of his supposed Anglo-Indian roots, then it would also be in keeping with the typical patriarchal proprietorial resentment of many Anglo-Indian men to intermarriages between 'their' women and British men. Films like *Mississippi Masala* (1991) involving a romance between a diasporic South Asian woman and an African American man similarly explore the prevalence of attempts to police marriages between individuals of different races from both sides of a boundary line, amid an amplified preoccupation with controlling women's romantic and marital choices. At the same time, on a political level, encouraging marriages within the community was also key to maintaining its numerical strength and building up a self-confident group identity.

Flawed as its literary and cinematic depictions are, *Bhowani Junction* was one of the few works where Anglo-Indians were openly given centre stage. Another example is Paul Scott's novel *The Alien Sky* (1953), which furnishes perhaps the most direct literary exploration of racial passing by Anglo-Indians. It is a work that never attracted the same level of attention as his subsequent *Raj Quartet* series (1966–75), adapted for television as *The Jewel in the Crown* in 1984. If we set aside Scott's growing literary flair since the earlier novel, it was arguably easier to present to a television audience the related theme of interracial sex and its offspring through the prism of a liaison between an Indian man and an English woman than to explain the complexities of passing and of a multigenerational community of mixed descent. Although Indian, its central male protagonist is 'culturally hybrid' as a result of his upbringing and education in England—this is also more easily and immediately communicated by his words, attitude and accent as soon as we hear him speak. It appears likely that, for much the same reason, the character of Captain Charles Munro, the Kenyan-born son of a Scottish father and an Indian mother, from Michael Crichton's novel *Congo* (1980), was replaced in the 1995 Hollywood adaptation with a black actor who plays 'Monroe Kelly', who briskly conveys his cultural hybridity to fellow characters and the audience with the line 'I'm your great white hunter for this trip, though I happen to be black', delivered in a refined Mid-Atlantic accent.[74]

When the 2015–16 television series *Indian Summers* attempted to briefly allude to racially mixed children in the setting of an orphanage, it made the mistake of presenting the mixed as being of intermediate or darker skin tones by default, rather than demonstrating the more complex reality that within mixed families even siblings can vary in complexion. This point comes across in the offensively worded limerick which Victoria repeats to Ranjit: 'There was a young lady named Starkey, who got herself hitched to a darkie. The results of her sins, was an eightsome of twins: two black, two white and four khaki.'[75] One of the few series to really take the time needed to attempt to explore the theme fully was the Second World War BBC drama *Tenko* (1981–4), in which a Singaporean Eurasian female character plays a prominent role throughout the show's three seasons, and a half-Swiss half-Indian male character appears in the third season. Despite the fact that neither is a precise fit with the Anglo-Indian community in India, many of the same issues and tropes as well as the pejorative term 'chi chi', more usually applied to Anglo-Indians and their accent, are transposed into a similar colonial setting. Although problematic in various ways, *Tenko* included a rare and genuine attempt to depict colonial racism towards the mixed throughout Asia, while making points considered progressive at the time by didactically evolving the attitudes of key characters through the first two series.

However, it seems that unless mixedness is chosen as a significant theme within a film or series, the added screen time required to explicate the subject often prevents its being shown at all, thereby contributing to a general erasure of the mixed. Casting directors have also perhaps not wanted to take on the task of locating suitably mixed actors, although this has not prevented mixed individuals such as the

British actor Ben Kingsley (born Krishna Pandit Bhanji to a Kenyan South Asian father and an English mother) from taking advantage of their appearance to play a range of roles. In Kingsley's case these were as varied as *Gandhi* himself in Richard Attenborough's famous 1982 biopic, the Polish-Jewish Itzhak Stern in *Schindler's List* (1993), and the German-Austrian Nazi Adolf Eichmann in *Operation Finale* (2018). It should be noted here, however, that neither the fictional Captain Munro nor the celebrated Kingsley can be regarded as Anglo-Indian in the sense in which the term is used in this book. The group that came to be known in the early twentieth century as the Anglo-Indian community or, more broadly and euphemistically, as 'the domiciled community' was never entirely coterminous with the so-called racially mixed peoples of South Asia. The internally and externally policed social boundaries of the new mixed-race Anglo-India excluded many kinds of individuals of mixed descent, such as individuals of Indian paternal and European maternal ancestry, and sought to include others who were, or who claimed to be, unmixed. Accordingly, this book is both a study of the history of the imaginative construction of a particular social, cultural, ethnic and political community which formed the predominant yet far from all-inclusive mixed-race group, constituency and identity in colonial India, and a history of the contestation of those very categories, internally and externally imposed, which sought to ascribe membership of this 'community' to certain kinds of individuals of mixed European and Indian descent.

The colonial British construction of this category was first substantially fleshed out in the electoral rules for the Bengal Legislative Council, which defined an Anglo-Indian as

> any person being a British subject and resident in British India, (i) of European descent in the male line who is not a European, or (ii) of mixed Asiatic and non-Asiatic descent, whose father, grand-father or more remote ancestor in the male line was born in the Continent of Europe, Canada, Newfoundland, Australia, New Zealand, the Union of South Africa or the United States of America, and who is not a European.[76]

The definition given in the 1935 Government of India Act, India's last colonial-made constitution, was to prove far more consequential and lasting, providing the template for article 366 of the Constitution of the Republic of India of 1949–50. It succinctly and ambiguously specified that '"an Anglo-Indian" means a person whose father or any of whose other male progenitors in the male line is or was of European descent but who is a native of India'.[77] The omission of any reference to presumed Indian maternal ancestry was carefully crafted to include all those of European paternal descent, whether or not they were willing to admit to being mixed. Thus, it drew in those who asserted a contested claim to be pure Europeans of Indian domicile, commonly known as 'Domiciled Europeans'. All of these attempts to codify the Anglo-Indian category officially elevated place of birth, domicile and residency above questions of race and ethnicity. Yet in practice these were inconsistently applied and usually functioned merely as proxies for socio-racial status, confirming the subordination of certain classes of 'country-born' Europeans alongside the mixed as inferior to the rest of the highly internally stratified colonial British society. The concept of an Anglo-Indian diaspora was also implicitly negated through the exclusion from these definitions of non-resident ethnic Anglo-Indians born outside India.

Although state recognition can never be the sole determinant of membership in an ethnic community, this raises the question of how diasporic individuals like William Henry Pratt, the British-born son of two Anglo-Indian parents, should be classified. Yet, whatever answer we give and however he may have chosen to self-identify, his story is inseparably bound up with the history of Anglo-India. Globally famous following breakout roles as the monster in *Frankenstein* (1931) and Imhotep in *The Mummy* (1932), he certainly merits his first-place position in a 2011 list of 'top classic horror actors' on the Internet Movie Database.[78] With a complexion too brown to attempt to pass as a straightforward Englishman, he had chosen Boris Karloff as his stage name. Implying that he had Russian or Slavic ancestry put him in a more ethnically ambiguous category, from which, like the part Buryat-Mongolian Russian-Siberian actor Yul Brynner, he could take on a wide range of roles. There is a curious connection between the two in that Karloff's great-aunt, a fair-complexioned Anglo-Indian, was the real-life Anna, who, as a result of her own efforts to pass compounded by subsequent myth-making, was turned into the quintessential Englishwoman character of *The King and I* (1956), in which Brynner played the King of Siam (modern Thailand). Karloff's light-brown skin was sometimes darkened with makeup, as when he played the suit-wearing Choctaw Native American Tishomingo in *Tap Roots* (1948). He also donned yellowface eye makeup to play the Yale-educated Sherlock Holmes-esque Chinese detective Mr. Wong in five films between 1938 and 1940. Karloff exuded charm and wit in this role, and despite its reliance upon problematic tropes, including his desexualisation as an Asian male, Wong's positive gentleman-scientist persona reflected growing American sympathy for China during the Second Sino-Japanese War of 1937–45.

By contrast, Karloff's menacing performance as the overeducated eponymous genius-supervillain in *The Mask of Fu Manchu* (1932) was more in keeping with the sinister or disreputable roles in which he was so often cast. Yet Karloff's later series of 'mad scientists' included more morally complex characters. Just as he had humanised Frankenstein's monster, Karloff's performance as Dr. Henryk Savaard in *The Man They Could Not Hang* (1939) explored the psychology of a man of science whose noble intentions give way to a spree of vengeful and meticulously calculated murders. Karloff's makeup discernibly lightened his skin—dramatically so for his better-lit scenes. Alongside the casting of the white former Miss Michigan beauty pageant winner Lorna Gray (born Virginia Pound) as Savaard's daughter, this would have encouraged audiences to presume that Karloff's character was European. Karloff's ethnicity did not preclude him from playing other British or European parts. His genteel accent became so familiar that he was particularly sought after for narration and cameo appearances on radio and television in his later years. Off-screen, Karloff's polite polish and refined English tastes, including his love of cricket, became well-publicised features of his public image. He certainly played on the perceived erudition so often intertwined with American and international perceptions of Britishness. However, this could not be said to reflect a cultivated artificiality. For, unlike most of his older brothers, Karloff had been born in and received all of his education in Britain. By upbringing he was what his immigrant father aspired and claimed (in his own words) to be: a 'coloured' Englishman—or, as we would now say, an Englishman of colour.

Karloff's father's disdain for being referred to as Eurasian, the predominant term for the mixed since the late nineteenth century, is easily understood given its by now pejorative and racialised inflection. Since 1880 the group's leaders in India had been campaigning for a change to 'Anglo-Indian', which was officially sanctioned in the 1911 census of India. Anglo-Indians in this sense are one of the oldest, most politically developed and self-conscious mixed-race groups to have emerged from the colonial encounter. Analytically they might also be considered as the most tangible human manifestation of the imperial connection. Despite this, their own story and their part in the wider drama of decolonisation have been consistently overlooked in both British and Indian accounts. Their small numbers relative to the great Indian masses no doubt provide part of the explanation for this— Satoshi Mizutani conservatively estimates that there were only 160,000 Eurasians and 47,000 Domiciled Europeans in 1911.[79] According to the census of that year, there were only 100,451 returns for Anglo-Indians as against 185,434 European British subjects.[80] However, the census compilers themselves conceded that although accuracy had likely improved since the adoption 'of the term Anglo-Indian as the official designation of the mixed race, instead of Eurasian, their former designation, which was very unpopular amongst them', perhaps as many as 'three-tenths of the persons returned as Europeans were in reality Anglo-Indians', a factor only partly offset by the 'growing tendency amongst certain classes of Indian Christians to pass themselves off as Anglo-Indians'.[81] The individual stories and political disputes detailed in this book should help to make the case that the extent of racial passing has likely been underestimated, even if the community's leaders were at times just as keen to overinflate the numbers of their supposed constituency.

However we define the boundaries of the Anglo-Indian or broader 'domiciled' group, it was a micro-community relative to the population of India. Yet so too were the colonial British population and the even smaller number of British administrators and civilian state employees. The British prime minister David Lloyd George would tell the House of Commons in 1922 that there were a total of '2,500' Britons governing India, including '1,200 British civil servants' and '700 British police officers'.[82] In the years between 1911 and the outbreak of the First World War the Raj aimed to maintain a '75,000'-strong garrison of British soldiers, in a 'ratio of 1:2' with the standing army of '150,000 Indian troops'.[83] During that war India was denuded of British soldiers. At moments like these, and through periods of civil unrest and domestic insurrection, Anglo-Indians and Domiciled Europeans could become almost as disproportionately significant as the similarly minuscule British population.

The colonial authorities made maximum use of those they considered to be reliably loyal quasi-Europeans, by heavily employing them in the railways, telegraphs and customs departments, which underpinned military defence and internal security. In peacetime the domiciled were deployed as military auxiliaries to defend these vital transport and communications services from anticolonial terrorism and sabotage. During the two global conflicts of the early twentieth century, they were selectively allowed to take on more directly military roles. For these reasons alone, the subject ought to have attracted more attention within histories of imperialism in South Asia. With the growing interest in the history of race in relation to empire, these two intertwined and often conjoined 'domiciled' groups, at the intersecting boundary lines of race, colour and class, offer a unique and essential basis on which to build a more comprehensive understanding of the Raj's distinctive and relatively malleable socio-racial hierarchy. Revisiting the subjects of empire and decolonisation through Anglo-Indian eyes, through the prism of the lives and concerns of those who were never simply the colonisers nor the colonised, but something in-between—at times playing the roles of either, neither or both—enables us to re-examine that history from a new vantage point. Such a perspective is neither colonial apologia nor nationalist polemic but one which, in its complexities, contradictions and ambiguities, subverts the simplistic binaries of ruler and ruled, and will hopefully find broader applicability to, and wider resonance with, the complex identity debates of the twenty-first century.

During the twentieth century, Anglo-Indians had remained largely invisible to historians. If they mentioned the mixed at all, most histories would typically give brief summaries like the following from Charles Allen's *Plain Tales from the Raj*:

any station that was on the railway line had a 'railway colony' com-posed for the most part of Eurasians—officially termed Anglo-Indian—and domiciled Europeans. A specific number of subordinate posts in the central services—the police, customs, railways and tele-graphs—had been set aside for this twilight community, which saw itself very much as the 'backbone of the British administration'.[84]

The mixed received more substantial treatment within Kenneth Ballhatchet's *Race, Sex and Class under the Raj: Imperial Attitudes and Policies and Their Critics, 1793–1905* (1980), and David Arnold's 1978 article 'European Orphans and Vagrants in India in the 19th Century' in the *Journal of Imperial and Commonwealth History*. However, it was not until 1996 that a professionally trained historian truly put them under the spotlight in *Poor Relations: The Making of a Eurasian Community in British India, 1773–1833*. The author of this landmark study, Christopher Hawes, lamented that 'in many ways some of the hang-overs of British attitudes towards Eurasians still exist amongst histo-rians ... [and] they tend to be dismissed in a footnote or else described as marginal people'.[85] The change Hawes had inaugurated picked up steam in the 2000s with William Dalrymple's *White Mughals: Love and Betrayal in Eighteenth-Century India* (2002) and Durba Ghosh's *Sex and the Family in Colonial India* (2006). Foregrounding the position of Indian women in their relations with European men, Ghosh argued that colonial British determination to suppress the visibility of inter-racial relationships and their mixed-race offspring had been mirrored and supplanted within the Indian nationalist project's vision of caste purity, constructed around the figure of the Hindu woman as the guardian of the home, embodying the nation, and surviving the colo-nial encounter untarnished. During its long period of neglect, Anglo-Indian history had therefore been left mainly to Anglo-Indians them-selves. The result was that Herbert Alick Stark's *Hostages to India, or The Life-Story of the Anglo-Indian Race* (1926) and Frank Anthony's *Britain's Betrayal in India: The Story of the Anglo-Indian Community* (1969) came to be repeated 'lock stock and barrel' as the 'two "Bibles"' of Anglo-Indian history.[86] Hawes charged the sociologists Noel Gist and Roy Wright with having 'take[n] Stark at face value',[87] in their almost tautologically titled study *Marginality and Identity: Anglo-Indians as a Racially-Mixed Minority in India* (1973). To Hawes, this attempt to 'label Eurasians as marginal people' owing to their middling position 'perform[ed] … a sort of sociological trick', ignoring 'the extent to which the … [mixed] overlapped with the British the whole time'.[88]

Anthony himself had drawn heavily upon Stark's histories as well as *These Are the Anglo Indians* (1962) by Reginald Maher (whose son Gordon would later head the Australian Anglo-Indian Association and the International Federation of Anglo-Indian Associations). Rather than being cited as authoritative scholarly accounts, these and other key Anglo-Indian texts, including books and pamphlets by Cedric Dover, Kenneth E. Wallace, Dr. H. W. B. Moreno, Walter Culley Madge and others, should have been viewed, read and drawn upon as primary sources, reflecting the interpretations and arguments of men who were very much political actors in their day, and were often in heated, sometimes bitter contention with one another. Hawes began this process by cautioning that, although 'we owe a great debt to Stark, he was not actually a historian … [but] a polemicist'.[89] Based upon his own extensive archival research, Hawes found upon closer inspection 'many cases of repression' cited by Stark and Anthony to have been 'misleading' or overstated.[90] Wider interest in Eurasian-cum-Anglo-Indian history began to really take off in the 2010s, with notable contributions by Michael Fisher, Chandra Mallampalli, Satoshi Mizutani, Valerie Anderson and Liesbeth Jacobson. However, scholars in anthropology, human geography and literary studies, including Kuntalla Lahiri-Dutt, Lionel Caplan, Alison Blunt and Glenn D'Cruz, had already led the way during the two preceding decades, helping to account for the interdisciplinary flavour of the new field, which grew up around the online open-access *International Journal of Anglo-Indian Studies*, now edited by Robyn Andrews and Brent Otto. Nonetheless, much of the history written thus far has focused primarily on Eurasian origins and community formation through the eighteenth and nineteenth centuries. This book aims to fill the void and bring the story of the colonial-era Anglo-Indian community towards a conclusion at the final moment of disjuncture brought about by the sudden and precipitous British withdrawal at the end of empire.

The first chapter, on 'The Creation of a Mixed-Race Community', provides a broad overview of the origins of the group and the beginnings of a collective group consciousness across the three East India Company presidencies of Bengal, Bombay and Madras. Towards the end of the seventeenth century, with its tenuous footholds along the Indian coast, the Company was more concerned with religious, denominational and national rivalries with its European competitors. It was in this context that the Company issued an order in 1698 that the marriages of its 'soldiers to the native women of Fort St. George', Madras, would be financially incentivised by a payment upon the baptism of any resulting child into the Anglican Church.[91] 'Native women' here was meant to include partly Portuguese- and French-descended women as well as Indian women, and it was the risk of children from such unions being raised as Catholics that was one of the main impetuses for the order. Almost a century later, a series of orders between 1786 and 1808 attempted to prevent mixed children being sent to England for education and prohibited the mixed from serving in the Company's civil, military and marine services, except as regimental musicians. The reason for the dramatic policy reversal is one of the major questions which will be addressed. Alongside other injustices, the change gave rise to a series of petitions to colonial governors and the imperial metropole during the 1820s.

Their demarcation as a separate group had its roots in this economic disenfranchisement of mixed-race men and resulting social closure against them, which would become increasingly racialised as the nineteenth century 'progressed'. The chapter sets forth the rise of so-called scientific racism and the significance of negative literary tropes in this later period. However, during the early decades of the century the position of mixed-race women was less detrimentally affected, as, with the paucity of European women, they continued to be regarded as acceptable brides for British officers and soldiers. The history of orphanages for the mixed, previously explored by Hawes and Ghosh, is also briefly recounted, alongside more exceptional mixed-race men whose continued successes, especially in military service, defied the official Company ban. Nonetheless most mixed-race men in this period relied upon clerkships to fill the economic void, until the rise of a larger number of English-speaking Indian competitors caused another dislocation in their employment. Genuine and self-interested British attempts to address the so-called Eurasian question through charity and education accompanied and preceded the discovery by the mixed of a new economic niche in the rapidly expanding railway and telegraph networks.

The second chapter, 'A New Anglo-India', begins with the early nineteenth-century background to the internal debates among the mixed as to how they should be designated. The success of a campaign begun in the 1880s to redesignate the group from the increasingly pejorative and racially inflected 'Eurasian', used in the 1901 census, to 'Anglo-Indian', adopted for the 1911 census, represented a victory for those who emphasised their connection and loyalty to Britain as an imagined homeland. The more longstanding campaign to overturn the prohibitions on their military service, first put in place by the Company, was also temporarily satisfied by the belated approval of an Anglo-Indian Force to fight in the First World War. Monarchism and empire loyalism, combined with appeals to shared kinship with Britons and to colonial paternalism as Britain's sons, reached a climax in the enthusiasm of many within the community to serve in various capacities. However, the delays and the difficulties of enlisting Anglo Indians to fight, as well as ongoing discrimination, hampered official recruitment efforts, encouraging racial passing, amplifying pre-existing colourism, and exacerbating internal dividing lines among the domiciled. As the war drew to a close, political infighting ensued and the temporary unity between various Anglo-Indian political organisations broke down, paving the way for the rise of a more confidently mixed leader—Henry Albert John Gidney (1873–1942).

Beset by a new wave of unemployment for the group amid the compulsory demobilisation of Anglo-Indian soldiers and nurses, and the rising calls by nationalists in the Central Legislative Assembly for the Indianisation of the railways and other services at their expense, Gidney did his best to defend a racialised status quo which placed the domiciled in an intermediate position between Europeans and Indians, by reframing the question in the language of minority group rights. Gidney also made tentative moves towards encouraging Anglo-Indians to identify themselves more with the land of their birth by means of a dualistic assertion of loyalty to both their British father-land and Indian motherland. Yet even this proved a bridge too far for many of the old guard, associated with his predecessor John Abbott, who charged Gidney with abandoning the community's British heritage and organised resistance from both inside and outside his Association, challenging his claim to be the group's sole representative. Despite such opposition, Gidney was chosen as the community's delegate to the Round Table Conferences in London, where he made common cause with the other minorities, particularly the Dalit leader Dr. Bhimrao Ramji Ambedkar, to insist on constitutional safeguards and to resist the claims of Gandhi and the Congress Party to speak on behalf of all Indians.

The third chapter, 'Contesting Anglo-India', introduces the less politically potent challenge Gidney faced from what might be termed the 'Anglo-Indian Left', whose most prominent thinkers, Kenneth Wallace and Cedric Dover, still championed the community's older designation of Eurasian as part of an intellectual project to foster a wider pan-Eurasian mixed-race identity, solidarity and possible nation, by making common cause with the other mixed-race populations of the European empires in Asia—a topic which is given its own section. Wallace actually became reconciled both to Gidney and to the Anglo-Indian label, refocusing his energies on addressing the group's unemployment and rising within Gidney's Association to become his deputy and later biographer. Another area in which the two worked together was in attempting to dissuade Anglo-Indians from returning themselves as Europeans in the census and electoral rolls and from joining the European associations. How Karloff's elder brothers, highly placed within the Indian Civil Service, judiciary and British diplomatic corps, may have been regarded leads us into a deeper analysis of the concept and practice of racial passing by Anglo-Indians. Anglo-Indian women's careers in medicine and nursing also reveal much about the Raj's socio-racial employment hierarchy and the professional benefits of successful passing for those of fairer complexion.

After exploring the significance of Wallace's and Dover's pan-Eurasianist works, we turn to an analysis of the eugenics of both Left and Right. For one of Dover's most significant intellectual contributions on the global stage was to combat emerging racial purity theories with his own case for the genetic superiority of mixed-race peoples within a eugenicist framework. Another Anglo-Indian writer, Millicent Wilson, adopted a contrary approach, embracing the racial hierarchy that placed whiteness at its apex and arguing that Anglo-Indians could become a white community through mate selection and the supposed predominance of white genes. The final section deals with attempts to build up a more confident mixed-race identity and to foster a kind of Anglo-Indian patriotism, mainly along dualistic Gidneyan lines, and including a Gidneyite cult of personality. Symbols of Britishness, Anglo-Indianness, Indianness and mixedness were combined in various ways, to constitute the basis for a kind of communal sub-nationalism still predicated on the conviction that even a future self-governing India was destined to remain tied to the British Empire.

Chapter four departs somewhat further from the generally chronological narrative to draw out and weave together various strands of the mixed-race experience, such as agricultural colonisation schemes, which spanned a period of more than a century from roughly the 1820s to the 1950s. In the late-colonial era, attempts at manifesting Anglo-India territorially, whether within mainland India, in the Indian Ocean, or even further afield, increasingly took on the complexion of an attempt to retreat from the difficulties of the Anglo-Indian position during the later stages of decolonisation behind the real or imagined walls of a protected space. In this sense colonisation neatly fits with this chapter's title, 'Anglo-India under Siege'. Grouped together under this theme are several other areas which suggest both the real dangers of the Anglo-Indian position as auxiliaries of empire, put in harm's way to defend the vital security infrastructure of the British Raj, and the reasonable anxieties or imagined fears of the mixed as to their future economic, social and political position in a self-governing India, which might take on the menacing complexion of a caste-inflected 'Hindu Raj'.

Gidney's efforts to secure a place for Anglo-Indians within schemes for Indianisation of the officer ranks of the Indian Army met with official intransigence, foreshadowing another episode discussed later in the chapter when Anglo-Indians faced racial discrimination in their efforts to become pilots in the Royal Air Force during the Second World War. Gidney's desperate lobbying efforts in London to secure ongoing reservations for Anglo-Indian employment in the 1935

Government of India Act bore fruit with the help of sympathetic British parliamentarians. However, his subsequent wartime encounter with Sir Stafford Cripps, who envisaged no place for Anglo-Indians at all in his proposals to settle India's constitutional future, was a devastating blow to Gidney, most likely hastening his early death. We end by exploring the exceptional case of Cyril John Stracey, who became a colonel in Subhas Chandra Bose's Japanese-backed Indian National Army, in stark contrast to the general outpouring of pro-British sentiment among Anglo-Indians during the Second World War.

The title of the fifth chapter asks the question whether the blood-stained British retreat from empire would spell 'The End of Anglo-India'. It was certainly the death of the colonial Anglo-India. To reconcile most Anglo-Indians to inclusion within the incipient new Indian nation would require a dramatic reformulation of Anglo-India. This was to be the task of Gidney's successor, Frank Anthony, who attempted to radically reorient Anglo-Indian identity into a nested category within Indian nationalism. His formula that Anglo-Indians should regard themselves as Anglo-Indian by community and Indian by nationality, which can be described as communal nationalism, faced heavy opposition from within the group, as did his attempts to do away with the Domiciled European category altogether. Finding they could not prevail against Anthony, British-aligned empire loyalists were more likely to favour collective emigration to Britain or its anglophone 'White Dominions' such as Australia, or a colonisation scheme to resettle the community in the Andaman Islands. However, in the 1950s, pan-Eurasianist socialists in the mould of Wallace and Dover similarly concluded that the pressures for the creation of new linguistic states and attempts to de-fund anglophone education gave the community no choice but to attempt to create a Eurasian nation, suggesting New Guinea as a potential site. Before independence Anthony made final appeals to Britain for political and financial support to ensure Anglo-Indians' place in any future constitution and to endow Anglo-Indian education and provide land for colonisation within India, preferably building upon the existing McCluskiegunge settlement in modern Jharkhand.

Equally disillusioned by his experience with Cripps during the Cabinet Mission, who once again refused to concede a single seat to

Anglo-Indians in a future Constituent Assembly tasked with drawing up an Indian constitution or to entertain any of his other proposals, Anthony departed for London to meet with Attlee and the ministers of his new Labour government, as well as Churchill, who was now in opposition. Achieving no result from this, in a moment of despair Anthony concluded that this was 'the end of the Community'. Anthony's heartfelt reaction to this calamity, which also became instrumental in a broader decoupling of the Anglo-Indian identity from Britishness for those of the group who were to remain in India and embrace his message, was to construct a plausible and emotive narrative of British betrayal, which he could contrast with the magnanimity and foresightedness of the Congress leadership. I have previously explored the structural reasons for the granting of generous constitutional safeguards to the community in Indian constitution-making,[92] which were all the more remarkable for flying in the face of a general trend towards the curtailment of the expansive minority group rights of the colonial period. In this book I will instead focus on the high politics of Anthony's personal relationship-building with Gandhi, Jawaharlal Nehru and, more especially, 'Sardar' Vallabhbhai Patel, all of whom, in his account, recognised that Anthony had been trying to make a community who had almost been anti-Indian feel that they were Indians.

Since his appeals to the Sapru Committee of 1944–5, including a prophetically expressed denunciation of the Muslim League's call for Partition, Anthony had been inching towards this rapprochement. While Gandhi remained sceptical of the need for distinctive Anglo-Indian representation as a racial minority apart from their Indian Christian co-religionists, he agreed to support Anthony's ceiling-limit lawyer's bid for three seats on the Constituent Assembly. The success of Anthony's Association in the 1946 provincial elections enabled him to meet a commitment to Patel that in return for three guaranteed seats he would direct Anglo-Indian votes in other provinces towards the selection of Congress candidates. However, Anthony resisted Patel's call to re-embody the Anglo-Indian-dominated Auxiliary Force to attempt to quell Partition violence, fearing that this could make Anglo-Indians targets of the escalating intercommunal killings. Following Anthony's threat that he would otherwise resign, Patel, in line with his hard-headed and pragmatic dealings with the Indian princes, and in the face of considerable opposition within the Congress Party, lent crucial support to the retention of the provisions for Anglo-Indians in the constitution, while the minority subcommittee he chaired was in the process of withdrawing similar measures for most of the other minorities.

In contrast to Anthony's strategic embrace of Indian nationalism, in the Punjab Cecil Gibbon, seeing that most of his Anglo-Indian constituents were likely to fall on the Pakistani side of the new border, sought to reformulate their identity towards the new Muslim state by presenting them as a more aristocratically descended mixed community of 'Anglo-Muslims'. Neither this term nor 'Anglo-Pakistani' retained much currency, however. In the absence of specific safeguards for the group as a distinct minority from other Pakistani Christians, the shorthand term 'Anglos' became more common. This attempted redesignation followed on from the earlier rebranding of the mixed-race group in Burma—composed of both ethnic Anglo-Indians and ethnic Anglo-Burmans—from their official collective classification as Anglo-Indian to Anglo-Burman during the 1935–7 administrative separation of Burma from the Raj—another subject which I have addressed elsewhere.[93] The chapter concludes with Anthony's efforts to prevent the exodus of a substantial proportion of Anglo-Indians from India, and to dissuade Anglo-Indians remaining in India from attempting to register themselves under a British status as an insurance against any future deterioration in their position in the new nation, which he emphasised was likely to damage their employment prospects, especially in the service of the state.

The book ends with a brief epilogue, foregrounding the experience of Anglo-Indian pilots on both sides of the Indo-Pakistani conflicts that followed hard upon independence. By contrast with the discriminatory ceilings they had faced during the Second World War, individual Anglo-Indians were now enabled to rise to spectacular new heights in all three branches of the armed forces as well as the nursing services. The achievements of these fortunate few obviously cannot be the measure of Anglo-Indian employment more generally in the decades following independence. In general Anglo-Indian women fared better than men in entering new vocations, such as the travel and tourism and telecommunications industries. The substantial unemployed and underemployed component within Anglo-India that had existed throughout the colonial era persisted as well. Yet Anthony's efforts to set up new Anglo-Indian schools and defend pre-existing colonial-era anglophone institutions provided another key arena for the community's employment, and, alongside the group's new military heroes, a new generation of Anglo-Indian educators would become the most well-known representatives of the community in the new India.

1

FORGING A 'MIXED-RACE' COMMUNITY IN INDIA

Genesis

The emergence of an increasing number of individuals of mixed European and Indian descent had been the practically inevitable consequence of the long-term presence in the Indian subcontinent of European traders, soldiers and administrators since the end of the fifteenth century. Whether such people would come to form a distinct group, and how they would be viewed by Europeans and Indians, remained very much an open question. The subtitle of Christopher Hawes's doctoral thesis—'The Making of a Reluctant Community'— emphasises the near-universal preference among the mixed for inclusion within the emerging colonial British society, and their resistance to being separated out from it.[1] Among the Portuguese, French, Dutch and British, there developed divergent attitudes towards sex and intermarriage with local peoples, and the legal and civic status which should be accorded to the offspring of such unions. Were these children to be considered as Europeans, Indians or as something in-between? Religion was one important dividing line. As well as being a profit-seeking enterprise and an arena for national rivalries, early colonisation by Catholic and Protestant powers formed an extension of the wars of religion in Europe: conquest and proselytisation overseas were a potential means of compensating for the loss of souls and

33

a furtherance of the universalist claims of rival faiths. The prevalence of Irish soldiers serving the East India Company and subsequent British Raj, as well as early intermarriages between British soldiers and Indo-Portuguese and Indo-French women, helps to account for Catholicism ultimately becoming the majority denomination among the mixed. However, Hawes argues that in the early days, around 1773–1833, 'Most educated Eurasians of British descent were Protestant ... Where Eurasians of Portuguese descent were accepted into British Eurasian circles, such as Willoughby Da Costa and the Derozio family, they too were Protestants.'[2]

Henry Louis Vivian Derozio (1809–31), the young proto-nationalist poet, struck a particularly discordant note among the mixed. His burning patriotism for India and radical ideas inspired the 'Derozians' from among his students at the Hindu College, Calcutta, leading to the emergence of the Young Bengal movement. Derozio's engagement with the politics of his own group centred on the debate over what their collective designation should be, and how to define the nature and boundaries of a community of mixed descent. Dolores Chew attributes Derozio's strong preference for 'East Indian' over 'Eurasian' to his instinctive tendency to link the interests of the mixed 'with those of other native inhabitants of India'.[3] Makarand Paranjape sees it as being more reflective of Derozio's 'cosmopolitanism than [his supposed] proto-nationalism' at a time in which 'the national imaginary was as yet inchoate'.[4] Derozio was certainly comfortable moving between several milieus and inflecting his language towards the audience he was addressing. Before the First World War, most early Indian nationalists did not perceive expressions of devotion to the British monarchy as incompatible with their patriotism. Derozio had few qualms about the fervent royalism and imperial British patriotism of a 1930 petition to the British Parliament on behalf of his group—sentiments which closely reflected the then prevailing popular sentiment among the mixed. He subsequently endorsed its efforts not only to redress the group's grievances, but to restore them to a co-equal status with other British subjects. Derozio's concern, and initial opposition, understandably centred on whether the petition would also represent those, like himself, whose European paternal ancestry was not British. His grandfather Michael Derozio, a wealthy

'Portuguese' businessman, was recorded as Protestant,[5] but arguments persist over whether or not Derozio's mother was English.[6]

English references to settled 'Portuguese' populations in India were generally shorthand for either mixed Indo-Portuguese people or Portuguese-speaking Indian converts to Catholicism who might claim mixed descent. Rightly or wrongly, the English generally viewed such ancestry as either doubtful or extremely diluted. Darker-skinned Luso-Indians from Goa or South India were particularly singled out for ridicule, beyond the growing prejudice towards the British-descended or anglicised mixed-race population, being classed alongside 'the descendants of aboriginal Asiatic Christians from the Malabar coast, from Damaun, the Malayan Archipelago, and from Manilla [*sic*], Macao, &c.' who had merely 'assumed the European habiliments, and … [were] vulgarly but incorrectly called Portuguese'.[7] In 1843 Mrs. Postans described how

> the Portuguese … may be known by his sallow countenance, slovenly gait, and mimicry of European fashion. His garments are the worst-shaped things imaginable … [and] of the gaudiest tint; he affects a swagger, and desires to pass as a man of style and taste. Nothing can be more dirty and despicable than the Portuguese of the lower order, nothing more absurd and comical than the affected beau of the upper … Among the natives … the Portuguese is held in contempt, and considered capable of all sorts of depravity and wickedness. That he is weak and degenerate is certain, while all that energy and talent which originated the Portuguese government in India is wholly lost. The Portuguese encourage priestcraft … [placing] their foot upon the neck of the laymen … [While] admirable as a *cook* … [despite] his deficiency in cleanliness and his love of potent liquors … [this is where] his usefulness ends …[8]

Such prejudices operated to incentivise those with Portuguese-sounding names to anglicise themselves to enhance their social standing within the internal status hierarchy of the mixed and, aspirationally, in the eyes of British colonial society. Rudyard Kipling would later jest that his fictional D'Castries family had dropped the D' from their surname for 'administrative reasons'.[9] By Kipling's time a large proportion of such families had effectively entered into the mixed-race British-orientated Anglo-Indian group, and the issue of whether they were Protestant or Catholic had ceased to be as significant as whether they had culturally assimilated or married into this anglophone community.

However, Stephen Neill explains how the East India Company's early policies regulating marriage were primarily driven by intertwined anti-Catholic prejudices and the perceived need to uphold English dominance through their own state religion of Anglican Protestantism. In the late seventeenth century the Company sought to ensure that the 'many soldiers of the garrison' who married wives from the 'considerable population of Roman Catholics of Portuguese or part-Portuguese origin' did so in ceremonies conducted by its own Protestant chaplains, to ensure that any resulting children would belong 'to the English and not to the Portuguese community'.[10] The 'considerable population of Roman Catholics of Portuguese and part-Portuguese origin' in Madras were ministered to by 'French priests' who were 'made welcome' so long as they did not involve themselves with the English residents.[11] Neill recounts how in 1680

> an English merchant married a Portuguese widow ... [in a ceremony] solemnised by a Portuguese priest from neighbouring Mylapore. To this the authorities took the gravest exception. The priest had wisely fled to avoid ... disciplinary action ... Intermarriage as such was not objected to; many soldiers of the garrison had taken 'Portuguese' wives and had been married by the [Anglican] chaplains. It now seemed wise to the authorities to regulate the matter more exactly ...[12]

In March came their decision: 'That upon the marriage of a Protestant with a Roman Catholic, both the parties to be married shall solemnly promise before one of the Chaplains ... that all the children begotten and borne shall be brought up in the Protestant religion.'[13]

Doubtless influenced by the tenuous vulnerability of its strategic footholds along the Indian coast, the Company was eager that its soldiers should marry and thereby become grounded in the country, as well as give rise to a growing citizenry aligned with England and Protestantism. Much of the bloodshed in Europe since the preceding century had grown out of the European wars of religion. So long as their upbringing as Protestants could be ensured, within prevailing patriarchal and patrilineal assumptions about nationality as deriving from the father, there was no fundamental objection to wives and mothers being of different national, denominational, religious or ethnic backgrounds. At this point the English thought less in racial or colour terms than in religious ones. Such attitudes were in keeping with those of other European traders and colonisers, including the Protestant Dutch and Catholic Portuguese, French and Spanish, who would all continue to uphold relatively more inclusive attitudes to interracial sex, marriage and their offspring, so long as these were combined with conversion and baptism. Although they also developed their own socio-racial hierarchies, each in their distinct ways was more willing to fit converts and mixed offspring into their new colonial societies and strategic enclaves, according them legal statuses that effectively recognised them as co-nationals or co-religionists, although not co-equal citizens in the modern sense.

Among the English, 'a number of sailors and others had [already] married Indian women. [However,] so much trouble had arisen out of marriage with Roman Catholics that both the authorities in Madras and the directors in London agreed that marriage with Indian women was more desirable … [for] the troops in India',[14] leading to a seminal letter of 1698 from the Company's Court of Directors in London to the President of Madras that

> the marriage of our soldiers to the native women of Fort St. George, formerly recommended by you, is a matter of such consequence to posterity, that we shall be content to encourage it with some expense, and have been thinking for the future to appoint a [gold] pagoda[15] to be paid to the mother of any child that shall hereafter be born of any such future marriage, on the day the child is christened, if you think this small encouragement will increase the number of such marriages.[16]

This unambiguous evidence of a policy of incentivising mixed marriages would, as Glenn D'Cruz notes, become very important to 'most Anglo-Indian commentators', who later sought to establish 'the coloniser's moral responsibility for the welfare of the community' thus brought into being.[17] Equally, it points to early origins as a result of legitimate marriages sanctioned by church and state, in contrast to later attempts to denigrate their social and moral origins by intertwining racial mixedness with presumed illegitimacy. These are evident as early as 1803, in a letter by David Ochterlony, the son of 'a

Highland Scot who had settled in Massachusetts' but fled to Canada with other loyalists when 'the American Revolution broke out' and subsequently 'entered the Company's army in 1777'.[18] Ochterlony's letter explained the importance of sending his daughters by Mubarak Begum to Britain: 'My children are uncommonly fair ... but if educated [in India] in the European manner they will in spite of complexion labour under all the disadvantages of being known as the NATURAL DAUGHTERS OF OCHTERLONY BY A NATIVE WOMAN—In that one sentence is compressed all that ill nature and illiberality can convey.'[19] Although 'as many as a third of all births' in eighteenth-century England took place out of wedlock,[20] the charge of illegitimacy, even if applied to only one generation, carried considerable stigma in its own right.

By the twentieth century Anglo-Indian families were typically composed of multiple generations descended from repeated marriages among the mixed themselves. Nonetheless, a widespread ascription of illegitimacy to the mixed, based upon prejudiced speculations as to their origins,[21] had become central to a web of intersecting socio-racial bigotries which sought to construct them as a lower- or working-class group, with whom most of British colonial society would be less keen to associate than 'full-blooded' Indians from wealthier and more elite backgrounds. In upholding legitimacy, paternal descent and religious affiliation as primary determinants of social identity and civic status, Indian society was similarly patriarchal. However, Dorothy McMenamin contends that the predominantly Islamic population in north-western India was comparatively inclusive and accepting of interfaith unions between European men and Muslim women, an argument that finds some support in other locations like Hyderabad, where a few elite Muslim women managed to have their marriages to Europeans recognised and thereby retained their good standing in the eyes of late-Mughal courtly society. This would rarely, if ever, apply to Hindu women who married or cohabited with European men.

Unlike analogous 'interracial' and interfaith couplings in other parts of Asia, involving Burmese or Chinese women for example, Hindu women can be generally assumed to have effectively cut themselves off from their own caste and family as a result of their choice of mate. McMenamin goes so far as to suggest that they were regarded 'as outsiders, *mlecchas*, effectively outcastes', regardless of whether they continued to practise Hinduism or converted to Christianity.[22] Notable exceptions aside, it was, therefore, generally ordinary Muslim and lower-caste Hindu women, 'sometimes Christian converts, who married or lived with European soldiers ... the largest group of European males on the subcontinent'.[23] Durba Ghosh's work highlights how 'Anglican church records, baptismal and marriage records ... court records, such as wills and court cases' deliberately crafted a coded language which subtly pointed towards issues such as illegitimacy and racial status, because it was in 'the state's interest to suppress the visibility of subjects who threatened the whiteness of colonial society'.[24] Anglo-Indian families thus had scant means to recall and, perhaps, less inclination to speculate about the identities of Indian maternal ancestors. When they did so, it was pleasing to imagine them as Mughal princesses[25] or high-caste widows saved from suttee.

According to William Dalrymple, 'wills of East India Company officials from the time of Claude Martin show that more than a third of the British men in India were leaving all their possessions to one or more Indian wives, or to Anglo-Indian children'.[26] Hawes explains that

> in the early days ... if you were born Eurasian the odds on chance were that you would be taken from your Indian mother as early as possible and sent out to an orphanage because that was official policy ... [after which] if you were a lower class Eurasian, the son of a soldier, you would actually go back into the army as a bandsman, and you would marry the daughter of a British soldier. So, you would be completely institutionalised from the very beginning. If you were middle class, and shall we say, the son of an officer by an Indian woman, you would go to ... a higher class orphanage for sons and daughters of officers and you could get a clerical job in a government office, or you might become an apothecary, an engineer, or a surveyor or indigo farmer.[27]

This helps to explain why the bulk of what became the Anglo-Indian community were so profoundly culturally orientated towards Britain, and so effectively deracinated from Indian society and culture. While other loyalist groups that aligned themselves with the colonial state could be regarded as having anglicised themselves to varying degrees in response to material and social incentives, the mixed-race group were the direct inheritors of an intergenerationally transmitted British cultural package which remained at the core of their home lives and ongoing educational upbringing.

Between 1783 and 1820, the Lower Orphan School in Calcutta allowed private soldiers 'of good character and able to support a wife' to choose a bride from among 'the Cinderellas of the establishment' on a single brief visual inspection.[28] 'The girls from the Upper Orphan School most often married officers, local merchants, or returned to England to marry there'; better marriages for them in India were facilitated by special balls, which were hosted until the 1830s.[29] The Byculla school in Bombay continued a similar practice until well into the nineteenth century. Viscountess Falkland, wife of the Presidency's Governor (1848–53), attended the school's 'annual examination of the boys and girls' alongside 'the Bishop … and all the European gentlemen and ladies of the island'.[30] She judged 'the girls … [as] certainly singularly plain; their complexions being of all kinds of neutral tints and shades of yellow';[31] nonetheless she commended the school as

> in all respects an admirable institution. The children … all half-castes—many … orphans, and some foundlings … receive a very good education … [but are not] overeducated, merely learning what will be necessary … [after] enter[ing] the school when very young. The girls remaining either till they marry, or are engaged as attendants on European ladies. The boys when old enough, become clerks in government offices, or tailors, or butlers and valets to European gentlemen. The matrimonial arrangements for the girls are somewhat peculiar, but … [being] sanctioned … by the heads of the clergy … and the ladies-patronesses … they are not … deemed unbefitting … Should a European, or a half-caste, in the middling rank of life desire to find a wife, the mistress of this establishment … [invites him] to her tea table … [with] several of her pupils of fitting age … From among these dark beauties, the aspirant selects one … [and] is at once accepted … with the consent of the girl and that of the committee of ladies … [if] he is found to be respectable.[32]

By contrast, Calcutta's Upper Orphan School initially sent officers' children who were recorded as legitimate to a 'branch of the institution … in England'.[33] Ghosh interprets the differential treatment of officers' children and non-officers' children as being rooted in contemporary racial and colour prejudices, which led to the assumption that officers' children 'were more likely to be legitimate and by extension of this logic, of pure European extraction'.[34] Yet treating class as merely a proxy or cover for racial motivations would be anachronistic at this point. Despite the increasing salience of colour and race through the middle and late nineteenth century, ideas about race during the early decades were fairly inchoate, and it was still far from uncommon for class, wealth, religion and denomination to prove more consequential than colour.

Prasannajit de Silva emphasises that it was then 'hard to conceive of any sense of a single common identity between, say, the Eurasian children of a senior Company official and those of an ordinary British soldier'.[35] It is well to remember that British constructions of racial difference were never as straightforwardly binary as they became in the United States under the logic of the 'one-drop rule'. Even at its high-water mark, c.1880–1920, colonial British racism remained fundamentally class-inflected, preoccupied with social, moral and economic markers of respectability, and—crucially—malleable enough to admit of individual exceptions. Arguably, it was precisely this flexibility and nuance that made racial and colour prejudices so durable through the middle decades of the twentieth century, even as they became increasingly tacit and opaque. Dalrymple sees our surprise at the extent to which the earlier 'transformative period' of the late eighteenth and early nineteenth centuries 'was far more ethnically mixed and culturally hybrid than we imagine' as the product of 'the later Victorians … colonising not just India but also, more permanently, our imaginations, to the exclusion of all other images of the Indo-British encounter'.[36]

In 1782 thirteen Company officers founded and endowed the Military Orphan Society. They included Lieutenant Colonel William Kirkpatrick (1756–1812), who had also campaigned 'for the sons of English officers by native mothers' to be educated 'in England' under a general scheme that would prepare them to secure 'cadetships … in the Indian army'.[37] According to Ghosh, he had fathered 'several mixed race children … with native women in Bengal'.[38] However,

Dalrymple lists only 'two Anglo-Indian children', Robert and Cecilia, whose mother was 'Dhoolaury Bibi ... with whom he maintained a relationship until the end of his life, despite being married to an Englishwoman—Maria Pawson—for twelve years in the middle'.[39] Once 'aged eleven and four', they accompanied him to England where his father, Colonel James Kirkpatrick (1729–1818), 'agreed to take' them in.[40] This was surprising, given that William himself was illegitimate and hardly knew his father, having been 'born in Ireland' from 'a brief affair' with Mrs. Booth, 'the sister of a well-known anarchist'.[41] Despite never acknowledging him, William's father paid for him to attend an Irish boarding school and bought him 'a military cadetship in the Company'.[42]

For men like William with few prospects at home, Company service was a chance to attain rank, status and riches. His own father's career—from Madras cavalryman to 'Commander in Chief of Fort Marlborough' in Sumatra—was one to emulate. Born 'on a plantation in Charlestown, South Carolina', following the family's flight 'from Dumfriesshire after being implicated in the failed 1715 Jacobite uprising', James inherited 'good looks' and 'very dark brown eyes' from his mother, a 'Creole Lady from Georgia', which, combined with a 'rackety love-life', led to him being 'known universally as "the Handsome Colonel"'.[43] James also fathered two legitimate sons in India with Katherine, the daughter of Dr. Andrew Munro, founder of the Madras Hospital. These two, George (1763–1838) and James Achilles (1764–1805), grew up completely unaware of the existence of their older half-brother William. James Achilles became a major in the service of the Company and was appointed as Resident at the court of the Nizam of Hyderabad. An open-minded deist, he married a young aristocratic Hyderabadi Begum under Islamic rites. In 1899 a Madras civil servant placed the blame for the resulting scandal upon Khair-un-Nissa:

> She was of the purest Persian descent ... claiming relationship from the Prophet himself ... The wooing was effected in truly oriental fashion. Kirkpatrick was sitting alone one evening when, to his astonishment, he was visited by one of those old women ... match-makers ... [who told him that] Khair-un-Nissa ... had fallen desperately in love with him at first sight, as she watched him through the

purdah during an entertainment in her grandfather's house. The Englishman at first repelled the advances ... but the princess would brook no denial ... [and] at last resolved to take the matter into her own hands. A veiled figure was ushered by night into the Residency and pleaded her suit so passionately that Kirkpatrick's heart was melted ... [but] the outside world stared and scoffed and blamed and understood nothing. The storm which followed ... [was not] confined to Hyderabad. Extraordinary charges, not only of bribery, corruption and murder, but of abjuring his religion, were levelled ... The ears of the Governor-General in Calcutta were poisoned by Meer Allum, a former envoy of the Nizam ... A lengthy enquiry was held, with the result of completely clearing the Resident's character. The Nizam ... testified that Hushmat Jung was free from all suspicion of impropriety.[44]

That scandal and trumped-up charges would follow is perhaps unsurprising, for, as De Silva argues, 'the archetype of the eighteenth-century "White Mughal" living in relative harmony with his Indian environment is ... a modern recasting of the ... "nabob" ... originally an official in the Mughal Empire; but, from the eighteenth century ... increasingly used to refer (often in a pejorative sense) to senior East India Company employees in, or returning to Britain from, India'.[45] To the landed aristocracy, trade was hardly respectable, but 'nabobery' was worse—entwined with 'broader concern[s] about corruption, financial scandals, and misgovernment, which were widely portrayed as endemic amongst the British in India'.[46] It was a means for nobodies to return as wealthy potentates to Britain, where, it was feared, they would corrode the body politic. Negative stereotypes intertwined nabobs' 'oriental' mode of living with real and imagined vices of self-indulgence, opulence, ill-gotten riches, personal immorality, debauchery, and the supposed impropriety of their interracial and interfaith relationships. By contrast, Dalrymple presents Kirkpatrick and Khair's marriage in a sympathetic manner attuned to present-day multiculturalist sensibilities, emphasising its culturally syncretic flavour, with the 'sixteen'-year-old enjoying her relatively liberated role as 'mistress of her own zenana',[47] penning 'frequent letters', indulging traditional Mughal courtly hobbies such as pigeon flying, and sharing her husband's 'interest in precious stones'.[48]

Their two children, known as 'Mir Ghulam Ali, Sahib Allum' or 'William George Kirkpatrick' (1801–28), and 'Noor un-Nissa, Sahib Begum' or 'Katherine Aurora (Kitty) Kirkpatrick' (1802–89), were sent to England to be educated—a common practice for officers' children.[49] Given the distances and risks of long sea voyages at the time, Khair must have realised the probability of never seeing them again. She would have been devastated to learn of the fate of her son, who fell into 'a copper of boiling water in 1812 … was disabled for life, with at least one of his limbs requiring amputation … [and] lingered on, a dreamy, disabled poet, obsessed with Wordsworth and … Coleridge, before dying at the age of twenty-seven'.[50] Had she been able to foresee her more fortunate daughter's future, it might have provided some solace. Kitty settled near Exeter, not only doting upon a brood of her own and living to the ripe old age of eighty-seven, but also becoming 'the most literary of Anglo-Indian celebrities' as the muse for the Scottish historian, satirist and polymath, Thomas Carlyle (1795–1881),[51] who fondly recalled this

> strangely complexioned young lady, with soft brown eyes and floods of bronze-red hair, really a pretty looking, smiling, and amiable, though most foreign, bit of magnificence and kindly splendour … welcomed by the name of 'dear Kitty' … Amiable, affectionate, graceful, might be called attractive (not slim enough for the title 'pretty', not tall enough for 'beautiful'); had something low-voiced, languidly harmonious; placid, sensuous, loved perfumes; a half-Begum in short; interesting specimen of the semi-oriental English-woman.[52]

An 1899 source described Kitty as 'an East Indian of the type best summed up in the French euphemism "un peu tintée" [a little tinted]', concluding that 'it was precisely her un-English proclivities that charmed Carlyle', who made her the template for Blumine in *Sartor Resartus*, a 'philosophical romance' which parodied Hegelian idealism and Goethe's *The Sorrows of Young Werther* (1774).[53]

Blumine rejects the novel's protagonist, Diogenes Teufelsdröckh (God-born Devil-dung in Greek and German respectively), a professor of 'Things in General' at Weissnichtwo (Don't know where) University, and author of a lengthy tome of German idealist philosophy entitled *Clothes, Their Origin and Influence*, in favour of Togwood, an English aristocrat. Togwood's original is presumably 'Captain James Winslowe Phillipps of the 7th Hussars', whom Kitty married in 1829.[54] Carlyle's consolation prize fiancée Jane Welsh cattily commented that 'Kitty with £50,000 and a princely lineage … "never was out of humour in her life". With such a singularly pleasing personality you could hardly fail to find yourself admirably off.'[55] However, what amounts to a large dowry was not a prerequisite for making a good match in Britain. Around eighty years later, in 1910, Marie Cuyper, whose portrait reveals her complexion to have been considerably darker than Kitty's, married Sir Frederick Barthorpe, the banker and author of 'two books on Indian Currency'.[56] An Anglo-Indian 'possessed of a beautiful soprano voice', Marie had been 'educated in St. Mary's Convent, Naini Tal' before proceeding 'to England to specialize in music' where she 'sang at Queen's Hall concerts'.[57] Even had the future Lady Barthorpe been European, her profession would most likely have raised eyebrows among Sir Frederick's peers. However, it did nothing to prevent the couple's son attending 'Eton and Oxford'.[58] Although this was an unusually elevated match for an identifiably mixed individual by this later period, it reinforces the point that at no time was effective merger into British society entirely beyond reach for mixed-race *women* in Britain itself.

For a comparable but more solitary case involving a mixed-race man, we must go back to 1840, when David Ochterlony Dyce Sombre, a dark-skinned Catholic, variously referred to by Britons as an 'Oriental', 'European', 'Anglo-Indian', 'Indo-Briton' and 'Eurasian … as well as many more impolite epithets', 'married the much gossiped about daughter of an English Protestant Viscount'.[59] This circumstance could only be explained by the tremendous wealth he had inherited four years earlier as the adoptive heir of 'the infamous Begum Sombre, a Muslim courtesan-turned-Catholic princess who … ruthlessly ruled … [the] small but prosperous state' of Sardhana.[60] His fortune also enabled him to purchase 'election to the corrupt constituency of Sudbury' to become 'the first Asian and only the second non-White ever to be elected to Parliament'.[61] Supporters of Dadabhai Naoriji's more dignified claim to be considered the first South Asian MP might be tempted to imagine away the 'nine months' in 1841–2 it took the House to 'repudiate … [Sombre's] scandalous election',[62] but, as Hansard demonstrates, Sombre entered the division lobbies twice, once to cast his vote against the majority over the totemic issue of the Corn Laws.[63]

Although exceptional, such cases reflected significant differences between how the mixed were regarded at the imperial metropole and how they could expect to be treated in the colonial setting. In his evidence before both Houses of Parliament, John William Ricketts (1791–1835) described how

> many of my countrymen … educated in England, Scotland, and Ireland have, on … going back to India, been so much disappointed at the state of things, that they … returned to Europe to seek a living, finding that the door was completely shut against them in their native land. I mean men of first rate education. There was a son of a General officer, who returned in 1825; he had obtained the diploma of a doctor of medicine, but he found that the state of society was such as to compel him to return to … [practise] in England.[64]

In her *Scenes and Characteristics of Hindostan* (1835), the travel writer and poet Emma Roberts (1794–1840) described how the position of the two genders was diverging in Calcutta, as mixed-race women retained the possibility of 'marrying up' (hypergamy) while doors of opportunity were being closed to their economically disadvantaged brothers.

> For a very long period, no half-caste was admitted into Government-house; marriages with this class of the community were discouraged by banishment from society, and even by the forfeiture of office. Nevertheless, the charms of the dark-eyed beauties prevailed; a man of high rank contrived to introduce his wife; [after which] other married ladies were admitted … but it was still a long time before exceptions were made in favour of illegitimate daughters. Several succeeding Governors-general positively refused to admit them; and it is not exactly known how their entrance was effected at last. These young ladies form the only individuals of their sex who enjoy greater privileges than are allowed to the masculine portion of the same class. Emancipation from the restrictions which oblige them to move in a very inferior grade of society has been rigidly denied to the sons of Europeans by native women; their only employments leading to wealth have been wholly mercantile, and the greater number have been only qualified to fill the lower orders of clerkships. At the orphan schools, the sisters … are taught to dance; but that accomplishment

is not considered necessary in the education of the brothers, and the young ladies, conscious of their superior prospects, look down upon their male relatives with undisguised disdain. Nearly all the females aspire to marriages with Europeans, and are with great reluctance prevailed upon to unite themselves to persons of their own class. The men are less ambitious; they are afraid of being despised by … [European] wives, or perhaps, in consequence of the greater difficulty [for them] of forming alliances amongst persons of a different complexion, are content to match with those of their own condition.[65]

What is once again noteworthy as a social dividing line is the different degrees of acceptability into this most exalted circle of colonial British society that applied to 'married ladies' as distinct from 'illegitimate daughters'. In the face of such headwinds, it was the class of their father, the issue of actual and presumed legitimacy, as well as the gender of the child concerned, which usually proved most consequential to the life chances and career trajectories of the mixed. Almost a decade later *The Englishman* newspaper's owner-editor, Joachim Hayward Stocqueler, snobbishly observed the 'notorious fact, that their females prefer to marry with Europeans, and that, of the inferior classes, many are taken as wives by the British soldiery, and by the various English who are in the capacity of assistants, and the like; and in all these instances the real Eurasian people, as a race, are losers.'[66] However, in his novella *The Crime of Colour* (1855), Stocqueler acknowledged that

some of the girls … [possessing] the advantage of an education in England, obtain husbands from among the officers, and are thus recognised in the upper circles upon the same footing with English women; the young men, on the other hand, rarely having either the energy or opportunity of carving a way for themselves, linger out existence as clerks in public or mercantile offices, or take to the sea, or enter into life as small traders, forming alliances with girls of their own hue, and thus perpetuat[e] … a race of poor, puny mortals discarded by the very nations whence they sprung.[67]

Prohibition

The roots of the hardening dividing lines between the British and their mixed-race children, as well as the diverging prospects of girls and boys, had begun to emerge towards the end of the eighteenth century. The Company issued various orders: preventing children 'of the Upper Orphanage school at Calcutta ... from proceeding to England to complete their education and thus qualifying for the covenanted services' in 1786; prohibiting 'the Indian born sons of Britishers ... from being employed in the Civil, Military and Marine Services of the Company' in 1791; and disbarring 'all persons not descended from European parents on both sides [from service] in the army except as fifers, bandsmen, drummers and farriers' in 1795.[68] In 1808 the Commander-in-Chief issued a general order confirming their ineligibility to 'be recommended in India for any vacant commission'.[69] The purpose of these orders was to forbid the sons of deceased British fathers to be educated in Britain even when the means were available for them to do so, for the sole purpose of preventing their entry into higher grades of Company service. Having personally consulted the 'manuscripts of the India Office' in London,[70] Herbert Stark revealed how the 1791 order had revolved around the case of

> John Turing ... the son of the Company's Commissioner of the East Coast, and Resident at Ganjam, inferentially by a Tamil or Telegu wife ... [who] unfortunately had acquired his sable complexion from his mother ... [and] had been sent to England and was on the point of returning to India in the capacity of a commissioned officer in the army. The Proceedings of the Court of Directors dated the 19th April, 1791 ... record as followings:—'Mr. Turing was called, and having withdrawn—Resolved unanimously that no person the son of a Native Indian shall henceforth be appointed by this Court in employment in the Civil, Military or Marine services of the Company. S.O.' (Standing Order).[71]

However, as well as being inconsistently enforced, this ban affected mixed-race men and women differently. While young men's career prospects were blighted, if anything this only encouraged the continuing pattern of British officers and soldiers marrying the mixed-race daughters of their fellows. With so few European women in India in the early nineteenth century, cohabitation with or marriage to Indian or mixed-race women remained commonplace. As late as 1830 Mr. Wynn told the House of Commons that 'among the officers who held the highest situations on the staff in the Company's service at

Calcutta, there was not at present one who was not married to a female of Indian descent'.[72] In the same year the Company's critics were arguing that whatever evils it claimed to be combating were more likely to be brought about by reducing mixed-race men to 'virtually … a state of slavery … [as] outcasts from the parents to whom they owe the curse of their existence … [and impelling them] to break through the first and strongest law of their nature, and to look with abhorrence, scorn, and even horror, on the being who had nurtured them'.[73]

Stark's grand narrative, echoed in the speeches and writings of Anglo-Indian politicians like Kenneth Wallace and Frank Anthony, attributed this dramatic policy reversal to the avarice of the Company's directors, seeking to appropriate to themselves the full value of India patronage, at the expense of their officers and soldiers in India, who might naturally expect that their sons by Indian women should succeed them or at least be given the opportunity to serve and rise upon their own merits.[74] Valerie Anderson succinctly dismissed this interpretation 'that Eurasian exclusion was prompted by shareholder greed', countering that 'it is likely the decision was essentially political. Sons of natives might reasonably have been expected to have had at best divided loyalties'.[75] The year 1791 also saw the beginnings of a successful slave revolt in the French Caribbean colony of Saint-Domingue—the Haitian Revolution—whose instigation and leadership were attributed primarily to the mixed-race 'mulatto' offspring of the white planter class with their black slaves. Fear that 'East Indians, alias Eurasians, alias country-borns' might follow this example and, in the words of a mid-nineteenth-century issue of the *Calcutta Review*, 'combine with the natives and drive the English from Calcutta' was another oft-cited cause of the Company's U-turn.[76] Yet, given that the policy's roots went as far back as 1786, events in Haiti could, at best, have been taken as a confirmation of pre-existing fears—if they were not merely a convenient pretext for actions already contemplated for other, more material, considerations. Much the same applies to the supposed impact of Viscount Valentia's words following his 1802–6 tour of India:

> The most rapidly accumulating evil of Bengal is the increase of half-cast[e] children. They are forming the first step to colonization by creating a link of union between the English and the natives. In every

country where this intermediate cast[e] has been permitted to rise, it has ultimately tended to ... [its] ruin ... [as in] Spanish America and St. Domingo ... Their increase in India is beyond calculation; and though possibly there may be nothing to fear from the sloth of the Hindoos, and the rapidly declining consequence of the Mussulmans, yet it may be justly apprehended that this tribe may hereafter become too powerful for control. Although they are not permitted to hold offices under the Company, yet they act as clerks in almost every mercantile house, and many of them are annually sent to England to receive the benefit of an European education. With numbers in their favour, with a close relationship to the natives, and without an equal proportion of that pusillanimity and indolence which is natural to ... [natives,] what may not in time be dreaded from them? I have no hesitation in saying that the evil ought to be stopt ... by obliging every father of half-cast[e] children, to send them to Europe, prohibiting their return ... [This] expense ... would certainly operate as a check to the extension of zenanas, which are now but too common among the Europeans ...[77]

Fortifying Valentia's demographic anxiety, by 1837, an early census undertaken by Captain Birch, the superintendent of police, estimated 'Eurasians' in Calcutta to number 4,746, as against 3,190 'Portuguese' and only 3,138 'English'.[78] Every other group was dwarfed in size by the city's Hindu majority and significant Muslim minority, with 'Native Christians' only accounting for 49 of its 229,705 estimated residents.[79]

In the Central Legislative Assembly in 1946, Frank Anthony placed great emphasis on Valentia's 1808 report to the Company 'that the increasing wealth and number of Anglo-Indians constituted a menace to British supremacy in India and they must be crushed'.[80] Whether or not Valentia played any significant role in confirming or shaping ongoing policy-making, it is unsurprising that such a clear articulation of elite British thinking should become a landmark in Anthony's historical narrative of the Anglo-Indian community's origins, serving, as it did, to signal the extent of the reversal from the earlier scheme of financially incentivising marriages with Indian and mixed-race women, to a raft of measures that would operate to limit the size and growth of the mixed-race group. Rather than being read as mutually exclusive, the two explanations for the reversal—the prospect of material gain *and* anxieties over this fast-growing class—could be combined to support Stark's and Anthony's overarching theme of 'a deliberate policy of destruction, formulated by the British and aimed at eroding opportunities for the Anglo-Indian community'.[81] For, despite its ring of corporate conspiracy, Stark's emphasis on the Company's mercenary motives in depriving mixed-race men of their potential livelihoods remains deserving of serious consideration. In 1831 *The Extraordinary Black Book* documented how

> all the salaries in India are on a much more extravagant scale than in England ... [accounting for] the immense value of India patronage, and the wide field it opens for providing for children, relatives, and dependents ... [Trade] has never been an object of so much importance as the military appointments to an army of 150,000 men, the filling up of vacancies in the judicial and police departments, and the numerous situations in the collection and expenditure of a revenue of 24 millions per annum ... and so early as 1798, it was notorious that a very extensive and systematic traffic [in appointments] was carried on ... by public advertisements ... till at last an office was openly established for the sale and purchase of India patronage.[82]

That gaining full control of these lucrative patronage networks was a major, if not the primary, consideration remains highly plausible. As with imperialism more generally, actions undertaken in an earlier era to acquire wealth and power were frequently justified *ex post facto* on grounds of race. Indeed, the development and hardening of racial ideologies of rule through the nineteenth century were usually less cause than consequence of empire-building and territorial expansion. At the same time, following Anderson, we should not too quickly discount the Company's own justification for the discriminatory measures—part excuse, part plausible fear—that the dramatic growth of the mixed-race group, overtaking the British population, might lead them to align themselves with local Indian peoples in order to overthrow Company rule. Such a fear would have been more plausible to contemporaries than it may appear with hindsight, given the path-dependent trajectory which resulted from the Company's fateful policy decisions. The Company's severest critics predicted that its decision to strip away existing livelihoods and end future career prospects for the mixed could be the very cause of those fears being realised, citing the malign policy of Spain, which, severing the interests of the Creole from that of the government he contributed to maintain, gave rise to a deadly enmity which has terminated in its total overthrow ... [A] similarity of circumstances ... [exists] between the Creole of the East with the same class in South America ... [Both are] victims of the same species of injustice ... cruelty ... [and] arrogance ... In the same way it is usual to encourage erroneous impressions as to the future destiny of the Indo-Briton. The pride of his oppressors recoils at the idea of his ultimately attaining to a station of rank and independence ... Neither will they admit the probability, because they tremble at it, that men of lofty and commanding intellect may at length spring up among the race they continue so vitally to injure—that the genius of a Bolivar may yet arise.[83]

Among those who might credibly have filled such a Bolivarian role was Colonel James Skinner, or 'Sikandar Sahib', the founder of Skinner's Horse, which lives on as a tank regiment of the Indian Army. R. D. Mangles's testimony to the House of Lords described him as 'a very distinguished officer ... [and] a half-caste ... His mother was a Hindoo ... of the Rajpoot caste, which is the military caste, the second in the scale ... He has a jaghire of land ... [and] is a man of great influence among the native population ... [who] could raise ... 10,000 men at any time.'[84] Skinner and his brother Robert were initially granted 'Jagirs yielding Rs. 20,000/—a year. Shortly after this, however, when it was decided that British subjects ... [should] not hold land, the Jagirs were withdrawn and [less valuable] pensions granted', displeasing both brothers and 'their friend Lord Lake'.[85] Skinner reflected in his memoirs:

> I was ... still at the head of 1,200 horse ... in 1822 [when] I went to Calcutta, where I was very kindly treated by [the Governor General] Lord Hastings. He promised that he would not lessen my command by a single man; but no sooner had he left the country than my corps was at once reduced to 800 men. Rapid, indeed, has been my fall. In the Mahratta service from 1796 to 1803 ... no question was ever raised as to my birth ... When I entered the British service ... I imagined myself to be serving a people who had no prejudices against caste or colour. But I found myself mistaken. All I desired was justice. If I was not to share in all the privileges of a British subject, let me be regarded as a native and treated as such. If *I was* to be regarded as a British subject, did the hard labour and ready service of twenty years merit no more

than a pension of 300 rupees per month; without either rank or station? and after the distinct and repeated promises of the permanent
maintenance of my corps, was it fair that I should be left liable to be
commanded by the youngest subaltern in the army … But I thank my
Creator that … I have ever discharged my duty as a soldier with honour … that during the space of twenty years, in which I have served
with Europeans, no one can ever upbraid me with dishonouring 'the
steel', or being 'faithless to my salt'; that, finally, though I have failed
in gaining what I desired and deserved,—that is, *rank*,—I have proved
to the world that I was worthy of it; by serving my king and my country as zealously and loyally as any Briton in India.[86]

Having met Skinner during her Indian travels between 1836 and
1842, one English lady wrote of her 'savage amusement … at being
forced to endure the indignity of meeting self-styled Englishmen
and women who are actually "uncommonly black"'.[87] Although such
crude colour prejudice was increasing, it was still far from universal. Addressing the House of Commons in 1830, William Wynn
recounted how

the son of an English officer, by a lady whom he had married in
England, was darker than suited the taste of our military critics … [so
they refused] to admit him, though regularly nominated … There are
those who talk of the inherent unfitness of persons of Indian descent
to fill offices of trust and importance in India. I should be ashamed to
argue with those who uphold such doctrines. I should blush if I were
compelled to go through the names of those who, in spite of these
regulations, have worked out their way to greatness by the commanding force of their talents … Colonel Skinner, who, though he was
excluded … from serving in the East India Company's regular Army,
raised a corps of 8,000 men … earned for himself the rank of
Lieutenant-Colonel in the King's service, and obtained the cross of a
Commander of the Bath … Is it wise … to make such a man, with
such influence, the object of proscription? If such policy is to be permanently adopted, individuals in his circumstances will soon be animated with feelings of hostility to our Indian Government. If the
career of honor is shut against them, those talents which cannot be
used in favor of the Government will be used for its destruction.[88]

Almost as famous were the Hearseys and Gardners. The 'son of a
Jat lady by Capt. Henry Hearsey', 'Major Hyder Young Hearsey' was
'educated at Wool[w]ich', and overcame 'the ban against the admis-

sion of Anglo-Indians into the Company's Army ... [through] the influence of his cousin Col. Andrew Hearsey, Commandant of the Allahabad Fort'.[89] An archetypal 'White Mughal', the British Colonel Gardner wore 'Asiatic costume' at home and while 'associating with natives ... but while visiting a large military station, in company with the resident [that is, the British representative] of Lucknow ... [donned] a blue surtout, resembling the undress uniform of the British army, but profusely ornamented with silk lace'.[90] Gardner and other British and mixed-race officers were in service under the Maratha ruler Yashwant Rao Holkar at the outset of the Second Anglo-Maratha War (1803–5), apparently in the expectation that they could never be called upon to fight their own countrymen. Threatened with execution at the mouth of a cannon, Gardner fled, reputedly carrying off a pious 'Mahommedan princess, the sister of one of the lesser potentates of the Deccan' during his escape to the English lines, where he was soon put in 'command of a regiment of irregular horse'.[91] Like James Achilles Kirkpatrick, Gardner married his bride under Islamic rites. More unusually, he acceded to his wife's wishes that their daughters be raised as Muslims under purdah, making them 'eligible to match with the princes of the land'.[92] This ran counter to the efforts of most British fathers to have their mixed children accepted in either metropolitan or colonial British society.

A source from 1883 gave further instances of mixed-race military men:

> The soldier who commanded the Bombay Army during the campaigns of 1803, 1804 and 1805 was General Jones, a Eurasian. Colonel Stevenson, another Eurasian, was Quartermaster-General ... [There are also] Colonel Nairne, Major Deare, Captain Routledge, [and] Lieutenant Mullins ... of the Irregulars, all ... distinguished officers, notable for fearless bravery and gallantry in action, capable soldiers and leaders of men ... There are yet in the civil service, and still more largely in the army, members of the Eurasian community who, through family connexions with the Directors of the late Company or other high officials, found an entrance to these services; but if the fact of their birth is not denied or ignored, it has been frequently suppressed.[93]

The superintendent of the District Charitable Society's almshouse in Calcutta, who had served in the army until 1875, could also look back in 1890 on 'over 40 years' of acquaintance with the many Eurasians in my regiment … [who were] fully equal to Europeans—in fact some of the smartest and best educated non-commissioned officers and men in the corps were Eurasians, or, as I have been accustomed to call them, East Indians. In my regiment there were … nearly 200 Eurasians out of the 1,000 men. [But now] the outlet of the [British] army is closed [to them] … When I was serving with native regiments, about one-half the bandsmen were Eurasians. The band was the only portion of these native regiments in which Eurasians served.[94]

A handful found success in other fields, such as the famous and accomplished William Palmer, the son of

General William Palmer, by his beloved Mughal wife Begum Fyze Baksh of Delhi … As fluent in Persian and Urdu as he was in English and French, and educated in both India and England, where he had attended Woolwich Military Academy … equally at home in Mughal and English culture … extremely intelligent, with a flair for entre-preneurial innovation that would later blossom into a banking fortune of almost unparalleled magnitude.[95]

Similarly exceptional were the two mixed-race sons of Colonel Kyd, the chief engineer of the Company's military establishment in Calcutta, after whom Kidderpore district was named, who became 'famous ship-builders, and in 1818, launched … the *Hastings*, a seventy-four gun ship'.[96] According to Hawes, Palmer and the Kyd brothers freely mixed 'with the whole British society', their paternity, wealth and 'gentle-manly' deportment enabling class to 'surmount race'.[97] The few such individuals tended to be the legitimate children of more elite officer-class British fathers. The rest were relegated to a less than fully British civic status—particularly jarring to men like John William Ricketts, whose father, 'an ensign in the Engineers', had 'died at the Siege of Seringapatam, in 1792'.[98] This accounts for the emotive force of Ricketts's plea to be placed 'upon the footing of our fathers' while presenting an earnestly loyalist yet burningly reproachful petition to the British Parliament in London in 1830.[99]

Petitioning Parliament

After attending Calcutta's 'Military Upper Orphan School', Ricketts had risen to become the 'deputy registrar in the office of the Board of Customs'.[100] The first among his petition's litany of complaints was that '*a very large majority*' of his group were being excluded from the status of 'British subjects' by the 'rigid' interpretations of 'successive Judges of the Supreme Court of Judicature at Fort William', and thereby 'prevented from enjoying the benefits of the Law of England', while, as Christians, they were 'equally debarred from the adoption of the Hindoo or Mahomedan civil law', leaving their 'marriages', 'the legitimacy, or illegitimacy' of their children, and their rights of inheritance in a state of legal limbo.[101] The debate over the 'Petition of [the] Indo-Britons' on 4 May 1830 was sandwiched in-between those on the 'Emancipation of the Jews' and the civil disabilities of Catholics in England and Ireland, including impediments to Catholic marriages and charitable bequests.[102] The context was thus that anyone, nonconforming Protestants included, who was not a member of the established church did not at this time enjoy co-equal status. Although it probably did more than anything else to ensure the formation of a separate mixed-race group and identity, their disbarring '*from all superior and covenanted offices in the* [Company's] *Civil and Marine services*' was left to third place.[103] Ricketts's second complaint had been that exclusion from British status deprived many of habeas corpus protections, thereby subjecting them to late-Mughal sharia legal codes, which were painted as cruel and capricious. Civic status was thus elevated over economic concerns—for at its heart Ricketts's petition was a plea for all of the mixed to be accorded a fully British status.

Officially the dividing line for this was legitimacy, but in practice the variable application of an apparently legal test meant that assumptions based upon colour and class could place some mixed individuals in a less privileged or positively disadvantageous position, at the whim of the judge or official concerned. Although the employment prohibitions had been drafted in explicitly racial terms, the Company's supporters emphasised class and legitimacy, separating out a '*First Class*' among the mixed, who, in accordance with *jus sanguinis* legal principles, were fully recognised as British subjects as a result of their legitimate birth.[104] Ricketts, they insisted, could not claim to represent all of the mixed, but only a '*Second Class*' among them, the illegitimate children of British men and Indian, Asian or Indo-British women, who were to be regarded as 'natives of India, as the law now stands'.[105] This aimed at pairing down Ricketts's purported constituency to a mere '2,000 heads of families in all the provinces under the Bengal government'.[106] Nevertheless, they were forced to concede that even this subordinated class included 'four attornies of the supreme court', a barrister who had 'died a few years ago', 'a magistrate of Calcutta', and 'several [others] … high up in the King's army, who fought and bled in the [Iberian] Peninsular War, under the Duke of Wellington: and one of the colonels who so gallantly led on his Britons in the late storm of Bhurtpore'.[107] They noted that 'there would [also] have been a commissioner of the petit court, had it not been … for the opinion of the chief justice … that the candidate, not being a British subject, could not hold the appointment', despite his 'liberal education in England' and his brother serving as 'a lieut.-colonel commanding a King's regiment'.[108]

Stark would later call it 'an outrage that whereas illegitimacy in England forfeited inheritance but not civic and political equality, in India it should deprive an Englishman's son also of these'.[109] A late-nineteenth-century article also critiqued this defence of the Company as a legal fiction:

> Nor indeed, is the political disability, as applicable to East Indians, the sons of the European fathers and native mothers, really grounded upon the fact of illegitimacy … since there are … illegitimate sons of European parents on both sides who have been unscrupulously admitted into the … Company's service, both civil and military. The objection, then, is merely skin-deep, and destitute of all reason and justice; applying, as it does exclusively to persons descended from Indian mothers; but shall such an objection, alike absurd and unjust, continue to operate as a libel upon the British administration in India …[110]

Kenneth Ballhatchet reveals how class could provide cover for racial anxieties, as in the case of

> Josiah Dashwood Gillies … an outstanding member of the new generation of Eurasian Assistant Surgeons … [who] began as an Assistant Apothecary, worked his way through Madras Medical College, and in 1855 at the age of 29 went to Britain to be … admitted MRCS and … awarded an MD degree by the University of St Andrews. His examiners at the Royal College of Surgeons were so impressed … that they

made a special recommendation that he be appointed an Assistant Surgeon ... even though he had exceeded the age limit. He was duly appointed, and at first he seems to have had considerable success. But he decided to specialize in women's diseases—sociologically an unwise choice. He was attached to the 5th Regiment, Madras Native Infantry, and visited various civilians in the neighbourhood.[111]

When 'Mrs Stonehouse, the wife of a Lieutenant in his regiment, died of puerperal peritonitis while under Gillies' care', he was suspended and subjected to a campaign of vilification and dubious complaints alleging 'insulting and low-lifed behaviour towards his female patients ... abominably filthy habits ... [and] want of veracity'.[112] Ballhatchet argues that 'the root of the matter ... was the insistence of the English elite that their women should be protected from physical contact with Eurasian males'.[113] A few years later 'in the Bengal army several Apothecaries ... [were] promoted to commissioned rank in recognition of their services during the Mutiny', or Great Rebellion of 1857–8, resulting in a heated debate two years later between senior officials about medical men of mixed-race.[114] The Governor of Bombay declared 'that Eurasians as a class ought not to be excluded from the opportunity of responsible medical employment ... depend[ing] on character and education', while 'the Commander-in-Chief, the Director-General of the Medical Department and the Inspector-General of Hospitals all felt ... strongly that Eurasians should never have been given commissioned ranks as medical officers'.[115] As Ballhatchet explains:

> Walter Elliot ... took his cue from the Governor ... first ... [drawing] attention to his own tolerance by stating that he had met 'East Indians who were gentlemen in every sense of the word'. This was no question of race ... He would object just as much to being treated by a doctor who was 'a low born or vulgar Englishman'. Class prejudice, it appeared, was acceptable, even if race prejudice were not. One must have gentlemen. It was not a matter of medical skill, or even of moral integrity ... In short, 'the medical attendant of an English lady must be a Gentleman as well as a skillful practitioner'.[116]

Yet even if it was not 'the done thing' to admit it, by the mid-nineteenth century the question was increasingly racial. Despite variable enforcement and many individual cases that bucked the trend, the overall effect of the Company's prohibitions was to relegate the bulk of mixed-race men to junior clerical positions and place a hard ceiling upon their ambition.

For most, English-language proficiency was their one remaining selling point, and initially they did not face significant Indian competition. Hawes provides 'a comprehensive record of the Indo Britons employed in 1836 in the Uncovenanted Service' of the Madras Presidency, on a range of monthly salaries between 100 and 300 rupees, showing their more usual occupations, such as 'Assistant', 'Examiner', 'Registrar', 'Head Clerk', 'Superintendent' and 'Accountant', for various departments, including Military, Revenue, Judicial, Mint and Assay, among others.[117] By contrast, a commercial house, 'Messrs Arbuthnot & Co', replying to a query 'on what they payed [*sic*] their Indo British clerks', revealed one head clerk on Rs. 500, one writer on Rs. 200, seven other writers on Rs. 50–65, another on Rs. 35, and three on only Rs. 17½.[118] By 1844 the reliance upon clerkships was so great that Stocqueler's *Hand-Book* wove this association into negative stereotypes of the mixed as

> orderly and intelligent, and in one line, an industrious race ... but ... devoid of both mental and personal energy, and ... unlikely, therefore, to ever make a political class ... of any weight or importance ... Perhaps there is no class of men, with their educational advantages, and ... other facilities for acquiring local superiority (supposing the true mental vigour to exist), who have produced so few men of note ... their constitutional temperament is, by nature's own decree, a bar to the endeavour. Clerkships ... [are the] employment which the body of them *look to*, and ... [are] manifestly ... best suited to their quiet and unambitious turn of mind. We are aware that they have labored ... under the difficulties of position which might have repressed the advancement of a more aspiring race ... But has it ever been observed that they have been incessantly *trying* to elevate themselves in the social scale, or have they not been quiescent, and apparently attached to the sub-official employment which so easily gives them food?[119]

This anticipates the scorn-laden tropes later applied to the much-maligned figure of the 'Bengali baboo' clerk. That these imputations were keenly felt is evident from one particularly defensive source in 1878: 'We are aware that the Anglo-Indians are blamed for their predilection to desk-work, or ... "quill driving". It may be mere quill driving or copying of papers; but we know by experience that in many instances, it is not the mere mechanical use of pen and hand only, but purely intellectual brain work as well.'[120] Yet, despite their proficiency in English as first-language speakers, the mixed would be replaced in these roles for much the same reason as they had been so readily employed. Just as they were willing to do the work more cheaply than imported British young men, so too the fast-expanding number of Indians literate in English were all too ready to undercut them. An 1892 committee set up to investigate the growing poverty among the mixed in Calcutta recorded a dramatic decline in the employment of 'Indo-Europeans', from having held 99.6% of government clerkships in 1840, to 74.3% in 1850, 38.3% in 1860, 20.6% in 1870, and 18.2% in 1890.[121] The same trend saw the mixed lose most of their significant share in highly paid deputy magistracies and collectorships and all of their posts in the Subordinate Judicial Service.[122] As Hawes argued, this 'inexorable process ... started in the 1820s ... [with] the Western educations of Indians', begun by the Company to lower the cost of clerical work in English.[123] The loss of clerical positions as a mainstay of employment for the mixed through the second half of the nineteenth century echoed their earlier economic displacement.

Literary tropes

Fiction reflected but also reinforced hardening racial attitudes during the second half of the nineteenth century. Stocqueler's *Crime of Colour* (1855) clearly signalled that in India, if not in Britain itself, mixed-race men had come to be regarded as pariahs, who were not to be received socially by the gentlemanly and officer classes. Stocqueler's story begins with a young Horace Somers, an inexperienced young man, who stumbles upon the young daughter of a 'slain Pathan ... [who] like all the young females of the higher class of Indians, [was] exquisitely fragile and delicate' with 'a face radiant with beauty' and large dark eyes 'of a proud and fierce expression'.[124] Somers takes pity upon Peerun, behaving chivalrously until a predictable romance blossoms. He sends their son, 'baptized Walter', to

> England to ... a first-class academy ... Peerun was placed on a pen-
> sion; and Horace, obtaining leave of absence, quitted the station ...

Soon afterwards his marriage [to an Englishwoman] was announced … followed by his appointment to the Adjutant-General's department where he gradually rose to offices of more consequence … and, as a major in the commissariat department … contrived to amass a very considerable fortune … most miraculously … [as] invisible boats containing phantom military stores were totally lost in imaginary tempests; and herds of public cattle (on paper) were carried away by myths in the shape of ferocious wild beasts …[125]

Somers thus takes on the guise of a nabob, who could only have made his fortune by defrauding the Company state, rather than by straightforward gentlemanly officering. Stocqueler's narrative resumes:

The little half-caste, Eurasian, East Indian, or … whatever name the English delight to call the offspring of European fathers and Native mothers, has emerged from the academy and passed to the University of London … [having become] a polished gentleman and a liberal scholar. His father had always supplied him bountifully … [but] has died, [and] Walter finds himself the possessor of three thousand-a-year, a warm heart, a sensitive temperament, and a very dark complexion. He had inherited more natural peculiarities of his mother than from his proud English sire. The latter had bequeathed him a fortune, but the former had given him the aptitude to enjoy it.[126]

The moral of Stocqueler's story becomes increasingly clear as it hurtles towards its tragic denouement. Although lavished with education and wealth, Walter is foredoomed by the titular 'crime of colour'—the original sin of his father in having misguidedly brought him into the world. Members of Somers's family studiously ignore the young man, although, with money to spend, he makes friends easily enough in London. The chief among these is 'Lionel Stratford, the son of a merchant … [but] nevertheless destined … [by] his great natural talents … [to] cut a figure in the courts of law'.[127] Despite Lionel's anticipated upward mobility, his class origins are again significant. The friendliness of Lionel, in introducing Walter to his young cousin Julia, sets up a disastrous chain of events, as the two enter into a brief correspondence in which Julia agrees to make enquiries as to the fate of Walter's Indian mother and deliver a ring and ten-pound note to her if she can be found.

Walter begs Julia to write to him in all events, for he has already fallen for her at first sight—something Lionel absurdly attributes to his friend's oriental nature: 'The children of the sun, Julia, are the slaves of sensibility. Passion quickly ignites in their bosoms, and unhappily burns with distracting fury.'[128] Deciding that he must declare his love and propose to her, Walter, with a hastily employed working-class English manservant in tow, follows Julia to India, where unbeknown to him she adopts an entirely mercenary approach to finding a suitable husband, settling upon 'Mr. Montague Toodleton', not for love but because, in her own words, 'he is worth three-hundred a-year, dead or alive'.[129] In the comically named Muddlempore, home to 'a few Eurasians employed as clerks, [and court] interpreters',[130] Julia soon acclimatises herself to the expected racial aloofness of colonial British society. Thus Walter faces complete humiliation once he catches up with her.

> The reception which his card experienced realised all his fears that his 'colour' would stand in the way of a polite reception.
>
> 'Somers, Somers?' exclaimed Mrs. Cardamum ...
>
> The name struck Julia.
>
> 'I think I know the name—I remember a person—a dark young man—'
>
> 'Yes,' said the collector. 'Half-castes, as we call them. What could bring him here? He'll find the place very dull, for we can't possibly admit persons of that class into society.'
>
> Mrs. Cardamum condescendingly proposed to see him in the verandah. But the officers suggested that he should be allowed to come in, as it would be 'good fun' to see how a 'country-born' could comport himself in first-rate society ... Somers rushed in ... almost staggered—towards Julia, and disregarding the ... [others] exclaimed—
>
> 'Pardon—oh, pardon for ... a love that maddens me into a forgetfulness of all things but itself. To see thee I have passed over half a world. Julia—Miss Stratford—forgive me ... pray tell me—is the door still open—is your hand still free?'
>
> This sudden address perfectly astounded the auditors. Mrs. Cardamum had never seen such an unceremonious personage. Mr. Toodleton wondered where he had been bred. The officers thought it 'capital fun'. But to Julia it was anything but a subject of mirth. She was shocked; yet her quick interpretation of the feelings of Somers prevented her uttering a word. The first plunge over,

Somers recovered himself, and turned to Mrs. Cardamum, offering a hundred apologies. Then, drawing forth his letter of introduction, he handed it to her. The surprise of Mrs. Cardamum was unconcealed. What could Mr. Stratford mean by sending a person whom she could not possibly recognise on a footing of equality? What was *she* to do with the half-caste? Drawing herself up, she determined at once to let Somers understand his 'position'; and in a few words she expressed her regret that she could not recognise the introduction! From the manner of Somers, the officers expected that 'a scene' would ensue, and ... immediately withdrew ...[131]

Walter then accuses Mrs. Cardamum of 'extraordinary rudeness', while she responds by telling him that he has '*mistaken* his position'; having associated with 'a few people in England', he is obviously oblivious to how things are done 'in this country [where] it is not the practice to forget the origin of a certain class of individuals'.[132] Toodleton chimes in, commending the 'sound policy' of 'a broad line of demarcation between the European and the native' which renders '[him] who partakes even remotely of the complexion of the Hindoo ... quite beyond the pale of civilized society'.[133] 'Gracious God!' exclaims Walter, asking whether 'even here, in the land of my birth ... it is a crime to carry about one the mark of kindred with the descendants of the proud Timour and the wise Ackbar?'[134] Their reply is that 'even the Governor-General of India dare not ... attempt to drive half-castes down the throats of Englishmen of the upper ranks'.[135] Finally recovering herself, Julia expresses her 'regret—it was rash—in my ignorance of the usages of society here ... and it was foolish in you to cherish anticipations—so slight an acquaintance—really—what shall I say?'[136]

More tragedy is soon to follow in Walter's encounter with his mother, but we are left in no doubt as to what lessons readers were supposed to draw—that relations between British men and Indian women could result in nothing but misfortune. One source from 1847 celebrated that among the planter class in the interior the 'pure English wife' was coming to replace 'those wretched incumbrancers which here and there still usurp the place of a wife'.[137] In keeping with the Army's goals of controlling soldiers' sexual behaviour and formally and informally regulating servicemen's marriages, Stocqueler's novella was serialised in the *Patriotic Fund Journal* for the support of

British forces fighting in the Crimean War (1853–6). As in other government departments and the private sector, men were usually required to remain unmarried through the early stages of their careers unless they could obtain special dispensation. Nonetheless, a report of 1864 into the Army's 'sanitary state' drew the inference that 'a certain number of soldiers' were still marrying 'Indian wives', and that the wives of non-commissioned officers and soldiers included both 'women of English birth and Eurasians'.[138]

As these women were 'exposed to great hardship', housed in 'inadequate' accommodation, and, by implication, were at least partly drawn from the young women of 'the lower orphan school of Calcutta' and the 'Lawrence military asylum in the hills', we might question whether even many of those assumed to be 'of English birth' were actually fairer-skinned women of mixed descent.[139] Colonial British society did not wish to acknowledge ongoing interracial relationships but was content to ignore them so long as they did not intrude into its own social world. This was again refracted through the prism of class. The lives of common British and Irish soldiers were beneath the notice of colonial British society, and with no legal impediment to interracial marriages from church or state, there was no point at which they entirely ceased. Having founded the Eurasian and Anglo-Indian Association in 1876 with the aim of collapsing the boundary between the mixed and the unmixed, Dr. E. W. Chambers insisted that 'many a soldier marries among East Indians, and many there are who would gladly do so if they saw the prospects of making a happy home in the country'.[140] Hoping to encourage further British and European settlement in India into which the mixed could merge themselves, Chambers was no less biased than those colonial Britons who sought to downplay the phenomenon. Nonetheless, there was a steady decline in the number of interracial relationships amid the heightened racial and colour prejudices of the late nineteenth century, cementing earlier processes that had by now turned the mixed into a largely endogamous, self-contained and separate group.

A socio-racial hierarchy

The historian Trevor Royle advanced the argument that 'the British in India unconsciously adopted many of the Indian forms of caste and adapted them for their own use'.[141] Class was certainly constructed distinctively in the colonial setting, with ever finer gradations of status based around British men's careers, from which wives and unmarried daughters derived their own position in the pecking order. The resulting hierarchy was elaborated by Ian Stephens, editor of the Calcutta *Statesman*:

> British society in India ... evolved peculiar snobberies of its own, borrowing (no doubt subconsciously) from the Hindu caste-system, and creating distinctions undreamed of at 'home'. Civilians in the covenanted Government services, especially the I.C.S. [Indian Civil Service] became in effect Brahmins, calmly conscious of superiority over all the others ... Army officers assumed a stand-offish Kshatrya mien. These two constituted the topmost British castes; and ... held their fellow-nationals doing 'business' in contempt, sometimes opening up talkatively on the subject after dinner, when you'd hear them term even the chairman of some great mercantile firm a 'boxwallah'. This might be done half-jokingly ... but it could sting, and be meant to. Civilian officials were worse at it than the military, and the womenfolk than the men. Oddest probably however was the caste-cleavage within the business community itself ... [where] to be in 'commerce' gave vastly more status than 'trade'. The latter was thought degrading, it made a really low-level Vaisya out of you; and the manager of the city's chief department-store ... might be blackballed from the best clubs.[142]

The left-wing Australian war correspondent Wilfred Burchett similarly described a

> more rigid distinction between various grades of European society than the Hindus had with their caste system. Clubs open to 'burrah' [or big] sahibs, closed to 'Chotah' [or small] sahibs. All the infinite gradations from the pukkah pukkahs down the scale, to semi-despised Europeans 'of the country' and Anglo-Indians. The 'Saturday Club' where only 'pukkahs' could be members. Where one had to submit to examination by the Club Committee, and only if one's antecedents and reputation were 'quite-quite' irreproachable, could one become a member. If one married, one must resign and present one's wife to an examination board, which judged whether wifie's antecedents were sufficiently respectable to permit hubbie's re-acceptance as [a] member.[143]

A case in point is Vivien Leigh, whose father was 'required to resign from the Bengal Club and the Saturday Club' after marrying her mother, Gertrude Mary Frances Yackjee.[144] Although a Catholic, Gertrude's father was Armenian,[145] while her mother had come from the kind of orphanage background so common among the mixed, although possessed of a complexion sufficiently fair to give credence to her family's assertion that she was straightforwardly Irish. Although she was fair-skinned and reputed to be English, Leigh's mixed ancestry and birth in Darjeeling establish her as the first person of Asian descent to win an Academy Award—for Best Actress in *Gone with the Wind* (1939). India afforded many Britons the means of enacting or asserting more elevated class pretensions than would have been plausible in Britain. If a young man wished to retain his position—professionally and socially—and rise in his career, it was all-important that he not marry badly. Kipling delivered this message clearly in 'Kidnapped', a short story published in the *Civil and Military Gazette* in 1887. While 'a Subaltern or a Tea-planter's Assistant, or anybody who enjoys life and has no care for tomorrow' might marry a 'girl' of 'Spanish complexion' without 'a soul' caring, for 'a good young man—a first-class officer … with a career before him' such a thing was 'impossible'.[146] Yet if Virginie Saulez Castries's name had been more assuredly British and her complexion sufficiently fair to pass as white, then Kipling's allusion to the 'little opal-tinted onyx at the base of her fingernails', a supposed physiognomic marker of mixedness, could hardly have saved the fictional young officer Peythroppe from his determination to marry her.[147]

Anne de Courcy furnishes one particularly spectacular real-life example from 1889, during the highpoint of 'scientific racism' and high imperial Kiplingism. Infantry Lieutenant Alexander Trotter's will reveals his cohabitation with 'Khanam Jan, mean[ing] the equivalent of "noble princess"'.[148] Their 'natural son', born in 1814, became an 'Assistant to the [Company's] Military Board'.[149] He in turn married a 'widow of eighteen in the Cathedral at Calcutta', who De Courcy concludes also 'probably … had Indian blood'.[150] Alexander's grandson 'William Henry Trotter, born in 1837', became 'a stockbroker … for different banks', and married a fair-skinned 'young woman called Sarah Honoria Boot of a fairly humble background … both [her] father and maternal grandfather … [having been] non-commissioned soldiers'.[151] Yet Sarah too was 'probably' mixed, and of the couple's six daughters, four had recognisably darker skin.[152] The other two, Mabel and Grace, 'were pretty, light-skinned girls who could pass as English ... [and being] determined to do so ... cut themselves off' from their sisters and 'never mentioned [them] to their descendants'.[153] Grace was born in 1868. At nineteen she met 'William Henry Hoare Vincent'.[154] Vincent had been 'born in 1866 ... the third son of the vicar of Carnarvon', attended an elite public school on a scholarship, and went on to place 'seventeenth ... of about 200' in the ICS examination in London.[155] He underwent further study at Trinity College Dublin before travelling to India in 1887.

After having met Vincent, Grace and her sister received an incontrovertible stamp of their social standing by being taken on a 'tiger-shooting trip' which their shikari friend George Sanderson had arranged 'for Lord Clandeboye, the twenty-two-year-old eldest son of the Viceroy, Lord Dufferin'.[156] Vincent, who had been temporarily posted to Dacca, 'was still pursuing' Grace and, being 'only twenty-three', was granted the necessary viceregal 'special dispensation' to marry before thirty as an ICS officer in 1889.[157] Known as the 'heaven-born', members of the ICS were at the apex of the social pyramid of British India. Vincent's career went from strength to strength as he became 'a judge of the Calcutta High Court in 1909 ... was knighted in 1913', appointed to the Viceroy's Executive Council in 1916, served as 'Home Member of the Government of India and President of the Viceroy's Executive Council' the following year, and became 'Speaker or Leader of the Legislative Assembly'.[158] By concealing her ancestry, disowning her darker sisters, and husband-hunting as ruthlessly and effectively as any British woman of the fishing fleet, the by 'now Lady Vincent' had climbed close to the pinnacle of the highly stratified and superlatively snobbish social world of the old Anglo-India of the British.[159] From this perch she now felt herself able to look down upon boxwallahs and men 'in trade' like her daughter Dorothy's suitor, Charles Arthur, who eventually rose to become the 'Senior Resident Partner of Jardine, Skinner & Co., Managing Agents', and who was the nephew of Sir Allen Arthur, a former 'President of the Bengal Chamber of Commerce ... [and] the first Commerce Member of Curzon's Viceroy's Council'.[160] However, she didn't succeed in her attempt to thwart Dorothy's marriage to Charles. This and her separation from her husband, to live on her own in Cheltenham, no doubt contributed to the tragedy of her estrangement from her daughter. As with many other individuals who succeeded by 'passing', the price in personal terms had been high.

'Scientific' racism and the 'Eurasian problem'

The fiction of race as a scientific truth proved to be one of the most damaging and ill-fated ideas of the modern world. Emerging by the late nineteenth century as a means of sorting humanity into discrete and supposedly self-contained groupings of biologically distinct races, it superseded and overlaid previous ideas about the social, religious and cultural differences between humans. Races had long been taken to exist as tribes and nations, but by race something quite different had been meant. Prejudice on the basis of colour, culture and religion is as old as civilisation, perhaps older. It is rooted in the fear of the unknown that existed when any group of hominids encountered another that was unfamiliar; in the cautionary principle of protecting one's own social group from 'the other'. Scientific racism, however, was something new. It purported to identify real biological differences between discrete branches of the human species, which could be discerned by supposedly regular and distinctive anthropometric and physiognomic features, and mapped onto the more dramatic differences in skin colour between humans. Complexion is simply the visible manifestation of the melanin levels we have inherited from ancestors who evolved the appropriate concentration to regulate body temperature and shield their skin cells from sun damage while allowing sufficient absorption for the synthesis of vitamin D. Hence humans whose ancestors lived for long periods in equatorial regions tend to have darker skin and those whose lived in subarctic conditions with infrequent opportunity to absorb sunlight have among the lightest skin tones. Most of the rest of us fall somewhere in-between these two poles, on a blended spectrum of complexion, rather than in neatly defined and highly differentiated boxes.

The late-nineteenth-century assertion that these differences amounted to an immutable biological means of separating and categorising distinct 'breeds' of humans soon generated denials that 'race mixing' was sustainably possible or desirable. Like animal hybrids from two different species, it was argued, the offspring of such mixing could only be unhealthy or infertile. 'Eurasians' in India were subjected to the resulting pseudosciences embedded within colonial anthropology which sought to measure and categorise them anthropometrically, by measuring height, nose size and shape, and cranial circumference. Various new theories and insights had to be developed in response to this 'empirical' data and to the obvious fact that, far from dying out, such populations began to thrive and multiply. Indeed, as Malthusian philanthropists fretted, the problem was usually that the mixed had higher birthrates than Europeans and consequently ought to be restrained from early and improvident marriages. Both as objects of study and of charity, the mixed were dehumanised, infantilised and patronised by genuinely well-intentioned and supposedly disinterested scholarly types like Edgar Thurston, superintendent of the Madras Government Museum and a correspondent of the anthropological societies of Paris and Rome. In 1909 Thurston tabulated differences in the averages of height, length and breadth of head, and 'nasal indices' between the English, Eurasians, 'Muhammadans', Brahmins, Pallis, Velalas and Paraiyans,[161] from which he was able to draw such 'useful' conclusions as the following:

> The head of a cross-breed ... generally takes after the father, and the breadth of the Eurasian head is a persisting result of European male influence ... [which] is clearly demonstrated in the following cases, all the result of re-crossings between British men and Eurasian women ... [possessing average head lengths of 19.2 centimetres, as against the 'Eurasian average' of 18.6, as well as an increase of 0.3 in breadth.][162]

To which he added the observation of the 'Census Commissioner, 1891' that, compared with Europeans, 'Eurasians seem ... peculiarly liable to insanity and leprosy'.[163] Despite his being wedded to what we now understand to be dangerous and troubling racialised assumptions, Thurston's motives should be contextualised within his efforts to put what he believed to be validly scientific knowledge to good use, as he describes:

During a visit to Ootacamund on the Nīlgiri Hills, I ... examine[d] the physique of the elder boys at the Lawrence Asylum ... 'to provide for children of European and East Indian officers and soldiers of Her Majesty's Army ... and of Europeans and East Indians in the Medical Service, military and civil ... serving ... [in the] Madras [Presidency], a refuge from the debilitating effects of a tropical climate, and from the serious drawbacks to the well-being of children incidental to a barrack life; to afford for them a plain, practical, and religious education; and to train them for employment in different trades, pursuits, and industries'. [Having examined] ... thirty-three Eurasian boys, I was able to testify to the excellence of their physical condition ... [being] well-nourished and muscular, with good chests, shoulders, and body weight.[164]

The poorest and least-educated mixed children, including the 'kin-thal classes' of the Calcutta slums, generally received a few years of education in orphan asylums, before being thrust out into the world of work in a society in which manual occupations were strictly allocated along caste lines. By the late nineteenth century, charity and education had come to be seen as the primary prisms through which to perceive and attempt to redress the 'Eurasian problem'. Morally and religiously minded individuals who were genuinely humane and well-intentioned were usually at the forefront of such efforts. Yet even they had broader purposes in mind. A letter of 1866 to the *Bombay Gazette* addressed the reputational risks of European and Eurasian poverty:

The appointments in the public services hitherto filled with considerable credit by Europeans and Eurasians cannot now be regarded as the inheritance of their children, and it is now not an unusual circumstance to see John Brown superseded by Babajee Gopaljee ... These classes are ... connected with the Christian Church, and I hope they are not destined to become a standing reproach to that Church, or to be exhibited before the eyes of the heathen, as a poverty-stricken and inferior race ... [which] must necessarily lower the prestige of the English nation. Already we find many respectable Europeans and Eurasians living ... in the midst of filth and wretchedness, in the back streets inhabited formerly by natives only, and which are certainly most improper places for the residence of any European or Christian ...[165]

This helps to resolve any apparent paradox which might be supposed to arise from a period of hardening racial attitudes and ideologies coinciding with an increase in charitable provision for the mixed. While Anglican Church authorities were earnestly philanthropic on their behalf from the late nineteenth century through to the post-independence decades, one early call to action had been interdenominational competition for souls, as revealed in H. Skipton's case for the increased provision of Anglican education:

> In 1880 or thereabouts ... the Church of Rome ... realized the importance of the Domiciled Community as the ultimate key to the religious and political future of the country, and they threw themselves into the task of capturing them ... 'I believe', says a living missionary, 'that the Roman Catholics are buying up an opportunity that we have created, not by a willful policy of neglect, but by that all-too-English assumption that we ... are sure to come out victors.' ... Father Nicholson, Head of the Cowley Fathers ... in Poona, is equally emphatic. 'The importance', he says, 'of work amongst the Eurasians is very great; it is a tendency of Church of England missionaries to think that the only work of importance is that amongst Indian Christians. The Romans, on the other hand, are concentrating the greater part of their efforts upon the Eurasian Community ... with no slight degree of success.' ... The education which these Roman Catholics supply is far cheaper than that ... [of] the Anglican Church or the Nonconformists ... The Bishop Cotton School[s at Nagpur and Bangalore] ... were brought to the verge of ruin through unequal competition, and both were saved by money collected in England and India ...[166]

Religious authorities were, for the most part, relatively enlightened as compared with their contemporaries on issues of racial prejudice, drawing inspiration from biblical injunctions like Galatians 3:28, and emphasising the universal value of human souls. The colonial state sensibly co-opted them alongside other philanthropic elements within British 'civil society'. As a result unemployed and underemployed domiciled men in major cities could generally rely upon various charitable organisations. For, unlike undesirable Europeans, impoverished Indian-born 'Domiciled Europeans' and Eurasians could not simply be deported. The willingness of secular and state authorities to countenance a more charitable approach in India than was applied to the poor in Britain rested upon the more pressing concern of safeguarding British racial prestige in a colonial setting.

Aravind Ganachari makes clear that the liberally funded 'European Vagrancy Act XXI' of 1869 was motivated by the desire to conceal European poverty from Indian eyes. In the colonial setting, the usual Victorian concern with not being overly indulgent in the provision of charity for the undeserving, the professional pauper, the beggar, the loafer, the vagrant and the ne'er-do-well was tempered by a recognition that in India such men, some of them discharged soldiers who, in the words of a north division Bombay police commissioner, went 'from house to house begging [and] often ... [became] intoxicated in the bazar ... bring great disrepute on the European character'.[167] The naval Commander-in-Chief in India wrote in two minutes of 1862:

> [First:] I have long been alive to the shame and inconvenience to which we are exposed by the destitution of some of our countrymen in India ... It would hardly be unfair to say that these facts involve a serious stigma on the character of our government, which must suffer in native eyes accordingly, and putting aside the question of charity, we lose in prestige as the dominant race ... by permitting such a state of things ... [Second:] I would ask leave to remind those who differ from me in this matter that British existence in India is an artificial one, and therefore exceptional as compared with the state of things at home. We are compelled to regulate things out in this country ...[168]

Ganachari may not have realised, however, that one of the members of these charitable committees, 'Charles Forjett, the police chief of Bombay',[169] who wrote a book emphasising his centrality to preventing the spread of the Great Rebellion to Bombay, with an interpretation of those events that approached the most jingoistic and racialised of British rhetoric in its imperialistic fervour, was a 'dark-skinned' Anglo-Indian.[170] His complexion allowed him to actually enact the literary trope so prevalent in imperialist fantasies, of disguising himself to spy on insurrectionist agitators, before mounting the few European police and civilians at his disposal into an impromptu cavalry force to cow the would-be rebels. Given one Anglo-Indian historian's assertion that 'Forjett believed himself to be an Englishman', today's scholars can be excused for making the same assumption.[171]

The 1892 Calcutta Pauperism Committee operated on a wholly opposite set of presuppositions, which cast the mixed as innately incorrigible. Unsympathetically explaining away obvious racial discrimination, its report ended up, in its collection and presentation of evidence on individuals, deflecting blame back onto the mixed themselves. Individual cases were taken as illustrations of the supposed moral failings of the group as a whole. In the heightened racialism of the late nineteenth century, their problems were implied to be innate rather than situational. One such case was the thirty-two-year-old son of 'a European soldier' and a 'Eurasian' mother, who had achieved basic literacy at 'the Moorgehatta Orphanage' and 'the Calcutta Free School', been placed at eighteen in a 'fitting shop on the Eastern Bengal Railways … [on] Rs. 10' per month, before joining the circus, working as a barman in 'a native liquor shop', 'selling cigars on commission', 'playing in the "Foo Foo band"', doing 'ordinary coolie's work … on the jetties at night', working another temporary appointment 'on the Tirhoot State Railway as a second guard on Rs. 40 a month', before being reduced to sustaining himself on the leavings of British gentlemen's tiffin (lunch) boxes, which their servants sold for one or two pice at Dalhousie Square.[172] The committee's report sidestepped examples of racial prejudice which they themselves uncovered, such as one department store's argument that it was compelled to hire European rather than mixed women owing to the preferences of British lady customers. Despite the report's recognition that wage competition with the poorest of Indian labourers presented a challenge to those seeking to preserve any semblance of a European lifestyle, beyond anything comparable in Britain, the underlying cause of poverty among the mixed was nonetheless attributed to 'deficiencies of character, which are largely traceable among Indo-Europeans'.[173]

A return to soldiering?

One of the Calcutta Pauperism Committee's principal proposals was that the mixed be allowed to return to military service. This would provide a solution to the group's economic problem, while holding out the prospect of cost savings for the colonial state in return for a conveniently local pool of soldiers whose loyalty, they concluded, would be beyond question. This neatly dovetailed with the longstanding desires of the mixed themselves. During the Great Rebellion they, as well as Christians more generally, were given good cause to feel themselves at risk of being killed alongside the British, as anti-English and anti-Christian sentiment reached fever pitch. Perhaps it was predictable that in this existential crisis many mixed-race men would again rally to the British colours. Yet the more questionable claim that this was inevitable became key to Stark's construction of Anglo-Indian history and identity in *The Call of the Blood, or, Anglo-Indians and the Sepoy Mutiny* (1932). Whether or not they fully concurred with this, subsequent Anglo-Indian writers would continue to celebrate the bravery and martial prowess of young men like the 'Anglo-Indian Telegraphist—named Brendish—who ... heroically remain[ed] ... at his post of duty in the telegraph office at Delhi ... [to] dispatch that famous telegraph message which saved the Punjab for the British Empire',[174] and won him the medal of the Victorian Order.[175] This was not different in kind from the protestations of other Indian communities, especially up to 1919, who had sided with the British in 1857–8 and reaped the rewards of loyalty through ongoing military service, coming to be considered as so-called martial races.

Yet in the Anglo-Indian case this would carry the additional emotive force of claims to blood and kinship, and form a key plank of their political case for a return to military service—in short, an overturning of the original injustice of the Company's ban, which they hoped the post-Company colonial state would eventually accede to. As Walter C. Madge, the group's first nominated representative to the Viceroy's Imperial Legislative Council in 1910, would tell the Calcutta *Statesman*: 'sneers have been flung at certain classes of our people, but I feel that what man has done in the past man can do in the future, and the story of the Mutiny ... belongs for ever to our class ... with the evidence upon record of the fighting qualities of those of our race who claim some kind of reversion to the British type of character'.[176] This appeal followed on from a series of petitions during the nineteenth century, including a proposal of 1874 from the Anglo-Indian Aid Association of Bangalore and Mysore; repeated approaches from a Calcutta Association in 1879, 1883 and 1884; as well as an Allahabad Association proposal in 1883 and another approach from a body in Madras in 1884; and, finally, a combined 'deputation of the various Anglo-Indian Associations ... received by the Secretary of State at the India Office' in London in 1897, which had 'made the formation of an Anglo-Indian regiment one of the chief reliefs for which they prayed'.[177]

A War Office file of 1886 contains handwritten exchanges that frankly expose the extent of racial and colour prejudice at the time, opposing any attempt

> to enlist any Eurasian or other 'man of colour' ... [We] don't want men of any well known cowardly race ... Of all the dangerous proposals I have ever in my time heard ... this is certainly the most dangerous. By all means let India raise an Eurasian Reg[imen]t & officer it with British officers if its Rulers have faith in the[ir] fighting qualities ... but in the name of all that is dear to us let us keep our British Regiments strictly British ... [Once] we begin to fill our ranks with alien races, our downfall must soon follow. The India Gov[ernmen]t could call any Eurasian Corps it might raise a 'local' corps & so avoid the word 'Eurasian' which to the ordinary Englishman who has served in India—certainly to those who fought during the mutiny—sounds as a synonym for a coward of a very poor physique.[178]

Such aspersions appear more in keeping with Stocqueler's *Hand-Book* and *Crime of Colour* than actual direct experience. This is especially so if one considers that Sir Hugh Rose, who had commanded the Central Indian Field Force during the Great Rebellion, defeating rebel armies at Jhansi, Lahore and Gwalior, and Robert Napier, a veteran of both Anglo-Sikh wars and the chief engineer during the Siege of Lucknow, had both been 'strongly in favour of the employment of the Eurasians in the military system of India and [recognised] the excellent services rendered by them during the mutiny and the Bhutan campaign'.[179] The last Company Governor General and first Viceroy, Lord Canning, had apparently agreed to such proposals, according to the evidence of a memorandum of 1907 drawn up by Charles Stevenson-Moore, the officiating director of Criminal Intelligence, as he sought to make the case for the creation 'of special police reserves to be composed mainly of Europeans and Eurasians' in the wake of serious rioting in the Punjab.[180]

Bizarrely, even the proactive and persistent efforts of another Viceroy, Lord Curzon, to 'see the experiment' of establishing a fully military Eurasian force 'made on political grounds' were quashed by civil service obstructionism.[181] Curzon did not accept their arguments that the idea could not be cost-effective, nor did he believe that any of the potential obstacles, even that of 'carrying a Bill through the House of Commons', which was famously disinterested in taking up Indian legislation, were really 'insuperable'.[182] Relatively enlightened though he was on race, the arch-imperialist and self-assuredly aristocratic Curzon also took an incredibly condescending attitude towards the mixed, describing them in one missive as 'a feckless lot',[183] and responding with 'publicly expressed sarcasm' to a deputation in 1900 from the Imperial Anglo-Indian Association requesting official sanction for their desired communal redesignation from 'Eurasian' to 'Anglo-Indian'.[184] Curzon saw the mixed as an underutilised asset, even suggesting 'that Eurasians might be very useful in the peopling of many blank spaces on the map of the British Empire ... say in South Africa'.[185]

Thwarted in his military scheme, Curzon was instrumental in cementing the mixed in a less prestigious, but equally essential, security role—safeguarding strategically vital areas, most notably the still rapidly expanding railway network. Other than the army itself, there was no more vital representation and instrument of imperial power in India. Militarily, the railways were as important to the Raj as roads had been to the Roman legions. As Christian Wolmar argues:

> They were, first and foremost, a colonial project designed to serve British interests, both economic and military ... The railways were an instrument of control. The stations became fortresses, the white and Eurasian staff became an auxiliary army and the tracks became lines of communication in the event of conflict. The 1857 Rebellion, coming as it did at a crucial stage in railway development, had an enormous impact on its eventual shape and the attitude of the British colonial rulers to their Indian subordinates.[186]

In a letter of 1899 'to the Presidents of the various [Anglo-Indian] associations throughout India', Curzon sought to draw

> their attention to the great opening that appear[s] ... to be present to your community for employment, notably in the [Railway] Traffic,

Locomotive, and Engineering Departments ... Out of a total of 308,000 persons employed upon Railways in India, only 7000 are Eurasians, or less than 2½ per cent ... [In just] three Departments ... there are some 1150 posts on every thousand miles of line in India, the pay ranging from Rs. 30 to Rs. 400 a month, or 25,000 in all, for which Anglo-Indians and Eurasians are free and qualified to compete. Why do you not enter for these appointments? Why, on the contrary, do you allow the European and Native employés to increase ... while your numbers have only increased at the rate of less than ¾ per cent? You are mistaken if you suppose that the Railway administration can ever give you a fixed proportion of these appointments for which you can qualify at leisure.[187]

Employment on the railways, in key roles such as engineers, supervisors, rail inspectors, drivers of the most important mail trains, and stationmasters at more vital locations, as well as a whole host of lesser but still relatively well-remunerated posts as firemen, platform guards and ticket collectors, was soon to become the effective preserve of a conjoined 'domiciled community'. The railway colonies, with their own segregated institutes for their 'Domiciled European' and Anglo-Indian staff, their own company-provided bungalows and primary schools, substantially apart from both Indian and colonial British society, were to provide the bulk of the community's employment and the complacently self-contained world of the new Anglo-India.

2

A NEW ANGLO-INDIA

What's in a name?

Debates around what term to use for the mixed existed practically from the genesis of their politics. Rosinka Chaudhuri explores 'a series of letters on the subject of "naming" that appeared in the *Calcutta Journal* of November and December 1821' in which the relative merits of 'Eurasian', 'Indo-Briton', 'Asiatic-Briton', 'Anglo-Asiatic' and 'East Indian' had all been considered.[1] As some of the contributors were the sons of Germans or Americans, at this point 'Eurasian' and 'East Indian' appeared to be the most popular. Such debates grew more heated as a result of the East India Company's use of the term 'Half Caste' in an official order in 1827, which a group of petitioners in Madras complained to their Governor was 'highly insulting and intolerable'.[2] They requested that he 'sanction the adoption of a term in ... future records ... as a distinctive appellation for the class of people they represent[ed] ... recommend[ing] ... *Eurasian* as the one to which they ... [had] from choice been accustomed'.[3] However, internal correspondence reveals that the Governor's decision to opt instead for 'Indo-Britons' was motivated by the goal of getting those who were 'descendants of Dutchmen, Germans' or other continental Europeans to 'consider themselves as a branch of the great venerable British oak', as it was in 'the interest of such persons to identify themselves with the English nation, as they are permanently settled in a country under the dominion of England and are in fact Britons in language, [and] manners'.[4] The Madras petitioners initially responded to the decision by asking the Governor 'to suspend the publication' of his order, expressing themselves 'sorry to learn that one party who are favourable to the term "Indo Briton" have entered on private means to establish that term ... [in] a procedure ... improper and unjust'.[5] 'Mr. Kyd', presumably one of the mixed-race shipbuilding brothers in Calcutta, had apparently intervened to advise the government that 'Indo-Briton' was 'by far the most appropriate'.[6]

The Madras petitioners expressed regret that 'disunion and difference of opinion ... exist among our Brethren as to the term most proper to designate us' and 'a very large portion ... are inimical to the term "Indo Briton"'.[7] Expressing their preference for 'any [term] which embraces all classes of our mixed race and [would] thus obviate giving umbrage to any party', they suggested 'a general meeting ... be convened by advertisement ... to bring the clashing opinions on this head at Madras to a final settlement and ultimately to enter on a correspondence with those descended like ourselves in Bengal, who ... [are also] split into parties on the same subject'.[8] The Governor dismissed this proposal out of hand, and the petitioners were left to content themselves with the fact that they had done away with the more injurious term 'half-caste'. That the Madras petitioners saw this as a matter on which they should correspond with people like themselves in Bengal is noteworthy. With such petitions emanating from groups of mixed-race people in all three Company presidencies—Bengal, Bombay and Madras—between 1827 and 1830, some kind of meaningful collectivity was evidently crystallising. Widely geographically spread groups were already articulating the sense that they formed part of the same community. Another group petitioning the Governor in Bombay in 1830 had opted to self-designate as 'East Indians'. They requested assistance of a more practical kind—that is, support for an agricultural colonisation scheme. Yet, tellingly they had also resolved to approach 'the opulent, influential and respectable part of the East Indian Community at Calcutta and Madras ... [to] solicit their aid by contributions and general co-operation for the objects of' their planned project.[9] It is perhaps easier to imagine a relationship with those to whom you look for financial support, but in all three presidencies the mixed were already beginning to think of themselves as part of a broader collectivity. John William Ricketts had originally embraced the term 'Eurasians',[10] and Henry Derozio may have been among those who persuaded him to take his 1830 petition from Calcutta to London in the name of all the 'East Indians' of India. However, a 'small section of the … community' who preferred the term 'Indo-Briton', 'headed by Mr. Charles Reed and J. L. Heatly, the former a gentleman of considerable ability and possessed of a genius for litigation[,] opposed the action of the East Indian Committee, and did their best to invalidate and render abortive what had already been effected'.[11] Had the term 'East Indian' been maintained, it would probably have boded better for the community's future in postcolonial India, but its proto-nationalist connotations might not have been as self-evident at the time, for, as one Company official stated in 1827, 'Europeans who have long resided in India are often called East Indians'.[12]

It may appear surprising that the beginnings of a collective group consciousness could precede any widespread agreement about what the group should be called, or that the issue of naming would prove so consistently contentious within any group over the span of more than a century. Some might imagine that the lack of clarity on a collective designation somehow implies the absence of any identity or social existence as a cultural, social or ethnic group. Similarly, when individuals or families chose to distance themselves from the political claims made on their behalf, or to opt for other terms of self-identification, many historians might plausibly conclude that a category so contested and an asserted group so variable or porous in its boundaries did not enjoy a meaningful existence as a single 'community'. This would be to ignore how the very debates over what they should be called—unceasing and highly charged debates that would never entirely die away even after Indian independence in 1947—were themselves compelling evidence that a social group existed in which different factions shared the same overwhelming preoccupation with how they should collectively define themselves. Baked into those arguments were that they shared a common social existence, and that they could recognise one another as part of the same group across wide geographic spaces. As for other severely stigmatised groups, repeated changes of name could serve as a means of seeking to escape from the derogatory associations which were intrinsic to or eventually built up around particular designations. By the late nineteenth century 'Eurasian' had become the most prevalent term for the mixed in India, and as this was also the period of increasing racial stereotypes, exemplified by works such as Aleph Bey's novel *That Eurasian* (1895), the term itself was perceived by many within the group to have become almost as pejorative as 'half-caste'.

At the same time, those of their leaders who, from at least the 1880s, campaigned for another redesignation from Eurasian to Anglo-Indian were clearly desirous of appropriating a term which had long been used to refer to colonial Britons, and which therefore carried connotations of Britishness. Analytically, the demand to be recognised as Anglo-Indians could be seen as yet another strategy to break down the dividing lines that colonial British society had sought to erect against the mixed, and to blur the boundaries between them and the unmixed. After Lord Curzon's scornful rebuff in 1900, it was not until the viceroyalty of his successor-but-one, Lord Hardinge (1910–16), that the name change to Anglo-Indian would achieve official sanction through its use in the 1911 census. In 1915 Sir John Rees complained to the House of Commons that 'the Eurasians ... are now described as Anglo-Indians, which is exactly what nobody else calls them'.[13] Even the Scottish missionary, the Reverend Dr John Graham, who founded the St. Andrew's Colonial Homes at Kalimpong for fictively orphaned mixed-race children to prepare them for possible emigration to Australia and New Zealand, was to lament in 1934 that the annexation of the label 'Anglo-Indian' by the mixed had 'meant robbing Britishers, who had served in India, of a title of which they were proud and for which no satisfactory successor seems to have been discovered'.[14] Elizabeth Buettner notes that 'Graham accurately reflected the disparaging sense of entitlement many Britons felt *vis-à-vis* Anglo-Indians, a community widely seen as unworthy of either their privileges or their appellation'.[15] As Ian Stephens would later explain, this redefinition of Anglo-Indian to mean 'Eurasians, persons of mixed Indo-British blood ... didn't in this new sense catch on till a decade or so later ... among the public at "home"'.[16]

More instinctively sympathetic than most of his countrymen, Stephens described how far below the internally gradated hierarchy of colonial British society he perceived the 'domiciled' to be:

> Beneath all these [colonial British] castes, scarcely deserving of notice perhaps, were the British who'd been brought up in India, the 'domiciled European', descendants of men who'd made it their home, losing their U.K. domicile. You had to be very careful here, for just possibly some of them, though not obviously showing it, might have Indian blood. And of course persons obviously of mixed Indo-British parentage, the Eurasians or Anglo-Indians, were beyond the British pale altogether; out-caste; officially a separate community.[17]

Stephens employed an 'able young "domiciled European"' named Norman Devine as subeditor in the *Statesman*'s newsroom, whom he would promote to 'war correspondent' in 1942.[18] Despite those few possible cases which he conceded 'might have Indian blood', Stephens upheld the self-perception of Domiciled Europeans by stating that it 'meant someone of pure British stock, but born and educated in India and so—as it was termed—"of the country", and accordingly looked down on by most British people raised "at home"'.[19] However, Buettner outlines how 'country born' whites domiciled in India were referred to in popular slang as '15 annas', one anna short of the fully white rupee.[20] One British memsahib admitted that 'when I was very young I took the conventional attitude which everybody took—even enlightened people like my parents—of making jokes about "blackie-whites" and "twelve annas in the rupee"'.[21] In similar vein, 'some Indians made sneering remarks … [such as] *Kutcha Butcha* or half-baked bread',[22] or, as one Anglo-Indian explained, 'depending on the shade of your colour they used to talk about the Anglo-Indian as being *teen pao*, three-quarters, or *adha seer*, half a pound, if you were nearly white'.[23]

The spectrum of people claiming 'European descent were metaphorically valued at 8 annas or 15 annas', out of the 16 annas in a rupee.[24] Amid longstanding British biases against the '"country born" … as racially as well as socially inferior', Buettner contends that the distinction between Anglo-Indians and self-proclaimed Domiciled Europeans 'amounted to the same small change'.[25] That this more widespread judgement was rooted in colonial British prejudices does not make it untrue. If we were to judge by self-perception alone, there were also many Anglo-Indians who asserted that they were exclusively of European or British descent, however implausible this was, to judge by their colour. In 1928 the *Anglo-Indian Review*, the journal of the main organisation claiming to represent the interests of both Anglo-Indians and Domiciled Europeans, went so far as to claim that

> very few families who have lived in India for two or three generations, as 95 per cent of ... [Domiciled Europeans] have done ... have not intermarried into Anglo-Indian families chiefly of the 'albino' variety, and 95 per cent of these people, who spend their lives pretending to be pure Europeans[,] are Anglo-Indians and have mixed blood, but for obvious reasons they are anxious to remain aloof from their darker brothers. There are thousands of such Anglo-Indians masquerading under the euphonious name of 'Domiciled European', squeezing into clubs from which, if their coloured relations were known, they would be excluded ... We have seen ... and known enough of the[ir] antecedents ... to be able to put most of them to utter shame. One could even go further and say that 30 per cent of the officers in both the Indian Army and the I.C.S. and other Superior Services to-day are nothing but Anglo-Indians masquerading as Europeans.[26]

If there was hyperbole in these speculative statistics, there was also more truth to the thrust of the assertion than most historians have hitherto recognised. One interesting case in point was Roy Nissen (1924–60), a country-born railway accounts officer of Danish paternal ancestry who claimed to be a 'Domiciled European', but who acknowledged himself to have a 'swarthy' complexion.[27] He also admitted that most of his girlfriends and ninety per cent of his friends 'were Eurasians and we ... didn't consider ... [there to be] any difference between us at all really ... Of course they would never admit that we were a Domiciled European ... [To them] we were fair Anglo-Indians.'[28] Either Nissen was an atypical 'Domiciled European', a rare interloper, or, more likely, he was one of many who were in fact mixed but felt able to plausibly self-identify as being of pure European descent because of the social, material and career-advancing benefits of doing so.

Undoubtedly most 'Domiciled Europeans' genuinely believed that they were of pure European descent because that was what their parents had always told them. Though it must have appeared absurd to colonial Britons and more cosmopolitan and well-travelled Indians, many self-identifying Anglo-Indians, even some with darker skin, shielding themselves under the boundary-blurring prior association of the term with the British, clung to similar beliefs. The mixed were frequently ridiculed for making implausible claims of this kind, being thin-skinned, overly defensive and prone to imagining slights. Given the prevalence of more transparent insults, and the English penchant for subtleties of tone and inflection, understatement, snubs and barbs delivered in the polite language of supposed cordiality, a good proportion were probably more real than imagined. Yet despite the problematic pathologisation of the mixed from without, both at the time and in subsequent academic discourse, there were undoubtedly psychological tensions in the self-perception of the mixed. Some who held deep-seated convictions that they were unmixed most likely experienced cognitive dissonance in their desire to hold onto self-perceptions and inherited family traditions about their ancestry, which in other contexts and with other company they might feel compelled to concede were unlikely to be the whole truth.

Within the conjoined domiciled community, perceptions of subtle gradations of difference in colour, which were often found among siblings, were finely tuned. Colourism, even between immediate family members, was not unknown and might at times be manifested in favouritism towards, or greater investment in, lighter-skinned children who were likely to enjoy better career or marriage prospects. At the same time, it is important to recognise that within the conjoined domiciled community, colour might be perceived very differently from the way it was in colonial British circles. With few having been to Europe themselves, they perhaps assumed that Mediterranean complexions were darker than a British person would find credible. Most untravelled Indians were also capable of believing that light-brown skin tones could be congruent with claims to purely European ancestry. The plot of Rabindranath Tagore's short story 'The Babus of Nayanjore' revolves around the idea that an elderly Indian man from a family of great lineage who had lost their fortune could be deceived into thinking that a fellow Indian 'in disguise' and wearing a 'tall silk hat' was a British lieutenant governor. The old man in question is not blind but simply lacking any experience of the English or their language. Most gainfully employed Anglo-Indians (even of limited means) employed servants, who could be expected to treat them as Europeans. Manual labourers, workplace subordinates, door-to-door sellers, and shopkeepers, very likely behaved similarly, especially towards Anglo-Indians of intermediate and lighter skin tones. Thus the classes of Indians with whom Anglo-Indian and Domiciled European railway employees most frequently associated would be likely to validate the self-perceptions of objectively dubious claimants to a European status and complexion.

Roy Nissen's sister, clearly of the same 'domiciled' background as her 'swarthy' brother, but probably of fairer complexion, was a nurse who had risen to become a sanatorium matron in Karachi, and was therefore 'infinitely more qualified than a good many of' the British Queen Alexandra nurses (QAs) she worked alongside, yet they felt able to treat her 'as dirt'.[29] After she managed to marry up, to a 'covenanted' British 'junior clerk with Royal Insurance',[30] Nissen's sister relocated with her husband to Calcutta and attempted to pass herself off as a pukka British memsahib. This she did apparently with some success, for she soon felt the necessity of keeping her brother at arm's length. Nissen dubbed the entire class of British young men as the 'covenanted-wallahs' because of their 'covenanted' contracts, including preferential terms of service and better promotion prospects than those recruited locally. The Eurasian-cum-Anglo-Indian politician Kenneth Wallace recalled 'an Anglo-Indian holding a good appointment by virtue of his passing for a European' writing 'a pathetic letter to a friend to influence' 'an old lady who knew his family in the old days', to stop her from 'wagging ... her tongue, as if the fact of his blood got to be known his promotion would be jeopardized and even his job'.[31] Another 'acquaintance of' Wallace had 'enlisted in the A.I.R.O' (Army in India Reserve of Officers) during the First World War and, like Merle Oberon, felt compelled to pretend to 'his friends' that his 'not very dark' mother was 'a very old and faithful ayah' after she saw him off at the railway station.[32] Both world wars would bring unprecedented opportunities for the mixed and the domiciled to attempt to elevate their status. As individuals they could seek by means of passing to transgress the socio-racial dividing lines that the Raj had erected and sought to maintain, while their political leaders could also pursue collective strategies, in similar or contrary directions, which they hoped would result in better outcomes for the group as a whole.

The First World War

The advent of what was then known as the Great War appeared to offer the ideal opportunity for Anglo-Indians to realise their long-standing dream of overturning the prohibitions on military service which had formally been in place since the 1790s. However, they had never sought service on the humble pay and conditions of the Indian sepoy. They hoped ultimately to be offered the same terms as British soldiers, and to be given the chance of becoming officers as well. Nonetheless, the group's leaders had never been above highlighting how local recruitment from the domiciled, mixed and unmixed, would offer an attractive cost saving to government. This implied an intermediate position between British and Indian soldiers, under the implicit understanding that Anglo-Indian soldiers could be trusted to be as loyal as they had been in the past, and thus ought to be considered as on the European side of the 'ratio of 1:2 calculated to be the minimum to ensure a defeat of rebellious Indian troops', which the Raj had sought to maintain since the Great Rebellion of 1857–8.[33] Sensitive to criticisms of this in the Indian press, Walter C. Madge had appealed to his fellow members of the Imperial Legislative Council

> and especially the Indian members, to counteract anything like race animosity in this matter. Our Indian fellow-countrymen are stretching forth the tendrils of their hopes towards certain privileges and powers. We for our part are simply claiming the privilege of laying down our lives for our Empire and our King, and I think I may depend upon the goodwill of the Indian members ... not to add any bitterness to any controversy that may take place on the subject outside ... I have already seen some remarks ... characteristic of a type of feeling which I hope will never exist in this Council.[34]

When John Harold Arnold Abbott (1863–1945), a successful Jhansi-based businessman at the head of Abbott Brothers, a construction company which had been awarded contracts for large-scale dam projects, was nominated to the Council in 1913,[35] he followed in his predecessor's footsteps. As indicated by the name of the body he presided over—the Anglo-Indian Empire League—Abbott took his lead from the official government block, routinely voting against the Indian reformists on legislation not affecting his own community. High among Abbott's priorities were his pushes for Anglo-Indians to be admitted to British regiments, for the creation of an Anglo-Indian regiment, and for the attachment of volunteer railway units to the British Army for periodic training.[36] Accordingly, the day after the British declaration of war upon Germany, Abbott wired Lord Hardinge 'offering to raise an Anglo-Indian Regiment for service abroad, as well as a Corps of women Nurses ... [I]n a few days over five thousand names of volunteers had been registered, while some hundreds of women, trained and untrained, had applied for permission to serve as nurses'.[37] This was in keeping with the support for the war by the bulk of early Indian nationalists, who were still, for the most part, cooperationist reformists who desired constitutional concessions towards greater autonomy for India. Mohandas Gandhi, who attended 'a War Conference at Delhi ... [in] April 1918', wrote to the Viceroy's secretary the next day offering to become 'your recruiting agent-in-chief' and 'rain men on you'.[38] Wartime military service was widely perceived as a means of proving that Indians merited co-equal citizenship within the empire.

Even more defiant and outspoken early nationalists such as Bal Gangadhar Tilak, who founded a Home Rule League in Belgaum in April 1916, and the Irish-descended London-born Annie Besant, the leader of the Theosophical Society in India and the founder of another Home Rule League branch at Adyar in Madras in September, saw in the war a unique opportunity. In an article entitled 'To Arms', Besant explained how 'liberty may be contemptuously denied to a disarmed people ... [but] is secure for a strong and armed nation, who says calmly: "Liberty is my birth-right, I take it!" England's need is India's opportunity—her opportunity to show herself as the nation of warriors, of heroes, that she is too mighty to bear a yoke, to remain a dependency.'[39] Yet among the recruits to the Raj's large volunteer army and along a wide spectrum of Indian society, it was still more common to approach the authorities through genuine appeals to their presumed paternalism, often by invoking the concept of *Ma Bap* or 'mother-father'. Anglo-Indians, however, made a more literal appeal to shared ties of blood and kinship through collective assertions that they were Britain's 'sons'. Anglo-Indian recruiting speeches in Madras would later go even further, interpreting the belated 'sanctioning of the Anglo-Indian Force … [in 1916 as] the first definite pronouncement of the policy which identified the domiciled Community and made it what it claims to be [–] British'.[40] Thus, even when compared with the abundant loyalist, imperial-monarchist, and martial speeches of Indian princely rulers, aristocratic landowners and other well-to-do Indians, Anglo-Indian and Domiciled European support for the war was particularly heartfelt.

The prevailing sense of Britishness among most of their number had been validated by their redesignation as Anglo-Indians in 1911. C. T. Robbie, the Empire League's general secretary, invoked a transcendent vision of imperial British common citizenship, situating the community as part of a single family spread across

> the 'outposts of Empire' … loyal sons answering the mother-call. Class and creed distinction … alike forgotten in the hour of threatened danger. Forgotten also were former disabilities … For years the Community had clamoured for the right to serve King and Country as Anglo-Indian soldiers, but for years their cry had remained unheeded. Surely now their prayer would at last be heard …[41]

Many were swept up in this kind of naive collective patriotic fervour, mirroring reactions to the war's outbreak in the British Isles and the Continental European empires. Fred Murcutt, the Madras-born son of an anglicised Italian father and an Anglo-Indian mother, who had been educated at La Martinière College Lucknow, was employed by Abbott Brothers and served as wartime recruiting agent as well as honorary general secretary for the Empire League, described how 'in 1914, when the War burst … there were thousands of young men in India burning with patriotic zeal'.[42] Yet this initial wave of enthusiasm was met with cool indifference, as Robbie described:

> Incredible as it must ever be Mr. Abbott's offer was declined … Only those who really know the community can at all realise the unspeakable dismay with which the refusal became known. Wounded pride

... was nothing to the disappointment that even in the hour of the mother-country's direst need Anglo-Indians were to be denied the right to help. Only those who know the depth of the veneration of the Anglo-Indian for Great Britain and the universal desire prevalent to be somehow associated therewith can fathom just what the refusal meant to the better classes ... [Nonetheless] some thousands of Anglo-Indians found their way to one or other of the various fronts, in many instances there to make the supreme sacrifice.[43]

Robbie was alluding to the many individual Anglo-Indians and Domiciled Europeans who managed to enlist in British and Commonwealth as well as Indian forces. Amid widespread attempts at racial passing, recruiting agents in India had probably connived in their enlistment as European or British nationals, although some had found it necessary to travel to Britain in order to sign up. In his political memoir-cum-history Frank Anthony would later insist:

The achievements of many Anglo-Indians who joined as Europeans were lost to the Community. Even through the mists of time, however, some are clearly identifiable ... [Flight Lieutenant] Lief Robinson who joined the R.A.F. in World War I brought down the first Zeppelin over England ... [and was] awarded the ... [Victoria Cross]. [Flight Lieutenant] Warneford ... accounted for the first Zeppelin over France ... [receiving] the V.C. [and] ... the Croix-de-Guerre. Robinson and Warneford were lads from Bangalore. Percival Lovery, another Anglo-Indian from Bangalore, enlisted as a gunner and was [among several other Anglo-Indians] awarded the V.C.[44]

In making his case in London in 1930, Gidney would cite 'Robinson and Warneford' alongside his claim that 'in the Great War we gave 80 per cent. of our manhood to serve with the colours',[45] and 'hundreds of Anglo-Indian nurses ... [who] went to all theatres of war; many of them getting honours'.[46] As a British and Indian credentialled ophthalmic surgeon and lieutenant colonel in the Indian Medical Service (IMS), who had served in the Boxer Rebellion in China, Gidney ran a hospital during the war for Indian troops, which the Commander-in-Chief of the British Army in India 'complimented ... [as] the best he had ever seen'.[47]

After the war, Robbie cooperated with various schools and railways to compile a detailed list of the names and units of domiciled men who had, by one means or another, ended up serving in practically every theatre of the conflict, including the Western Front, East Africa, the Middle East and Mesopotamia. The La Martinière Calcutta school alone had four men in the Canadian Army, two in the Australian, sixteen commissioned officers in the British Army and nine in the Indian, fifty-eight on the Indian Army Reserve of Officers, two British naval officers, sixteen British Army NCOs or privates, and thirty-three Indian Army NCOs or privates.[48] Many others were attached to a wide array of war-related support services, such as the Electrical Mechanical Section, the Royal Engineers, the Motor Ambulance, a telegraphist unit, the interpreters section, and the Indian Subordinate Medical Department (ISMD) Field Force. Not all railways and government departments would release their employees, as these were considered essential services, as one recruiting officer noted: 'A large number of men ... employed in the various Railways ... offered themselves but failed to obtain their employers' permission. The same applies to ... the Telegraph and Police Services.'[49] However, both the Jodhpur–Bikaner Railway and the Darjeeling Himalayan Railway sent some of their staff to East Africa or Mesopotamia. Dehra Doon listed nine domiciled women, one of whom was head of the station's Ambulance Brigade and in charge of Munro soldiers' canteen, another a clerk at Army HQ Simla, and the rest mainly working in hospitals.[50]

Thus when, in 1916, the imperial authorities' desperation for front-line recruits finally induced them to sanction an Anglo-Indian Force (AIF),[51] of infantry, cavalry and artillery, comprising 19 second lieutenants and 1,090 NCOs and privates, it proved challenging to find domiciled men who were not already serving in some capacity. 'Government of India Order No. 6293, 1st June 1916' had already removed the official (but widely circumvented) ban on domiciled enlistment to British regiments, enabling the Dorset Regiment to scoop up 'large numbers' before AIF recruiters had a chance to begin their work.[52] The loss of their 'services which might have counted for much to Anglo-India', and also 'their identity' as Anglo-Indians, was lamented.[53] Yet recruiters were reluctantly compelled to admit that the 'bare Rs. 25' per month of the AIF was a hard sell to 'the poor Anglo-Indian, with invariably several' dependants, when compared with the higher salaries of the Nursing Orderly

Corps, Supply and Transport, Mechanic Corps, Machine Gun Sections, Volunteer Artillery and Railway deployments to East Africa and Mesopotamia, which paid between Rs. 70 and Rs. 195 per month.[54] Robbie also described 'the strength of the temptation to the Anglo-Indian to be considered a European and while it was possible for Anglo-Indians to join British Regiments as Europeans the wonder is that any of the fairer men came forward for the Anglo-Indian Force at all'.[55] Nonetheless, Abbott and other Anglo-Indian leaders responded to the challenge to supply 1,200 men by invoking 'British grit', coordinating the efforts of the Empire League and rival Anglo-Indian associations to deploy recruiters to as many centres in India and Burma as possible:

> and after earnest, blood-stirring speeches, amidst the wildest enthu-siasm the first one hundred volunteers were obtained ... Recruiting agents threw overboard private business work, and scampered all over the country, pleading, cajoling, urging, threatening and obtain-ing volunteers in hundreds ... but now came to be seen how many of these volunteers could be spared ... from Government offices and Departments, from Railways, from businesses and the like. And the results froze and disheartened even the staunch keenness and enthu-siasm of the leaders of the community.[56]

With India denuded of a large proportion of its colonial British population, the colonial state had good reason to wish to keep domi-ciled men at work in their strategically sensitive roles on the railways and telegraphs. George Morton-Jack documents how vexed the Viceroy became at the 'gamble' London was willing to take in deplet-ing the Raj of such a high proportion of its military forces, complain-ing to a friend of 'the evil tendency at Whitehall to regard India as a milch cow'.[57] Hardinge was especially worried about the loss of the European element, thereby destroying the peacetime '1:2 ratio of British to Indian troops'.[58] Amid this tenuous racial balancing act, the small domiciled community of mixed and apparently unmixed people of European descent became all-important. Yet the approval of the AIF created some confusion among British commanders such as General R. G. Strange, who oversaw

> a largely attended Recruiting meeting ... [in] Calcutta ... At the out-set there was a great rush of applicants ... [But] owing to the attitude

adopted by the Fort William Authorities ... many were lost to the Force who might have proved a decided acquisition in-as-much-as Domiciled Europeans who offered themselves for enlistment in the Anglo-Indian Force were declined on the ground that they had no Indian blood in their veins. In most cases these joined other units. Descendants of European fathers and Assamese mothers were simi-larly rejected.[59]

This awkward racial categorising by colonial British authorities, seeking to exclude domiciled men who appeared white, amplified pre-existing dividing lines and set the tone for a perception that the AIF was to be only for Anglo-Indians 'of colour'. This almost became a self-fulfilling prophecy because, amid prevailing colourism, it put off lighter-skinned members of the community, and even those with darker skin may have taken its implications amiss. Robbie's com-ments are unintentionally revealing about the prejudices prevalent within the group at the time:

> recruitment has brought the recruiter a much deeper insight into the advantages and disadvantages peculiar to the Anglo-Indian Community than he could otherwise have obtained. IT HAS PROVED BEYOND ALL DOUBT THAT THE PATRIOT IS NOT ALWAYS WHITE-SKINNED ... Even when War, the great leveler of mankind, has held the country in its iron grip I have seen the sneer of the fair-skinned decry the man of colour, despite the fact that the traducer was not half the man the traduced was.[60]

Combined with rumours 'that non-Anglo-Indians' (Goans and Indian Christians) 'were being enlisted wholesale' in South India, lighter-skinned Anglo-Indians, especially from North India, were deterred from signing up.[61] The reason for the even more bizarre exclusion of partly Assamese individuals was probably that they were more likely to look like East Asian Eurasians than typical Anglo-Indians. One recruiter expressed frustration that

> a large number were lost owing to ... rigid adherence to the pre-scribed chest measurement and weight. Many of these also joined other units being good enough for the ordinary British Regiments but not so for the Anglo-Indian ... Quite 75% of the men rejected for being under weight and chest measurement were otherwise of good physique, healthy and sound and are now in the General Service Class of the Indian Defence Force.[62]

This emphasis on chest measurements, while not unprecedented in wartime recruitment, appears to have been applied with greater fastidiousness in the Anglo-Indian case. Evidently, racially inflected pseudoscientific anthropometric and physiognomic assumptions were blended into the standard Army concerns about the height, health and physical qualities of mixed-race recruits. This context created an amplified desire to prove Anglo-Indians' martial qualities, bravery and physical fitness as soldiers during the conflict. Robbie was over-joyed that the AIF's 'honoured warriors' had 'discredited [the] claims of [British] *fathers*', and 'gloriously vindicated' their Anglo-Indian '*sons*'.[63] He spoke of 'the return of the victors to their *native land* ... [their Indian] *homeland*'.[64] By contrast, others like Fred Murcutt referred to themselves as 'the descendants of those Britishers who had helped to bring the priceless Indian gem to the crown of Britain, who had fought, bled and died on a *foreign strand* for the sake of honour and prestige' and had now been 'allowed to emulate the deeds of their forebears when another far more serious crisis had arisen, which needed the whole hearted help and aid of all the *sons of the Mother Country*'.[65] This sense that India was still 'foreign' and that Britain was 'their Mother Country' contrasts strikingly with Gidney's evolving trajectory towards a dualistic discourse which would combine a British fatherland with an Indian motherland.[66] At this point Gidney was the president of the Empire League's Bombay branch, and made a speech at the dockside to the community's returning heroes.

> In our welcome we do not forget our Gallant lads ... whose graves adorn other lands ... Their death has meant our victory; their sacrifice the undying honour of A[nglo-India] ... To all their relatives we offer our deepest sympathy. From their tribulations springs a new life for the Community and *surely* the Community will live that life nobly and well. They *cannot* do less, in honour to all who have fought and fallen ... It is the one opportunity we have wanted, and to which we have been look-ing forward to show the whole world (and particularly India, in which country we have suffered from inherent handicaps and disqualifications) that we are indeed sons of the Old Country; that the fighting qualities transmitted to us from our forefathers, still run in our veins; are still at the service of our King and Country; and that, as such, we are entitled to take our proper place in India as second to none. On behalf of the Anglo-Indians of India and Burmah I salute you![67]

Alongside its infantry, the AIF had first been established with two field troops of cavalry, each comprising one second lieutenant and thirty NCOs and men, but in 1917 these were converted into cavalry signal troops. This decision is readily explained by the fact that the Indian Army was already abundantly oversupplied with regular cavalry, which were mostly stationed on the North-West Frontier with Afghanistan. They included those famous regiments originally founded by Colonels Skinner and Gardner. Morton-Jack recounts how Indian cavalry outflanked and encircled the Turks at Megiddo—'the last time in western military history [in which] mounted troops played a leading role'.[68] More surprisingly, to those familiar with the standard accounts of masses of foot soldiers advancing against immovably static entrenchments, they even played a significant mounted role on the Western Front, with charges 'at the Somme, [in which] they galloped ahead of British infantry to make rapid local gains.'[69] At the Battle of Cambrai, 'the 2nd Gardner's Horse jumped rows of German barbed wire, a trick they had specially trained their horses for'.[70]

However, the Indian Army had entered this global conflict 'particularly weak in artillery. The Indian Mountain Artillery had just seventy-two guns and the British artillery in India 336 field guns and howitzers.'[71] The British were evidently reluctant to entrust ordnance to Indian sepoys following the Great Rebellion, believing that outdated, inferior or lower-calibre technology would remain sufficient for fighting colonial frontier wars. Thus the AIF Battery, deployed to Mesopotamia (modern Iraq) as part of Indian Expeditionary Force D, came to play a particularly prominent role at the Siege of Kut, south of Baghdad, in a campaign which turned into one of the largest disasters in British military history. After 147 days with no relief or food left to feed what was left of the 13,000 British, Anglo-Indian and Indian defenders, General Townshend surrendered, whereupon the already malnourished survivors were force-marched to POW camps, with many dying en route. One young British officer who was injured in a failed attempt to break the siege, having earlier survived the similarly colossal disaster at Gallipoli, was the future prime minister Clement Attlee. A secret report circulated by the Secretary of State for India gave the following account of the role played by the AIF Battery four months before the surrender:

> On … Christmas Eve, the Turks attacked the fort in mass … The action … was most bloody, and the way the men of the Bombay Artillery (*Eurasians*) handled their guns in its defence was worthy of the highest commendation. Twice the Turks gained a footing in the north-east salient of the fort, but each time they were driven back with heavy slaughter. The attack … continued throughout the day and night …[72]

Even before seeing action, the Battery's popularity had led to it being dubbed 'the Corps d'Elite of the Anglo-Indian Force'.[73] Abbott's own son Roy—touted as 'the first Anglo-Indian Recruit to join up, the first non-commissioned officer to be appointed, and the first to receive a commission in the Anglo-Indian Force'—had chosen the Battery.[74] Yet as Gidney's dockside speech indicated, the bulk of its recruits had come from Burma:

> The only Anglo-Indians who went out at the outset, were the Volunteer Artillery … The deeds performed by that Battery are as glorious as they are undying. They breathe a spirit of true Loyalty and magnificent heroism. They fought bravely,—no matter what the odds—and they died bravely, for they represented the honour of the British Army (the finest soldiers in the world) as well as the honour and name of Anglo-Indians. Only one third of these lads from Burmah are left! What finer record of service could we expect from them?[75]

As president of the Burma branch of Abbott's Anglo-Indian Empire League, French-born and naturalised British subject Jules Emile DuBern had spearheaded its recruitment. His son Terence, then studying in England, enlisted in 'the 2/13 Battalion London Regiment', before being recommended for an AIF commission by Abbott.[76]

Burma had been governed as a province of British India since its conquest was completed in 1885. Alongside a larger number of Indian merchants, money-lenders and manual labourers, many Anglo-Indians had migrated there, most to work on the railways, and others in various government departments and private businesses. Burma had thus become an extension of the imagined space of Anglo-India. In the census and for electoral purposes, the collective designation for mixed people of European paternal descent in Burma was 'Anglo-Indian', grouping ethnic Anglo-Indians together with those whose

Asian ancestry was actually Burmese or ethnic minority Burmese. This encouraged a shared social and political existence for two closely intertwined but potentially distinct groups. Wartime recruiting experience had brought home to Robbie the true extent of caste- and class-inflected socio-racial prejudices towards the mixed among the educated Indian middle classes—he 'noted the contempt of the well-to-do Indian for the man who is neither an Indian nor European if perchance the latter were not overendowed with this world's goods'.[77] By contrast, the lack of specifically caste-based prejudice among the Burmese, and the high level of autonomy of Burmese women in marriage, divorce and property ownership, created a very different climate for interracial relationships and their offspring. According to customary Buddhist practice, cohabitation and eating from the same bowl created a common law marriage, which the woman herself was free to terminate. Burmese women who lived with European men were thus far better placed than their Indian counterparts in seeking to maintain respectability and familial ties with their Burmese relatives for themselves and their children. This could not but foster distinct attitudes and relatively muted socio-racial prejudices towards the mixed among the resident colonial British population. Also in keeping with Burma's later acquisition, the ongoing prevalence of interracial and interfaith relationships more closely resembled the situation in India a century or more before.

Charles Campagnac, who would eventually wrest leadership of the mixed in Burma away from both DuBern and the India-based leaders, was ethnically Anglo-Indian himself, although firmly embedded in Burma's national life and married to an ethnic Anglo-Burman. Around 1926 Campagnac established an Anglo-Indian Federation of Burma to rival DuBern's Anglo-Indian Association Rangoon branch, which, as the *Review* observed, mirrored 'the same communal schism as India experienced at that time'.[78] By September 1932 the remnant of the All-India Association in Burma agreed to formally dissolve itself by amalgamating 'to form one united Body' with Campagnac's Federation.[79] To better situate the community to face rising Burmese ethno-nationalism and anti-Indian sentiment, its name was eventually changed to the Anglo-Burman Union. Anticipating the constitutional separation of Burma from India with the implementation of the 1935

Government of Burma Act in 1937, Campagnac had the foresight to seek to rebrand his conjoined community, reversing the prior position by having ethnic Anglo-Indians accept a new joint status as Anglo-Burmans. However, over the following decade Anglo-Indian leaders in India still hoped to maintain their own presence in Burma, and in 1932 the *Review* had expressed the 'hope one day to effect one big union and understanding between the mixed races of India, Burma, Malaya, Federated States and others ... [for] who will deny the potentialities for power of such a combine of communal forces?'[80]

In neighbouring Bengal, Lionel Ingels had brought his Calcutta Association into a temporary federation for wartime recruitment under Abbott's leadership. Anticipating that the arrangement would not long survive the peace, Robbie insisted on the need for a single and explicitly political Anglo-Indian organisation with 'ONE AIM' and 'ONE HEAD', 'if life in India is to be at all possible for the Anglo-Indian in POST WAR TIMES and under POST WAR CONDITIONS'.[81] Failure would see 'the Anglo-Indian barque ... "tossed about with every wind of doctrine" ever journeying yet never reaching its desired haven'.[82] Predictably, negotiations between Ingels and Abbott soon broke down, officially over the proposed organisational structure, but really over who would be in effective control of an amalgamated body.[83] The Empire League's change of name to the All-India Anglo-Indian and Domiciled European Association at its 1918–19 AGM may in part have been an attempt to give Ingels's side the face-saving semblance that the Associations had won the day. Yet it was not Ingels but Abbott's deputy Gidney who emerged from the pack to make a successful leadership challenge, his surprise triumph in a bitterly fought contest adding fuel to ongoing factionalism through the 1920s. Lord Lloyd, who served as Governor of Bombay at the time, later recalled how

> it was under my aegis that Sir Henry [Gidney] first abandoned a lucrative medical practice ... to champion the cause of the then ill-organised and scattered Anglo-Indian community ... I remember well ... to my cost—and also pleasure, the energy and assiduity with which in the earliest days of his public career, he espoused the cause of those ... who, on the demobilisation of the Anglo-Indian Units from Mesopotamia and elsewhere, found themselves confronted by economic disabilities and difficulties.[84]

Anglo-Indians had no doubt expected that the confirmation of their eligibility to serve in the British Army would continue, and that, failing this, their earmarked jobs on the railways would be awaiting their return. Instead, the AIF was permanently disbanded. No alternative routes for continued service in the British Army or British Indian Army were substituted; nor were serious efforts made to assist Anglo-Indian veterans resuming civil or railway employment. It is not a stretch to imagine Anglo-Indians feeling betrayed by the lack of recompense or lasting recognition for 'the acknowledged successes and good services rendered by Anglo-Indian units in the War'.[85]

Gidney would later recall the plight of the large cohort of 'Anglo-Indian nurses ... [who had] freely enlisted in the British Army ... The moment the War was over the door was closed and they were demobbed. To-day the rules prevent an Anglo-Indian nurse being employed by the British Army.'[86] Paul Scott's fiction describes how '"the rulers of the roost" in civilian hospitals were Queen Alexandra nurses sent from Britain: "You should see the airs some of the QAs give themselves. At home they'd simply be ordinary ward nurses ... Here they rank as sisters ... [and] are[n't] supposed to do anything menial. That's all left to the poor little Anglo-Indian girls."'[87]

Generally, as Buettner highlights, colonial British women were less likely to work than their metropolitan counterparts. While many careers deemed suitable 'for unmarried middle-class women had slowly shed some of ... [their] stigma in Britain', such as 'teaching, nursing, working in ... department stores, and as typists and receptionists', in India these were associated with 'the racially mixed'.[88] Nursing was one of the few careers that British women, generally from less 'pukka' families, pursued in India during peacetime. By 1923 Gidney was arguing 'that the recruitment of hospital nurses from England for British Station Hospitals is unnecessary, and ... should be stopped on the ground that sufficient nurses' could be obtained in India.[89]

Constitutional politics and Indianisation

Even before the war's conclusion Robbie was bemoaning the unfortunate 'tendency ... in high places to give way to the agitator at the expense of the peaceful loyalist'.[90] With the implementation of the 1919 Government of India Act under the Montagu–Chelmsford Reforms, the colonial state came under enormous pressure from the provincial Legislative Councils and the reconstituted Central Legislative Assembly (henceforth 'the Assembly') to Indianise government services and the railways, not only at the expense of colonial Britons and Europeans (domiciled or otherwise), but also of Anglo-Indians. Fortunately for the domiciled, the colonial state reserved the railways as a 'central' subject under the new diarchic system, while devolving other areas (like education) that were considered less vital to the Provincial Councils. M. Rashiduzzaman's doctoral research reveals that this concentrated demands for railway reform in the bicameral central legislature, leaving the railways as 'the single department on which the maximum number of questions was asked in both the chambers'.[91] The retention of centralised control over the railways is a reminder of how crucial this infrastructure was to the Raj's military and security system. Yet when colonial authorities felt compelled to give ground to demands for Indianisation, they were more willing to surrender the lower management level currently occupied by Anglo-Indians than to give up the command structure dominated by 'gazetted' or covenanted British officers.

The pressure for 'Indianisation' had begun long before. It was in keeping with Gopal Krishna Gokhale's earlier scrutiny of Curzon's budgets, in which the Viceroy had sought to defend himself from the charge of being 'personally [involved in] the appointment of this or that European or Eurasian to some post or other in some part of India'.[92] Growing expectations for greater participation by Indians in public service were catalysed by the First World War. Already in 1918 Indian reformists like V. S. Srinivasa Sastri were moving resolutions on subjects such as 'Recruitment in India for the Public Works Department and the Railway Engineering Service'.[93] In the debate over Sastri's bill, Mr. B. D. Shukul complained that

> these posts in theory are intended for the children of the soil; yet in practice ... are manned mainly by Anglo-Indians ... [with] the higher appointments ... practically shut out to the children of the soil. This constitutes ... a longstanding grievance which is greatly resented by those ... already in the Service ... [who] are smarting

under an insult as they rightly regard the preference shown to the Anglo-Indians to be ...[94]

Although since 1911 'Anglo-Indian' was officially meant to refer to the mixed, and not to colonial Britons, here the word was still being used in the older sense. Shukul referred to the mixed as 'Eurasian'.[95] This revealed the perils of the three-decades-long push among the mixed for redesignation to a term still commonly understood to refer to the British. Indian nationalists could plausibly blame Anglo-Indians for orientating their demands towards claims to a British status that would elevate them above their Indian compatriots and that could be read as confirming their alienness. Although the British defined Anglo-Indians and Domiciled Europeans as 'statutory natives of India', Sastri and Shukul were not prepared to recognise this Indian civic status. Sastri argued that for the purposes of Indianisation 'the word "Indians"' should be 'used in the sense of the Public Service Commission's Report, as meaning Indians of pure Asiatic descent'.[96] Thus the mixed were caught in-between two contradictory definitions that excluded them. While they were denied recognition as British or as Indians, it was arguably rational for them, either individually or collectively, to make apparently contradictory claims in both directions themselves, for advancement into superior colonial British-dominated rungs of service, and for retention of those junior subordinate roles they currently held, for otherwise they would find themselves in the unenviable position of being trapped between the conflicting interests of the two sides.

Similarly in 1921 Rai Bahadur Sinha asked for 'the number of posts in the higher grade of services in the Railway, Postal and Telegraphs Departments, and ... the number of such posts held by Indians and non-Indians, respectively, according to nationality'.[97] Mr. C. A. Innes responded that only 228 of these were 'held by Indians' as against 611 'held by Non-Indians'.[98] On those occasions when the proposition was put in this straightforwardly binary way and neither side was willing to fully embrace the mixed or concede them an Indian or a British status, they were in danger of being overlooked entirely and squeezed out altogether. Shukul further complained that 'in certain departments such Indians as are allowed admission are required to possess higher educational qualifications than the members of other communities, such as Eurasians and Christians'.[99] With middling jobs on the railways having been effectively earmarked for the mixed since the days of Curzon, few Anglo-Indians had hitherto seen the need to encourage their children to attend Indian or British universities, even if they had the means. Those whose children attended the better European and Anglo-Indian schools already paid far higher fees than Indians at the secondary level. These schools prepared students for the external Junior and Senior Cambridge examinations, not the matriculation examination for Indian universities. In response to Shukul's charge that Indian university graduates were better-qualified applicants for railway jobs, Gidney could only answer that the Senior Cambridge or European school leavers' examination should be treated as equivalent to the Indian matriculation examination. This was a suggestion the authorities generally agreed to, but it could be a limited protection to a community whose poorer classes had long been accustomed to leaving school early, often without passing the Junior Cambridge, expecting to be apprenticed on the railways, learn on the job, and be promoted to become train drivers and firemen.

Anglo-Indians could clearly ill-afford to lose either these more physically arduous railway jobs or the middle-management rungs of railway, telegraph and customs administration which the better-educated among them then held. Taken together, these were their bread and butter—the economic lifeblood of this small commu-nity—the loss of which would have meant another radical displace-ment of the group's existing employment structure. Anglo-Indians were thus fortunate to have Gidney waging his one-man war in defence of these vital niches. One British colonial official purported to have dreamed that

> I had died ... [and gone] to heaven ... I asked admission from the outside custodian and I was terrified he would not admit me. He asked who I was. I replied I was John Coatman. He asked what I had done and I said I was Director of Public Information. 'Very sorry, I cannot let you in', was the answer. 'We have no message from earth.' 'What shall I do', I thought. I 'better go to hell'. And as I was thinking of what I should say I heard a stentorian voice, in a wordy warfare with somebody ... the voice of Sir Henry Gidney ... How he got in I do not know but he was inside and suddenly I heard his voice raised, 'Is that John Coatman outside? Let him in.' The gates were opened.

There I saw him with the inside custodian examining the books and he demanded to know the percentage of Anglo-Indians in heaven. Here was your leader totaling up the number of Anglo-Indians ... and after a while he said, 'Sir, I demand ten per cent. more for my community.' This is how he fights for you in heaven and earth.[100]

This comic anecdote reflected the reservations that Gidney's persistent lobbying efforts ultimately enabled him to secure for Anglo-Indians in certain grades of railway and telegraph employment. The system in which Anglo-Indians were employed had been openly and explicitly socio-racial at the start of the century. Under pressure from Indian legislators and their allies in the press, these patterns would persist in a more limited way while being rendered increasingly opaque, partly through being reframed as a communal question, in which Anglo-Indians would retain a smaller share of their existing employment as one of several Indian minorities. Whatever the justice of Indian demands and the inequities of the system, Anglo-Indians did have their own structural economic problem. They faced a ceiling on their own employment above which the vast majority could not rise, unless they were of fairer skin and succeeded in passing as European.

There was also an ever-present underclass of the unemployed and underemployed, heightened by downturns in the wider labour market, and particularly acute because of demobilisation following the First World War, as well as increasing Indianisation during the 1920s, with the global depression following the Wall Street Crash of 1929 still to come. Thus while Anglo-Indian leaders might want to encourage their flock to pursue other careers and thereby make the group less collectively reliant upon state employment, giving up those well-paid or relatively well-paid positions in the middling rungs of the public sector and the more lowly yet still privileged positions they held on the railways as train drivers, firemen and guards, before finding viable alternatives, would have amounted to collective economic suicide. When Gidney first addressed the Legislative Assembly at length in the budget debate of 1921, he resisted Indian demands to reduce railway expenditure, stating:

as the representative of a community which ... forms the backbone of all the railways ... I feel ... entitled to speak with some authority on this matter ... The racial distinction that has been made is very unfortunate and undesirable ... My community forms a very large percentage of the members of the Great Indian Peninsula [GIP] Railway and ... [if there are] not a sufficient number of Indians in the engineering staff of the grade of Rs. 450 to Rs. 3,000 per mensem ... The same ... applies to my community for there is not a single Anglo-Indian employed to-day in this grade ... Railway employees will not tolerate any reduction of their pay ... The last five years ... have shown an enormous amount of railway unrest ... [Reducing] the pay of all the railway employees ... [would] only ... add ... fuel to the fire ... I consider this demand as suicidal, and if the House passes it, we would be cutting our nose to spite our face.[101]

Dr. H. S. Gour, who would become the leader of the nascent Democratic Party grouping in the year that followed, responded:

the Honourable and Gallant Colonel ... has let the cat out of the bag by saying he is watching the proceedings in defence of his own community ... [Are they] not classed apart and paid higher wages for discharging the same duties for which Indians in this country are equally efficient but for which they are paid much lower wages? ... Are not the scales for the remuneration of railway employees classed as Europeans and Anglo-Indians, and Indians, and are not the wages for doing the identical work different[?] ... It is a well known fact that the engine drivers and guards of all mail and passenger trains are members of the European or Anglo-Indian community ... If a European or Anglo-Indian Guard is paid in the neighbourhood of Rs. 300 a month, the Indian Guard would probably be paid little over Rs. 100 a month ... and the same may be said of ... the staff in the first class and big stations, which are meant exclusively for Europeans and Anglo-Indians, and only Indian subordinates.[102]

Although Anglo-Indians were often posted to remoter and smaller railway stations than imported British and Domiciled European staff, Gour's facts were difficult to counter. Gidney could only state that he wanted to 'avoid any racial distinction', proclaim his support 'for equality of treatment', and reiterate his point that in the posts above Rs. 450 on the GIP railway, Anglo-Indians were 'suffering from the same disability as the Indians ... [as] the portal to this grade is the passing of an examination in England.'[103] Gour responded that he was 'glad to hear this expression of opinion from the Honourable and Gallant Colonel. He is also like myself for "fair play and no favour".'[104] However, like the colonial state, Gidney would actually seek to reframe racial distinctions as communal ones. If Punjabi Sikhs, Rajputs and other martial races could be allowed to maintain their disproportionate preponderance in the Indian Army, why could not the same apply to the railway and telegraph niches that Anglo-Indians currently held? To ask any community to suddenly give up its main source of existing employment or to radically reduce its wages and standards of living would undoubtedly have provoked a similar opposition or perhaps an even graver reaction. Britons whose jobs were being Indianised always had the option of going home. But this was not so for the vast majority of Anglo-Indians. Their wartime dreams of having firmly established their right to a British status had proved illusory.

Indian reformists like Sastri, correctly or incorrectly known as 'moderates', tended to become more sympathetic to Anglo-Indians' difficulties through greater familiarity, while not giving up on the justice of their demands for equal access to railway jobs. During his 1923 address to

> a well attended meeting of the Domiciled European and Anglo-Indian Community ... [Sastri] said that he considered it a privilege ... to speak to them ... though it was impossible to unite all the various communities in India into one homogen[e]ous whole and sink all their differences, it was practicable to so unite them that they would mutually tolerate, befriend and co-operate with each other ... He had personal friends among Anglo-Indians for whom he had the greatest admiration, but, speaking frankly, he must tell them that owing to the actions of some ... the impression had gained ground that the community considered themselves aloof from the rest of the country as they had privileges above others which they felt they must defend. The Government, by giving the community special concessions, had weakened ... [them.] No community could develop itself if it looked to the Government for special favours. The Anglo-Indian community had the brains and energy to take their place in the life of the country. Let them give up the desire for special privileges and they would find the other communities in India would embrace them as brothers and as co-operators in the uplift of India. He reminded them that the colour bar in the Colonies operated against them as well.[105]

Not many Anglo-Indians at the time would have been receptive to Sastri's message. It appears that Gidney had arranged this meeting to try to nudge his constituents in his desired direction. He had probably also invited Sir Montagu Webb, knowing that the typical Anglo-Indian would more readily take advice from a colonial Briton. Webb reinforced Sastri's message while commending 'the work that the community had done in the war. He exhorted … [them] to cease looking for Government patronage, but to turn their attention to private enterprise', although he was more sanguine about potential emigration, advising them 'to keep … [their] eyes open to opportunities overseas'.[106]

Gidney's success in gaining the sympathy of Sastri for the difficulties of the Anglo-Indian position was by no means exceptional. As his more radical protégé would later reflect, 'many sections of Indian opinion' appreciated the 'constant theme in Gidney's speeches' of denouncing 'race and colour discrimination' and 'regarded [him] as liberal and advanced in his thinking'.[107] In Madras in 1934 and Lucknow in 1937, Gidney would be hosted by 'civic bodies … dominated by members of the Congress Party … [where] he was welcomed and honoured as an Indian … [and proved himself to be] no narrow communalist'.[108] Nonetheless, while expressing 'high regard and esteem' for Jawaharlal Nehru, Gidney wrote to the *Statesman* in 1929 denouncing Mr. Barton, 'President of the Anglo-Indian Federation' and 'General Secretary of the Indian Telegraph Association', for his 'unauthorised' 'luncheon' meeting with 'the leader of the Independence Party'.[109] The *Review* was less diplomatic, attacking any possible 'alliance' or political 'flirtation' with 'the extreme section of the Congress' as 'sheer noonday madness'.[110] The conservative forces which formed the main opposition to Gidney might easily have resorted to harsher rhetoric. Anthony would later defend his political predecessor and mentor as

> a progressive leader in the context of the then obtaining attitudes … complexes … [and] certain inhibitions in the Community. Gidney's policies certainly represented a striking advance on the position taken up by [the] Anglo-Indian leaders who preceded him. He was unqualified in his emphasis that the Anglo-Indians are nationals of India and could only find their proper place if they moved with and accepted the other peoples of India without the inhibitions and complexes of the past. Gidney was ahead of the hard core of Anglo-Indian thinking.

Yet he could not go too far ahead for fear of being misunderstood and misrepresented in his own Community.[111]

Anthony's euphemistic allusion to 'inhibitions' was intended to convey his reading of Anglo-Indians' complex psychological hang-ups, which he sought to diagnose later in his book. Part of what was really at issue was the group's deep-seated cultural, racial and colour-based prejudices, as well as its still overwhelming primary allegiance and loyalty to Britain and its corresponding reluctance to develop any real understanding of, let alone sympathy for, the concerns of Indian nationalists and the Congress. Anthony also cited a key speech which Gidney gave in Bangalore:

> Deny the fact that you are sons and citizens of India, disclaim it, conceal it in your efforts to ape what you are not, and you will soon be the 'not wanted' of all. The opportunity is yours today to more closely associate yourselves, from early school life with the rest of India, to realise that you, with all other communities, have a right to live in this, your Country, and that you are first and last sons of India … But if there is one thing which you must completely eradicate from yourselves it is the retention of the 'superiority' and 'inferiority' complexes; and you should bring about their replacement with a complex of equality.[112]

The effects of education

Many of the franker and more illuminating interventions on the subject of education actually took place in the 1940s, but these are indicative of how much more culturally conservative things were likely to have been earlier in the century. The Reverend L. J. Hopkins, a former president of the 'Kolar Gold Field Provincial Branch' for 'three years' up to 1931, who had expressed himself 'glad … to identify himself with the Association and the community',[113] took issue with the standard line from Anglo-Indian politicians that 'Anglo-Indian schools … were mostly controlled by Europeans, [who] taught the pupils to look away from India and things Indian, to look up to everything British and to look down upon most things Indian'.[114] The now Bangalore-based educationist instead blamed parents and home influences, declaring in 1943:

Even where there is no actual contempt of things Indian, there is too often a staggering lack of interest ... I asked two young people ... if they knew which man of letters of international reputation had just died ... I told them it was Rabindranath Tagore, and to my horror I discovered they had never heard of him! But what exasperated me still more was that they made it pretty clear, when they knew he was an *Indian* poet, that they did not *want* to know about him.[115]

A rather discordant Anglo-Indian socialist writing as 'McNeelance' preached that the community should broaden its cultural horizons beyond Shakespeare, George Bernard Shaw, W. B. Yeats and Beethoven by reading Tagore; learning to 'read an Urdu newspaper'; going 'to a ballet by Menaka'; or listening 'to Indian Music without laughing at it or saying "It is just noise ..."'.[116] McNeelance complained

that our failure to appreciate the culture of our land ... is due to a false set of values, which finds anything Western perfect and anything Eastern beneath one's notice ... an attitude that is stronger in the Anglo-Indian than ... the European. This turning away from Eastern culture is stronger in Anglo-Indians because the urge to like and appreciate it is stronger ... When an Anglo-Indian declares vehemently against Indian culture, nothing seems more apt than Shakespeare's phrase, 'the lady, (or gentleman) doth protest too much, methinks'. The average member of the community prefers Spanish, Hungarian or Slav Music to any other. But it seldom occurs to him that his reason for doing so is the fact that this music is very Eastern ... a synthesis of East and West and shows up Kipling's 'East is East, and West is West' as a lie ... This is something the Anglo-Indian must realise. He too is where East meets West ... At present the Anglo-Indian's behaviour is neurotic; it is a vain attempt to run away from one half of himself ... [We should be] steeping ourselves in both Western and Eastern ideas. It is not a question of repressing the 'Anglo' in us but a question of releasing the 'Indian', and making something different, something truly Anglo-Indian, that will enable us to realise the best in the community and take our rightful place in our land India and in the world.[117]

Although basic literacy was nearly universal among Anglo-Indians, placing them far ahead of almost every other Indian community, Fred Corbett's assessment and prescriptions were probably more realistic:

we are a politically lazy and indifferent community, with an inbred conservativism [*sic*], and live in a little world of our own, remote from the stir of the political and intellectual life of the country ... with most of us, our education ceases when we leave school or college. Most of us forget that ... education is a never ending process, for all ages ... Very few Anglo-Indian homes possess a well stocked library of useful and instructive books, as most of us are satisfied with reading a few trashy and ephemeral works of fiction ... Very few of us even study the daily papers closely ...[118]

Nonetheless, Anglo-Indians were a potent force in the performing arts. With Calcutta's 'schools of dancing ... run almost exclusively by' Anglo-Indians, colonial British women steered clear of 'teaching ballet' to avoid any 'risk' of their being suspected to be mixed themselves.[119] Although 'our culture is one-sided and mostly confined to Western music and Art', insisted Corbett,

> We are a cultured community. There is hardly an Anglo-Indian family of any standing but has at least one accomplished musician, painter or singer, and there are many instances where whole families are accomplished musicians. There is no concert of European music given anywhere in India, but there are Anglo-Indians in it. Not a day passes but Anglo-Indian artists broadcast over the various Indian Radio stations ... The results of the various musical examinations held in India by the Trinity College of London and other bodies show a very large number of successful Anglo-Indian candidates.[120]

It was from this rich well of talent and training that so many individual diasporic Anglo-Indians propelled themselves to global prominence in cinema and classical and popular music. Corbett suggested that Anglo-Indians try to broaden their cultural horizons by attending the performances of 'Uday Shankar, Ramgopal and other exponents of Indian dancing'.[121] The Anglo-Indian education system and culture closely mirrored that of the anglophone West Indian middle classes who Anne Spry Rush argued came to see themselves as black imperial Britons.[122] Having 'been born and raised (and ... to some degree prospered) within a British imperial system', the West Indian middle classes constructed their identities within a broader conception of Britishness.[123] In claiming co-ownership of cultural products that were British in origin, they were not only looking for practical means of self-advancement: 'For them,' argues Rush, 'the nature of civilization itself remained essentially British—encased within a class structure and an imperial world outside of which culture seemed impossible.'[124] Though there were no doubt differences between black imperial Britishness of this kind and the Britain-orientated identity and common citizenship claims of a sizeable majority of Anglo-Indians, Anglo-Indian attachments if anything ran deeper as a result of the emotive invocation of shared blood, kinship and history. Both education systems taught for the same Cambridge external examinations. Describing the curriculum, one Barbadian felt himself living 'the lives of those great men in the History of England book. My mind crawled with battles and speeches ... Magna Cartas ... Anne Boleyn ... Elizabeth Tudor ... Mary Queen of Scots—all these were women with whom I was in love. I painted their faces black and put their huge crinolined dresses on the girls I saw around me.'[125] West Indian parents staunchly resisted the attempts of the British drafters of the Kandel Committee Report of 1943 to sever them from a system deemed to be an 'external ... veneer'.[126]

Anglo-Indian parents probably were, in the main, just as conservative, and the cultural content of anglophone education in India followed much the same pattern, with emphasis placed upon the teaching of British history, English literature, and the names and types of European flowers. Within a system modelled on elite (fee-paying) public schools in England but with an added Christian emphasis, 'French or Latin' frequently took precedence.[127] Provision for Indian languages, when available, was often paltry; this inadequacy did not well equip Anglo-Indians to compete with Britons taking examinations in London for entry into colonial service. As 'an old Baldwinian', Gidney was intimately familiar with the kind of privileged boarding-school education that better-off members of the domiciled community enjoyed, although with a distinctive American Methodist inflection.[128] Around the same time as Gidney's Baldwin Boys' School, Bangalore, was founded in 1880, senior Anglican clergy became anxious to extend educational provision for the mixed in response to the 'Eurasian Question'. One observer wryly complained 'that there are many more important things to be attended to before the question of establishing a system of Etons and Harrows in the hills for Eurasians can seriously be taken up'.[129] However, as Elizabeth Buettner explains, with the increasing association between the domiciled and even the most elite of European schools, colonial British parents who

could afford to do so preferred to send their children, and more especially their sons, to Britain at a young age to establish their non-Asiatic
domicile, secure their future employment and marriage prospects,
and avoid them becoming associated with the mixed.[130] Although
there are examples of Anglo-Indian women being employed as nan-
nies, British parents were often advised that it was better to employ
only Indian ayahs and servants to avoid their children contracting the
supposedly highly catching 'chi chi' accent.

In 1939 the anticolonial socialist writer and journalist Ela Sen
intermingled middle-class Indian prejudices towards the mixed with
her assessment of

> so-called European schools ... In reality, such schools are filled with
> Anglo-Indians, usually of low culture and parentage. With their infini-
> tesimal drop of 'white blood' and deliberate ignorance of the land of
> their birth, they treat their fellow Indian students with scorn and
> contempt for their 'dark blood'. From the school authorities them-
> selves Anglo-Indians got preferential treatment, and the Indian child
> is at first bewildered by this ... Birth and breeding are of no conse-
> quence in such schools, which are dotted all over the length and
> breadth of India, and it was in just such an atmosphere that Subhas
> [Chandra] Bose began his schooling at the age of five.[131]

Defending Anglo-Indians from frequent charges of exhibiting a
sense of superiority towards Indians, Gidney similarly implicated the
colour and cultural prejudices of their Western educators. Combined
with the inferior position and limited number of Anglo-Indian teachers in these schools, these contributed towards inculcating an equally
damaging sense of inferiority towards Europeans in Anglo-Indian
children, he argued. However, when addressing his own flock Gidney
was just as apt to lay blame on Anglo-Indian parents themselves. As
well as advocating reform of its cultural content, Gidney bemoaned
the lack of technical and vocational training available to prepare
Anglo-Indian youths for realistic and practical areas of future employment, which would be especially crucial for the majority who were
not expected to undertake further study.

Although anglophone schools in India employed increasing numbers of Anglo-Indian teachers, mostly women, as the century progressed, there was a decided socio-racial and cultural hierarchy in

place. British, European and American educationists and religious organisations were firmly entrenched in management and leadership roles, and were almost entirely resistant to any change on that front. Gidney would of course have wanted the management to open up through the promotion of Anglo-Indian teachers. Anthony would later reiterate many of the same points more forcefully, asserting that 'most of the ills of the community ... were directly traceable to the obsolete and outworn system of education obtaining in Anglo-Indian and European schools'.[132] He told a meeting in Mussoorie in June of 1943 that 'our schools ... taught our children to look away from India and our community. The teaching of Anglo-Indian history, which should form the first and basic ingredient of the curriculum, has been completely ignored. Not only European but Anglo-Indian education-alists also are utterly ignorant of the history and achievements of [t]he community.'[133]

Conservative Anglo-India

Gidney's position was highly triangulated. Although he habitually spoke of Indians as a category of 'other' when addressing fellow Anglo-Indians, he increasingly deployed a dualistic emphasis on famil-ial connection to both Britons and Indians, reflected in the use of terms like 'our Indian kinsmen'[134] and 'our Indian brothers'[135] in his Association's journal, the *Anglo-Indian Review*. Deep significance was read into the most subtle of changes in his rhetoric by his more emphatically pro-British, arch-loyalist opponents. Since 1920 rival 'leaders in Bengal' had denounced him as 'the self appointed Bombay Leader who has tried to pose as President-in-Chief of the Community', and waged a 'paper war ... in the public press ... culminating in one party dubbing the other "Pro Indians"'.[136] As late as 1930, while 'addressing a public meeting', Gidney placatingly referred to 'England' as 'the homeland', even as he tried to persuade Anglo-Indians that it could offer them 'no haven across the seas' or 'safe retreat when our life-work is done', that they had 'no ties ... which necessitate a permanent link with England ... All our interests lie here in India.'[137] Even such carefully calibrated appeals to Anglo-Indians and the gradual moves Gidney made towards courting Indian opinion were attacked by 'his political opponents, particularly Abbott and Stark', who clearly believed Gidney to be more pro-Indian than he was publicly willing to declare, and continued 'to accuse Gidney of abandoning their British heritage'.[138]

The defeated and displaced former Empire League president still nursed a grudge and retained his own faction of sympathisers and supporters, during a period when Gidney was still struggling to amalgamate various Anglo-Indian organisations under his leadership. Most of the political challenges to Gidney came from conservatively minded forces of this kind who were bellicosely pro-British. They not only set up rival organisations, but also formed entryist factions within his Association, at times capturing significant geographic strongholds. Some of these individuals appeared to be operating as cat's paws for Abbott, while organisations calling themselves leagues or federations, harking back to Abbott's Empire League and wartime Federation, continued to be established through the interwar years. As late as 1929 'Mr. H. W. B. Moreno' attempted to revive an 'Anglo-Indian League' in Calcutta, with 'a compendious ... 21st Annual Report' backdating its foundation to 1909, thereby arousing the *Review*'s jeers that this long history of operations had been kept 'such a close secret that we were not even aware of its existence'.[139] This was characteristic of a multitude of localised and regional power struggles, which resulted in the reincorporation of long-defunct organisations, the secession or disaffiliation of Association branches, and the setting up of duplicate corporate structures by rival leadership slates each claiming continuity with the original body. The *Review* denounced 'separatist camps', 'Loyalist Legion[s]', 'so-called Federations', 'other mushroom organizations ... [and] strange societies with high-sounding names, ideas and ideals', 'movements [which] spring up and die down in a night, like Jonah's gourd, and may be ignored by an institution which has its roots planted throughout India and Burma'.[140]

At the 1918–19 AGM, 'some Domiciled Europeans [had] demanded to know why the "Domiciled European" had been left out' of the Empire League's new name, which was to have been just the Anglo-Indian Association, 'as there were many covenanted and Domiciled European members ... who were obviously not Anglo-Indians'.[141] Following 'a very heated and prolonged discussion', a resolution was passed 'by a small majority' that 'Domiciled European' should also be included in the Association's name.[142] In 1928 the *Anglo-Indian Citizen* reflected: 'The possibility of a split between Anglo-Indian and Domiciled European has threatened before. Much feeling was aroused among Domiciled Europeans by the uncharitable gibe *Albino-Anglo-Indian* levelled at them by' Gidney.[143] The *Review* defended Gidney's coinage as 'never [having] been applied to the Domiciled European *proper*, but to that unfortunate unpigmented Anglo-Indian who takes advantage to deny his birth-right and is thus able sometimes to force himself or creep into a community from which his own darker-skinned brothers and sisters are ostracised'.[144]

As Anthony would later comment, Gidney 'lost few opportunities to criticise those Anglo-Indians who posed as domiciled Europeans', mocking them as 'Rear-Rank Europeans' or 'Domestic Occurrences'.[145] In this context, it is easy to imagine how the shift in leadership from men like Abbott, who had apparently been born in Edinburgh, to the Igatpuri-born and visibly mixed Gidney would have irked both Domiciled Europeans and those colonial Britons who had chosen to take on paternalistic leadership roles on behalf of the domiciled and who were very likely accustomed to being treated with deference. Gidney relished being the centre of attention, boasting to Australasian newspapers of having shot two tigers in quick succession without reloading in the presence of the 'late Maharajah of Mymensingh'.[146] One presumably British diarist mocked the grandiloquence of the

> gallant Col. Gidney, or Ginday, as some admirers dub him, I.M.S. (RETD.), C.I.E., J.P., E.T.C., M.L.A., E.T.C., etc. ... [explaining that] I wrote to the *Englishman* about this notability saying he used those sub-sections of the alphabet because he considered the donkey looked better with all his harness on and he threatened to horsewhip me but changed his mind and became almost more than friendly ...[147]

There was a double standard here, for many colonial British officials were similarly well-armoured with postnominals and would have taken far greater offence at such jests.

Sir Cecil Walsh, a colonial British judge of the Allahabad High Court, was the president of the Association's branch in the United Provinces, which had effectively seceded in 1920 in protest over Gidney's takeover. In 1922 they complained at having been 'overlooked' in the government's consultation for nominations to the Legislative Assembly—'even tho[ugh] we do not recognise Col Gidney as our Head', 'we represent the Community in the U.P. in a far greater measure than does any other existing Representative Body', and 'venture to place before you the names of two tried and trusty leaders whose past service to the Community is well known viz (1) J. H. ABBOTT of JHANSI and (2) H. A. Stark, Armenian College, Free School Street, Calcutta'.[148] There is evidence from Walsh's own pen to suggest a prejudiced predisposition against Gidney on grounds of colour alone. In 1913 Walsh had presided over the trial of an infamous double-murder case involving two couples who 'belonged, directly or indirectly, to' the ISMD, which Walsh described as a 'body ... recruited entirely in India; partly from amongst domiciled Englishmen, but mainly from amongst the Eurasians, or Anglo-Indians, as they are now known'.[149] Walsh wrote a whole book on the case, which implied that the chief male perpetrator's criminal tendencies and sexual immorality were linked to his 'general physiognomy' as a man 'of pronounced Eurasian stock'.[150]

Unfortunately for Gidney, he had opened himself to attack through his private life. Admitted by his successor to have been 'a polished performer on the dance floor' who could 'put to shame much younger exponents of the waltz and the tango', and a 'sparkling raconteur' with 'a connoisseur's eye for beautiful women' and 'a reputation as a lady-killer',[151] Gidney was named as a third party in a 1922 divorce case adjudicated by Walsh. Unsurprisingly Walsh took the opportunity to pass 'serious strictures upon Colonel Gidney in the course of his judgement'.[152] Gidney responded by promising 'very shortly to vindicate his personal honour to the satisfaction *of the whole world*',[153] instructing Sir Tej Bahadur Sapru to bring a case 'asking that certain passages in the judgement ... be expunged from the record ... under Section 107 of the Government of India Act'.[154] Despite Sapru's famous legal skills, the Chief Justice rejected the legal premise on which the case had been brought, while expressing the views that 'Mr. Filose, for reasons not very apparent, may have deliberately lied and may have completely deceived the Judge' and that 'the question as to the propriety of Gidney's conduct in this family dispute was ... irrelevant to any issue, but was a matter which was of such importance to Colonel Gidney that he offered … [him] the opportunity of explanation'.[155] Even after Walsh's subsequent departure for England, Allahabad appeared to remain a hub of anti-Gidney agitation. In September 1932 the *Review* offered

> our hearty congratulations to our Allahabad Provincial Branch on its success in the appeal moved against it by Mr. McGowan. We are much impressed with the business-like manner in which the recent meetings … have been conducted. Every item breathes of solid work, a desire to work in conjunction with the Governing Body, to co-operate with each other and work as a team … for and with the District Branches and, what is more to the point, to get rid of disloyalists and nonco-operators. The Association has tolerated these renegades quite long enough and it is the recognition given to them that has helped to keep alive … such organisations as 'Federations', 'Leagues', 'Legions' and others who pretend to co-operate and be loyal at meetings, but whose true voices and opinions are heard in their homes or at public places … The new Allahabad Branch Council … is an example to many other Provincial Branches … [who] spend their time in petty wrangles and in evolving means of nonco-operation or side tracking the desires of the Governing Body.[156]

While entryism and obstructionism of this kind by the remnants of Abbott's faction persisted, Gidney's Association was in the process of establishing its pre-eminence across much of India. Only a couple of major rival organisations remained to contest its representative claims. One of these was the London Anglo-Indian Association, of which Stark claimed to have been the 'Founder and First President',[157] which sent a deputation to the Secretary of State for India in 1923, and was in contention with Gidney over who had the right to speak on behalf of the group during the run-up to his own deputation in 1925. Its membership likely comprised mainly wealthy and successful Anglo-Indians who had retired in Britain and British well-wishers, some of whom had paternalistically adopted leadership roles on the community's behalf during their careers in India. No doubt to Gidney's increased consternation, by 1930 it was presided over by Walsh. Gidney was angered by the London Association's continuing tendency to submit its own ideas about the group's future to the British government, thereby implicitly claiming to speak on behalf of Anglo-Indians in India. There was also a powerful and independent

Madras-based Anglo-Indian Association of Southern India, which in Anthony's words, was the

> only ... organisation in the South [which] continued to stay out, to plough a lonely, dissident and completely ineffective furrow. Its claims were based on its alleged ancient character and little else. Throughout Gidney's struggle and achievements ... it had not helped ... It lost no opportunity, however, to attempt to stab Gidney in the back. The same policy was continued after I assumed Gidney's place. In all the critical phases through which the Community passed, it never raised its voice. But it came to my notice that, furtively, whenever a memorandum was submitted by Gidney or me a dissident note would be struck by this body.[158]

With the help of a travelling secretary, Gidney had sought to strengthen his position, by reviving moribund or defunct Association branches as well as setting up new ones in smaller stations up and down the railway lines. By 1929 Gidney's Association claimed '88 branches dotted over the country with a membership of over 10,000' across India and Burma.[159] Two years later the *Review* was proclaiming that 'after generations of disunion and discord', Gidney had achieved 'Anglo-Indian and Domiciled European ... unity and representation as one corporate community in India and Burma'.[160] However, in reality Gidney still faced ongoing challenges from rival organisations. Even some branches of his own Association, notably the Bangalore branch, were at times willing to defy his authority, contradict him in their statements to the British press, and enlist the support of politicians in both Houses of Parliament. Affectionately known to many Anglo-Indians as 'Bangy', or more widely as the 'garden city' or 'pensioner's paradise', with its spaced-out leafy cantonment suburbs bearing names like Richmond Town, Fraser Town and Cooke Town, its clean streets and neat rows of bungalows with large enclosed gardens, Bangalore was described in 1934 as enjoying

> an exceptionally good climate ... [and the status of a] civil and military station ... Occupied for considerably over one hundred years, not only by British troops but by many civilian residents, British and Anglo-Indians. When Mysore was handed back to the present dynasty in 1881, a Treaty was made under which it was agreed that the civil station would remain under British administration so long as British

troops were kept there ... There are said to be about 130,000 residents in the tract of land in question, 2,700 of whom are Europeans, [and] 5,500 Anglo-Indians ...[161]

A year before, Gidney had implied that the real figure was closer to '20,000' or 'nearly one-sixth of the Anglo-Indian community of India'—an expansive figure that perhaps included those in Mysore in addition to Domiciled Europeans and others of lighter skin believed to be posing as British.[162] Following a visit by Gidney in February 1929, the Bangalore provincial branch's annual report lamented the 'utter want of interest in important matters concerning the Community ... [as] so disheartening, yet so characteristic that one despairs [that] the Community will ever arrive at a right sense of its responsibility to itself and to its children'.[163] Estimating its local 'domiciled community' at '10,000' in 1928, the branch had previously complained that only '300' of these had signed up for membership, 'cry[ing] shame on' the remainder, whom the president categorised 'as, (1) "grousers", (2) "disinterested", [or] (3) "cowards", ... [who had] taken so much out of Anglo-India and refused to give anything back in return, for the pitiful fear of being known as Anglo-Indians'.[164] However, Bangalore Anglo-Indians were recalcitrant, with most remaining aloof from the politics of Gidney's Association. Many among the mixed were more apt to self-identify as British or European, or to use the ambiguity inherent in the Anglo-Indian category's prior association with the colonial British population to situate Anglo-Indianness within Britishness—that is, in their view, to be Anglo-Indian was to be British. Even those within the Association took more fervently pro-British positions than Gidney did. At an Anglo-Indian Conference in Calcutta in 1930 'to give instructions to ... [Gidney as] the Anglo-Indian delegate to the Round Table Conference' in London,[165]

the Delegate from Bangalore moved a resolution restricting the grant of any further political advancement until incontrovertible proofs were shown of India's unswerving loyalty to the British Crown and connection, of real homogenity [sic] among the various communities ... and greater tolerance between Hindus, Muslims and other communities. After some considerable discussion ... [this] was rejected by a majority.[166]

Subsequently in 1934 Gidney found himself opposed by the leaders of the local branch of his Association, when he decided to support Mysore's Diwan (or prime minister) in his attempt to reincorporate the hitherto British-administered civil and military station back into the large, surrounding princely state. As he privately wrote to the Diwan: 'Words fail me to tell you how upset ... [and] annoyed I am ... It seems as if my good work is being frustrated by a few people who call themselves Europeans, but who are nothing else but Mulkies [meaning natives] or more correctly "Albino" Anglo-Indians.'[167] However, these fairer-skinned Anglo-Indians were able to obtain the help of the 8th Duke of Atholl, previously elected on a Unionist ticket to the Commons, and now willing to present their case in the Lords. Atholl contradicted a statement Gidney had given to 'a well-known newspaper', emphasising 'that the Anglo-Indian Association in Bangalore "dissented entirely"' and was 'opposed to this transfer'.[168]

Another acrimonious legal case in which Gidney became embroiled illustrates the continuing challenges he faced on his conservative flank. *Graham v. Henry Gidney* involved 'a youngish man of fine physique and meritorious war-record' named Graham, who had apparently been assisted by Gidney 'in obtaining employment', and who had until recently 'professed to be an admirer and follower of' Gidney.[169] However, in the wake of Gidney's return from the Round Table Conference in early 1931, a 'split' had emerged within the community, and the attitude and feelings of Graham and 'a considerable number of Anglo-Indians' had apparently turned sour.[170] They were angered 'by the discharge by the railway and other authorities of a considerable number of Anglo-Indian[s] ... in order to replace them with Indian employees'.[171] Graham ended up leading a faction of disgruntled and unemployed young men who began 'to agitate' for Gidney to fire his Indian staff, and especially his longstanding secretary Mr. Iyer, in order to give these jobs in the Anglo-Indian Association's head office to Anglo-Indians.[172] They held meetings and passed resolutions, during which Graham 'spoke with considerable heat', before it was decided that they would collectively descend upon Gidney's office in Park Street, Calcutta, to convey their demands.[173]

When Graham arrived with 'a body of followers' to find Gidney was not present, '20 or 30' of them began a sit-in, while the rest loitered 'in the court-yard or on the stairs'.[174] Graham refused to believe that Gidney was not due back that day, and menaced his staff, threatening one named 'Mr. Chandler' that 'I have only to raise my finger and my 200 followers will pull you to pieces', and shouting, 'You, N[-word]' or 'Damn N[-word].'[175] The court report clarified that between fellow Anglo-Indians this had 'no ethnological or special significance'. However, we may infer that the insult actually meant either to deny another Anglo-Indian their Europeanness or Anglo-Indianness, and thereby classify them with 'native' Indians, or to condemn their pro-Indian orientation. Iyer, Gidney's Indian secretary, who Graham was demanding be fired to make way for an Anglo-Indian, testified that 'the apprehension was that he would visit again with a mob'.[176] Upon his return Gidney reported the matter to the police, resulting in Graham's arrest, whereupon Graham brought a suit against Gidney for false imprisonment.[177] Yet if Gidney had been guilty of any embellishment in reporting events he had not himself witnessed, he could hardly be blamed when his staff were being threatened by a mob. Graham's suit was accordingly 'dismissed with costs' by Judge Ameer Ali.[178]

At the imperial metropole

London proved to be one of the most consequential arenas for Gidney's extensive lobbying efforts during the 1920s and 1930s. In 1925 Gidney led a deputation to Lord Birkenhead, the Secretary of State for India, to seek solutions to what appeared an existential problem. His memorandum appeared to keep open all options, including collective emigration, and a new distinct intermediate status rather than the contradictory 'trinity of existence' imposed upon the group to suit colonial British administrative convenience. His submissions implicitly looked to the British for firm guidance on questions of identity, nationality and civic status, which he would be able to present to his constituents. It appears likely that had the British wished to take a bold approach to supporting the creation of an Anglo-Indian colony as the nucleus of a future Anglo-Indian state, or had they put their weight behind a scheme to resettle Anglo-Indians in some other part of the empire, or to grant Anglo-Indians some kind of unique but more clearly defined legal and civic status, Gidney would have remained open to endorsing a radical or imperially orientated solution to the grand question of how the community should situate itself to face the challenges of devolution and decolonisation. However, it was not until 1928 that the government's full response finally came. It evaded responsibility for the 'anomalies' which arose from Anglo-Indians' 'exceptional position' as a 'community ... intermediate between pure Europeans and pure Indians', arguing that the multiplicity of statuses which were applied to them in different situations and for different purposes arose 'from the attempt to accord recognition' to this unique position, and therefore could not 'constitute a grievance'.[179]

Anglo-Indians were firmly advised that any attempt to create some kind of 'third category' in law was impractical and unlikely to be advantageous.[180] They should therefore accept their existing 'legal status ... [as] "natives of India"' with 'a permanent stake in India and in no other country'.[181] This was essentially an instruction that they had no claim to British nationality nor should they hold out hopes of official support for their collective resettlement to other parts of the empire, such as Australia. They were instead to focus on 'achieving for themselves an integral part in the economy and society of the country in which they live', with the assurance that accepting what amounted to Indian nationality would be in no way 'inconsistent with the maintenance of their individuality as a separate social entity, or with the position which is theirs by virtue of their ancestry, history, and peculiar conditions and aptitudes'.[182] It was confirmation for Gidney that his efforts should be principally directed towards achieving the best constitutional protections possible as an Indian minority community, in line with the so-called communal politics of the Muslim League and other smaller minority groups.

The tone of the *Review*'s response to the Irwin Declaration by the Viceroy towards the end of 1929, holding forth the prospect of Dominion status without any definite timeline, indicates both Gidney's fervent monarchism and the bridging role he optimistically thought Anglo-Indians might play in bringing the two sides together:

> our efforts must be redoubled not only in the open expression of our loyalty and allegiance to the King Emperor, but also in the ready co-operation with our Indian brothers to make that loyalty and allegiance

all the stronger. Had we but realised the farsighted ordination that brought the Anglo-Indian into being and served both faithfully, loyally and equally we would today have been of infinitely greater importance as a cementing force between the European and the Indian than we are, but it is not yet too late to show the Viceroy and India that with Mahatma Gandhi we are 'dying to give and secure true heart co-operation', and as a community so closely linked both with the European and the Indian we unhesitatingly ask and expect a place in the framing of a scheme for Dominion Status—a constitution suitable for India's needs. We urge no time should be lost in establishing a superlative trust between England and India and that the Round Table Conference should be a perfectly representative one of all communities in India ...[183]

Gidney had long publicly professed himself to be sympathetic to greater devolution of power into Indian hands, so long as the interests of the minorities were not to be sacrificed in the process. The meeting he had held in Calcutta in 1923 concluded that 'it was time for Anglo Indians while maintaining their distinctive communal and civic rights, to join hands with Indians in working for the attainment of self-government ... within the British Empire by constitutional means'.[184] Gidney therefore reacted to the Congress Party's decision to boycott the first London conference with expressions of regret and concern that it would be difficult to reach a final settlement without them. Clearly, however, he was immensely pleased to have been chosen as a representative, and declared his belief that no lasting settlement could be reached that would ensure future peace, stability and good government unless the Muslims, Europeans, Anglo-Indians and others were granted adequate guarantees of their future position in any new constitution. He expected ample and liberal safeguards for the protections of the linguistic, racial and religious distinctiveness of the minorities and took it for granted that the British Parliament could not divest itself of its responsibility to ensure such protections. At the first conference Gidney told the Minorities Sub-committee:

Whatever may be the future of India, the Anglo-Indian community is, for better or for worse, an indissoluble part of that future. We are an Indian community: we are the sons of the soil who not only have our roots in the country's past but live, work and die there ... We accept the implications of our Indian nationality and we look forward to a glorious future for our mother country … [but] in our politics there is one fixed star from which no considerations of communal or personal advancement or benefits will ever make us deviate and that is our inexpungible loyalty to the Crown of England … I am talking not as an Englishman but as an Indian and I want my Indian brethren to try for a moment to put themselves in my place. By law, by residence, by environment and circumstances, I am an Indian. But by blood I belong also to Britain. For me, therefore, there is no antagonism between India and Britain. They are both my countries. I am unable to see any difference between the welfare of the one and the welfare of the other. Unfortunately, of late … speakers in India have not hesitated to draw a distinction between Indian-Indians and Anglo-Indians as though there were some fundamental clash between the interests of India and Britain. But I would ask you to think over the sayings of some of the finest spirits who have graced the history of Indian India … Ram Mohan Roy, Keshab Chunder Sen, Sir Saiyid Ahmed, Mr. Gokhale … the late Mr. C. R. Das … and innumerable other great Indians [who] had in their hearts an ideal England which they loved and to which they gave their wholehearted devotion.[185]

Gidney then repeated Das's endorsement of 'Dominion Status … [within] the great Commonwealth of Nations called the British Empire' in his last public speech at Faridpur in 1925 as expressing 'all the elements of Swaraj … To me the idea is specially attractive because of its deep spiritual significance.'[186] An editorial in the *Review* reflected Gidney's persisting belief that 'the root cause of all the disaffection in India … [was] the consciousness of inferior treatment' and remained wedded to the hope 'that the Indian nation … [could] be won over to loyal cooperation by the promise of equal status' within the empire.[187] This was in keeping with the politics of reformists like Sastri, who had taken over the leadership of the Servants of India Society in 1915 after the death of its founder, Gokhale, and had sought to reassure Anglo-Indians in his 1923 address of his commitment to one of its 'fundamental postulates … that the British connection with India was providential and must be maintained'.[188] However, it was out of step with the Congress Party's 26 January 1930 declaration that Purna Swaraj (or complete self-rule) was now their goal. Nonetheless Gidney made the following heartfelt appeal:

My Indian brothers, you know that that is the England which holds your loyalty and, therefore, you must not blame us in whose veins the blood of this people runs for holding steadfastly to the country which holds your devotion who are children by adoption and not by nature as we are ... our attitude has been so often misunderstood ... We hold to the British connection because there is that in us which will allow us to do no other. Through fair weather and foul, we have stood by England and we shall continue to do so.[189]

In his opening address he had spoken to his fellow delegates 'in a dual capacity as an Indian, speaking for India, and as a member of the Anglo-Indian community'.[190] He went on to emotively explain: 'We are ... a synthesis of India and Britain, as no other people are or can be ... I assure you that the decisions now being taken ... are matters of life and death, literally life and death for us.'[191] *The Times* singled out Gidney's 'striking epigram that "a reformed India must not result in a deformed Anglo-India"'.[192] The staunchly conservative *Daily Telegraph* judged the whole 'a moving appeal to Great Britain for the protection of his community, whose loyalty has rendered such service to the Empire, from the Mutiny down to the present day'.[193] The *Morning Post* described Gidney's speech as

one of the most moving and pathetic ... These people, the children of mixed unions, owe their birth and being to the presence of the British in India ... There is no guarantee or safeguard, nothing but our presence, which could protect this minority from a fate even more cruel than that of the Loyalists in Southern Ireland. The Hindu would call them aliens; but they could not exist outside of India.[194]

It was left to the *Daily Mail* to take on the less serious matter of the 'enormous fires' kept 'alight for the past three weeks' in the conference rooms at St. James's Palace, 'the idea of the authorities ... [being] to get the rooms to as near 70° [Fahrenheit] as possible', prompting Gidney's remark 'that the place was a little too like India to be pleasant in his winter clothes'.[195] The somewhat corpulent colonel, known for his well-tailored three-piece suits, was, asserted the *Mail*, 'looked on as the glass of fashion and mould of form in the Indian Legislative Assembly'.[196] Doubtless Gidney relished wearing full rig, including top hat, pin-striped trousers and spats when he visited the King-Emperor at Buckingham Palace at the end of the third and final conference to have his knighthood conferred. Masters's *Bhowani Junction* described Gidney's fictionalised stand-in in this way: 'no one except Sir Meredith Sullivan actually … [got] up in public and … [said], "I am an Anglo-Indian." They'd made him a Sir for that.'[197]

It would have been difficult to find a more pronounced visible contrast to Gandhi, who braved the cold streets of London's working-class East End neighbourhood with a white homespun shawl in addition to his usual austere attire, having arrived as the sole representative of the Congress Party in time for the second conference in September 1931. With less than usual sagacity, Gidney had prophesied the year before that

> the ultimatum presented by Mr. Gandhi to Lord Irwin lets fall the curtain on his last public action … Mr. Gandhi and his lieutenants in their campaign of civil disobedience may delude themselves, that it will not lead to violence and bloodshed, but unless they are checked, and at once, they will soon realise, as he has done before, that the fuses they lay throughout India for irresponsible and inflamed youths to set alight will not consist of sodium chloride, but of gunpowder. The duty of the Government of India is equally clear … Rule or get out.[198]

Gandhi's attitude towards the Anglo-Indian community's future in a self-governing India was made clear several months before his arrival in London in a public response to Gidney's rival H. W. B. Moreno:

> every community would be on a par with every other under the swaraj Constitution … The Anglo-Indians … would come in where their merit would take them. There would most decidedly be nothing to prevent them from occupying the highest position that any other Indian may be capable of occupying. The fact however is that the Anglo[-]Indians as a class have occupied or attempted to occupy the position of rulers. They have not as a class taken part in the national movement. They have isolated themselves in their favoured position … Hence like the Englishmen whose cry for equality means retention of favoured position the Anglo-Indians may feel aggrieved that they would be at a disadvantage under swaraj if they did not have the present favoured position guaranteed … [If] Dr. Moreno … seeks information about the submerged Anglo-Indians … I should be surprised if they did not in common with the submerged of the other communities find themselves in a better position than they are in today. Anyway, there are enough Congressmen who are pledged to the abolition of all unjust privileges, all unnatural inequalities. If the con-

dition of the masses is found to undergo rapid improvement ... the Anglo-Indian poor must share it to the fullest extent possible. The Congress aims at swaraj for the whole nation and not a section ... I therefore invite all the minorities to join the national movement ... Let it not also be said of any of them that in the hour of the nation's trial, they stood aside and came in to enjoy their share of the happiness. They will get the share but they will not relish it even as a man who has not toiled for his meal cannot enjoy it though it is placed before him.[199]

Claiming to speak for all of India, Gandhi was somewhat contemptuous of and embarrassed by what he saw as the supplicatory well-dressed assortment of Indian notables hand-picked by the colonial government to attend the conference, most of whom he believed did not have a sufficient constituency of support.[200] The opulent extravagance of the Indian princes appalled him. Gandhi was particularly dismissive of the representatives of the smaller minorities like Gidney, perceiving them as pawns of British imperialism. On the Federal Structure Committee, Gandhi's first speech made it plain 'that as a representative of the Indian National Congress he was not prepared to give political recognition to any community other than the Muhammadans and Sikhs'.[201] In Gandhi's own words, 'In spite of appearances to the contrary, especially in England, the Congress claims to represent the whole nation, and most decidedly the dumb millions, among whom are included the numberless Untouchables.'[202] Dr. Bhimrao Ramji Ambedkar, the British- and American-educated leader of the group now known as Dalits, angrily responded:

The Mahatma has been always claiming that the Congress stands for the Depressed Classes, and ... represents the Depressed Classes more than I or my colleague can do ... It is one of the many false claims which irresponsible people keep on making ... To put it plainly ... we are not anxious for the transfer of power; but if the British Government is unable to resist the forces that have been set up in the country which do clamour for transference of political power—and we ... are not in a position to resist that—then our submission is that if you make that transfer ... [it] be accompanied by such conditions and ... provisions that the power shall not fall into the hands of a clique ... an oligarchy, or ... a group of people, whether Muhammadans or Hindus; but that ... power shall be shared by all communities in their respective proportions.[203]

In one form or another, power-sharing, in place of majoritarian democratic rule, was what most minorities wanted, for otherwise they felt that their position might well be worse under a Hindu Raj than under the British, who for their own imperial purposes had been happy to co-opt and reward them. Many of India's Muslims nursed memories of their association with the rulers of the Mughal Empire though it was the long-downtrodden and cruelly abused Dalit community whose fears were the most justifiable. Accordingly, their leader Ambedkar addressed the British Labour Party 'Prime Minister, [Ramsay MacDonald, to say] that the Depressed Classes would regard it as the greatest betrayal on the part of His Majesty's Government if it were to leave us to the mercy of those who have taken no interest in our welfare and whose prosperity and greatness is founded upon our ruination and degradation'.[204] In his initial surprise at the forceful tone of Ambedkar's eloquence, Gandhi initially assumed him to have been a higher-caste sympathiser with the 'untouchables' rather than one himself. He now declared:

> I can understand the claims advanced by other minorities, but the claims advanced on behalf of the Untouchables, that to me is the unkindest cut of all. It means the perpetual bar-sinister. I would not sell the vital interests of the Untouchables, even for the sake of winning the freedom of India. Let the whole world know that to-day there is a body of Hindu reformers who are pledged to remove this blot of untouchability. I would far rather that Hinduism died than that untouchability lived.[205]

Ambedkar had little faith in such protestations. Back in February, Gidney had told a meeting of the Empire Parliamentary Association:

> No one can deny that the reason why they have been held in a position of slavedom is to be found in the cruel and merciless religious and caste prejudices that still pervade Hinduism. The fact that over 50 millions of Indian subjects are considered to be unfit to be touched by their Hindu brothers is ... the blackest spot in the history of India, and certainly does not fortify its claim for Dominion status, or even responsibility in the centre.[206]

Responding to a follow-up question from a Unionist MP as to 'whether there can be any constitutional advance so long as the caste system remains', Gidney stated: 'They are absolutely the antithesis of each other. I do not think India can become a nation or develop a true national Government so long as the caste system remains as it is to-day.'[207] All of this was no doubt music to the ears of (metropolitan and colonial) British officialdom. While Gidney also dwelt at length on 'the Hindu–Muslim problem', he argued that the British delegation at the first conference had 'not sufficiently appreciated ... that the settlement of the problems of the other minorities is of almost equal importance to that of the Hindu–Muslim, and that unless these problems are dealt with in a resolute and generous manner, the new conditions in India will result in the creation of a number of Ulsters'.[208]

During the second conference Gidney and Ambedkar were drawn into a close cooperation by their common interests. When Ambedkar made his case in the various committees and subcommittees, Gidney would echo, 'I join in that statement too, Sir', 'I agree with and support everything that Dr. Ambedkar has said', and Ambedkar would respond in kind with 'I associate myself with what Col. Gidney has said'.[209] Though they had a curt disagreement on the extension of the franchise,[210] this tag-team effort was the result of their common complaint that, in the words of Ambedkar, 'Mahatma Gandhi told us on the first day that he spoke in the Federal Structure Committee that ... he was not prepared to recognise the Anglo-Indians, the Depressed Classes, and the Indian Christians ... [and] when we ... had the chance of talking to him yesterday in his office, he told us in quite plain terms that ... [this] was his full and well considered attitude.'[211] Gidney immediately followed with:

> On behalf of the community which I have the honour to represent, I associate myself entirely with my friend Dr. Ambedkar. I am also in the unfortunate position of having been refused recognition by Mahatma Gandhi as far as a separate community is concerned ... Yesterday, when we met Mahatma Gandhi upon this matter, he impressed us in terms that left no doubt in my mind that as a community he and the Congress were not prepared to recognise us ...[212]

There is a historical irony in the fact that in India's 1949–50 Constitution Dalits and Anglo-Indians were, alongside Adivasis, the only minorities to be substantially recognised. However, at this point Gandhi's efforts were concentrated on achieving a grand settlement with India's Muslims. Attempting to convince his fellow delegates that more could be accomplished 'by being closeted in one room and by heart-to-heart conversation' with one another privately 'than by sitting stiffly at this [conference] table',[213] Gandhi declared:

> I fear that Dr. Ambedkar, Colonel Gidney and other friends are unnecessarily nervous ... Who am I to deny political status to any single interest or class[?] ... I have undoubtedly given expression to my own views on these points ... [and] I hold to those views ... [but] please disabuse your minds ... of the idea that there is going to be any steam-rolling in the Conference and ... give your wholehearted co-operation to the proposal that I have made in connection with these informal meetings.[214]

Gandhi hoped to present his grand bargain as a fait accompli, exposing the British-imposed conference as a charade of procedure rather than the real forum of decision-making. This ultimately backfired when the smaller minorities began to organise collectively outside the conference halls, to formulate their own private pact and thereby reject Gandhi's efforts to corral them. Despite his rhetoric of ostentatious humility, Gandhi's strategy had required supreme self-belief in his own abilities of persuasion. But in the event MacDonald was able to take advantage of the general disunity that prevailed, in his concluding remarks that the 'communal problem is a problem of fact ... and you had better go on trying to take your own responsibilities upon your own shoulders and see if an agreement can be come to ... But supposing I said to you ... "Take this business over to yourselves," why, you know perfectly well that you could not go six inches without coming to a deadlock.'[215] Gidney interrupted, 'Not one inch.'[216] It was not the last time Gidney felt so uninhibited with the prime minister, and an unfazed MacDonald directly replied, 'Well, I am generous as regards your enterprise and your successes. I give you six instead of one.'[217] MacDonald suggested to the small minorities that they should 'try their hands', to which Gidney replied that they had already 'been trying' and had 'almost succeeded'.[218] MacDonald then requested that 'any common agreements' they had devised be circulated.[219]

One of the two Indian Christian delegates, the Protestant Dr. Surendra Kumar Datta, ended up 'bitterly opposed' to the 'Five-Party Agreement ... between five Indian minorities—the Moslems, depressed classes, Indian Christians, Europeans, and Anglo-Indians', which the *Manchester Guardian* concluded had 'played a not unimportant part in ensuring the break-up of the Conference', arguing that its proposals 'must be utterly repugnant to the feelings of the most rational of Hindu Nationalists ... Each minority has put in the most definite form possible its full demands ... slightly modified in consultation so as to dovetail into each other and fit as closely as possible. Thereafter the demand of each minority has been generously granted by its fellows—at the expense of the Hindus.'[220] An 'indignant' Raja Narendra Nath charged Gidney with arranging 'secret meetings' and treating Hindus 'with contemptuous disregard', prompting the prime minister to respond: 'Arguments and no heat, please.'[221] Gidney proclaimed that there had 'been no secrecy about these meetings', offering his 'grateful thanks' to the Muslims 'for their loyalty and adhesion ... during very difficult proceedings', having earlier explained 'that every means had been taken of getting the Sikhs to join in the agreement. He had consulted with the Sikh member who was in possession of the memorandum three or four days ago.'[222] Sardar Sant Singh would later cross swords in the Assembly with 'the Knight of the Anglo-Indians', expressing pride 'that the Sikhs never joined the unholy Pact'. Gidney retorted that they had not been slow to take advantage of it and that the Sikh representative 'gave us a surfeit of communalism and ... was the real cause of the minorities at the First and Second Round Table Conferences not being able to arrive at a settlement' over 'the Muslim–Sikh problem in the Punjab' by haggling 'over one seat'.[223]

Sir Hubert Carr, one of four delegates representing 'Europeans in India', sardonically thanked 'Mr. Gandhi for his share in brin[g]ing the minorities together', by attributing the genesis of the Minority Pact 'very largely ... [to] the failure of the information committee which sat under ... [his] chairmanship'.[224] Gandhi had previously addressed MacDonald 'with deep sorrow and deeper humiliation' that he had 'to announce [the] utter failure on my part to secure an agreed solution of the communal question through informal conversations among and with the representatives of different groups'.[225] Just as he had alienated Ambedkar with his claims to be a better representative of Dalit interests, Gandhi had claimed to 'know' Anglo-Indians much better than Col. Gidney does. I have seen them weep before me. They come to me and say, 'We are bastards. Englishmen do not recognize us; Indians would not adopt us.' I say, 'Come to us, discard your tinsel and we will adopt you.' ... They would be pariahs and untouchables with a separate electorate under National Government. Sir Henry Gidney may be all right but others won't be knighted. But if they would come and claim the suffrage of our people they are quite welcome ...[226]

Needless to say, this was insulting, and whether or not any Anglo-Indian had actually confided such tortured emotions to Gandhi, he was unlikely to win hearts and minds by making them public while reinforcing stereotypes of Anglo-Indian illegitimacy. However, according to Charles Campagnac (another bitter Gidney rival), over the course of 'many conversations' on board a steamer travelling from Rangoon back to India,

> Gandhi told me that he thought that Eurasians were the rightful leaders of India and that they would be, if they threw in their lot wholeheartedly with Indians. He said that it was the ancestors of the Eurasians who had helped to conquer India and their double blood, double intelligence and double sympathies could do much to bridge the gulf between East and West. He said that one reason why Indians did not trust the British was because of the manner in which they treated Eurasians ... 'You are their own flesh and blood and see how they treat you. How can we, who are in no way related to them expect any better treatment than your community.'[227]

Of Gandhi's three visits to Burma in 1902, 1915 and 1929, this may have been the second, before Gandhi had become well-established on the Indian political scene, and when he might be regarded as imaginatively casting about for allies. Gandhi's words certainly represented an appeal more shrewdly crafted to flatter the self-perceptions of the mixed. His concluding note, whether or not it really had much to do with Indian attitudes towards the British, played upon the same theme of egregious treatment of the mixed by their blood relations.

CONTESTING ANGLO-INDIA

The Anglo-Indian Left

Gidney faced an intellectually fascinating but less politically potent challenge from a few discordant voices on his left flank, including the pan-Eurasianist socialist Kenneth Wallace. In 1930 Wallace was a 'stalwart of the Calcutta Federation',[1] a persisting thorn in the side of Gidney's Association. Wallace contested Calcutta's municipal elections against the Gidney-backed (presumably Jewish) incumbent 'Mr. V. D. Cohen', whom the *Review* described as having 'always been a friend to the [Anglo-Indian] community'.[2] Gidney's mouthpiece journal crowed over Wallace's poor showing, unable to suppress its delight at his having secured

> a mere 83 votes as against 336 ... [for] Mr. Cohen ... Possibly ... hail[ing] ... from the Federation Camp did not prove as prejudicial as the fact according to the *Englishman* [newspaper] that ... [Mr. Wallace] received open Swarajist support ... 'In Ward XV where Mr. Cohen had an easy walk over on previous occasions, Mr. K. E. Wallace with the support of the Congress was a keen rival. Leaflets in Bengali, strongly commending ... [him] to the Indian voters, were largely distributed. They had, however, very little effect, although bearing the name of Mr. Subhas Chandra Bose.' We deplore the fact that in his zeal to enter public life Mr. Wallace had to resort to Congress support.[3]

At some point after his electoral bruising, Wallace crossed over to the Association, becoming a member of its governing body in 1931, and eventually rising to the role of Gidney's trusted vice president. This dramatic rapprochement highlights both men's political pragmatism and flexibility. Despite Gidney's instinctive aversion to socialism, he remained amenable to embracing all manner of specific policies if he could be persuaded they were in Anglo-Indian interests. In late 1930, shortly before Gidney's departure for the first Round Table Conference, Wallace led a deputation to present him with his own detailed proposals for the community's economic reconstruction. Enlarging upon an idea put forward 'many years ago' by Herbert Stark for 'an educational cess', Wallace proposed a broader communal tax.[4] Marketed as 'a small communal cess upon incomes' over a hundred rupees a month, it would compel a large swathe of those gainfully employed above entry level to pay an additional 'three pies in the rupee'.[5] Aware that defining an Anglo-Indian 'for the purpose' was likely to be a stumbling block, Wallace refrained from 'suggest[ing] that it should be made compulsory on Europeans (Domiciled or otherwise)', but insisted the scheme's 'benefits' be correspondingly restricted to those on 'a communal register as is the case of the minority communities of Europe'.[6] Alongside European minorities who had been 'given the right to tax themselves for their own particular needs, through the agency of their country', he furnished 'the precedent of the Talukdars [landlords] of Oudh', to argue that the colonial state would be able to collect the tax on Anglo-Indians' behalf.[7] The proceeds would

> be used for … [the] improvement of education, technical training, institution of farms, financing of co-operative societies, and such other measures but not the mere giving of doles to unemployed members. The primary intention should be reconstruction on a well planned programme over a period of about five years … [on] the analogy of the New Economic Programme (N.E.P.) of Soviet Russia …[8]

Wallace included his radical plan in a memorandum submitted to Motilal Nehru 'asking for certain assurances regarding the position of the Anglo-Indian community in free India', to which Congress's Working Committee replied: 'As regards the assistance of the State being given to particular communities to raise funds by taxing them-

selves for educational or other purposes intended for their own benefit, this Committee is of opinion that this may certainly be done
provided that the purpose is not inconsistent with national policy.'[9]

Noting that 'Mr. Wallace has often been in opposition to the
Association … [the *Review* commended his] largeness of spirit …
initiative and political sagacity'.[10] Far from flinching at Wallace's
Soviet template, Gidney devoted four of the *Review*'s pages to reprinting Wallace's memorandum, and himself authored a further two
pages on Anglo-Indian unemployment statistics to undergird
Wallace's approaches to government. Communal taxation appears to
have gone no further than this. However, shared support for technical
and vocational training for Anglo-Indian youth as part of wider educational reform led to Wallace's appointment as chairman of the
Gidney Higher Education Fund Committee, established as a scholar-
ship-granting trust in May 1931 with 'Rs. 44,000 in Government
paper and Rs. 2,500 in cash' from about five years of fundraising.[11]
Nonetheless, a year later Wallace was still expressing 'grave anxiety'
over the 'economic position':

> In the past the Eurasian Community was cut down in its prime. But
> for the proscriptions of the East India Company and the prejudice
> with which they have been regarded, they might to-day have had their
> roots in the soil as agriculturalists and … in the higher administration,
> industry and commerce … but to-day their economic position is
> undermined by the pressure of Indian competition in the services on
> which they have mainly depended … Even in normal times, the inci-
> dence of unemployment among Anglo-Indians is high, while in times
> of severe trade depression, as at present, fully a quarter to a third …
> [are] rendered unemployed.[12]

Nationalists had long called for 'Government to differentiate
between the *Indian-Indian* and the *Anglo-Indian* in all schemes of
Indianisation'.[13] This was now taking on an increasingly communalist
inflection, with legislators like Maswood Ahmad complaining 'that
though Muslims form[ed] over 26 per cent. of the whole Indian population, their total employment on railways … [was] 17 per cent.',
and that in Muslim-majority areas where they 'constitute[d]
71 per cent. of the population they form[ed] only 7 per cent. of the
total'.[14] While colonial authorities undoubtedly trusted Anglo-Indians

more than Muslims, if they had to give way to pressure for Indianisation, then parcelling up railway posts through communal reservations (positive discrimination or 'affirmative action') would provide the next best form of security against sabotage or industrial unrest. Underrepresented ethnic minorities would remain dependent upon state and railway authorities for patronage and retention of their employment and were less likely to make common cause across communal dividing lines. Chandulal Trivedi outlined recent colonial policy, involving 'reservation of one-third of vacancies for minority communities ... [with] 25 per cent. of total vacancies ... reserved for Muslims' in the Superior Railway Services.[15] This had come largely at the expense of Anglo-Indians, whom Maurice Hallett admitted he had 'forgotten' during the recent discussions over the respective percentages for each minority.[16]

Having recently been appointed 'the advisory President of the National Union of Railways', Gidney participated in 'the general meeting of the all-India Railway Federation' in Calcutta and its Simla Conference with the government-appointed Railway Board.[17] Despite its 'national' pretensions, this union, of whose '3,000 members' '9/10ths' were 'Anglo-Indians and Europeans', was mainly confined to the GIP Railway.[18] Accordingly, in August 1930 the *Review* announced the registration of a new Anglo-Indian and European Railway Union of India, which it argued was necessary to counter 'other communal Railway Unions, such as the Muslim Union on the Bengal–Nagpur Railway'.[19] To drive recruitment, it even rebranded itself as the *Anglo-Indian and Railway Union Journal* from October 1930 to July 1931. As Anglo-Indians and Domiciled Europeans mainly held better-remunerated posts as drivers, firemen, guards, ticket collectors, stationmasters, engineers, workshop overseers and other lower-middle managers, any union to defend their interests would seek to preserve their relative privilege under the existing status quo. Arguing that 'strikes strike the strikers the hardest', Gidney won support from cautious, conservative or pro-administration unions.[20] Ramlal B. Naglai, a member of two battling unions in 'the Karachi Division', commended him for 'enunciating certain principles which are consistent with our method of work and will absolutely smash the basis on which our rivals are trying to wreck the interests of railway staff'.[21]

In response to a threatened general strike across all railways, Gidney compared 'Jamnadas Mehta ... with Lenin' and lambasted 'the All-India Railway Federation' as 'a Hindu caucus'.[22] Gidney's attempt to brand the strikers as violent communists or communalists would have been more appropriate to the South Indian Railway strike of 1928. For, as the historian Kanchi Reddy concludes, a 'most remarkable feature of the 1932 struggle of the railway workers ... was the non-violent and non-communal character of the movement ... despite the efforts of the railway administration to divide the working class on communal lines'; its leaders proved themselves 'moderate ... in contrast to the militant and violent struggle' inaugurated by the 1928 strike's 'left radical leadership'.[23] One of Wallace's Indian correspondents condemned Anglo-Indians' 'strike breaking activities', expressing himself as 'anxious to see the Eurasians take their place in India, not as strike breakers and railway guards, but as the leaders of the modernist movement ... if they only had a national outlook' and shared 'my vision of a future India ... [as] a modernised country frankly adopting European standards but keeping its own culture ... Anglo-Indians should be natural leaders.'[24] However, Wallace remained preoccupied with Anglo-Indians' own unique challenges, including a glass ceiling extending across

> Government services ... private firms ... social relations, [and] even the church ... [although] things are more subtly effected [than before]. We do not to-day have Government saying in effect, 'this service is closed to you', but if you realise the practical handicaps you will see how well adapted they are to European interests and ill-adapted to ours ... Mercantile service employers do not say to-day 'Mr. so-and-so, no Anglo-Indian can expect to rise above Rs. 100 in this firm', but we understand the position and others have remarked on the caste-ridden and cast iron structure of European society in India. Occasionally, we do have a lad taking a good degree at an English university, but if he is at all unable to hide his identity ... the question of promotion is a vexed one.[25]

Wallace and Gidney were well aware of the fortunate few who, as a result of their fairer complexions, managed to evade these strictures. Some even succeeded in having themselves classified as Britons or Europeans of non-Asiatic domicile in order to receive 'overseas and other privileges' in employment, thereafter remaining 'fear[ful]' of being identified as Anglo-Indian in any context lest they 'forfeit' their higher salaries and perquisites.[26] Aspiring to join these privileged ranks, realistically or otherwise, a large number of Anglo-Indians declared themselves as Europeans in decennial censuses or sought membership of the European Association. Anxious to combat these trends, the *Review* stressed that 'the census returns are confidential documents and will not be available as evidence in any such connection', less persuasively insisting that 'the test for such overseas privileges is not race, but domicile'.[27] However, individual Anglo-Indian claims to 'European British Subject' status had definite advantages in the legal arena. Anglo-Indians and Domiciled Europeans of lighter skin tones, extending slightly beyond what might typically be regarded as 'white', could expect to be granted a European jury trial by default, which practically all Anglo-Indians regardless of complexion appear to have trusted to be less biased towards them than an Indian jury. Darker-skinned Anglo-Indians and Indian Christians attempting to pass as Anglo-Indians were more likely to be challenged to provide evidence of proximate European descent, even if, in many cases, their request for a European jury trial had a good chance of being granted.

The colonial state also classified Anglo-Indians as European British subjects for 'defence of empire purposes' in order to compel their service in auxiliary railway battalions. This was not taken to be contradictory to their position as 'Statutory Natives of India', which functionally meant Indian 'nationality' and, in a strictly legal sense, was equally applicable, regardless of race or colour, to anyone who was born with or was deemed to have acquired Indian domicile. Questioned about these various overlapping terms, Gidney asserted 'that at least 85 per cent. of those who claim to be Domiciled Europeans are none other than the fairer members of the Anglo-Indian community', including 'hundreds' in the membership lists 'of any Branch of the European Association'.[28] Gidney insisted that he had

> always contended that [it] is morally wrong for the European Association to enlist such people ... [for] it certainly would not be the[ir] duty ... to defend the claims of an Anglo-Indian passing as a

European ... [So] what benefit does the European Association derive by entertaining such members? To my mind, (1) it swells its number; (2) it increases its electorate ... and (3) it increases ... [its] revenue ... In short the advantages are entirely for the Association and certainly none for its Anglo-Indian member even though he imagines that he is a European because he is accepted as a member ... I addressed the European Association of Calcutta ... and said that it was poaching on ... [our] preserves ... and that it weakened the position ... of the Anglo-Indian community, especially the strength of its electorate and its demand for adequate representation on the Legislatures. Moreover it prevented a correct census being taken ... for I estimated that at least 20,000 Anglo-Indians are to-day posing as Europeans.[29]

The European Association was not a social organisation but a mercantile lobbying and political body, whose finances and numerical clout translated—when combined with inflated census returns for those claiming to be Europeans—into greater electoral representation at the expense of the Anglo-Indian group. The *Review* would later complain that

one very serious handicap ... is the absence of a correct electoral roll, the result of the extraordinary and inexplicable desire, amounting to insanity, of the fairer members of the Anglo-Indian community to enrol themselves in the European electoral roll. We wonder if they think that by joining the European Association ... they improve their status or conceal their identity from the European? Their communal brothers and sisters know them as 'Bhai Bhunds', but they deny their origin and vainly try to assert they are of either French, Italian or Spanish ancestry—anything rather than admit being an Anglo-Indian ... [Having] escaped the colour handicap ... [they] live their lives concealing their identity, lest European firms look down upon them and hopeful that they may, in time, be mistaken for the imported covenanted article; lest European Clubs black ball him and lest European ladies ignore him as many of them are wont to do with hybrids, such as we are, and ... lest ... their leave and pay be reduced ... They promptly deny their connection with the community and, in some instances, deny their very parents. It is to such depths that the fair complexioned Anglo-Indian has sunk in his efforts to conceal his identity and we boldly assert this cowardly deception ... is encouraged by his admission as a member of the European Association and courted by his European employer and Railway officials ... We know of many European firms in Calcutta who, in the full knowledge that two-thirds of their subordinates are Anglo-Indians, return them *en masse* as Europeans. This ... creates a schism in the community ... accentuates that already cursed inferiority complex from which so many ... suffer and deprives the community of its best men.[30]

By 1939 Wallace, now vice president of the Bengal provincial branch, was writing to ask the secretary of the European Association, Calcutta, to 'make a public announcement ... that the European Association does not seek the membership of others than Europeans and that anyone who happens to be a member by either deliberately or unintentionally disguising the fact that he is not a European will not be entitled to any assistance from the Association should need arise'.[31] The European Association represented a powerful and influential group—politically, socially and economically—and Wallace's manner of addressing them was somewhat deferential in its reluctance to cast any aspersions on their bona fides, collegially asserting that in 'drawing up ... our separate communal electoral rolls you and we have always cooperated with each other ... and it has, we believe, been your policy to discourage members of the Anglo-Indian Community from joining the European Association whenever the fact that such a person is not a European is known to you'.[32]

Wallace claimed: 'It is not that this Association seeks to strengthen its own membership by people of this disloyal nature towards their own community but that ... [European Association membership] encourages in them false hopes of economic and social advancement, especially if they happen to be in mercantile service.'[33] The secretary of the Calcutta branch of the European Association attempted to reassure Wallace that he would have their full cooperation both with regard to proper voter registration and 'in avoiding recruitment of Anglo-Indians to the European Association', acknowledging that Anglo-Indians were occasionally admitted in error, but stressing that 'the Administration rarely, if ever, interviews candidates for election and ... it is not possible without arousing ill feeling to carry out searching enquiries into the parentage of new or existing members ... The Committee is not willing definitely to refuse assistance in advance to any Anglo-Indian just because he is an Anglo-Indian, as each case must be considered on its merits.'[34] On the face of it, this reply appeared very creditable and reasonably cooperative, while declining to behave punitively towards those of its members who might be Anglo-Indians engaging in passing. Unlike the European Association, colonial clubs were more than willing to carry out the kind of probing inquiries that, because they were exclusionary and discriminatory in nature, Wallace was in the odd position as a 'progressive' community leader of calling for.

Confronted with the question 'What is the strength of the community?' at the Round Table Conference, Gidney had felt his case weakened by the 'inaccuracies in the census of 1921'.[35] Demonstrating numerical strength remained crucial for a micro-community seeking to retain disproportionate political representation, which in turn provided the best platform for demanding the continuation of reservations or quotas in government and railway service—especially seeing that, in the Anglo-Indian case, these amounted to positive discrimination (or affirmative action) for a group whose average standard of living was in advance of the population as a whole. As the 1931 census approached, the *Review* printed propagandistic reminders at the bottom of its pages, such as 'Remember the interests of your future generations will depend on your strength in the country. Protect posterity by returning yourself as an Anglo-Indian'; 'Your future is at stake. Experience has shown that numbers are important in the changing India. You gain nothing by returning yourself as a European and gain everything by returning as an Anglo-Indian. Do so in the 1931 census and so help your leaders in their efforts for the community'; and 'To have a voice we must have numbers and this can only be secured by every Anglo-Indian returning himself as such in the forthcoming census. Nothing will be gained by describing yourself otherwise.'[36] A full-length, front-page editorial informed Association branches

> of the procedure to be followed .... We cannot sufficiently stress the necessity and importance of an accurate numbering of our own community ... There is still an erroneous belief that it is advantageous for Anglo-Indians to adopt a European disguise ... [However,] whatever you declare is quickly forgotten by the census officer ... Thus, from the individual point of view there is nothing to be feared—social or other advancement—but from the communal point of view an accurate census is vital ... While relative to the millions of other communities ... our numbers may be insignificant, they ... may be of

tremendous consequences when it comes to proportions in such Services as the Railways, Telegraphs, etc. ... [and to our] voting strength in the various provinces ... But for this deprivation ... in Calcutta, Rangoon, Ajmer, Nagpur and the United Provinces, the Anglo-Indian vote would be a very important factor ... An Anglo-Indian who considers himself to be a European even for purposes of census may satisfy his false pride but it will be to the great harm of his own children and himself ... Anglo-Indians ... calling themselves Europeans ... is detrimental in all cases, but grievously detrimental in the case of the census. Let us appeal to your pride, to your good sense, the interests of your children and particularly your regard for the truth.[37]

Passing

The concept of 'passing' relates to one of the key facets of the mixed-race experience in India, Burma and other British colonies in Asia. Passing is usually defined as the attempt to pass oneself off as being from a group to which one does not belong. However, it is perhaps more helpful to define it as also encompassing the attempt to pass oneself off as not being from a group into which one has been born, from which one is wholly or partially descended, or to which one has been ascribed by prevailing systems of racial, religious and ethnic classification within the society in which one lives. Conscious passing can constitute a transgressive act against the racial order and hierarchy that is being imposed and that is seeking to police one's life opportunities across multiple spheres. If so, it is usually the strategy of an individual, a family or a couple of family members to elevate themselves, often while hoping to maintain a low profile. Of course, at other times, as in the case of Merle Oberon, it may be something that enables one to be supremely visible in a way that would not otherwise be possible. Success may require a multitude of active steps and deliberate fabrications, but there is also the intertwined and normally more passive experience of being 'passed'—that is, when others knowingly or mistakenly ascribe you to a group from which your background might otherwise exclude you. Being 'passed' may happen unexpectedly when no attempt to pass is being made. It may constitute the beginning of an ad hoc decision to 'go with it' and use the unanticipated opportunity to begin to consciously pass. Alternatively, it might constitute the moment when a quiet strategy of positioning oneself in the hope of passing has finally paid off. Or it might be a brief experience, deliberately or accidentally derailed within moments, either by inadvertently revealing one is not of the group to which one has been ascribed, or by taking a stand and objecting to it.

If the mixed are often rendered invisible in the colonial archive, passing as a strategy of self-elevation has been even harder for scholars to detect. It is the contention of this book that passing was far more widespread than has been generally assumed. Both through ongoing interracial unions between British soldiers and mixed-race women and the under-recognised phenomenon of passing, the socio-racial dividing lines of the Raj were continuously contested and transgressed. To the story of Grace Vincent explored in the first chapter, we could add the exemplary case of the Pratt brothers, for whom migration was key to a more variable degree of passing or being passed. William Henry Pratt (1887–1969), known as Billy in childhood, would later become famous to the world as Boris Karloff. His father and his father's father shared the same name, Edward John Pratt. The senior Edward joined the 'East India Company's Marines ... in Bengal on October 15, 1815', becoming a first lieutenant, and, after the death of his first wife, married an 'unidentified Indian woman' – Billy's grandmother.[38] The younger Edward (1827–95), Billy's father, had been 'appointed Assistant Collector of Salt Revenue' in 1874, and ended up partnering with four women, at least three of whom he had married (though the third of whom remains 'unidentified'), and siring twelve children, two of whom sadly did not survive infancy or childhood.[39] Billy was the youngest.

Billy's mother, Eliza Sarah Millard, may have had a European complexion, but she was also mixed, as well as being the niece of Anna Leonowens (née Crawford). In *Bombay Anna: The Real Story and Remarkable Adventures of the King and I Governess*, Susan Morgan reveals how upon disembarking at Singapore in 1859 Anna immediately 'reinvented herself', making 'up a new "history" of her origins and identity, a new biography', a character which she then became and continued to perform 'for the rest of her life'.[40] Though Anna came to be famous in fictionalised form, a fiction that built a second layer upon the fiction she had created herself, as a British woman, her background was in truth like that of many other Anglo-Indians. She was the granddaughter of 'a lieutenant in the First Battalion of the Fourth Regiment N.I.' of the Company's army in Bombay and, as Morgan argues, 'a local woman' whose absence from the records confirms 'that she could not have been European. The most likely possibility is that … [she] was an Anglo-Indian (of mixed race), born in India.'[41] Anna, however, being fair enough to pass as European herself, disapproved of her sister's marriage, and even more of her niece's marriage (to Billy's obviously mixed-looking father), 'eventually disown[ing them]'.[42] As Scott Allen Nollen suggests, 'Anna's prejudices … affected her family relationships … [and] young Eliza's marriage to twice-widowed, half-Indian Edward Pratt at the age of 16 may have contributed to Anna's distaste for her sister'.[43] Eliza's first child was 'Edward Millard, born in India on August 29, 1865', who would become a member of the Indian Civil Service (ICS), an eminent legal scholar, and ultimately a Bombay High Court judge (1918–25).[44]

Of the two surviving daughters and seven surviving sons, all but two were the children of the 'prolific' Eliza.[45] We can assume that most of the children were born in India 'before Edward retired and moved the family' to England, after which his last two sons, Richard Septimus and Billy, were born, in 1882 and 1887 respectively.[46] Thus there was a large age gap between Billy and his older siblings, one of whom, 'his half-sister, Emma Caroline Pratt, a spinster only two years younger than his deceased mother',[47] took him in at age seven when his father abandoned him in 1894, crossing the Channel for France and eventually dying in Paris without meeting his son again. Billy's mother had died two years before. Prior to abandoning his son, Edward wrote to the India Office protesting against 'the "supercilious commiseration or compassion for the class of Coloured Englishmen to which I belong". Arguing that "Eurasia has yet to be discovered by the geographers", he claimed that he and his fellows deserved to be called "English or Indian".'[48] Clearly, Edward shared the dislike of the label 'Eurasian' then widespread among the mixed. Wishing to be accepted as an Englishman of colour, who had migrated home to Britain, was a distinct, though understandable, alternative to the various strands of mixed-race identity as they would continue to evolve in India.

It is not clear how far Edward's attitudes influenced his children and their perception of themselves in racial, national and cultural terms. A couple of them went 'back' to India to enter colonial service in the judiciary and elite ICS. Charles and David worked together in the administration of 'the Argentinean Railway'; while John and Richard entered Britain's diplomatic corps in China, where they 'experienced a political falling out ... the former having sympathized with the Communists while the latter organized the evacuation of women and children from the upper Yangtze in 1927. A staunchly conservative Victorian moralist, Richard became absolutely misanthropic, refusing to communicate with his family and turning down a knighthood', while his communist-sympathising brother became Sir John.[49] Despite high-flying careers, both diplomats had had to endure racialised jibes; as British Consul in a port city Richard was repeatedly invited by a 'leading British subject ... to perform the Indian rope trick.'[50] In his school photos in England, Billy stood out in stark contrast to his classmates. Nollen described how he 'had inherited a dark, somewhat greenish, complexion from the Anglo-Indian Pratts, but his facial structure, prominent brow and brown eyes made him the very image of his mother'.[51] Billy's childhood experience of his brothers was generally as intermittent overbearing figures who encouraged him to take the more sensible kind of career paths that they had pursued. Accordingly, he avoided them during the formative stages of his tenuous and impoverished acting career.

Billy and three of his most 'respectable' brothers gathered for a reunion in 1933 and are depicted in a monochrome photo as the 'four brothers Pratt'.[52] Although they had all been educated in Britain after their father relocated the family there, only William is known to have been born in England. Taken together, they are clearly mixed or South Asian in appearance, with a range of skin tones that would make them plausible as contemporaries of the Kashmiri-descended Nehrus. However, on their own and in other settings, they might have attempted to pass or have been passed, depending on the background of the person with whom they were interacting. Sir John, the only one of the four sporting a bow tie, waistcoat and pocket-watch chain, became a Knight Commander of the British Empire (KBE) and Companion of the Order of St Michael and St George (CMG), as 'an expert on China for the British Foreign Office and a lecturer at Cambridge'.[53] As Consul General in Tsinan and Nanking his complexion may have passed for Mediterranean, but in cosmopolitan Shanghai he 'was said to have encountered some colour feeling among the British community and behind his back the Chinese staff called him the black consul'.[54]

Standing beside him, Frederick Grenville Pratt has the lightest skin, although his imposingly large and unusually dark eyebrows stand out all the more as a result. 'Fred' had had a distinguished career in the ICS, 'first as District Magistrate and then Settlement Commissioner and Director of Land Records in Bombay, where he sat on the Legislative Council from 1915–25'.[55] In late February 1922, just over two weeks after Mohandas Gandhi called off his first non-cooperation movement, Pratt was arguing the government's case against a motion from an Indian legislator to defund the budget by Rs. 15,50,000 on the grounds of excessive taxation upon the 'Bhils of ... [a] poor district of Gujarat' who had suffered three years of drought and crop failure.[56] Pratt blamed 'political agitators' for threatening and intimidating 'many of the landlords' in 'a disloyal campaign ... for the purposes of cutting down the revenues of Government'.[57] Some landlords, not wishing to 'sacrifice themselves ... on the altar of a political shibboleth', voluntarily 'paid the second instalment as well as the first', with the result that 'during the whole of last year ... even before the political embargo was called off, our local officers had been so successful in fighting this agitation that they had collected sums 300 per cent. in excess of ... previous years'.[58] If the members of the Indian opposition benches did not assume that Pratt was a typical colonial British ICS man, then any historian coming across his name in the proceedings of the Bombay Legislative Council almost certainly would.

That several of the Pratt brothers were British-educated children of mixed-race Anglo-Indian parents, including a father who wanted to be regarded as a 'Coloured' Englishman rather than a Eurasian, does not really tell us what their identity was or how they would have described themselves. For Billy, the man who was to become Boris Karloff, his British birth and upbringing in Britain and more tenuous connection to a father who had in any case abandoned him make it even less likely that he would have felt any affinity with India or with the rival identity categories of mixed-race peoples in India. He always described and deported himself as British, and, notwithstanding a childhood consciousness of standing out as a result of his colour, this was true to his education and upbringing. His personal habits and tastes were British in many respects and he played up to the Hollywood media's desire to portray him as the quintessential English gentleman. While he lived in California surrounded by foreigners, any tensions between his identity and his performance of a public-facing persona would have been easier to reconcile. Nonetheless, his life is part of the broader story of the Anglo-Indian diaspora, and how migration and passing (or being passed) could affect the lives of mixed-race people of European and Indian descent in a wider world.

Movement from one locality to another, or migration from one country to another, either temporarily or with the intention of permanent settlement, is often a key ingredient of successful passing. By moving, one escapes from those who are familiar with one's background and who may be acquainted with one's relatives. A place where one is already known is a more difficult environment in which to seek to change one's existing status. What is more, those advertising positions in distant localities, in unpopular and remote postings, often find it harder to attract suitable candidates. In such circumstances, employers and recruiters may be willing to consciously look the other way, or at least will not be actively looking for reasons to disqualify a much-needed candidate. For example, the colonial authorities in British Honduras (modern Belize) were desperate to attract young European doctors, but found that their advertised salary of £300 for an assistant medical officer was insufficient.[59] They therefore internally debated whether they could afford to increase the figure or whether they should consider 'well qualified but inexperienced Eurasian or coloured creole doctors'.[60] If a pale-skinned Anglo-Indian member of the Indian Medical Department had shown up claiming to be a European British subject born in India, we can easily imagine few questions being asked.

One British missionary's wife recalled a tragic story of an Anglo-Indian doctor who settled in Britain:

> if a girl is fair so that she can be a European, by all appearances she
> would be accepted, she might have a sister who is dark and she would

not be accepted. We had a friend who came home [to Britain] to train as a docter [*sic*] and she is a very clever doctor, she was very fair but she had a brother and a sister who were dark, and she found on the boat that she could be friendly with all the Europeans and all the people accepted her, and then someone asked where were you born, and she said in India, and from then on they dropped her, because they realised that she was an anglo-Indian, although she was white, and after she got to England she was very bitter, and it was so sad because ... her brother and her sister, she just refused to acknowledge them, so it broke up that family, which is dreadful because the angl[o]-Indian is a very ... [devoted] member of his family, they look after each other, the old people ... are cared for by their daughters and sons, right until the end, and they set a wonderful example of family life. But that's [the] sad thing, this was forced upon her because she felt that if she was going to make a success of herself as a doctor she must never, never let anyone know that she had anything to do with India.[61]

The antennae of colonial Britons were finely tuned to detecting domiciled and mixed-race backgrounds among those who could plausibly pass as European. But in the Indian princely states colour and racial status mattered less, which helps to account for the number of women doctors from domiciled backgrounds who sought service there. Even if there were prestige benefits for princely rulers and their wives in claiming to employ Britons and Europeans, the perception of Europeanness and even of the range of complexions that could fall within its ambit would be significantly less discriminating among those Indians who were not so widely travelled. The British-mandated 'Annual Return[s] of Europeans and Eurasians Employed' in native states provide some interesting contrasts. The Punjab States returns record Miss Angelina Thomas as headmistress of a local girls' school on Rs. 90 per month, and Miss J. Reid of another on Rs. 50, both of whom were listed as Eurasian and as British subjects.[62] Bahawalpur in Punjab in 1922 lists 'Miss Z. E. Decosta', 'Lady Doctor', as employed since 1908 on a salary of Rs. 700, along with her personal assistant, Miss Brown.[63] Both were reported as British subjects but in this case as Europeans, although Decosta's Portuguese surname would have created the strong presumption among colonial Britons that she was either mixed or an Indian Christian. Such prejudices are apparent in Shelland Bradley's novel *An American Girl in India* (1911):

'It is not that our Mofussil Clubs are at all exclusive ... In fact, they generally err far too much the other way. But even they have to draw the line somewhere. Why, actually only the other day there was a talk of proposing the Peninos.' The Peninos, I found, claimed to be Portuguese. It's wonderful how many Portuguese there are in India. Considering the fewness of the original Portuguese adventurers they must have been a wonderful race. 'Mrs. Penino is large and fat ... All Eurasians grow large and fat very soon if they don't get skinny and wizened. It's hard to know which is the lesser evil of the two.'[64]

The 1921 records for Kapurthala State classify 'Miss G. M. Friend Pereira M.D.', 'Lady Doctor to Her Highness the Maharani Sahiba and Ranis and in charge [of the] Female Hospital' with a salary of Rs. 425 per month, plus 'house and carriage', as Eurasian.[65] Given the geographic distance and differential finances of these princely states, we cannot be certain that Decosta's higher salary was straightforwardly the product of her classification as a European British subject rather than as a Eurasian, but it would be entirely plausible for this to be the case. Women with Portuguese names would have been more clearly marked out in British eyes as racially suspect whatever their skin colour. So it is hardly surprising that they sought refuge and superior employment opportunities in the princely states, where no doubt any claims they might make to a European status would also be more readily entertained.

However, nursing was the professional field which was by far the most representative Anglo-Indian women's vocation at the time. Irene Green provides an exemplary case of a successful nursing career aided by willingness to migrate across long distances, face new challenges, and, wittingly or unwittingly, be drawn into the process of passing.[66] Green first relocated from her small railway colony home in South India to the dauntingly large metropolis of Bombay. Her more sophisticated and worldly fellow nurses during her first three years of training at St. George's Hospital teased her mercilessly by repeating her initials 'I.M.' as *I am Green*.[67] Born in 1906 in South India at the lower end of the Anglo-Indian class spectrum, she had only attended railway schools to primary or elementary standard. The family fell upon hard times when her father died in 1923. Still she knew more about her ancestry than many Anglo-Indians: 'My maternal grandmother [was] a Hindu. Her husband was a Portuguese Veterinary surgeon in the Bombay Cavalry.'[68] She initially referred to her father as 'an Englishman', before clarifying that he was 'a Scot[t] ish man' or 'of Scot[t]ish ancestry', something that appeared to have been confirmed in her mind by his having been 'brought up in the ... Scot[t]ish orphanage in ... [Secunderabad] in south India.'[69] Green's father worked on the railways and the family lived in a railway colony. The life she describes was fairly typical:

> My father, a railway man, was transferred very often, every two or three years and we used to love ... the train journey ... [in our own reserved] second class compartment ... [with an] adjoining ... coupe ... for our servants. We were also given two wagons in which to take all our furniture, flower pots because in some places, we did not live in the place long enough to start a proper garden ... also the poultry ... in cages, when the train stopped at various stations, I can remember running along with great pleasure and my father used to hoist us up and we'd go in and feed and water the birds ... Our dogs travelled with us in the compartment. Our food was ordered and reserved by railway telegraph and at the big stations the trays would [be] waiting, and we'd take them through the window ... Our servants travelled with us because some of them would not want to leave us. Some stayed with us for years, going from one station to the other.[70]

Thus the lowest class of gainfully employed Anglo-Indians, the railway families, upon whom the British, and even other more afflu-ent Anglo-Indians and Domiciled Europeans, were apt to look down, in fact lived a very privileged life within their own small and relatively sheltered world. Many, if not most, of the remoter stations on the branch lines hosted a small railway colony of Anglo-Indian families, with their own primary-level railway school and Railway Institute. Green fondly recalled Christmas as

> a wonderful time ... in the Railway Institute ... [with] a whole week's of entertainment, we had sports one day for children, sports one day for adults, we had a fancy dress for children, fancy dress for adults, a huge tree ... [with] candles ... Father Christmas came either on a railway engine, when we had to go to the loco shed and meet him. Sometimes he came on a camel ... [or] an elephant and then, we all went into the hall and he cut down the presents and gave ... [them] to us ... We picked a ticket out of a bag and we got the same number

that was on the tree ... After that there used to be a treat, plenty to eat ... then there was ... a railway picnic when all the community of the station ... got into a train and went far away up the line ... to a beautiful ... spot and ... had a picnic which lasted all day long.[71]

Naturally childhood memories are often nostalgic, particularly for diasporic emigrants, but this extract gives us a flavour of community life. Alongside churches and schools, the ubiquitous Railway Institutes were central to the social world of Anglo-Indian railway families. Modelled on colonial clubs, they often had their own bars, dance halls and sports facilities such as tennis courts. Green described herself and her younger sister, born in 1907, as 'railway children. All our lives, until I married we were railway.'[72] Unlike other families they had never been able to afford the hill station boarding schools which a significant number of Anglo-Indian children attended, and so, as she said, 'we stopped our education when we were still at the primary stage. My mother educated us actually by giving us the Bible to read. We were brought up, our education came from ... reading the Bible.'[73] The hammer blow came in 1923:

After my father died we had to leave railway quarters. We were very poor because his Provident Fund did not come to much. My mother looked for cheap lodging ... There were three unmarried daughters ... Our circumstances were getting ... desperate ... My sister was working in the railway stores, and I decided I had to do my bit. I wanted to nurse. I went to St. George's hospital, and [was] lucky, very, very lucky to be taken in because my ... education was below ... the usual standard ... but ... because I wrote a pathetic letter to the matron, I was accepted ... The problem [a]rose about [my] uniform. My mother could not afford new stuff ... so she decided to go to one or two of the officers' wives. She used to make hats for sale, and she begged them for their old tennis dresses ... cut [these] up and I was fitted up in this way ... A watch was needed. An old friend of ours gave me a watch. Another ... decided to give me ... a pair of scissors which were needed ... [I] took the train ... to Bombay ... [then a horse tonga] into the hospital grounds. This was [a] mistake ... because straightaway they knew I was not of the standard expected. Matron, however, was very kind. She decided to give me a chance. I had to struggle with the education ... I had to study harder than most ... I never went out. My head was stuck in a book and ... I was teased a lot because I was so naive, brought up up-country, never having moved out of the railway colony and garrison stations. I'd never been to a big, big ... town like Bombay or Calcutta or Delhi in my life, and I was bewildered. In the hospital, looking around, the other girls were all so sophisticated, that I was teased unmercifully ... because I was frightened to enter a lift. I'd never seen a lift before ... I did not know how to use a telephone. I was terrified of a telephone. Going into the men's ward, I wanted to keep my eyes down all the time because I'd never seen men in pajamas.[74]

She was similarly afraid of night duty at first, when all the beds were draped in translucent white mosquito nets, and the matron would suddenly emerge like a 'perambulating ghost ... [from] between two rows of beds'.[75] But she found some comfort in furtively smoking Indian cigarettes and drinking tea with an elderly Dalit sweeper named Gadbut who became 'a very great friend'.[76] Eventually her hard efforts to make up for her own lack of education paid off, although education wasn't the only thing that counted. Green's assessment of her colleagues and patients is particularly revealing:

> The other nurses were well-educated. A ... very very few of them were coloured. St. George's Hospital was really called the European General and coloured nurses were not accepted except for two or three of them who got in there because the nuns had written to the Matron ... The majority ... were like myself, what we called white Anglo-Indians. About a dozen or so were really English girls ... of English parents born in India ... Our patients were mostly Europeans ... Anglo-Indians were accepted, generally in large numbers, if they were white or off-white or beige-coloured ... Indian Christians came in, usually in their master's trousers, pants and shirts, and they called themselves Anglo-Indians. Our doctors, who were themselves Anglo-Indians in the major part, were not able to draw a line. It was a difficult situation and so these Indians were really accepted as Anglo-Indians or Eurasians. Mostly they suffered from ... [tuberculosis.] The European patients were mostly cases of malaria, typhoid; the Anglo-Indians were all the diseases of India.[77]

St. George's was the premier hospital of the city and province. Already we can see the importance and complexity attached to colour and categorisation within and between different groups. Green provides a more detailed and substantiated version here of the common Anglo-Indian charge that upwardly mobile Indian

Christians, and especially Goans (some of whom might have distant Portuguese ancestry, but most of whom did not), with European conversion names, also sought to pass as Anglo-Indians. The predominance of 'Europeans and Anglo-Indians' relative to 'Indian Christians' and 'Other Indians' in the nursing profession was cause for complaint in the Bombay Legislative Council in 1928.[78] In this case the complainant was a British doctor named M. D. Gilder, and the respondent, on behalf of the government, was 'the Honourable Dewan Bahadur' Harilal D. Desai, the Minister for Education.[79] Desai was asked 'to state why four European and Anglo-Indian sisters' had been appointed to the senior position of 'sister-in-charge of wards' at the Gokuldas Tejpal (or 'G. T.') Hospital, while the remaining six Indian Christians and two 'Other Indians' were only 'nurses working in a subordinate capacity'.[80] The tabulation 'of nurses employed in the administrative grades as matrons and sisters in charge of wards, operation theatres, and out-patients' strikingly bore out Gilder's assertion, with eighty-seven 'Europeans and Anglo-Indians' (it was either not thought necessary or possible to separate the two), fifteen 'Indian Christians' and only twenty-seven 'Other Indians'.[81] It is probably true that middle-class Indians at the time would have been unlikely to consider nursing as a suitable or respectable profession for wives and daughters, but the fact that the bulk of Indian nurses could expect to be confined to the most menial and subordinate roles, many of which are not even included in these figures, cannot have helped to raise the prestige of the profession.

In Bombay's own hospitals, whether they catered for Europeans or Indians, European and Anglo-Indian nurses generally predominated, while in Poona, for example, judging by these figures one of the largest civil hospitals in the country, there were fifteen European and Anglo-Indian management-level nurses, only three Indian Christians and none from other communities. Similarly in Karachi there were eight, one and zero respectively. Several smaller civil hospitals in remoter cities, such as Bijapur and Ahmednagar, defied this trend. But in the prestigious European hospitals, including Green's, there were no Indians in the management levels of nursing. These figures go a long way towards confirming the picture presented by Green herself. After three years in Bombay, Green took an even greater leap in the dark, undertaking 'a journey of over 1,000 miles' to reach her new posting in Peshawar near the border with Afghanistan.[82]

> I was lucky enough to get a job as a Nursing Sister on the North West Frontier ... not really intended for an Anglo[-]Indian girl but because the Matron was either short of staff or because I sent a photograph which showed me as near white ... I was given this job ... I found in the Mess not only that I was the youngest ... I was the only one, an Anglo-Indian, born in the country. The others were all English Sisters, and I had an awful lot to learn from them ... to speak correctly ... to lose my chichi accent ... something peculiar to Anglo-Indians ... [rather like a Welsh accent.] Here [in the UK] it might sound alright, but in India in those days it was a terrible handicap, especially in the Mess. I had to learn not to offer my hand ... [or] say 'Pleased to meet you' ... to just bow and to say 'How do you do?' ... to say 'Goodbye' and not 'Cheerio and chin-chin'. These were all Anglo-Indian sayings ... I had to learn ... a new way of speaking. Manners.[83]

One possible alternative was set out by the *Review* in 1932 in its denunciation of a Calcutta *Statesman* advertisement for nurses to staff King George's Hospital, Lucknow, and the Lahore Mental Hospital, which specified

> that the vacancies of Matron and Sisters can only be filled by British qualified and trained nurses, in other words, no nurse, however brilliant and experienced she may be ... who has had the misfortune and tragedy to be trained in India, can ever hope to secure these appointments ... We feel we must again protest against the ruthless manner, in which our Nurses and Sisters are being ignored—indeed ostracised from suitable employment in our Hospitals in our own country and the continuation of recruiting Matrons, Sisters and Theatre Sisters from England ... What are our Nurses doing to silently submit to this degradation? Are they prepared to grovel in this position of inferiority to the imported Nurse? ... Surely it is time our nurses got together, formed a Nurses Union or joined the ... Association and demanded their rights ... 'Woman, know thyself, value thyself and do not, for a moment longer, tolerate this open insult flouted [*sic*] in your very faces. Shout, demand and even strike but do not submit to this insult a day longer.[']'[84]

However, this was hardly a feasible strategy for a solitary individual, and gradually Green found that over a 'period of time not only my manners, deportment, but my accent was changing, I was gradually losing the … [chi chi accent], this was not deliberate, it was because I was mixing with the sisters in the mess, I was mixing with the officers and their wives' in the 'burrah' club, to which nursing sisters were automatically admitted.[85] Yet even her hopes of helping another fair-complexioned Anglo-Indian who 'was white with blue eyes' to join the club met with failure. This was precisely because her friend's parents lived in Peshawar and she was therefore

> known to be Anglo-Indian … [She wanted to join] because I used to talk about the parties there … [and] I wante[d] … her company … [so] I asked a … lady doctor who had influence … to try and get Celia in, and she told me I don't think we'll succeed it's no use trying, because everybody round here knows Celia is an Anglo-Indian. I told this lady doctor, well so am I, she said yes, but people don't know it here … you have passed, in the crowd … but Celia won't, so therefore this crowd—this club was tabboo [sic] … We were not bitter … we accepted it because this bar, not only the colour bar, but the class bar, cut right across India, we as Anglo-Indians did not allow the Indians into our institutes, we were allowed … as members of the corporals clubs—corporals messes, even some sergeants messes, allowed Anglo-Indians, other sergeants messes did not … [and] we knew that the … [burrah] club for officers was absolutely out of [the] question … not only for Anglo-Indians, but for all white people who were not officers …[86]

In spite of her growing confidence, revealing that she herself was an Anglo-Indian to a British doctor was itself quite risky. However, it was hardly the greatest risk she took. Despite their immensely privileged lives under the special protection of the army garrisoning the restive borderlands of the Indian Empire, in what is now Pakistan, these women were accepting greater physical dangers than their counterparts in Bombay. They came under sniper fire during intermittent conflicts with the Afridis. On more than one occasion a wealthy local Pashtun tribesman whom Green was nursing sinisterly jested about her Western ways and dress: 'I could easily have you kidnapped … you'd have to marry me … and then you would be in a [burka].'[87] Following the kidnapping five years earlier of a woman named Molly Elliot,[88] Green might have been alarmed had she chosen to take such comments seriously.

Without her fair complexion Green could never have advanced her career so spectacularly, but even so she

> had to learn to take a certain amount of digs, from some of the sisters … Because I was the youngest … the men had a soft spot in their hearts for me, I saw this, I knew it, I was popular with them, but not so with a lot of the women … all the women I met outside … But particularly in the mess … My only friend was the Scottish sister Miss Harding who … when I was 22 … took me under her wing. One of the sisters was particularly catty, when she found [out] that I had a boyfriend, one of the Sub[alterns] … she would deliberately speak about things in England, she talked about home, because she knew I was lost, she'd speak about different things in England, that I did not know. So letting him know … it never came out in the open, but it was there all the time.[89]

Contradicting the literary trope of the newly arrived Englishwoman as a relatively liberal and enlightened critic of colonial British prejudices,[90] this and other historical testimonies from multiple vantages attests to the uncomfortable reality that memsahibs were generally more anxious to police the socio-racial boundary between the domiciled and themselves than their male counterparts.[91] This is easily explained by their desire to exclude domiciled women as competitors, in the context of British women's livelihoods being almost entirely dependent on securing a husband with the highest status employment within the Raj's elaborately gradated class hierarchy. Roy Nissen similarly felt that in their eyes we 'were just muck', and he gave examples of memsahibs referring to Anglo-Indian women as '*kutcha* cobras', and one snapping at an 'Indian shopkeeper "I'll come back again after you've finished with this Eurasian woman over here" … [before she] just simply stamped out … we had quite a lot of that.'[92] 'Kutcha' means unripe, half-cooked or unfinished in Hindi, while 'pukka', a term colonial Britons appropriated to connote their own better classes and model behaviour, implies ripeness, readiness, or food cooked to perfection.

Green's experiences call to mind several scenes in Paul Scott's *The Alien Sky* (1974), which is set amid the imminent departure of the last few remaining British residents of a small fictional town. Here Scott constructs the tragic story of Dorothy Gower, a pass-white

Anglo-Indian woman whose unhappy marriage to a colonial Englishman rests upon the shaky foundation of her deeply buried secret that she is mixed. She does not wish to go 'home' to England for fear of being found out. When another, more visibly identifiable Anglo-Indian named Judith Anderson is brought to a party at the couple's bungalow by her older British lover, Frank Milner, who on the verge of Indian independence in 1947 is either unthinking or careless of how others might react, she is cruelly mocked by an English memsahib named Cynthia Mapleton, who goads her into explaining where exactly in Brighton she had lived, and asks her whether Brighton is 'on the west coast'.[93] Unrelenting in her 'interrogation', Cynthia asks whether the street which Judith gave, 'Lewes Crescent[,] is just opposite the pier'.[94] By now on the verge of tears Judith answers a question about her parents' background by saying that although her father had always lived in Brighton, her mother 'was Italian'.[95] With her partner Frank too drunk to walk her home, Judith is accompanied by a visiting American named MacKendrick and, during her exchange with him, reveals that Dorothy, the party's hostess, is actually a fairer-skinned Anglo-Indian with whom she had been 'at school in Assam', but who had succeeded in passing and thereby married a still unwitting Englishman.[96]

Mixed-race pan-Eurasianism

Pan-Eurasianism was another important intellectual counter-current to the Anglo-Indian mainstream. Its two most fervent proponents were Kenneth Wallace and Cedric Dover. Dover's post-Indian career has attracted substantial attention from Nico Slate in two academic monographs.[97] Slate presents Dover principally as an exponent of an expansive 'coloured cosmopolitanism', which embraced people of colour worldwide, especially African Americans with whom he built extensive contacts through extended visits to the United States, which he kept up following his migration to Britain. A friendly correspondence grew up between Dover and Nehru as fellow socialists.[98] In a letter of 1938 to Nehru, Dover expressed his clear identification with and continuing interest in India, while encouraging Nehru and Gandhi to forge greater connections with African Americans by suggesting they send 'Dr. W. E. B ... Du Bois ... one of the great pioneers ... of the movement for closer contacts between coloured peoples' their best wishes for his imminent seventieth birthday.[99] A year later in a speech on 'race problems' at the Indian Students' Union and Hostel, in Gower Street, London, Dover emphasised the

> oppression that the 'Coloured' people have to face ... when the Englishman talks of black and coloured race. Here, I must tell you what I experienced in America. I was addressing a Negro meeting ... [whose] audience did not know that my home was in India and not in England as the majority of it thought. Thinking that I came from England they were very polite and reserved with me, they listened to me as they would listen to an Englishman. But when in the course of my speech, I said that my home was in India they felt excited ... almost thrilled. There was thus a feeling of what I may call colour unity.[100]

However, what principally concerns us here is Dover's evolving attitudes towards his own mixed-race group in India. His first political and intellectual project was squarely aimed at building up the self-esteem of his own mixed group within India. In his seminal work *Half-Caste* (1937), Dover linked himself to the similarly discordant early nineteenth-century figure of Henry L. V. Derozio by presenting the poet as a role model for how he wished the group's politics to develop:

> This youthful genius left so profound an impression on the culture of Bengal that I have included a biographical account of him ... as a sort of type-study of the influence of hybrid genius on social evolution ... Derozio's poetry and teaching sprang from a deep love for India, 'my own, my native land', and ... no comparable personality has arisen in the century of increasing Anglo-Indianism following his death. Nor has the intense intellectual and philanthropic activity of his time ever been renewed in the community. There is a moral in this phase of Eurasian history which deserves to be learned ... that culture springs from attachment to one's motherland and the causes of humanity, not from parasitic services to a ruling minority. And a people is judged by its cultural worth.[101]

Despite the group's redesignation as 'Anglo-Indian' in the 1911 census, Dover still preferred to call himself a Eurasian. He was aware that following its adoption in the late nineteenth century, 'Eurasian' 'soon came to have a derogatory implication, which the Eurasians sought to elude by appropriating the label "Anglo-Indian" from the resident Britishers who had invented it for themselves'.[102] Nonetheless Dover denounced 'the painfully smug Anglo Indianism of to-day'.[103] Whether or not he accepted it, Dover had already lost the battle within his own group to restore 'Eurasian' as a positive self-identifier and reinject it with a sense of pride. His persisting adherence to the older designation was, perhaps more importantly, rooted in his first truly cosmopolitan project, the attempt to weld together a broader 'imagined community' from the peoples of mixed descent from across the European colonial empires in Asia. This pan-Eurasianism formed the basis for a prospective mixed-race nation and a new kind of nationalism in search of a homeland, comparable with contemporaneous Zionism, whose adherents were, during the 1930s, predominantly fellow socialists known as Labour Zionists. Before shifting his focus and efforts towards international socialism and 'coloured cosmopolitanism', Dover was, like Wallace, wedded to the narrower, but still expansive, creed of mixed-race pan-Eurasianism.

At the Indian Students' Union, Dover propounded his view that 'those who were anxious to style themselves as Anglo-Indians were actually moved from an imperialist outlook to do so'.[104] 'British Imperialists and their counterparts in India', Dover argued, had been 'very much cleverer than the Congress leaders' in flattering Anglo-Indians that they were 'a great and noble race' whenever it suited imperial 'interests … to get the[m] … back to the fold of Britain as if they were "British"'.[105] Dover sought to persuade his audience that though the 'many Anglo-Indians who fall easy prey to this wooing … may deserve the contempt of the average ordinary Indian they should not be treated with contempt by thinking and progressive Indians'.[106] Dover was referring to Ela Sen, whose recently published *Testament of India* (1939), had concluded:

> In the Anglo-Indian community the British will leave behind a legacy that will be nothing more than an additional burden … They have clung for so long to the skirts of the British and so deliberately alienated themselves from all things Indian that it is difficult for Indians to be patient with them. Yet it is hardly likely that Britain will provide them with a sanctuary, if ever she gives up India. How, then, is India

159

to deal with these people? Most of them are devoid of culture and education and come from the lowest strata of both nations ... Their lot will be pitiable, for with their 'white' complex they cannot possibly fit into the trend of present-day affairs in India.[107]

This followed Sen's disparagement of the supposed 'low culture ... parentage ... birth and breeding' in Anglo-Indian schools.[108] Having come to see discourses on 'racial culture', 'superiority or inferiority', 'blood-relationship', and other 'racial problems' as 'a clever Imperialist and Fascist move', Dover accused Sen of having 'talked of races and found something to hate ... [in] the Eurasian community', cautioning his fellow 'Socialist and ... anti-Imperialist' that this was 'a dangerous attitude for her to take' towards 'one of the most important communities in India holding an important position in the country ... [and] the daily life of the people'.[109] While making his own criticisms of colonial British racism, Wallace also pushed back against Indian prejudices:

A Brave New India cannot be built on the quicksand of communalism ... One complaint I have against these Indian communities. Not knowing us sufficiently, or caring to know us, many of their members have imbibed the European prejudice towards us, thus doing an injustice to what is after all one of their own Indian peoples. Also, we suffer ... from the prejudice of the caste system against exogamy.[110]

One 'prominent Indian gentleman' and self-proclaimed 'aborigine by race and an animist by religion', after commending Wallace's *The Eurasian Problem, Constructively Approached* (1930) as an 'extremely brilliant book', proceeded to take both pan-Eurasianists to task.[111]

... the Eurasian ultra Montanism that you and Mr. Dover seem to preach. You want to make a Eurasian community all over the East. It is significant that your vision of this Pan-Eurasianism extends only to those countries where the Europeans are dominant ... [not] to Turkey, Egypt and Persia, where ... the ruling classes are half-castes ... So far as Physical Eurasianism is concerned, the Pashas and Beys of Turkey and Egypt are even more Eurasian than our own friends. But still Mr. Dover's and your idea of a Eurasian community extends only to Java, Malay, Indo-China; but presumably not to Japan. The reason is clear. In Turkey and Egypt, the Eurasians (Physical) are Turks and Egyptians, because the Europeans are not governing races there. In

India, Indo-China, Java and Malay, the Europeans are the dominant people and the Eurasians think that they gain credit by dissociating themselves from the people of the country. This is the fundamental fallacy of your position … What is the reason for your loyalty to Britain as against India? I do not mean, of course, yours personally. But the question is why is it as a community you are attached to Great Britain? Has the community any ambition for India … your [own] country? I do not suppose many Eurasians would now be so foolish [as] to deny that their country is India.[112]

Thus, what might be interpreted as progressive within the context of internal struggles over identity among the mixed was decried from an Indian nationalist perspective as still being rooted in an underlying sense of superiority over colonised Asian peoples. Pan-Eurasianism was plausibly read as antithetical to Indian nationalism. Rather than identifying with the specific anticolonial struggles and identities of each colonised Asian nation, the mixed were seeking an escape in dreams of self-determination in a national homeland of their own, whose territorial embodiment would presumably come at the expense of the land claims of others.

Wallace's reviewer was even less restrained in his condemnations of the group as a whole, asserting that 'Eurasians have so far been hangers-on of Europeans'. 'They have no pride in their own country and their own people … All their pride was for their European (sometimes supposed) connection. They were ashamed of their own country and their own mothers.' Most damningly, 'Eurasians do not hide their contempt of … [N-word, plural] and naturally this feeling creates its complement among Indians.'[113] He recounted a story of a 'Eurasian individual I met at Oxford [who] was asked by the head of his college where he came from … [and] said from India, "but my father was Irish and my mother was Scotch" (he himself was very dark). The head of his college smiled and said "No doubt it was so: but do keep the fact to yourself."'[114] Seeking to counter Wallace's implication 'that Indians look[ed] down upon … [Eurasians] for their mixed blood',[115] his reviewer cited cases of

Indians whose mothers are Europeans … [who might be] physical … half-castes; but they do not belong to your community, because the essence of the idea of the community is common tradition and ideas.

I have a few relations and many friends who are married to European girls; their children are Indians; they are accepted as such. They belong to our community. You may ask why. The answer is their name ... If a man is called Ramaswamy and his brother is called Ramsey, then you will realise the difference. The sons of Indian fathers having to sport the names of their Indian fathers remain Indians. They have no pretensions to be different, any more than the child of a Mussalman father and a Hindu mother. But the son of a European father and an Indian mother accepts the European name and thinks that he has inherited the whiteman's burden! That is the difference in a name and that is why the children of my cousin by his Lancashire wife will grow up genuine Indians whatever their physical characteristics may be.[116]

By 1935, as the title of his second book suggests—*Brave New Anglo-India, in a Brave New India in a Brave New World*—Wallace had largely reconciled himself to the group's 1911 redesignation. Revealing his own flexibility of thought on the naming and boundaries of the group in India, Wallace's second work proclaimed:

There has always been much controversy as to a definition of Anglo-Indian. For electoral purposes ... [it] really amounts to a residential test. Whether you are of (so-called) pure European descent or one of 'mixed' blood of European paternity, so long as your parents are 'habitually resident' in India ... you are an Anglo-Indian ... but ... [this] is too restrictive and reflective of narrow communalism in a community that is kin to all ... exclud[ing] ... many who are of mixed blood but European in the maternal line, though culturally perhaps more 'Anglo' than many of us ... [This] is only justifiable on the grounds of narrow nationalism which arbitrarily accords a child the nationality of its father, except in the case of illegitimate issue. It is also absurd that many who never have and never will see the shore of Europe should be returned [in the census or electoral rolls] as Europeans ... I would have preferred the way of the League of Nations which requires only a simple declaration, which is subsequently unalterable—you abide both by its advantages and disadvantages ... All it asks is 'Do you feel you are an Anglo-Indian,' and that, after all, is all that matters. What if others should come into the community on this basis? Is it an evil or an advantage in the long run?[117]

Wallace's argument for widening the group's membership further to embrace individuals descended from Indian fathers and European or mixed-race mothers was unusual within the context of the internal politics of his group. A similar proposal from the Bombay branch of the Association at the 1947 All-India AGM would be voted down.[118] Despite his reluctant acceptance of the term 'Anglo-Indian' and co-option by Gidney, Wallace continued to maintain a Doveresque catholicity of mixed-race identity and sympathy, penning a letter to the editor in 1936 soliciting the cooperation of others 'in the preparation of a representative anthology of Eurasian verse' which would extend 'to all Eur-Asian poets, living and dead, including those whose white ancestry is derived from the maternal side'.[119] 'Cullen's *Caroling Dusk, An Anthology of Verse by Negro Poets* (Harper, 1927)', combining brief biographies with representative samples of each poet's work, was cited as a model.[120] Wallace did not wish to confine its scope to 'Eurasian poetic genius alone, but ... [wanted it to] express in verse the thoughts and aspirations of the Eastern peoples of "mixed blood"'.[121]

The eugenics of Left and Right

Intertwined with Dover's pan-Eurasianism was his intellectual involvement with the eugenics movement. While pan-Eurasianism served as a basis for a positive mixed-race identity, Dover's eugenic theories sought to debunk others working within the same field who championed 'racial purity'. At the time as well as for decades to come, eugenics was still seen to promise vast improvements in public health, and therefore attracted eminent scholars and public intellectuals from across the political spectrum. In the United States the socialist, feminist, birth control activist and progenitor of 'planned parenthood', Margaret Sanger, was a firm advocate of negative eugenics, including the segregation and sterilisation of those deemed to be genetically defective to achieve the racial betterment of various populations. She was influenced by progressive British eugenicists like Havelock Ellis, the vice president of the Eugenics Education Society, who argued for 'the eugenic guardianship of the race' in part through recognising the synergies between individualism and socialism.[122] In *The Task of Social Hygiene* (1912), Ellis expressed his view that 'the superficially sympathetic man flings a coin to the beggar; the more deeply sympathetic man builds an almshouse ... but perhaps the most radically sympathetic of all is the man who arranges that the beggar shall not be born'.[123] In 1895 the London School of Economics (LSE) had been founded by a group of Fabian socialists including Sidney and Beatrice Webb and George Bernard Shaw—all fervent supporters of eugenics. Shaw even declared that 'the only fundamental and possible Socialism is the socialization of the selective breeding of Man'.[124] By 1932, the year in which the Nazis became the largest single party in the German Reichstag, Shaw ominously declared that 'the majority of men at present in Europe have no business to be alive'.[125]

At the First International Eugenics Congress held at the University of London in 1912, an Italian professor delineated

> a hierarchy of the human varieties and races ... It is always the races strongest biologically and most evolved psychologically which impress their characters upon the descendants of ... [mixed] unions. This fact renders difficult the formation of truly mongrel or hybrid races ... A certain degree of difference amongst the parent varieties or races is necessary for the vitality ... of mixed ... populations: nevertheless, too great a difference ... proves always injurious to the descendants as much in physique as in mind ...[126]

Charles Benedict Davenport of Long Island, New York, who had founded the Eugenics Record Office in 1910 and would go on to establish the International Federation of Eugenics Organisations in 1925, compared marriage laws covering 'incest', 'first cousins', 'idiot[s]', 'the insane', drunkards, 'the feeble-minded', epileptics, imbeciles, and those 'with criminalistic tendencies' with the anti-miscegenation laws in 'most of the States'.[127] Davenport denounced 'the Missouri law that provides that proportion of negro blood is to be determined by the jury from the appearance of the person' as 'unjust' and one-drop rule legislation in 'Georgia' as 'futile'.[128] Accepting the contention that the American South had a 'huge "feeble-minded" coloured population', he argued that this 'problem ... [was] of the same order as ... in the north and in England', telling his audience to 'forget unessentials, like skin colour, and focus on socially important defects' through 'sterilization or segregation, [to] prevent the reproduction of the socially inadequate', a process he claimed would eliminate 'mentally incompetent strains' so that 'the good physical traits of some of the black races [would] be added, as a valued heritage to enhance the physical manhood of the south'.[129] However, this questionable early 'progressivism'—relative to thoroughgoing racial essentialists—diminished as Davenport's work on *Race Crossing in Jamaica* (1929) moved to demonstrate statistically that racial mixing between black and white populations resulted in biological and cultural degradation. This trajectory helped him to establish and maintain contacts with sympathetic Nazis during the 1930s.

The Nazis pioneered their own distinctive theory of racial purity within a eugenic framework through the fanciful concept of the supposedly 'Aryan' Germano-Nordic *Herrenrasse* (or master race). In Europe 'race' was more commonly used to refer to national or ethnic groups rather than groups defined by colour. On this basis the Nazis attempted to categorise a plethora of racial types to detect supposedly regular physiognomic identifiers of Jewish, Gypsy, Slavic and Oriental ancestry. This approach was influenced by colonial anthropology, racial anthropometry and the international eugenics movement, and particularly by contacts with American eugenicists, who had carried out the most extensive campaign of forced sterilisation in California. Dover entered into this global discourse by developing an antithetical theory of 'the natural vigor of hybrid groups' within the same eugenicist framework.[130] In *Cimmerii?, or, Eurasians and their Future* (1929), Dover declared:

> the scales of biological evidence clearly swing in favour of the theory that the carefully nurtured hybrid is superior to either parent. And those who hold this view … rightly believe that the inter-racial difficulties of the world will be solved by the development of mixed breeds, and that the removal of racial friction by marriage will ultimately lead to the peaceful occupation of the whole world by one composite race … For the 'menace of colour' exists only in the tortured minds of selfish capitalists and the unthinking rabble … Perhaps in centuries to come the despised half-caste will be instrumental in securing international amity and prosperity.[131]

As a defence against what was then near-universal denigration of mixedness and as an effective counter to the prevalent celebration of supposed racial purity, it was obviously empowering for Dover to dream of the universalisation of mixedness. At the same time, this line of argument held the potential to develop into a kind of mixed-race chauvinism, arguably evident in Dover's perception of

Booker T. Washington and Du Bois as strengthening his case for the superior qualities of people of mixed-race, in his assertion that 'the Negro owes his rapidly advancing position mainly to the efforts of mulattoes'.[132]

Along with Henry E. Roseboom (presumably the editor of the *Malayan Daily Express*, Kuala Lumpur, during the 1920s,[133] and quite possibly of mixed-race himself), Dover contributed to the Third International Congress of Eugenics, held in 1932 in New York, with a paper on 'The Eurasian Community as a Eugenic Problem'.[134] The subjects of their research furnished the imaginative basis for Dover's pan-Eurasianist collectivity and a potential network of mixed-race peoples from across the European colonies in Asia. The article rejected supposedly 'euphemistic names such as Burghers, Anglo-Burmans, Anglo-Chinese, Anglo-Indians' and Anglo-Malayans in favour of a broader 'Eurasian community extend[ing] ... throughout the Orient, blending in itself the characteristics of East and West. At a conservative estimate ... [the community] number[ed] ... 0.5 million, [with] more than one hundred and fifty thousand Eurasians being found in India alone ... [and their numbers were] increasing rapidly ... [to become] undoubtedly an important factor in Eastern economics'.[135] Dover and Roseboom called for a 'eugenic survey of Eurasians in the more important centres in the East ... [involving] a year's earnest work, by two or three investigators, in the principal towns of Japan, China, Borneo, Sumatra, Java, the Malay Peninsula, India, Burma and Ceylon' to 'evaluate their physical and psychological characteristics, compare them with those of the parent races, assess the importance of the environmental factor, and indicate the methods by which improvements may be effected'.[136]

Unlike many Western eugenicists, Dover and Roseboom were seeking to use this new science to discredit then prevailing 'deliberate vilification[s]' intertwining Eurasians' supposed indolence, irresponsibility and 'lack of energy' with their physical weakness and small stature.[137] The pair did concede that Eurasians' 'political, economic, and social positions are precarious and unhealthy ... [and] in their character make-up there are many weaknesses and defects', though 'there seems to be no proof in support of the contention that the half-caste is inherently inferior to either of his parents'.[138] But they

sought to prove instead that 'the causes of the unfortunate characteristics of the Eurasian community are to be traced to environmental
conditions, to generations of repression, prejudice, and economic and
social boycott'.[139] As Glenn D'Cruz notes, Dover failed to take heed
of the warnings of G. K. Chesterton, the most prominent English
opponent of eugenics of his day. A deeply religious and frequently
contrarian author, Chesterton laid great stress in fictional works like
The Wisdom of Father Brown (1914) on the notion that well-intentioned
people frequently get things wrong, and that those who overthink
matters may be more prone to error. A close friend of Shaw's and a
one-time member of the Fabian Society himself, Chesterton pulled
no punches in attacking his intellectual contemporaries in *Eugenics and
Other Evils* (1922), prophetically diagnosing 'this persistence in the
wrong path of progress ... [whose] moral attitude has taken on something of the sinister and even the horrible'.[140] At the time Dover
believed that

> Mr. Chesterton is alarmed for nothing. If eugenics was what he thinks
> it is, if I were acquainted with half as much experimental fact against
> it as there is for it, I would be as much an anti-eugenicist as
> Mr. Chesterton is, and so would hundreds of thoughtful people who
> now see in Eugenics the salvation of the future, and the amelioration
> of present, humanity. I am not a professional eugenicist, but only one
> in the sense that I appreciate the value of science.[141]

In his glowing 1930 review of Wallace's *The Eurasian Problem*,
Dover had gone so far as to state that 'there is abundant scientific
evidence to prove the superiority of mixed or hybrid peoples',[142]
citing 'an elaborate anthropological and ethnological study' by
'Dr. Shapiro ... of the Pitcairn and Norfolk Islanders, who are the
hybrid descendants of the mutineers of the "Bounty"'.[143]

In Dover's *Half-Caste* (1937), Slate detected a shift from the term
'race' to 'ethnicity' and interpreted this as a marker of Dover's 'move
beyond race and toward a cosmopolitan conception of colour ...
During the 1930s his focus expanded from the Eurasian community
to encompass people oppressed because of their color throughout the
world.'[144] Yet *Half-Caste* was a text in which Dover shifted between
many different registers, exploring poetry, engaging in political
polemic, ranging over anthropology and eugenics. D'Cruz has simi-

larly interpreted the work as a belated recantation of Dover's earlier eugenicist views, citing his reflections that eugenics had been 'hijacked by specific "vested interests" that destroyed the movement's socially progressive agenda', and his belated praise of 'Chesterton for "detecting in the use of science an enormous potentiality of misuse"'.[145] However, the chapter in which Dover had supposedly recanted concluded with the injunction that 'it is the duty of those who value the scientific ideal, who hope for an equalitarian society and the restoration of eugenics to a position of dignity, to protest with all the emphasis at their command'.[146] Dover clearly remained wedded to a theory generally known as 'hybrid vigour', which posited that mixed populations, being more genetically heterozygous, were biologically healthier than more homozygous populations, whose inbreeding would eventually 'encourage an increase of undesirable types, since numerous disorders are carried as recessive characters, which only become manifest in the children of unions between similar recessives'.[147]

Only two years earlier, in an article on 'Population Control in India' for the *Eugenics Review*, Dover was insisting that 'sterilization and legalized abortion is imperative in a country where the increasing incidence of such diseases as leprosy and insanity has not proved susceptible to treatment and research'.[148] Such arguments were entirely in keeping with the kind of eugenics advocated by the Fabian socialists in England. D'Cruz observes that 'Dover's faith in scientific truth is steadfast',[149] and for Dover eugenics remained a soundly scientific field, perverted by those engaged in 'supposedly eugenic endeavour[s]'.[150] Dover was seeking to combat what he believed to be misapplied, erroneous or falsified eugenics when he argued that 'it is certainly difficult to justify supposedly eugenic measures, involving a considerable increase in familial misery for several generations, on the grounds of a rational morality'.[151] His broader complaint was 'that in a capitalist and Christian democracy the rational application of scientific discovery is only too often superseded by the rationalized application of pseudo-scientific ineptitude, when it is not outrageously abused for the creation of the more violent instruments of power, parasitism and banditry'.[152]

If we consider the survival of anthropology as a respected discipline into the present in spite of its historical connection with racialised anthropometry in the colonial period, we may come closer to understanding his perspective. For Dover, the existence of politicised pseudoscience was no more disproof of the utility or veracity of 'good science' than the prevalence of low-quality literature could be taken to count against the prospect of composing great literature. Despite his observation that 'racialism and nationalism reside in every eugenic organisation today', Dover still perceived a great distance between the English approach to eugenics, focused on 'birth control and voluntary sterilization for the degenerate poor', the Italian push towards boosting population growth to provide 'more fodder for Il Duce's dream of a new Roman Empire', and the Nazi emphasis on its capacity to save 'the Nordic Race'.[153] He characterised these approaches as each being intertwined with the religion and culture in which eugenics was operating. While English and Italian eugenics had Protestant and Catholic inflections, the Nazis had substituted their new ideology of 'Nordic' racialism for religion in determining the shape of German eugenics.[154]

Dover deployed his own extensive engagement with eugenics, biology and anthropology as the intellectual toolkit with which to combat the growing cult of the supposed 'Aryans and Nordics' that had taken over German science.[155] He next turned his guns upon the American eugenicists Madison Grant (1865–1937) and Lothrop Stoddard (1883–1950), attributing the latter's 'prolific' success to 'an infinite capacity for mental gymnastics and subtle appeals to popular prejudices … [including] bogeys … [like] yellow perils, black menaces, [and] the nefarious designs of Soviet Russia … Above all Mr. Stoddard has a thoroughly mediocre mind, which has earned him the distinction, among other mediocrities, of being "a brilliant thinker".'[156] To Dover, Stoddard had 'failed to keep abreast of his anthropological reading', relying instead upon 'propagandists of another generation', with Nazi thinkers like '[Hans] Guenther, whose work stinks in the nostrils of every anthropologist who cherishes the ideals of his science … transmuted by the magic of Mr. Stoddard's pen into "one of the most scholarly members of the Nationalist-Socialist party"'.[157] Dover sought to refute Stoddard's contention that 'race is physiological fact, which may be accurately determined by scientific tests such as skull-measurement, hair-formation, and the colour of eyes and skin. In other words, race is what people *really* are

... as *proved* by the biological sciences.'[158] Against this, Dover explained 'races' as hereditary clusters in which

> specific traits ... [are] transmitted along Mendelian lines, but genetic segregation is also responsible for the perpetuation of characteristics, such as wooly hair, so common in a large number of individuals in a particular area that it is usual to speak of them as 'racial'. Therefore, miscegenation does not produce truly intermediate types of blends, but variable populations in which innumerable original features remain as heritable units, which may reappear in later generations, or be fortuitously recombined to produce new types. That is why the outward or *phenotypic* appearance of a group of more or less similar individuals is no guarantee of constitutional or *genotypic* similarity.[159]

Dover understood that scientific answers are only ever provisional. His deconstruction of the fiction of distinct or pure races in biological and anthropological terms reaffirmed his belief in the scientific method. Even in his attempts to combat race and colour prejudice, Dover retained more than a hint of the eugenicist's ambition for sexual and social control to achieve his desired outcomes. In *Half-Caste*, Dover had blended his politics with his empirical assertions on the issue of mate selection among the mixed:

> In the streets of Madras and Calcutta ... one is struck by the frequency with which the darkest Eurasians of one sex are observed with the lightest Eurasians or 'Domiciled Europeans' of the other. This 'attraction of opposites' may be partly a biological phenomenon, in which case we would have further proof of natural provision for the obliteration of ethnic differences, but in many cases the explanation must be sought in the contiguity of a highly privileged white group, which puts a premium on depigmentation. In fact, the phrase 'Improve the breed' is commonly used among certain classes of Eurasians, often with a psychologically significant bitterness, but not infrequently as affectionate advice to select the fairest skins in the matrimonial market.[160]

An Indian nationalist correspondent shared Dover's inclinations to police women's marital choices to achieve their shared political objectives:

> The crux of the Eurasian problem in India lies in the Eurasian women. If half a dozen of them ... [would] set up as leaders of Indian society

and ... of social movements ... not as mere sympathisers but as Indian women, then the whole question ... [would] assume a new aspect. But the women folk ... [are] as you will admit, the more *Anglo*-Indianised of the two. The Eurasian men—including my most charming and dear friend Col. Gidney ... though they may consider themselves Europeans ... [are professionally compelled] to associate with Indians. But Eurasian women—well, I have not yet heard of any of them having to do with Indian women ... Even when they have to attend on Indian patients as nurses their attitude is so supercilious that no sympathy of any kind is possible. I agree with you that propaganda is necessary, but that should be mainly among women. The most important thing for Eurasians ... is a self-respect League for their women; not to have as far as possible anything to do with Europeans for one generation ... A very dear friend of mine—a charming and cultivated lady closely associated with Du Bois—told me ... that the motif and purpose of most of the 'young negro' literature of America were to prevent the fairer women among them from having a weakness for the white Americans and to generate among their womenfolk in general a respect for their race. A movement of that kind in India seems to be an immediate necessity. With the development of that racial consciousness the community will take its place in the rightful leadership of India.[161]

An earlier book written by Millicent Wilson, an Anglo-Indian from Bangalore, commended Anglo-Indian women for pursuing precisely those marital strategies that Dover and his Indian correspondent found so objectionable. Embracing the eugenicist categorisation of a hierarchy of races and asserting that inherited white genes would prove dominant over non-white genes, Wilson argued in *The Anglo-Indian and Domiciled European Race of India* (1928) that this group was engaged in a deliberate strategy of whitening itself. Rather than celebrating the ultimate universalisation of mixedness and the inherent genetic superiority of hybridity as Dover had done, Wilson held up whiteness as the ultimate goal of Anglo-Indians' reproductive strategies: 'just as Americans and Australians now claim to have no mixed blood but are considered a white race ... [in spite of] a certain amount of miscegenation at the start', so too Anglo-Indians would eventually be able to 'claim to be a *white* people, quite as much as Americans and Australians claim to be white people'.[162] How might this be achieved? Non-white blood could be eliminated by repeated intermarriage with white 'pure

Europeans and pure blooded Anglo-Indians' over the generations, just as it was 'steadily being removed' in these white settler societies.[163] She explained how 'decent Anglo-Indian families, with coloured blood' and lighter-skinned Anglo-Indians of 'the best type ... [could] ultimately evolve and become fixed' in their whiteness.[164]

> Most Anglo-Indians ... are trying to work back to the pure white category ... There is a decidedly strong sentiment amongst the coloured Anglo-Indian for racial purity, and thus, what might easily have been a stupendous problem for this community is gradually solving itself, and in another century the majority of Anglo-Indians will be of pure blood, even though coloured to some degree.[165]

Despite being a mirror image of Dover's case against racial purity, Wilson's racial purification theory dovetails rather neatly with its inverse. Both draw on observations of the same phenomena, both operate within a broadly defined eugenicist framework, and both were potentially destabilising to the fictions that had arisen in the white settler colonies they cited, which had sought to efface their earlier history of racial mixing. It is a measure of how wide and receptive an audience such views were likely to command that Gidney, in spite of his own brown skin, gave his name to a preface generally endorsing Wilson's book as one of 'the few books of merit written on the Community', heralding 'an awakening in the Domiciled European and Anglo-Indian Community ... [in its] desire ... to learn more of itself, [and] its past history'.[166] He particularly commended her chapter celebrating the group's sporting achievements, especially in hockey and boxing, which were taken as evidence that Anglo-Indians could not be claimed to be physically inferior to Europeans.

Gidney was probably addressing her racial theories when he added: 'We may not all agree with some of the opinions expressed by Mrs. Wilson ... [but they are] obviously an honest and frank expression of her opinions'.[167] Wilson was certainly fiercely devoted to identification with the Anglo-Indian community, as opposed to trying to distance herself from it, like many fairer-skinned Anglo-Indians and Domiciled Europeans. Unlike the pan-Eurasianists, who often advocated collective emigration and the founding of Eurasia outside India, or other conservatively pro-British Anglo-Indians who supported the sending of Anglo-Indian children to Australia and New

Zealand and were sympathetic to the idea of a wider emigration of the group to one of the white settler colonies of the empire, Wilson was also determined that Anglo-Indians should make their home in India, where she anticipated they would be eventually recognised as an essentially white community among the other settler populations of empire. She advocated colonisation within India, expressing her belief that Anglo-Indians would play a pivotal role in the eventual Christianisation of India. Arguably Wilson's ideas provided a space for the large number of Anglo-Indians who sought to deny having Indian ancestry, to remain associated with the group and its political Association. Essentially, she was speaking for or to a significant constituency within Gidney's flock that he could not afford to permanently alienate. In contrast to Wilson's vision of Anglo-Indians' future within whiteness, Gidney's attempt to create a confidently mixed Anglo-Indian identity actually held more in common with Dover, in spite of the great differences in their political orientation, relative degree of attachment to Britain and India, and their adherence to rival designations.

Ongoing 'interracial' marriages

Dover's and Wilson's divergent prescriptions for the marital preferences of Anglo-Indian women were formulated in the context of two persisting trends. The first was for individual domiciled women, generally of fair complexion, to combine passing with marriage to the kind of Briton with whom they could ascend into one or other class of the highly internally stratified colonial British society in India, thereby effectively exiting from their own group—the path taken by Nissen's sister when she married one of the British men he referred to as the 'covenanted-wallahs'. As a self-identifying Domiciled European who admitted to being of 'swarthy' complexion, Nissen could not stand the superior attitudes of his brother-in-law towards him even as his sister increasingly distanced herself from him. He sadly described how 'she became very covenanted, and, of course she was a member of all the clubs there, and she was my elder sister and I did feel that she used to ... because of the influence of her husband she had to conform with him'.[168] Nissen's first application to the

Calcutta Swimming Club was rejected, and he was only belatedly accepted during the Second World War once they became desperate for members. He complained that the Anglo-Indian women whom he dated were happy to go out with him during the week, but at the weekend they were always booked up with the 'covenanted-wallah', even though there was little prospect that these men would actually marry them. So perhaps there was a touch of resentment in his assertion that an Anglo-Indian woman who made the more achievable match with a British soldier wasn't 'very particular so long as he was white ... didn't care whether she loved him or he loved her, so long as he was white'.[169]

Nissen described an apparently typical scenario reminiscent of Mr. Jones in *Bhowani Junction*, in which an Anglo-Indian father might be a 'station-master' on the railway and would be prepared to 'spend quite a lot of money ... buying a British Tommy out of the regiment' and do his best to secure the young man a job as 'a ticket-collector, guard ... fireman, working the cabin, something like that'.[170] This second trend of British, typically working-class men, who were usually non-commissioned soldiers, policemen or imported railway staff, marrying Anglo-Indians effectively meant their entering into the domiciled group. Ian Stephens disliked how the term 'BORs', for 'British Other Ranks', had become a class-inflected term of abuse.[171] The American-born Vicereine, Lady Curzon (1899–1905), described them as 'less than dust',[172] thereby supporting Trevor Royle's contention that 'as far as the British community was concerned' the British Tommy in India 'was little better than an outcast', and 'certainly no Brahmin was ever more disdainful of a sweeper than was the Collector's wife of a British private soldier or a Eurasian ticket clerk'.[173] Such men had no chance of courting a memsahib, but if they chose to marry into the similarly internally stratified world of Anglo-India, they entered at or near the top of its parallel socio-racial hierarchy. Lieutenant Colonel A. A. ('Tony') Mains, who had served in India since 1934 and become very familiar with the community through his military intelligence work, observed both phenomena:

> on the one hand, [Anglo-Indian] girls often married Europeans and went back to Britain and on the other, time expired British soldiers took jobs in India and remained there with their families ... particu-

larly ... in the thirties when there was mass unemployment in Britain, but an Anglo-Indian youth was ensured employment in India, either in the police or railway service ... My GSO II in Central Command ... was a Battery Sergeant Major RA, who took his discharge in India to join the Bengal Police as a Sergeant, married an Anglo[-]Indian girl and had no intention of returning to England.[174]

Royle concluded: 'With time hanging heavily on their hands soldiers would often turn for company to the Eurasian community who were happy to welcome them both as representatives of the British people and as potential husbands for their daughters. The ordinary British soldier was considered by many families to be the only escape route for their daughters as he occupied much the same social position in India as the Eurasians.'[175] Irene Green, the fair-skinned Anglo-Indian nurse who had successfully passed, married a British man and returned with him to the UK, candidly recalled her youthful dreams of around 1930:

As Anglo-Indians in our railway community ... an unwritten rule was for the girls to try and marry ... the British soldier, the idea was ... to improve the strain, so our aim was to marry British soldiers, not to marry Anglo-Indian men ... When we were about 14 or 15, we started playing Tennis in the railway institute ... We went to dances, our greatest ambition then was to dance with ... and to marry British soldiers. That was the aim and height of an Anglo[-]Indian girl ... She never danced with an Anglo[-]Indian man if she could help it. She preferred to dance with the soldier. Very often, they married soldiers, sometimes even sargeants [*sic*] never above that ...[176]

While she was still a child, her older 'sister ... married a British soldier' who took them both to Agra 'and we lived in the Fort, over looking the ... [Taj Mahal.] It's my greatest lovely memory.'[177] However, not all of these marriages ended happily. In 1926 Gidney wrote to Army Headquarters to complain of the

very serious and delicate matter ... [of] young women of the Domiciled Community ... [being] lured into secret marriages with British soldiers ... [which] are not recognised by the Officer Commanding the regiment ... [so that when] their husbands leave India when their regiments return to England ... they are stranded penniless and without a home, in many cases with one or two or more children ... The practice has created quite a tragedy in some stations in which British troops are quartered, particularly in Bangalore, Belgaum, Poona, Allahabad, Rawalpindi, Peshawar, etc.[178]

Mary (one of Alison Blunt's interviewees) similarly recounted being abandoned by her Scottish fiancé, a teacher, who 'purposefully left' behind his mother's letter instructing him not to 'come back with any black lady from India'.[179] Mary explained that Anglo-Indian women considered it 'all right' to marry a British soldier even though 'many of those soldiers let those girls down ... [but] it was absolutely taboo, it wasn't heard of, that an Anglo-Indian would marry an Indian boy'.[180] However, this should not lead us to imagine that desertions were the norm. During the Second World War, the Reverend J. A. Bower apparently argued for 'something like absorption in the European community'.[181] Hopkins responded by observing:

> With many this is taking place, and the war has increased it among the young women. An aspect of the Anglo-Indian problem ... is the obvious fact that the problem of the girls is in many ways quite different from the problem of the boys and must be dealt with differently. It is largely true that re-absorption into the European community is a possible solution for the girls to a much greater extent ... I do not suggest re-absorption ... What is needed is a wise and skillful opportunism— not to be wedded to any consistent policy, but taking advantage of every opportunity that offers itself.[182]

This echoed the divergences between the experience of mixed-race men and women a century before. Hopkins's comments were framed within the context of his wider criticism of the 'ineradicable, instinctive feeling [among Anglo-Indians] that everything British and Western is necessarily superior, and that everything Indian and Eastern is inferior—even soap and beauty preparations!'[183] Beverley Nichols was more explicit:

> 'Four shades whiter in four weeks!' So run the headlines of one of the innumerable advertisements for skin-whitening products. The Anglo-Indian girls spend a large proportion of their incomes on these preparations ... 'Don't for one moment imagine that because you were born with a dark skin you can do nothing about it,' proclaims the inventor of a popular bleacher. 'The technique of beauty treatment has been revolutionized with the introduction of X ... the skin tonic which acts scientifically on the pigment cells.'[184]

The same uncomfortable theme was raised within the group, with Evans lamenting that 'most of us try to present ourselves as "English roses"' through 'misuse of makeup [which] usually makes a company of women look like a troupe of clowns', and criticising 'the swarthy girl' for 'peroxide … bleach[ing her] luxuriant raven tresses', suggesting she instead confine herself to subtle additions, such as 'a slight touch of clove oil on her cheek bones'.[185] The community's political leaders, alongside Anglo-Indian communal patriots of various stripes, who were predominantly men, wanted to maintain the numerical strength of the group. Although this often took on the gendered inflection of seeking to censure and regulate women's behaviour, the criticism was usually targeted at those women who effectively exited the community through marriage and passing rather than those who married British men willing to become part of the domiciled fold. Anthony would later assert that Anglo-Indians had always

> shown an intense herd consciousness … perhaps … in imitative emulation of the social exclusiveness practiced by the British or even to some extent an inherited quality from the caste-conscious British and Indian social patterns. Marriages were jealously confined within the walls of the Community. It was regarded as a social anathema to marry even a light-skinned, most highly placed member of another community in preference to an ebony-hued poor Anglo-Indian. For generations there has been no intermarriage with other Indian communities.[186]

Deliberately omitted here, however, were ongoing marriages to Europeans, some of which were welcome additions to Anthony's numerical constituency, while others could detract from it. Although he expressed vehement criticisms of passing, dubbing it 'renegadism', it was not the done thing to 'out' those who had successfully passed. Fred Corbett implicitly argued that 'social climbing … or marrying into higher strata of society, and forgetting and neglecting the stratum' one came from was much the same whether practised in class, 'colour' or caste terms.[187] Such behaviour was hardly unique to Anglo-Indians; it was 'a natural process of evolution', which happened among other Indian groups, and was 'much more common in Europe and America'.[188] Criticised for his emphasis on mixedness by 'a fair Anglo-Indian' who had told him 'A mixture is not liked and is not good … we should try to forget it', Corbett responded with:

Why? ... We are a mixed community, there is no reason why we should hide or deny it, as there is nothing wrong in a mixture, on the contrary, a mixture is all to the good ... And it is now our duty, not to hide or deny our mixed origin, but to point it out with pride, and tell our traducers ... that a mixture ... gives the offspring additional strength and vitality. If any proof were required ... it is in the very separate existence of the Anglo-Indian community in India today, in spite of several centuries of neglect and calumny and deprivation of rights on the part of the European and of hostility and suspicion on the part of the Indian.[189]

The potential range of identities it was possible for the mixed to adopt essentially operated along a spectrum between two polarities. One involved aligning themselves with the British, European and Western side of their heritage, which was what their education and culture had thus far tended to emphasise. The other meant trying to reorient themselves towards a more Indian identity and culture, a change which, as a result of their prior history, could not now come naturally to them, and would accordingly require positive effort. Yet in reality neither of these extremes was fully in accord with their mixed heritage, and attempts to inculcate a sense of communal patriotism within the group generally meant building up a composite identity of some kind, which sought to encourage pride in mixedness, regardless of whether this identity was to remain primarily British-aligned or was reformulated towards greater embrace of India. Gidneyan dualism remained most at ease in the complacent belief that the connection between Britain and India was destined to continue, because it was within this context that all three intersecting patrio-tisms could be made to align with one another in a manner which facilitated pride in their mixed origins, history and current position within the colonial order responsible for their existence.

Pride and patriotism

With the word not yet having acquired its negative sting, the Association openly wrote about the need for effective 'propaganda' to change attitudes and behaviours. Taking up the challenge, in 1930 the Chakradharpur branch asked:

Why is the grafted mango the most delicious? Why is the blended tea the most expensive? Because they are a fusion of two distinct species. Then ought not we, who are the fusion of two great races be a race to be proud of ... Perhaps the inferiority complex so widely attributed to our race is due to our schooling. We leave these institutions, pregnant with pride of a land so few of us ever walk upon and when we do, it is as 'Furriners'; yet, the land of our birth and growth is so deliberately despised and ignored when really it is 'Wonderland' and by all the laws of logic we number among its component parts. Tell the Anglo-Indian young man, just left school, that he has Indian blood in his veins, which is the reason of his tinted skin and he'll punch you on the nose (*and he can punch hard.*)[190]

During the same year the *Review* published several full-length articles by J. S. Turner of the East Indian Railway, Moghalserai (Mughal Sarai). Turner bemoaned that 'the Anglo-Indian ... [is] proud of [Britain,] a Nation of which he is but a very remote offshoot ... [and] which has disowned him ... proud of a land that is not his own', yet 'devoid of all sense of Pride of Nationality ... to his [Indian] Motherland'.[191] Remarking that 'we find many of our people actually ashamed to acknowledge themselves Anglo-Indians, and only too ready to pose as Britishers, Americans, Russians and even Mexicans— anything but Anglo-Indians', Turner asked:[192]

Is it because of our mixed descent that we are ashamed of our Nationality ... of our very parents, who gave us being ... [and] of our birth? What Nation is there of absolutely unmixed blood? ... With civilization comes the intermingling of blood ... Turn your eyes to England and consider the British Nation, do we find that nation of pure Blood? Far from it! Perhaps it would be difficult to find another nation with a greater degree of admixture ... and yet we find the Anglo-Saxon—as much a hyphenated race as the Anglo-Indian—... proud of being an Anglo-Saxon. Why should then we be ashamed of being Anglo-Indians? The mingling of the East and the West in blood is not peculiar to India alone. Look at the American Continents? Look at Java? ... The Anglo-Indian race is not one bit inferior to any other race on God's earth ... [but] a match, and more, for any other race physically, morally and intellectually.[193]

This argument had much in common with Wilson's deconstruction of the supposed racial purity of white America and other British settler societies. Corbett would similarly argue that 'Britishers or Americans are not considered inferior because of these mixtures. It is only when the mixture happens to be coloured that it is considered inferior, because of colour prejudice, and it is our first duty to challenge this and prove ... that the coloured mixtures are no whit inferior to the two great white mixtures that girt the two sides of the great Atlantic.'[194] McNeelance celebrated 'the principles of equality and humanity and the absence of racial prejudice' in 'the U.S.S.R.', 'Lenin (with his western name and his Asiatic eyes and cheekbones) ... being conscious and unashamed of both sides of his blood and culture, and making a synthesis of both', and Stalin's declaration 'I am an Asiatic'.[195] This comparison was not best calculated to appeal to the average Anglo-Indian, but Anthony—no socialist, communist or pan-Eurasianist himself—would later appeal to his fellow Indian legislators by asserting that 'Russia is an Asiatic country. Her leader is a fellow Eurasian like myself, proud to call himself an Asiatic', while lambasting 'the South African Government' for its 'arrogant racial discrimination and ... shabby anti-Indian policy'.[196]

At first glance Turner appeared to be making a straightforwardly nationalist case for Anglo-Indians to embrace their Indian nationality:

Is not India as good and fair a country as any and better, by far, than most? ... People from a far off come every year at great personal inconvenience and expense to view her greatness, but our vision is blurred by proximity and, being her children, we fail to appreciate her worth. Teach yourselves to be proud of India and India will be proud of you ... If Anglo-India wants to take her rightful place in the body politic of India, she has got to change her present day callous attitude. She has got to learn to be proud of her Nationality ... proud of India. She must doff herself of all assumed airs of superiority and cease being the laughing stock of all her sister-communities ...[197]

However, on closer inspection, Turner's understanding of the nation is more complex and layered. He proceeded to call for a distinctive kind of Anglo-Indian communal patriotism, effectively a sub-nationalism, able to nest within a broad construction of patriotic devotion to the Indian 'Motherland': 'Anglo-India alone of all cultured races possesses no Day, no Flag, and no Emblems. These are essential elements towards inspiring pride of race and I am positively of opinion that it is up to the leaders of the community of all shades of opinion to get together, for the good of the entire race, and, after serious deliberation, inaugurate these National necessities.'[198] Anglo-India too required its own symbols, which were to include 'Anglo-India Day'; an Anglo-Indian 'National Emblem'; and an 'Anglo-Indian National Flag'.[199] These call to mind the words of 'Johann Wolfgang von Goethe [when he] told the designer of the Venezuelan flag ... "A country starts out from a name and a flag, and it then becomes them, just as a man fulfils his destiny."'[200]

Turner proposed 9 June, Gidney's birthday, to be known as 'GIDNEY DAY', to 'Let the rest of India know that we are proud of being GIDNEYITES'.[201] A 'floral Emblem', for 'a hyphenated Race by mixed descent', he argued, 'must likewise be hyphenated' by incorporating 'something to emphasise our British connection and something to signify our Indian descent, birth and interests'.[202] He therefore suggested a 'partly opened' lotus bud superimposed 'on a back ground of Rose foliage', which 'would not only be a very pretty button hole, but would be appropriately emblematic of our dual descent, connections and interests'; it could 'be made up and sold by our ladies on the Anglo-Indian National Day'.[203] His proposed flag was to be even more British in flavour, because, as he asserted,

our culture, education, habits, mode of living and, above all, our sentiments being all predominantly British, it is but natural that no rag, green, white, yellow, pink and blue will ever appeal to us ... The only flag that can, and always will, command our respect is the UNION JACK ... [which] must of necessity be the basis of our National Flag to emphasise our British connection. The Anglo-Indian floral emblem of the Rose leaves and the Lotus bud emblazoned in the corner of the Union Jack will suffice to make it the distinctive National Flag of the Anglo-Indian Race. I now appeal personally to Dr. Mrs. May Shave, M.L.C. of Lahore and to Mrs. N. H. S. Barnard, B.A. of Meerut (two of our most prominent lady workers) to organize a party of ladies, to work the first National Flag ... Coming from the ladies, I am sure, the flag will be valued, and cherished ... Chivalry is a special attribute of our Race, and you may rest assured, Ladies! that coming from you, your men will not only value the Flag, but, if needs be, they will uphold the honour of their National Flag with their life's Blood ... I appeal to every Anglo-Indian and Domiciled European ... [to] help this scheme of mine to materialize.[204]

Anglo-India appears here to be the nation, a constituent nation within the Indian motherland. If Turner's rhetoric may have appeared contradictory to outsiders, both its dualism and its proposal for the creation of a Gidneyite cult of personality evidently appealed to the president-in-chief. Dr. May Shave, heading the provincial branch in Lahore, warmly embraced the suggestion of inaugurating Gidney Day with 'a Social and Dance at the Roberts' Club … [to which] the railway contingent with all their lady folk arrived in lorry loads'.[205] Around '200 persons' attended the gathering, during which Shave

> eulogised the work done by the worthy Colonel and said she was pleased to see that the Anglo-Indians of Lahore were not slow in appreciating and honouring the man, who at much sacrifice had done such a lot for the community. The President then called upon one of the Vice-Presidents to read Mr. … Turner's article publicly and also stated that although she was in favour of 'Gidney Day' and the sentiments [he] expressed … she did not agree with his suggestion to have a national Flag, as she considered it was too early to think of such a thing, and that when the suggestion did take shape at some future date she hoped the design would include an emblem … represent[ing] all races of mixed blood.[206]

Did Shave mean all mixed-races in India, or across Asia, like Dover and Wallace? There obviously were different shades of opinion as to the balance to be struck in constructing a self-confident mixed-race Anglo-Indian identity. Yet despite differences in relative emphasis between identification with Britain and with India, most Anglo-Indianist constructions adhered to the kind of dualism promoted by Gidney and Turner. To jettison the British component of their identity and the sense of loyalty to Britain and the imperial monarchy would, at this point, have been anathema to most run-of-the-mill Anglo-Indians. Turner's dualism, his combination of predominant British feeling and embrace of Indian status, was not too far from Gidney's own sentiments. Any push towards greater identification with India as a component in this British-aligned and fundamentally colonial identity would have been a hard sell for a significant faction of Anglo-Indians— which helps to explain why many preferred to call themselves Domiciled Europeans, and to distance themselves from Gidney and his Association, or even set up rival political organisations.

4

ANGLO-INDIA UNDER SIEGE

Auxiliaries of empire

In 1912 Mazharul Haque declared: 'It must be in the knowledge of the Hon'ble Mr. Madge that a great many inspectors of police are recruited from the ranks of the Imperial Anglo-Indian community to which he has the honour to belong.'[1] Madge had just delivered a lengthy speech in the Imperial Legislative Council in which he said that he stood 'between the two classes [of Indians and Britons] with a real, an earnest and sincere feeling for both' while encouraging 'the whole of Indian society' to stand 'by the side of Government and come forward boldly … to detect crime' throughout the Police Administration itself as well as among 'the educated young gentlemen who speak in English and who go to villages in Bengal armed with good weapons and commit riot amongst their own countrymen, and rob them and ill-treat them.'[2] A decade later Gidney would also express support for law and order and strictly constitutional change, declaring himself to be 'in rather a peculiar position. Being the representative of the Domiciled Community … between two stones … [not knowing] which one is the bigger … [and] occupy[ing] a position between the devil and the deep sea.'[3] This medley of rhetoric fundamentally upheld the status quo in a manner typical of Anglo-Indian leaders' general support for law and order, and congruent with the

183

group's occupational affiliation to the strategic transport and communication infrastructure of the colonial state, as well as their prominence within various police forces across India.

Beverley Nichols asserted that 'a fair proportion of posts' were reserved for Anglo-Indians 'particularly in the police and on the railways'.[4] However, Philip Mason objected to a similar assertion with the reflection that

> we, who served in a particular district at a particular moment, are bound to grumble at *something*; it wasn't, we are bound to say ... like *that* in my time and in my province ... I am astonished to find someone saying that many posts in the police were reserved for Anglo-Indians. I don't think there was one Anglo-Indian in the police in Bareilly, a fairly average UP district.[5]

The military intelligence officer 'Tony' Mains clarifies that

> there were not a great number of Anglo[-]Indians in the police, as the force was, except for senior Officers, almost entirely Indian, Anglo[-]Indians and time expired British soldiers could join direct as Sergeants, a rank reserved for them and ranking equal to a Sub Inspector, they could expect promotion to Inspector and in a few cases to Deputy Superintendent. Sergeants were used in large cities to deal with Europeans and also they served in the armed and mounted sections of the District Police.[6]

Eric Stracey became one of the most successful. Born in 1920 in Bangalore, where he completed his schooling, Eric secured an economics honours degree at Madras and passed the All India police exam in 1942, enabling him to enter the force the following year.[7] He was unusual both in having taken a degree and in becoming 'fairly fluent in two [Indian] languages ... Tamil in the higher standard, [and] Urdu in the lower'.[8] In 1974 Eric reflected on how atypical this was for an Anglo-Indian of his generation:

> I was born and spent my formative years in a British cantonment. The entire atmosphere ... [and] conditions were much more British than they were Indian. My language was English. My literature ... was English. My music was western. My religion was Christianity. The curriculum ... [was] designed to make us pro-British and not particularly pro-Indian, if anything anti-Indian, and this was a gap to be bridged as we grew up and realised the essential wrongness of

that ... It gave rise to some very unfortunate situations where we adopted a superior attitude and insulted the feelings of our fellow Indians ... Our only contacts with Indians were with servants or the shopkeepers, and there would be one or two ... members of other Indian communities who would live amongst these essentially Anglo-Indian localities but they would be almost Anglicised themselves. They would talk English as well as we. They would have gone to our schools. Their religion would almost certainly have been Christianity ... We were not in touch with the cultured Indian of the other parts of the country ... The servant class in a place like Bangalore cantonment was drawn very largely from ... [lower castes or converts] to Christianity.[9]

Having passed his exams in 'English, general knowledge, Indian History, Maths, Geography, and, of course, a very stiff interview for which they gave us quite a heavy weightage in marks, particularly for policemen', Eric became 'a gazetted officer', underwent a year's training 'at Vellore, another six months in the field ... and then ... took charge of ... Erode [subdivision] in Coimbatore district'.[10] At only twenty-three, he was made an 'Assistant Superintendent of Police', with 'fifteen police stations, each with about twenty men ... [and a] total complement ... [of] about three hundred constables and fifty Officers' serving under him.[11]

Eric was one of five high-achieving siblings. His sister became a doctor, having had her start at 'the Good Shepard [sic] Convent and the Sacred Heart High School in Bangalore'.[12] All four Stracey brothers had attended St. Joseph's European High School, Bangalore, one of the best Anglo-Indian schools. However, their father made the unusual decision to transfer Eric's older brother Ralph to an Indian institution:

It was usual for Anglo-Indian boys going to College to carry on at St. Joseph's ... but my father thought that we ought to have a little wider horizon and so sent us to the Presidency College in Madras where, for the first year, my elder brother and I had to live in an Indian—that is non Anglo-Indian—Government Hostel sitting on the floor, eating off a plantain leaf and generally sharing the life and thoughts of young Indians of the intellectual classes.[13]

Ralph's 'all-round record' during his studies included having been 'Captain of the Hockey eleven ... Editor of the College

Magazine … [and] the champion shot of his Company and of the whole Battalion in the U.T.C. [University Training Corps] in which he was a Sergeant'.[14] He went on to win Laurence D'Souza Anglo-Indian scholarships of £100, then £300,[15] which supported his studies at King's College London and the London School of Economics and two attempts at the Indian Civil Service (ICS) examinations. In his first attempt in 1931 Ralph 'passed 70th', missing the cut,[16] but the following year he came thirty-third to secure his ICS place. Six other Anglo-Indians sat for the examinations in London that year. D. A. Bryan from Punjab came 'first among those candidates who appeared from India' and tenth overall, while Mr. 'Fletcher stood 41st'.[17] Being ahead of Frank Anthony, Gidney's nephew, and Mr. D'Mello, all of whom 'obtained qualifying marks, but did not pass high enough',[18] Fletcher was presumably the third Anglo-Indian whom Ralph recalled entering 'the Service the same year as I did' and 'for an Anglo-Indian, a young fellow, that was indeed an achievement'.[19] Even before the admission of the third 'out of 7 Anglo-Indians' to the heaven-born had been confirmed, the Anglo-Indian Association was celebrating 'a result of which we never dreamt, but which has, nevertheless, given us great satisfaction and pride'.[20] Although ICS examinations had also been held in India since 1922, a decade later no Anglo-Indian had succeeded via that route; the *Review* explained in 1933 how 'our candidates although they have done very well in most other subjects have all come to grief in the [Indian] Vernacular paper. This is to be expected considering the fact that the vernacular is taught in such a perfunctory manner in the European Schools.'[21]

Ralph's first posting was 'to Bengal where I went with a certain amount of trepidation because the Bengalese had developed a habit of shooting their District Magistrate and Collectors'.[22] One night that same year 'the female revolutionary Pritilata Waddedar … led an attack on the Pahartali Railway Institute outside Chittagong, an Anglo-Indian club patronized primarily by the subordinate staff of the railways. The revolutionaries threw two bombs and fired revolvers that killed one woman and wounded several others, including two police officers.'[23] Michael Silvestri notes that the Intelligence Branch (IB) responded to such incidents by employing Anglo-Indian (Eurasian) clerks … who defined themselves as Britons rather than Indians, [and] were [thus] deemed to be more unswerving in their loyalties than Bengali Hindus. By 1936, all of the forty-four clerks at the Central IB in Calcutta were Anglo-Indians; [and] so were the majority of the fifty-five clerks throughout the province's DIBs.[24]

Back 'on the evening of Good Friday, 18 April 1930', which Silvestri describes as 'perhaps the *annus mirabilis* of Bengali terrorism', the Indian Republican Army (self-consciously modelling themselves on their Irish counterparts) launched a series of carefully planned and targeted attacks upon the colonial regime, seizing 'weapons from the armories of the police and Auxiliary Force of India in the port town of Chittagong in eastern Bengal'.[25]

The Auxiliary Force (India), or AF(I), was predominantly recruited from the domiciled. The creation of this part-time unit was a poor recompense for the loss of the community's much-celebrated Anglo-Indian Force, which had been officially classified as 'an integral part of the British Army',[26] but was immediately disbanded upon the conclusion of the First World War. The replacement of the old Indian Defence Force with an AF(I) exclusively drawn from Anglo-Indians, Europeans and Britons, while relegating Indians to a separate Territorial Force, was also so transparently racial that it faced colossal Indian objections from the beginning. The new AF(I)'s role as a second line of imperial defence against domestic insurrection and civil unrest was reminiscent of the never-enacted 1907 plans by Charles Stevenson-Moore for quasi-military reserve police units composed of Europeans and hand-picked 'Eurasians'.[27] As Kenneth Wallace noted, this would prove 'a sore point to the Indian'.[28] However, as the *Review* complained,

> enrolment into this Force in the *Railway Battalions* is compulsory, that is to say, conscription is enforced in a Volunteer Force only from Anglo-Indian and Domiciled European employees … Government … [nevertheless] maintain that racial discrimination is not practiced … Added to this the insult constantly being hurled at the Community by the Army Department that Anglo-Indians are not a martial race.[29]

Ignoring Anglo-Indians' front-line wartime service, colonial officialdom continued to assert through the 1920s that 'as a result of the

Great War, from the purely military point of view, Anglo-Indians must be placed amongst the non-fighting classes. The formation of Anglo-Indian fighting units is not a proposition which can even be considered.'[30] It was unsurprising therefore that the Army evinced scant respect for the AF(I), regarding them 'as amateur soldiers' and encouraging them 'to look upon themselves ... as such'.[31] Gidney was also vexed that despite Association estimates that Anglo-Indians made up between 'two-thirds'[32] and 'three-fourths' of the AF(I), 'very few' had been granted commissions.[33] Anthony would later describe its role during the Second World War as

> the second line of defence in India ... There were no British troops left. But there were forty or fifty thousand Anglo-Indians in the Auxiliary Force ... to maintain ... law and order. There were forty or fifty thousand of us ... We were able to do it impartially. We had no predilections. If the Muslims were killing Hindus we would prevent it, if necessary by using extreme methods. If the Hindus ... were killing ... we would prevent it ... [making] us ... equally disliked by both communities, but we maintained it ...[34]

At the Royal Commission on Labour in 1929, Gidney tried to make the best of Anglo-Indians' unique obligation to serve in AF(I) railway battalions, attempting to leverage it in his defence of the group's existing higher starting salaries. With drastic pay cuts taking place across the board, Gidney asked a 'driver' and a 'retired station master' of the Bombay, Baroda and Central India Railway the leading question whether reduction to the Rs. 33 monthly salary received by some Indian ticket collectors would amount to 'a starvation wage for an Anglo-Indian lad' 'living [alone] in Rajputana or Ajmer'. His response was that this would be 'a ridiculous wage' for 'no [Anglo-Indian] boy can live under Rs. 70 a month ... [and] even then he cannot feed himself too well'.[35] This buttressed Gidney's demand for a de facto communal or racial 'minimum wage' for Anglo-Indians of 'at least Rs. 75 p.m.', which the Bombay provincial branch recommended be increased to 'Rs. 100' in the city itself.[36] In 1937 the *Servant of India* complained that Gidney was still calling for 'open discrimination in favour of Anglo-Indians' and argued that financial 'losses' from spending on 'strategic railways ... maintained for military purposes' should 'be borne by the Defence Department'.[37]

However, this last suggestion was hardly antithetical to the persisting complaint that 'Government refuses to sanction the formation of an Anglo-Indian unit or one or two Anglo-Indian Batteries ... [yet] expects us not only to be prepared but feel ourselves honoured by being made use of when the exigency arises'.[38] One of several resolutions passed on the subject by a Calcutta meeting convened by Gidney in 1923 similarly protested against 'the exclusion of the community from the Indianisation of the army'.[39]

The government had long maintained that Anglo-Indians and Domiciled Europeans were Indians by statute. In essence this meant they were both residents and nationals of India, regardless of colour, race or culture, and therefore officially exempt from displacement in railways and civil departments by means of Indianisation. However, in the military sphere neither the colonial authorities nor those in London were keen to apply the same principle by allowing Anglo-Indians to enter into schemes of Indianisation that would open up new opportunities for them. As only seventy places for cadets had been established at the new military college at Dehra Dun to prepare Indians to take the examination to qualify for an initial ten annual places for officer training at Sandhurst in the UK, it was understood to be impolitic for any of these new openings to go to Anglo-Indians. That Anglo-Indians supposedly held 'a large number of ... King's Commissions in the Indian Medical Service', or IMS, was defensively asserted.[40] Having seen action in China during the Boxer Rebellion of 1899–1901 and achieved promotion to a lieutenant-colonelcy in the IMS, Gidney was a prime example. However, as an obviously mixed-race man, his position in the IMS, almost all of whose officers were either British or Indian, was exceptional. Anglo-Indian medical men were usually relegated to the Indian Subordinate Medical Department (ISMD or IMD), an almost exclusively domiciled outfit which had only dropped its unpopular 'Subordinate' title following sustained pressure from John Abbott. Attending to the needs of the British Army units in India, it effectively served as a cut-cost local substitute for the Royal Army Medical Corps (RAMC).

The Adjutant General further argued that if Anglo-Indians were to be given the chance of entering the officer ranks of the Indian Army on the same terms as Indians, then 'Anglo-Indians now employed in the Supply and Transport Corps and Ordnance Services as Apprentice Storeholders under special terms would have to accept Indian competition for these appointments', as their counterparts in 'Mechanical Engineering' and 'Ordinance Factories' already did.[41] Lieutenant General Sir Andrew Skeen, Chief of the General Staff, and chairman of the Sandhurst Committee (1925–6), believed that 'any announcement that Anglo-Indians were eligible on level terms with Indians might materially affect the number of Indian boys of the right type coming forward for admission to Dehra Dun'.[42] Sir Charles Alexander Innes, head of the Commerce Department, which oversaw the railways, pointed out that Anglo-Indians might be allowed to compete for one of the ten Indian places at Sandhurst after attending 'their own semi-military schools', as he was 'not at all sure how the high caste Indian boy would view the admission of Anglo-Indians to the Dehra College, and it would be very unwise for the sake of being logical to imperil the prospects of this College'.[43] Satish Ranjan Das, who laid the groundwork for the foundation of the Doon School along British elite 'public school' lines, concurred, expressing his fear of

> great dissatisfaction in the country if the number of Anglo-Indians entitled to participate in the 10 vacancies is not restricted ... [and] if Anglo-Indian boys, by reasons of the [educational] facilities they already possess ... are in a position to compete for these vacancies, I would rather keep them out ... Indians of good family, while welcoming opportunities for their boys to mix with boys of pure English parentage, dislike the idea of their mixing with Anglo-Indian boys, whose habits and manners in their view, are not always desirable. I am afraid they do not consider these boys healthy minded. In Calcutta, in the Boy Scouts' movement, it has been found necessary to have separate associations for Anglo-Indians and Indians, because Indian parents could not be induced to send their boys to Anglo-Indian troops. If there is an influx of Anglo-Indian boys into Dehra Dun, it will affect the number of Indians willing to send their sons to that school.[44]

The colonial Government of India had initially tried to put Gidney off pressing for inclusion in both the Dehra Dun college and the new Indian routes of entry to Sandhurst via a selection board or examination held in India. They first responded to Gidney's approaches by questioning his representative capacity, consulting the rival London Association, and suggesting that Anglo-Indians would have to make a binary choice and elect to be regarded as either European or Indian. Their internal deliberations show that they thought Gidney would have a hard time persuading his flock to declare themselves as Indian, which was rather perceptive, given that after 'a referendum in Madras in which Anglo-Indians were asked whether they considered themselves Indians or Europeans' Gidney was accused of asking 'Anglo-Indians to denationalise themselves'.[45]

Ernest Burdon proposed threatening Anglo-Indians with expulsion from the AF(I) if they elected to be regarded as Indians, something he snidely anticipated 'that many Anglo-Indians would resent'.[46] That this was either ill-informed posturing or bluff is suggested by William Malcolm Hailey's response that as the AF(I) was 'largely Anglo-Indian in composition ... it does not seem right to refuse Anglo-Indians, purely on the ground that they have access to Auxiliary Force commissions, the privilege of seeking King's Commissions as Indians. King's Commissions and Auxiliary Force commissions are not in the same plane.'[47] The Commander-in-Chief, Lord Rawlinson, agreed. Though he remained opposed to Anglo-Indians 'being admitted to the Dehra Dun College', Rawlinson acknowledged the impracticability of excluding Anglo-Indians from a force in which 'numerically they form the great majority', which would amount to 'practically abolish[ing its] ... Railway units'.[48] Innes would later complain that

> logic is impossible when you are dealing with Anglo-Indians, or ... it is dangerous. For if we were to push to its logical conclusion the Anglo-Indian claim to admission to the ... College, we should abolish all our separate schools for the[m] ... The real truth of the matter is that the Anglo-Indian community appeals to logic only when it suits them. What they really want is the best of both worlds ... To begin with, I believe that as it is they may get most of the 10 vacancies. They have their own schools where they get much more of the Dehra type of education than most Indians get ...[49]

Tej Bahadur Sapru, then law member of the Viceroy's Council, similarly concluded that Gidney was trying to 'have it both ways' by claiming 'a share in that which is meant for Indians' while seeking to hold on to 'certain privileges which Indians have not'.[50] Bayya Narasimheswara Sarma acknowledged that 'Anglo-Indians domiciled in this country are statutory Indians and I do not see how we can object to their entry into these schools, but I agree that this can be done only if they share the privileges and the disabilities ... As I understand that they are not willing to forgo the existing additional facilities open to them.'[51] Sarma thought that Anglo-Indians should be given 'an option' and be compelled to make a choice.[52]

Burdon had earlier insisted: 'There is no doubt that ... the concession which Colonel Gidney really desires to secure for his community' is to make 'Anglo-Indian boys ... eligible for entry to Sandhurst by means of the examination held in India, which also was designed in the first instance for Indian boys', and that Gidney's demand 'for admission to this School' was merely intended as a stepping stone.[53] Burdon therefore wrote to Gidney 'to ascertain definitely which of ... two means of admission' to Sandhurst he was seeking, 'namely, the competitive examination held in England, or nomination and examination in India under the arrangements applicable to Indian candidates, but not both'.[54] This choice, alongside the demand that Gidney provide evidence that it had been made by his community as a whole, was intended to deter him, or at least kick the ball into the long grass. It was expected that, if a decision was forthcoming, Anglo-Indians would most likely prefer, presumably for reasons of prestige, to sit for the examinations in London, and thus the whole problem for the Government of India would go away. This was to underestimate Gidney's tenacity, as he continued to press his case alongside other grievances in a 1925 deputation to London, creating 'a sense of alarm' at the War Office.[55] The initial answers the War Office supplied to the Government of India's questions as to the eligibility of Anglo-Indians had stated that 'pure European descent is not necessary for [the] Indian Army' and that while nominated Indian cadets were examined in India, 'other candidates from India [were] examined in England'.[56] This crucial telegram was, however, deliberately crafted to mislead. For when 'an Anglo-Indian named [Eric] Pounde, son of Herbert Pounde, Deputy Postmaster General, Bihar and Orissa, Patna, domiciled in England', applied and was rejected, the Government of India was informed by the Secretary of State that it had been in accordance with an explicit regulation 'which states that candidates must be of pure European descent' unless they were 'Indian candidates'.[57]

Finding it 'quite impossible to reconcile what ... [was] now being said with what ha[d] ... been said before', the authorities in India now feared 'the possibility of grave embarrassment'.[58] Burdon expressed genuine exasperation that he had spent 'the last three years' in extensive correspondence and exhaustive discussions with 'both the Deputy Secretary and the Adjutant General … based entirely on the postulate that Anglo-Indians, as such, are eligible to compete at the entrance examination for Sandhurst held in the United Kingdom, provided only that they intend to enter the Indian Army and not the British Army'.[59] In a total about-face, the War Office now claimed that its telegram had merely been congruent with the fact that Indians who were not of European descent at all were admitted to the Indian Army, while 'other candidates from India', by implication only those who satisfied the test of pure European descent, were 'examined in England'.[60] A communication marked 'urgent' was fired off to the Secretary of State for India complaining that the

> Commander-in-Chief's questions referred specifically to Anglo-Indians and since there was no question of Indians being handicapped or ineligible we cannot understand how War Office replies can be held to refer to nominated Indians. Since 1921 we have assumed that this … telegram constituted authoritative interpretation of Sandhurst regulations as affecting Anglo-Indians and have based on this assumption all our recent correspondence …[61]

Burdon contented himself with the thought that in prompting the War Office's rejection of 'an Anglo-Indian on the ground[s] … of [his] mixed descent' by 'the letter of their regulations', Pounde's 'concrete case' had smoked out their true position.[62] This would have come as no surprise to Gidney, whose reply to Burdon's original demi-official letter had requested that he be supplied

> with a copy of the letter you received from the Army Council or Home Government in which you told me a definite statement had been made that Anglo-Indians were eligible for admission into the Army *as such viá* Sandhurst. I would also like to be furnished with one single instance in which an Anglo-Indian, declaring himself as such, in his application … has secured entrance … I may be wrong—I hope I am—but I am yet to know of a *Colored* Anglo-Indian who has …[63]

Gidney knew that any Anglo-Indians who had hitherto gained entry were almost certain to have been fair-complexioned individuals engaged in passing. 'Gidney urged that although there was no written rule against such entry[,] he had never heard ... [of] a single instance of an Anglo-Indian declaring as such, having secured admission ... and was of opinion that any hopes of making the Army a career was entirely illusory for 99 per cent. of the youths of the Community, even if their colour was not a practical difficulty'.[64] The closest example to which the War Office was able to point in a February 1923 communication to the India Office was 'the case of Mr. Donald Sarkies Matthew whose mother was an Armenian born in India', who passed the Sandhurst entrance exam in 1918 and was 'now a Lieutenant in the Indian Army'.[65]

Burdon condemned the apparent willingness of London official-dom to sanction the 'continuance of an irregular, not to say a fraudu-lent, practice' of admitting those able to satisfy 'the War Office that they were not Anglo-Indians but were of pure British descent', describing the Secretary of State's role as 'hardly becoming', and accusing him of having been 'distinctly disingenuous'.[66] The Secretary of State struck a somewhat apologetic tone in saying that he felt the 'greatest difficulty in telling ... [Pounde that] he has neither the opportunities of an Englishman nor of an Indian'.[67] Lord Birdwood, the new Commander-in-Chief in India, felt that the case illustrated the need for a firm decision 'under what category Anglo-Indians are to come in future. No one, I am sure, can help feeling sorry for the boys of this community, as they have never been regarded either as purely British or purely Indian.'[68] The 'home member', Sir James Crerar, conceded

> that the question is not so much of Anglo-Indians 'getting the best of both worlds' as of 'being done down both ways'. The decision of the War Office has radically altered the situation and it seems no longer possible to ... treat the Anglo-Indian for Army purposes on racial lines and not on lines of domicile ... It is [now] inevitable that the ten Indian vacancies should be open to Anglo-Indians. Some of the practi-cal difficulties alleged ... could be met by placing a reasonable restric-tion ... on the[ir] number ...[69]

In principle at least, Gidney appeared to have won his point. However, much of his energy in the years to come would be directed towards protecting Anglo-Indians' existing position in the AF(I) amid further rounds of budget cuts. In 1933 Gidney called attention to 'a belief ... current in the community' that 'thousands of Anglo-Indians' were being laid off 'to the benefit of Britishers in ... favoured units ... [including] the Calcutta Scottish and certain Light Horse Units and other such exclusively British sections'.[70] In 1940 most of the AF(I), including 'the port defence Artillery, Engineers and Signals, at Bombay, Madras and Karachi', were embodied into regular army units. According to Mains, 'Anglo-Indians were very much in majority in these units, for example 16 Europeans to 84 Anglo Indians in the Bombay Coast Battery and 17 to 105 at Madras.'[71] However, towards the end of the Second World War, 'these men were discharged ... for no adequate reason', before being compulsorily re-enrolled by the Railway Board in 1946, triggering 'a storm of resentment among Anglo-Indians on all the Railways'.[72] This administrative see-saw presumably aimed at downgrading their terms and conditions from embodied Army status back to an inferior civil position. Anthony wrote to the Commander-in-Chief to complain that their discharge should have removed any further liability for re-enlistment, pointing out that such 'exceptional service has only brought us antagonism and hostility' whenever Anglo-Indians were deployed 'to break strikes and also to act as military personnel ... [using] armed force against members of other communities'.[73] Anthony's letter concluded: 'Since we are being continually told that we must take our place with other Indian Communities, it is illogical for the Administration to single us out for this delicate and thankless work.'[74]

Anglo-Indian colonisation schemes

Empires as broad conceptual spaces allow for the concept of multiple constituent nations or, when 'nations' is used to refer to distinct ethnic groups, they may be said to coexist within the same geographic space. This flexibility is evident in the Aga Khan's 1915 'memorandum pleading that ... East Africa might be reserved for Indian colonization and development in recognition of India's war services', and his conception of such colonies as forming part of a future federation of British territories across Asia and East Africa that could become autonomous within the empire.[75] The colonial authorities habitually rewarded with land grants those who recruited for and manned the Indian Army. Apart from railway construction and telegraph laying, one of the major projects of the colonial state during the late nineteenth and early twentieth centuries was large-scale irrigation schemes that made possible the creation of agricultural 'canal colonies' in hitherto arid regions of western Punjab. By 1918 a total investment into just one of these, the Chenab Colony, 'amounted to more than Rs 325 lakhs'.[76] Estimated 'at over 2.2 million acres', it carried a population that had already grown 'from 112,000 in 1891 to over 1.1 million in 1911', with an 'annual value of crops … more than twice the total capital expenditure incurred on the colony' by 1915.[77] George Morton-Jack details how many First World War veterans 'received the promised land grants from the 178,000 acres of canal irrigated land in Punjab earmarked for them during the war', on the basis of their length of service, record of merit, and the number of casualties their regiments had suffered, with an attempt being made to award land to men from the particular regiments together in 'the same retirement villages or Canal Colonies named after their units'.[78]

Their predominantly Sikh settlers were not only composed of ex-soldiers, however. One British colonisation officer expressed the exasperated hope 'that Government will some day be able to devise a more appropriate method of rewarding the retired Meteorological Observer, the superannuated ticket collector, or the blameless but very unagricultural individual whose life has been passed in the cloistered retreats of the Accountant-General's Office'.[79] He might just as well have been describing many of the would-be settlers of McCluskiegunge, the most substantially realised Anglo-Indian colony and the only one which came even remotely close to becoming the nucleus of an expanding Anglo-Indian territorial state. It was led by another Anglo-Indian politician, who was also a property agent, Earnest Timothy McCluskie. As the Calcutta *Statesman* observed, McCluskie, like John Abbott, presented 'farming … [as] a means of investment'.[80] Named after Gidney's predecessor and rival for All-India leadership, Abbott Mount is a scenic spot in the Himalayan foothills of the Champawat district bordering Nepal, around 224 kilometres south-east of Dehra Dun. Before becoming the secretary and manager of Abbott Brothers, Fred Murcutt had been 'deputed to organise and carry through the great ABBOTT MOUNT COLONY SCHEME which in the face, oft times, of seemingly super human difficulties he successfully carried through' from December 1913 to 1915.[81]

Ralph Stracey provides an insightful overview of this major but somewhat discordant theme of the Anglo-Indian story, which ran from the earliest petitions to the Company state in the 1820s all the way through to the 1950s, but which became particularly potent in the decades following the Montagu–Chelmsford Reforms:

> The Anglo-Indian ... has always been resentful of that early prohibition from buying land and taking to farming but after the First World War there were several movements by D[avid] ... White of Madras, Abbott ... and later McCluskie in Bihar to found farming colonies ... These did not prosper because most of the people who went to settle in these places were retired from Government Service or the railways and very often their sons did not take kindly to being out of the range of the sound of [Calcutta marketplace's] Bow Bells ... It's very difficult for a railway fireman or driver to turn his hand to the plough and milk cows ... So these just became [retirement] settlements ... It is the pensioner who mostly settles down ... in a place like Whitefield or Dehra Dun, or Abbott's Mount ...[82]

This was an astute assessment of the reasons for the failure of colonisation schemes to fulfil the more grandiose, even utopian, visions of their founders, and it bears out Kuntala Lahiri-Dutt's conclusions.[83] Practical failures did not prevent them, however, from conjuring up elaborate plans for community- and state-building. Closely mirroring what David Gilmartin calls the 'social engineering rhetoric of canal colony settlement[s]' through which scientific agricultural modernity would 'transform the settlers themselves',[84] Anglo-Indian colonies were perceived as sites of individual and collective self-transformation and self-actualisation. There is also a striking parallel in Faisal Devji's account of early Indian Muslim political mobilisation as

> so much about creating ... 'a set of colonies' ... [or] spaces in which Muslims can reform or dynamise or enthuse ... their Islam and what it means ... We use the word colony in many ways ... in South Asia—there is a housing colony, there is the Canal Colony in the Punjab especially, and of course there is the colony ... in the sense of the colony of an empire ... When you think of the way in which

there were plans ... [for] a medical mission which was sent to Turkey in 1912 ... to help with the Ottomans, and they planned to create colonies in Anatolia for refugees coming from the Balkans ... Pakistan itself can be seen as the last in this line of experimental colonies ... in which Muslims can transform themselves, and remake themselves anew.[85]

Just as early Muslim colonies and Pakistan itself could serve as laboratories of Islam, providing the means to remake the self in social-ist, secular, religious, modernist or conservative ways,[86] Anglo-Indian colonies also provided spaces for various reformulations of the self and of the group.

The Whitefield colony (near Bangalore) in the Princely State of Mysore was begun in 1879 amid extravagant talk of attracting 'a few Swiss and Flemish peasants' to join in forging a 'Europeanised' future in which 'Eurasians and Anglo-Indians' would become the 'natural leaders' of India.[87] And an even earlier precedent is to be found in 1829, when the Bombay 'East Indian' petitioners approached their sympathetic Governor, Sir John Malcolm, for support in establishing their youth 'as farmers' aiming to apply 'superior intelligence' and the latest methods of improved agriculture, and he made over the Palace of Phoolshair, its accompanying buildings and forty-two acres, includ-ing fruit orchards, 'rent free for ten years'.[88] A work of 1878, *The Fortunes of the Anglo-Indian Race*, cited Phoolshair along with similar schemes in Calcutta and the Shevaroy Hills of the Madras Presidency, arguing that 'the great panacea for existing evils among Anglo-Indians is, in the first place, to discourage their predilection for desk-work; secondly the establishment ... of Industrial Schools ... Schools of Agriculture, [and] Model Farms'.[89] White hoped that Whitefield would ground the mixed in the soil of their birth, attributing

the fault ... not ... in the country but with those who were unable to shake themselves free of the influences which surrounded them. The indigenous population never seeks to be what it is not ... It treads its native soil ... without affectation ... enjoy[ing] ... a vitality which defies Time. The Association desires that Eurasians and Anglo-Indians should be what the indigenous population is, and ... has [accordingly] made such strenuous efforts to obtain land. With a collective footing on the soil ... an equivalent change of character will take place ... [and] all else will follow ... Eurasians and Anglo-Indians ... are—hothouse plants, passing phenomena like the figures in a kaleidoscope. The land of their birth or adoption has not owned them, and they have often sung 'Home! Home! *Sweet* Home!' feeling the magic of the sentiment, but, alas! without ever having realized what Home is, and without even the chance of doing so. Home, with all its sacred associations, it is now sought to create—Home towards which children will look with longing ... Home in which to pass the evening of life, and in which to rest amidst those we have loved.[90]

In 1882 the 'Mysore Branch (Bangalore)' of the Eurasian and Anglo-Indian Association published a 208-page *Guide to the Eurasian and Anglo-Indian Villages, Proposed to Be Established in the Province of Mysore*, including detailed architectural drawings of an idealised layout of the colonies involving a school, alongside chapters on the farming of fish, cattle, sheep, pigs, and ostriches, the breeding of horses, ponies and mules, the rearing of silk worms, coffee-growing and bee-keeping.[91] Their approach to the state's maharaja, His Highness Chamarajendra Wodeyar, had stressed how 'improved methods ... [of] Western Agricultural Science', based on the prior experience of an 'Experimental Farm', would 'ameliorat[e] ... the condition of the poorer classes of our Community'.[92] While consenting to become their society's patron and lauding agriculture as 'the healthiest and most ennobling occupation for any class of people', he cautioned that it required 'steady and patient industry, moderate aspirations, and provident habits to which people accustomed to miscellaneous pursuits are not trained without considerable difficulty', and would inevitably entail 'occasional failures and disappointments' and very modest rates of return unless they could succeed in outcompeting Indian *ryots* (peasant farmers) through 'increased labour, greater intelligence, and the application of science, and machinery'.[93] Nearly half a century later when Mysore's Dewan (prime minister), Sir Mirza M. Ismail, visited the colony in 1930, he celebrated its 'settlers ... as the best subjects of the Mysore Durbar', informing Gidney's Association that 'the State would welcome [more] Anglo-Indians colonising in Mysore'.[94]

Intellectually, there were various strands to these projects, some of which were realised and others never went beyond utopian fantasy. To generalise, nineteenth-century schemes were supremely confident of India's Europeanising future as a potential site of more extensive settlement in which the mixed could play an equal part. This was of course antithetical to the purposes of the East India Company and the subsequent colonial government, which continued to reject the idea that India should become a colony of widespread European settlement. Whitefield's founders had declared that colonisation 'means the birth of a new race to a position of physical and mental independence, one which will find scope for its energy in the country at large'.[95] Judging by Abbott's politics and the heightened wartime British imperial patriotism during its founding, it appears likely that Abbott Mount was intended to provide a secluded and healthy space for the uncontested assertion of the group's Britishness, where Anglo-Indians could work out or realise their own formulations of identity without fear of contradiction within a longed-for sense of economic and physical security.

By contrast, with its use of the Hindi term 'our Mooluk', the *Colonization Observer*, the journal of McCluskie's incorporated Colonization Society of India, presented a more dualistic vision of the mixed discovering and creating a home within mainland India, but imaginatively detached from it.[96] The assertion 'Independence is the goal we are striving for', alongside the society's slogans of 'unity', 'self-help' and 'co-operation',[97] probably only meant to imply self-sufficiency and autonomy, rather than constitutional separation. One letter to the *Colonization Observer* opined:

> the best thing possible is to start all over again ... on our own little plot of land, and ... do for ourselves what we have done for India, and the British Empire. As descendants of Britishers we will combine our loyalty to the Crown, and any Government, Indian or British, can depend on us ... But as fast as India is Indianizing ... let us Colonize and build a Nation, and thus do for ourselves ... It is like a beautiful dream, everything your own, and in a lovely spot with no dogmatic treatment and no dread of the sack ... no ... Dewalies, Mohorrums and riots ... [nor] any fear of Dacoities and Bomb throwing. It would be just splendid: Farming, Commerce and Industry, Dance Halls and Picture Houses ... Wake Up Anglo-Indians, and help in NATION-BUILDING.[98]

As early as 1931, debates over colonisation reflected profound and deep-seated anxieties about the prospects for Anglo-Indian survival as a Christian minority:

The Hindu is a product of the East, and we are of the West ... Will it then be possible to fuse these two distinctly divergent types into one great whole, yet owning a separate existence? I hardly think it can be ... and in my opinion there is ... only one means ... Christianity ... [But will] the Community ... be able to survive long enough[?] ... The Hindu is as much opposed to Christianity as we are to his faith and ideals. It would be far easier for the Mohommedan to fuse into the Hindu race, or *vice versa*, than for us to ever do so ... East must sink to what the East is, for it is not the policy even of the most enlightened Indian to cut adrift from ... [its] fetters ... There are no doubt some who have been to Europe, ... adopted Western polish and Western outlooks, but in their home lives may be seen the[se] fetters ... Our Christian culture cannot permit us to accept with equanimity some ... Indian customs, which, though they may be more ancient than ours, yet give rise to an intense feeling of disgust ... Either East must become West, or we must merge into the East. But let us remember Kipling's words. 'For East is East, and West is West, And never the twain shall meet.'[99]

Antithetical to Turner's dualistic celebration of hybridity, this binary Kiplingesque polarisation sought to construct Anglo-Indians as fundamentally Western. Christianity was the only basis of future unity, and, unlike Wilson, this author, writing under the initials T. D. A., was not confident that Christianity was destined to take hold in India. Drawing on chapter 9 verse 21 describing the servitude of the Gibeonites under the Israelites in the Old Testament Book of Joshua, T. D. A.

tried to visualise our Community after fifty years of Hindu rule, and the picture makes me shudder, for I see ourselves as their *hewers of wood and drawers of water*, exactly what we have been to the British ... The difference ... is this ... We despise the one and respect the other, and we do not mind serving those whose morals and traditions are more or less synonymous with ours, and whose children we claim to be, but it goes intensely against the grain to visualise our children working side by side in poverty with those whom we at one time engaged as our servants. The principle of Government in this land will be to bring living down to the Indian standard. This must necessarily react on those ... who have Western habits for it will not be possible for any one Community, unless endowed with much wealth to so separate itself into an unconnected entity, prosperous and Western in its living and habits.[100]

Almost two years earlier Turner had invoked the same biblical words to exclaim that 'Anglo-India is heading straight to the position of "DRAWERS OF WATER AND HEWERS OF WOOD"', appealing to the

> ladies ... [and] mothers of Anglo-India, to ponder ... what would be *your* fate with your Bread-winners ... out of employment and unable to find work? Would you be enjoying the merriments of to-night? Far from it! On the contrary one meal a day ... of the very poorest, would be a Godsend. Mean little hovels, dirty, unhealthy, smelling and vermin-infested, would take the place of the present Railway-provided accommodations ... we have been accustomed to call 'Home'. It would break our hearts to see ... [our] children ... on whom ... we dote, and for whom there is nothing too good ... clad in shreds and tatters.[101]

Both T. D. A. and Turner were haunted by similarly nightmarish and apocalyptic visions of possible Anglo-Indian futures. The main difference was in Turner's positive prescription for fostering a dualistic mixed-race pride and reorientating towards a kind of communal nationalism through which 'Mother India' would embrace her Anglo-Indian 'sons and daughters'.[102] By contrast, T. D. A. fatalistically concluded that economic discrimination and a consequent collapse of Anglo-Indian living standards were inevitable:

> there will be new laws ... drawn up to meet the requirements of the masses and not any small Community, tribe, or clan ... The Government will demand that we either become their hired servants according to their standard of living, in the lowliest positions, or fend for ourselves ... This would be entirely ruinous to us ... With all power vested in the hands of such caste believers, what tolerance of our Christian principles may be expected? May not an intensely intolerant Government enact by Statute 'No Christian may be appointed'. To-day ... conditions satisfying all classes may prevail under compulsion with a third power administering; may however the same be anticipated a hundred years hence? ... I have a firm belief that the ruling power will, in order to create a single united whole, endeavour to pursue a policy of exterminating those who will not voluntarily merge into their individuality.[103]

Of 'Mr. Gandhi' himself and 'his worthy Lieutenants', T. D. A. was positive, but noted that they were 'not Immortal'.[104] The Congress leaders were not in a position to vouch for the *bona-fides* of those who may be in power fifty or a hundred years hence … Remember the treatment accorded to the Israelites by the Egyptians … So also may the future Rulers of India say, 'These Christians are gradually spreading themselves over our land, and drawing away our people and taking away some of our living, we must exterminate them.' They are almost saying it to-day. Did not the British adopt a policy of suppression in the early days … which is … responsible for the invidious position we now occupy? Was it not because the half-bred races in America rose and overthrew the Governments of the unmixed rulers which relegated them to the lower ranks, that the British decided to adopt a policy … which has resulted in our relegation to those ranks from which we have tried in vain to extricate ourselves? Is not our present position in India precarious in the extreme owing to that policy? … If then our fathers … adopt[ed] such a policy, can we with any degree of certainty expect anything merciful from those whom we have hitherto treated as something less in importance than ourselves? … Suppose in the future India, an Extreme National Party should come into power, do we think to expect much mercy and tolerance from them? The Hindu with his own class distinctions and his scorn of what he designates the Untouchables is sufficient answer … His very attitude towards his brothers reveals his mentality.[105]

The invocation of biblical and genocidal themes is particularly striking here. T. D. A. also explicitly cited Herbert Stark's *Hostages to India* in support of this argument, revealing how constructions of the group's history fed into its ongoing politics. With rare frankness, T. D. A. confronted the uncomfortable subject of Anglo-Indians' own ill-treatment of Indians—past and present:

We have been taught by example to be intolerant and to despise, and we have well learnt the lessons, and are if anything more intolerant and scornful than our teachers. We have not treated the Indian as our second blood brother, but as something to be thrust aside as being inferior … He has for years writhed under this indignity, and our conciliatory attitudes towards him to-day in no way lessens the bitterness which he has cherished … [and] shews whenever he is given the opportunity. Do you think he will ever forgive or forget all the insults … heaped upon him … which he has patiently stomached? I say no. Emphatically No …. The Communal hatred against the White man and his Eurasian offspring is much more deep-seated to-day than it was fifty years ago, or after the Mutiny which we helped suppress.[106]

'Communal pressure' from 'the Majority Communities' was compared to 'volcanic forces. Deep in the body of the Earth ... [that] roll and move ... burst[ing] forth ... [in] fiery floods', bringing 'utter destruction'.[107] The caste system 'in the future Hindu India' was an ever-present threat to a Christian people who might eventually sink 'to the lowest social ranks ... the same level as the converted Chamar and Bhungi, whom ... [higher-caste Hindus] loathe and despise'.[108] T. D. A. concluded that 'the best home for the Anglo-Indians is a Christian home ... which acknowledges all men as equal ... a home where the Anglo-Indian will himself discard certain bad habits which he has inherited from his mixed parentage'.[109] Anglo-Indians should seek 'to break forever from the yoke of service and to make a bid for independence' through colonisation 'away from India, [where] we would be able to work out our own salvation in the same way as other colonies have done'.[110] A colony within India might prove just as vulnerable to a Swaraj government, placing them in a position 'even worse than serfdom'.[111] Therefore, if Anglo-Indians wished to preserve their own culture and traditions, emigration to a colony overseas was the only safe course:

> After all we are responsible to the generations which we shall leave behind and they will question our wisdom, and curse us for the yoke we may leave them to shoulder. Children now, may live long enough to suffer the evils of the depression to which we may in our short-sighted policy leave them ... If we are settled in India, we are by no means assured of the co-operation of the Indians ... If we as a community are to make good, we can only do so by making ourselves independent, and so long as we stay in India, we must of necessity be somewhat dependent upon the co-operation of the Indians ... to attain property, if we ever can ... [and] must strictly adhere to their requirements ... For you and for me, and for our children and grand-children, India which has been our much loved home, is home no longer. It is a land where if we wish to dwell, we must forever discard our culture and ... Western traditions, which will remind the ruling power of what they shall always consider the yoke which they bore silently, and re-educate our minds into a National Eastern groove, with Eastern traditions, aspirations and ideals.[112]

Writing from 'Johore, Malaya', J. W. Moore, a self-proclaimed 'Eurasian patriot', drew the same conclusion from the threat of 'extinction' posed by 'violent ... rabid nationalism'.[113] The title of his article—'Utopia via "Eurasia"'—played upon that of his Renaissance humanist near-namesake. In pan-Eurasianist vein, Moore asserted that 'the problem of the Anglo-Indian is the same problem facing all Eurasians' and that all the 'mixed races in the East' shared more in common with one another than with the peoples of their 'supposed native home[s]'.[114] Obviously not enamoured of 'the dog-like loyalty ... the Eurasian has always ... paid to an overlord', Moore desired to ultimately break free of both European colonial masters and colonised Asian peoples and thereby secure lasting Eurasian 'emancipation!'[115] Looking to other historical parallels, Moore identified three possible outcomes:

a) An intellectual and superior minority overcoming a very numerous but inferior majority and eventually dominating a new state.
b) A minority being absorbed by a dominant race or ... being compelled ... to merge into or being exterminated by an overwhelming alien majority ...
c) Emigration with a view to building a new and unhampered home ...[116]

Between these outcomes, Moore concluded that (b), merger or extermination, appeared 'inevitable ... unless we can, before it is too late ... devise means to preserve our entity', while (c) offered the only historically proven 'salvation for minorities'.[117] He identified 'the Jewish race' as 'the only minority race which has been able to survive as a separate entity and to keep its religion and customs without a home of its own ... in spite of all manner of disabilities and repression'.[118] Anglo-Indians were socially and economically similar to Jews in India and occasionally intermarried with them. Some common Anglo-Indian names, such as the partially anglicised Rosemeyer, are suggestive of Jewish ancestry. Moore regretted that Eurasians lacked 'the tenacity ... [and] freemasonry of Jewry' and their steadfast 'loyalty' to their own race.[119] However, his choice of 'the despised Jew' as 'a splendid example' of survival amid a hostile majority was a tragically misguided conclusion to draw nine months before the introduction of the Nuremberg Laws in Germany.[120] Not long before Moore's article, the *Colonization Observer* had republished a *John Bull* piece celebrating 'the New Palestine Homeland ... [as] a very bright spot in the black Jewish world of oppression and tyranny'—a means of 'salvation of the Jewish victims of the Nazi Terror'.[121] By July 1941 the *Colonization Observer* was reprinting accounts of Gestapo round-ups of Jews, 'dead' bodies being 'taken out' of overcrowded 'train after train', and a 'camp of horror for German Jews' operating in Vichy France where the elderly were 'left to die'.[122] '*India* ... [was warned to] *remember*' these '*NAZI crimes* ... [and] *do everything* possible to stop their *repetition in India itself*.'[123]

The *Review* also tackled mounting antisemitism,[124] directly comparing 'the situation of the Jews' with the need for Anglo-Indians to find their own 'Palestine'.[125] Having apparently regarded 'a colonization scheme with scorn as a crazy experiment', Jews were 'now flocking in thousands to ... Palestine'.[126] Crowning '200 ... agricultural settlements', 'Tel Aviv[,] ... the first and only completely Jewish city in the world. From the street dustman to the Jewish Mayor',[127] was inspirational. The 'astonishing racial cohesion' of the 'world-scattered' Jewish people, overcoming 'untold trials and sufferings',[128] resonated with Anglo-Indians, who were similarly conceptualised as 'a homeless and wandering Community', for whom colonisation would provide 'the chance of getting a real stake in their own country'.[129] One letter from a few 'young unmarried' Anglo-Indian men in the 'little jungle station' of Pyinmana, Burma, looked to 'McCluskieville' as 'an answer to prayer ... our only salvation ... Our visions of an independent Anglo-Indian settlement, happy and prosperous ... the Mecca of generations to come. Its stabilising influence should soon rout the sense of insecurity of a hitherto nomadic people.'[130] The official 1931 census figure for Anglo-Indians (still including Burma) was 138,395, but given the prevalence of passing, Anglo-Indian leaders believed this was seriously underestimated, and the census compilers themselves concluded that the true number was probably closer to 168,400.[131] The figure of 200,000 Jewish settlers therefore almost invited the *Colonization Observer*'s explicit parallel with the

> scheme of colonization in Palestine, which illustrates how the Jews have taken advantage of opportunities and have thus brought about the foundation of excellent towns and settlements in the Holy Land, by sheer enterprise. Does it not stand to reason that if a barren country, in the

Illustration 1: Anglo-Indian women of the Friis Browne Family c.1920s, showing characteristically differing complexions among sisters, courtesy of Rebecca Calderon.

Illustration 2: First Communion for Mary Philomena Keating (seated fourth from the left in the longest dress, b. 20 November 1936) and other children presumed to be Anglo-Indian at the Sacred Heart Convent in Dalhousie, courtesy of her granddaughter Susie Longstaff.

The Anglo-Indian & Domiciled European Association, All-India & Burma.

INDIA

OUR 88 BRANCHES
DOTTED OVER THE
COUNTRY WITH A
MEMBERSHIP OF
OVER: 10,000.

Illustration 3: Map of the 88 branches of the Anglo-Indian & Domiciled European Association in 1929, still including four affiliated branches in Burma (*AIR*, August 1929, back cover).

Illustration 4: Ethnically caricatured communal cartoon making the case for temporary safeguards for Anglo-Indians and Domiciled Europeans during the Simon Commission (*AIR*, Christmas 1928, p. 17).

Illustration 5: Sir Henry Gidney (left) meeting Sir Stafford Cripps in 1942 (LIFE Magazine, Mansell Collection).

Illustration 6: Close-up of Sir John Pratt, Consul-General, Shanghai, attending the Boy Scouts Parade at the British Consulate, Shanghai, on Armistice Day, Tuesday 11 November 1924.

Illustration 7: Wide-shot version of Sir John Pratt (foreground left), along-side (left to right) an unidentified Royal Navy commander, Sir Skinner Turner (1868–1935), Chief Judge of the British Supreme Court for China (1921–7), and Sir John Fitzgerald Brenan (1883–1953), British Consul-General, Canton/Guangzhou.

Illustration 8: William Henry Pratt, better known as Boris Karloff, in 1913; the youngest of his father's twelve children and almost uniquely having been born in England. Like Merle Oberon (who features on the cover of this book), Karloff's illustrious film career was enabled by his adoption of a name which would obscure his ethnicity and provide greater freedom to play a variety of roles in Hollywood. Both Karloff's parents were Anglo-Indians in the sense of being 'mixed-race', but his father objected to being called 'Eurasian', preferring to be thought of as an Englishman of colour.

Illustration 9: The D'Vaz family in Bangalore c.1929; my great-grandparents Mary and John seated (centre) with Great-Uncle George standing in between. My grandmother Virginia seated on the chair to the right with Great-Aunt Merlin standing in between. Great-Aunt Gladys seated on the leftmost chair with Great-Uncle Olvin standing in between. Great-Aunt Lottie, Great-Uncle Tom and Great-Uncle Patrick seated in front.

Illustration 10: My paternal grandparents, Virginia and Edward, in their Second World War officer's uniforms.

Illustration 11: My grandmother, Virginia (seated in the centre chair), with fellow members of her Women's Auxiliary Corps (India) unit during the Second World War.

Illustration 12: Recruiting advertisement for the Women's Auxiliary Corps (India), offering a choice of a sari- or skirt-based uniforms (*AIR*, April 1943, p. 7).

Illustration 13: My grandfather (Edward) in a dress uniform, possibly of the Princely State of Mysore; his sword was brought to the UK after his death in 1948 and has remained a family heirloom.

Illustration 14: My great-uncle Dr George D'Vaz (seated centre) in Dehradun in 1955 upon his retirement from the Army Medical Corps (India). He would go on to practise as a GP in England.

Illustration 15: My uncle (Paul), aunt (Sylvia) and father (Stuart) in 1950s Bangalore, before their emigration to the UK.

Illustration 16: My father on his call to the Bar, Gray's Inn 1970, going on to become a Head of Chambers later in his career.

course of less than 20 years, can ... be made to support a population of 200,000 souls, the Domiciled Community can also achieve the same result by the same perseverance and determination.[132]

Implicit here is the *terra nullius* construction of sites of colonisation as empty or underutilised—English common law justifications for settlement and 'adverse possession' going back to Sir Thomas More's *Utopia* (1516) and John Locke's *Second Treatise of Government* (1690).[133] This line of thought also underpinned British settler colonialism in Australia and other so-called White Dominions, which appeared to be more popular models for Anglo-Indian colonisation, than the more obvious near-at-hand templates of the colonial state-backed Punjab canal colonies, precisely because they embodied the imperial Britishness to which so many Anglo-Indians aspired. Another author in 1934 described how

> since the beginning of the Anglo-Indian movement no suggestion gained greater popularity ... because it seemed to guarantee ever-lasting happiness. No one thought of its practicability, everyone frantically voted for it only because the scheme very effectually appeared to segregate the Anglo-Indian from the Indian ... [However,] nobody can give a correct estimate of the cost, and above all if the colonisation is to be done in India itself the Anglo-Indian will soon realise painfully that even after Colonisation the Indian figures very prominently in his life.[134]

More than a decade later, Narayan Jog compared 'Pakistan and ... Anglo-India', insisting that 'both *are* in Hindusthan and both deny it!'[135]—before reflecting, more sympathetically, that

> the habits, thoughts and feelings of centuries cannot ... be changed in a decade or two, and Anglo-Indians find the journey from Father Britain, who has disowned them, to Mother India, whom they disowned so long, full of doubts and difficulties, heart-burning and even frustration. Many of them frequently raise the issue: 'Why not cut ourselves from both the parents? Why not emigrate *en masse*, say to Australia or even to the Andamans and strike out on our own? Why not stake out a little bit of the world which we can proudly name Anglo-India?' Alas! It is a wishful thought, a forlorn hope ... Anglo-India is thus undergoing the pangs of rebirth. It is humanity uprooted—or rather humanity yet unrooted, in spite of two centuries of existence.[136]

Through the latter stages of decolonisation, and even following independence, colonisation schemes based upon collective emigration would continue to be put forward. The Andaman Islands in particular were envisaged as a potential site for retaining a British imperial connection and orientation. Ralph Stracey soberly reflected upon

> a movement, originating in Calcutta, called the Brit-Asian League ... They asked the Government of India to let them have the Andamans after ... the Great War ... but the British Government for good reason, and that is that the Anglo-Indian had not been trained to an agricultural life, refused. There might have been some political reasons underlying this but this scheme never got off the ground ... The Andamans are not very conducive to the settlement of any people, although now the Hindus of East Bengal who were thrown out of Pakistan have been settled ... [there] and are doing very well ... [But] the main industries ... are timber, very large coconut plantations, and ... fishing ... It was a primitive way of life that they would have had to lead and so many of them, having been born and bred in the roaring cities of Calcutta and Madras, just didn't come forward.[137]

Ralph was actually compressing an earlier abortive attempt between 1923 and 1924 to settle the Andaman and Nicobar islands by the 'Ex-Services Association', which Gidney supported but attempted to distance himself from after its failure,[138] together with later attempts in the 1940s. Feeling burned by the first Andamans effort, Gidney was reluctant to support McCluskiegunge, especially seeing that the similarly larger-than-life McCluskie became one of the community's MLAs in Bengal and an increasingly prominent rival within Gidney's Association. Gidney remained worried that another unsuccessful colonisation attempt could fritter away the community's precious resources. However, after McCluskie's death Gidney lent his support to the project already under way, even allowing the settlers to make (presumably abortive) plans for a large president-in-chief's residence, to be dubbed 'Gidney Castle'. One snide onlooker mocked Gidney for posing for 'photograph[s] ... in nine different positions, waving a 3d. Union Jack while the colonists were starting off to work for 2d. a day, [and] even then payment was doubtful'.[139] Kenneth Wallace explains that although Gidney opposed emigration and 'especially' any further attempt to colonise 'the Andamans ... he was all in favour of a reserved area in India itself for Anglo-Indians'.[140]

In 1940 B. Leadon, president of the Anglo-Indian Association's Delhi branch and a prominent radio journalist, spelled out clearly the goal:

> Britain could … create in some very small corner of India an Anglo-Indian State or colony. It would be a very small price to pay the community for its past services … Such a State could be developed with loans granted by the British Government. If the Indian Legislature could be induced to agree to such a scheme, and I have every reason to believe that there would be little or no objection … [it could become] a protectorate of the Indian Government …[141]

In late March 1942, a letter to the editor from a retired major in the Indian Medical Department declared that the community's 'first and second line of defence' ought to be 'colonizing in the Andamans' to create 'a new ARCADIA, a real ANGLO-INDIA, all our own'.[142] S. F. Perry countered that 'puerile games … imagining ourselves as self sufficient … "Lords of all we survey" in an island of our own', in 'a Utopia … should be left to the School Children'.[143] They represented 'a policy of isolationism, distrust and segregation … that given publicity would only aggravate and increase the distrust of the Indian mind and make them bear towards us a feeling of contempt'.[144] Even if such a scheme could overcome the many practical impediments which had reduced earlier 'Anglo-Indian Colonies' to 'farce', the territory would become 'fair game for any government or nation'.[145] Perry pointedly asked whether 'we [are] to be in the British Commonwealth of nations or subject to the Government of India—or are some insane enough to think of forming a republic?'[146]

Great waves

Concurrently with 'Anglo-Indianist' and pan-Eurasianist discourses on collective emigration and colonisation, Gidney was still attempting to secure the Anglo-Indian future in India along more tried and tested lines. His energies and efforts were principally targeted towards the next great constitutional change on the horizon in the 1930s, the drafting of a constitution which would present the form, though not the substance, of a comprehensive devolution of power into Indian hands. From his position on the Central Advisory Committee for Railways, Gidney observed many self-proclaimed nationalists whose demands, he argued, exposed them as 'ultra communalists'.[147] Gidney told the Assembly that

> 70 to 80 per cent. of the questions asked in this House are pregnant with communalism, bias, [and] prejudice ... The nationalists are communalists in disguise ... Communalism is the direct negation of nationalism, but so long as it exists ... we must face it and safeguard the evils attached to its practice, *i.e.*, from a majority rule ... India ... can rightly and solely be called the Home and Playground of minorities, a land in which each one is separated from the other, expressing different languages, customs and religious faiths and entirely devoid of ... common cementing factors ... with each one of us fearing the majority community when the new Constitution operates and when possibly the Congress Party is in power ... India is nothing else, but a collection of minorities ... stand[ing] in peril of being swamped out of all employment ...[148]

Once again Gidney turned to the imperial metropole. Travelling to lobby British parliamentarians, he found allies in Lord Hardinge (the Viceroy during the First World War) and Lord Lloyd (the former Governor of Bombay). Both were key to the almost miraculous success of Gidney's desperate effort in London to secure justiciable reserved employment quotas for Anglo-Indians in the railways, telegraphs and customs departments in the face of stern and initially implacable resistance from both the colonial Government of India and the British Government's India Office. Lloyd, who was instrumental in the passing of a last-minute amendment to the 1935 Act, emotively asked his fellow members of the House of Lords:

> Who stood by us in the general strike in Bombay on the railway, and during the Amritsar disturbances? I have the bitterest memories of those anxious days and nights ... when all the telegraph staff up the lines who were not Anglo-Indians were tapping out Congress and disloyal messages ... paralysing the railways, spreading the strike, leaving the Anglo-Indians alone to do their best in great danger. Many of them, or at least some of them, fell at their posts ... This is the community who are going to be scattered among the minor classes and taken away from their jobs. They are a small community, but they are utterly vital to our existence in India.[149]

Perhaps unsurprisingly, among those with less recent first-hand experience, it was predominantly ardent Unionists and those of the imperialist 'die-hard' faction within the Conservative Party, including the Duchess of Atholl and Winston Churchill, who were most willing to speak up on Anglo-Indians' behalf. They had generally opposed Irish Home Rule, stressed the plight of Irish loyalists, and were intent on resisting even such devolution as the 1935 Act would deliver for India. If Churchill remembered their earlier encounter, when Gidney joined the Indian trade union leader Narayan Malhar Joshi and former Swaraj Party leader Makund Ramrao Jayakar, in grilling him on his resistance to any substantive further devolution before the Joint Committee on Indian Constitutional Reform back in 1933, he certainly held no grudge.[150]

Churchill would later lend his personal support to Muhammad Ali Jinnah, for much the same reason that he supported Gidney—he saw Muslim and Anglo-Indian interests as more aligned with Britain's in resisting, delaying or shaping the nature of decolonisation. None of this meant, however, that Churchill and other Conservatives and Unionists were not personally moved by Gidney's appeals, playing as they did upon Anglo-Indians' heartfelt patriotic loyalty to Britain, the Crown and Empire, in the face of betrayal by callous officialdom. Churchill was known to be a deeply emotional man himself, even in politics. He would later work himself up into the mood to compose his crucial wartime speeches on a diet of alcohol and martial music. Churchill's patriotic and imperial sentimentalism dovetailed with his more rational calculation that retaining Anglo-Indians was 'essential' to 'the defensive arrangements of … British power in India'.[151] He recounted to the House how he had 'had the pleasure of making … [Sir Henry Gidney's] acquaintance and of having some conversation with him on several occasions, and … when I looked into … [his] eyes I saw fear, and grief, and almost despair'.[152] At which Lord Eustace Percy interjected, 'You must have depressed him.'[153] Churchill fired back that he wished he 'could inculcate a similar disciplinary effect upon the Noble Lord by the mere power of a glance.'[154] Churchill proceeded to accuse the government of giving Anglo-Indians 'a good, Liberal whack on the head' while pretending to sympathise with their plight.[155] With characteristic eloquence, Churchill delivered a lengthy speech, beginning with a description of Gidney's approach to him:

I thought when I saw him that he was a man in a most unhappy position ... Here was a great National Government, with a majority of hundreds ... with all the Conservative party joining with the Socialists and Liberals to carry this Measure, taking over Socialist schemes and ramming them forward with their mighty force; here was all the power of the Government ... and the Secretary of State and the Viceroy, exercised through a thousand channels ... to shape and turn and smooth the passage of this policy; and here was this poor Sir Henry Gidney come over here to represent the Anglo-Indian community. Anything more unequal I cannot imagine. And you say he is satisfied with what he has got. I believe that to be a most profound misrepresentation ...

With this particular Government and this particular Parliament, you can get away with anything, but their day of accounting will come, and these statements will be brought home. You say the Anglo-Indians are satisfied with the treatment you are giving them in thus stereotyping them at this disastrous level to which they have fallen. They have fallen into the pit, and all you say is that they are to remain in the pit, but not to fall to a deeper deep which still opens to devour them. That is all you are doing for them, and because they dare not say a word, because they are prostrate before your conquering footsteps, you say, 'We have had no complaint from the Anglo-Indian community. Here is Sir Henry Gidney, who represents them, and he has not made to us any recriminatory representations ...' The Government know well that this particular case of the Anglo-Indians is poignant. We who know India can see what their lot will be. We can see the terrible future which awaits them.[156]

From the other end of the political spectrum, and from another man who, likewise unbeknown to anyone at the time, was also destined to become prime minister, came a similar acknowledgement of British moral obligation. Informed by his more recent first-hand experience in India as a member of the group of seven MPs who made up the Simon Commission of 1928, Clement Attlee reasonably argued that

everybody must be impressed with the very unfortunate position of the Anglo-Indians. I was in very close contact with Sir Henry Gidney for many months in India, and I saw a great number of that community. One has to recognise the enormous difficulty of their position—a position for which they are not responsible. They are people of a certain standard of life … Years ago they were … in a simple position, because they were the only English-speaking people who took these posts. Now every community is competing for these posts and it is a competition between people of different standards of life. I am opposed to the Amendment, because if this obligation is on anybody, it is on the British people, and you are trying to put it on to the Indian people. You are saying that certain posts must be reserved for th[is] … small community, while there are a very large number of other communities … You say that this community shall be given a privileged position as against other Indian communities. I say that if there is a moral obligation—and I think there is—it should be shouldered by this country … By taking this kind of line in respect of this community vis-à-vis the rest of the inhabitants of India, you would make the[ir] position far worse than it is now. By all means let us meet this obligation, but let us meet it ourselves, and not put it upon someone else.[157]

Unfortunately for the Anglo-Indians, this appears to have left little imprint on Attlee's perception of the nation's postwar priorities amid far weightier concerns once he became prime minister. Yet Gidney could no more see into the future than Churchill or Attlee. His limited moves to persuade Anglo-Indians to embrace a connection to the Indian soil, to the land of their birth, were not about abandoning their English-speaking culture or their existing ties to the colonial power, but making them more self-confident within the late-colonial world in which they existed. Like many political figures in India at the time, Gidney did not anticipate the coming of another world war and the transformative effect it would have in accelerating British withdrawal.

While expressing his public support for 'the proper development of India along constitutional lines', Gidney emphasised 'the loyalty of the Anglo-Indian community to the established Government … [as] a stable and indispensable element to the preservation of the peace, safety and tranquility of the country'.[158] Following the passing of the 1935 Act, elections were held in eleven provinces during the winter of 1936–7 under an increased but still very limited franchise based on property qualifications. The Congress Party emerged with majorities in five of these, and pluralities in a further three. Although the largest single party in Bengal, it was unable to form a ministry there, while in the North-West Frontier Province Congress formed a minority government, so that with the help of various coalitions Congress took power in eight of eleven provinces. Gidney had originally been associated with the founding of the Unionist Party, which won a majority and formed a government in Punjab. However, seeing that Anglo-Indian representation was mostly achieved through their own separate electorates, for Gidney what mattered was that his Association, rather than rival Anglo-Indian organisations, should pick up most of these communal seats. This they did, but Anglo-Indian representatives, whether inside or outside Gidney's Association, generally found themselves lonely voices in opposition to the de-funding of European and Anglo-Indian schools, and in debates over religiously motivated sumptuary legislation targeting alcohol consumption and cow slaughter.

When war against Germany was once again declared on India's behalf by the Viceroy in September 1939 without even a fig leaf of consultation with the Congress Party or its provincial premiers, there was outrage, followed by demands for Congress participation in a national government alongside a firm commitment to postwar independence. Lord Linlithgow's proposals for a mere consultative committee were insufficient to prevent the Congress ministries from resigning in protest. Muhammad Ali Jinnah, the Muslim League leader, whose party had failed miserably even among Muslims in the 1936–7 elections, greeted this event as a day of deliverance, promising 'honourable cooperation' in return for increased protection for Muslims. As might be expected, the mood among the vast majority of Anglo-Indians was more genuinely pro-British than Jinnah's tactical gambit. The Second World War, and the widespread participation by Anglo-Indians in the imperial war effort, once again amplified their monarchical, empire-loyalist, and pro-British patriotism. For the vast majority of Anglo-Indians at this juncture, fighting in a common cause with those they claimed as blood relations validated their own sense of self-identification with their British 'kith and kin'. In this context Gidney saw an opportunity to contrast such demonstrable loyalty with the bargaining position adopted by Gandhi and other Congress leaders:

> I regret ... the absence of any realisation of this vital part that we play in the life of this country on the part of those who profess to speak for the nation ... To them we do not exist ... Mr. Gandhi ...

[recently stated] that no community in India needed help except the Depressed classes ... the only real minority ... The Anglo Indian does not fear the loss of the right to practice his religion ... he fears ... the deprivation of his right to live and thrive in the country of his origin and development into an Indian community with British traditions and traits ... The other day, the Education Minister ... [in] Madras declared that ... a readjustment between the grants of Anglo-Indian Schools and Indian Schools may be effected ... Let those who claim self-determination ... sacrifice something in order to ensure the bread and butter of others ... [Then] I have no doubt that the Anglo-Indian will join hands ... in the attainment of ... Dominion Status for India, but as a partner in the British Commonwealth of Nations. But under no circumstances can we and shall we surrender our birthright, our loyalty to Great Britain, our family traditions, our standard of living and our mode of life, the maintenance of which in turn depends on our protected existence in the economic sphere. If the new order should demand the surrender of these, we shall become the Ulster of India and fight to the last ditch. In any case, our co-operation with a party which has adopted a bargaining attitude in ... according support to the King Emperor when His Majesty is at war is entirely out of the question.[159]

As the only Conservative acceptable to the Labour Party, Churchill became the head of a populist Left–Right wartime coalition in May 1940. Almost two years later, under pressure from his American ally, President Franklin Roosevelt, Churchill sent an envoy to India to negotiate with the Congress leaders to obtain their support for the Allied war effort. At this point Gidney found himself entirely wrong-footed, for if there was one person who would, in Anglo-Indian eyes, become the face of what Anthony would later term 'Britain's betrayal', it was the angular, dour and rimlessly bespectacled Sir Stafford Cripps. As a socialist who had been expelled from the Labour Party for his efforts to foster a cross-party movement with communists and other elements of the Left, Cripps's political capital in Britain during the war was such that Churchill felt compelled to include him in government, if only to muzzle and constrain him. Cripps believed, more plausibly than seems credible with hindsight, that he could displace Churchill as prime minister. 'There, but for the grace of God, goes God,' Churchill 'once muttered as Cripps strode by'.[160] Accordingly, Churchill lost no opportunity to get Cripps out of the way or place him in a position where he might fall flat on his face, first by sending him as ambassador to Moscow, and then on the ill-fated mission to India, which the old arch-imperialist was hoping would fail.

Cripps's devoutly Christian high-mindedness, humourlessness, relative asceticism, teetotalism and vegetarianism made him insufferable to many of his cabinet and parliamentary colleagues.[161] However, combined with his socialist and anti-imperialist convictions, these traits also made him a natural sympathiser of the religiously syncretic Gandhi and the secular socialist Nehru. This obvious partiality to one side in the negotiations deepened the suspicions of Jinnah. Despite Gandhi's rejection of the idea of any Briton playing an arbitrating role, this was the inescapable reality of the position in which even those British politicians who wished to further the cause of decolonisation felt compelled by circumstance to play. Cripps found, however, that no amount of well-meaning sentiments or statements on his part, no cleverly crafted legalistic or diplomatic formula, could reconcile his brief with what Gandhi wanted, nor overcome the Mahatma's antiwar principles. Gandhi rejected talk of postwar Dominion status as a 'post-dated cheque drawn on a failing bank'; and the shrewd elder statesman still held enough sway over his colleagues to torpedo Cripps's proposals in any form, even though Nehru, Patel, Maulana Azad and, more especially, Chakravarti Rajagopalachari had been willing to support the British war effort in return for immediate self-government and postwar independence.

An entire chapter of Wallace's biography of Gidney was devoted to the subject under the heading 'Armageddon—Britain's socialist envoy', outlining Gidney's fateful interactions with Cripps.[162] Gidney composed 'letters and memoranda', stressing the need of the 'minor minorities' for representation in the Constituent Assembly tasked with drafting the new constitution.[163] In the year of Cripps's mission, Gidney lost control of the agenda of a large conference in Calcutta. Invoking the biblical exodus of the Israelites from Egypt, the Reverend J. A. H. Bower advocated 'the mass emigration of Anglo-Indians'. 'Well may Gidney have asked: "Where is the promised land?",' commented Wallace.[164] The Calcutta faction won the backing of the Anglican Bishop of Calcutta and Metropolitan of India, who 'undertook to write [to] the Archbishop of Canterbury' endorsing a 'financially aided' scheme.[165] Their hopes of petitioning Cripps on the same basis, however, were pre-empted by Gidney's own request for a land grant 'of 200,000 acres' within India, preferably centred on the existing 'McCluskiegunge' colony, to form the nucleus of an Anglo-Indian state.[166]

It was still far from evident that a prospective Pakistan would not become part of an Indian federation, and Gidney argued that 'if Muslims, despite their numbers and the advantageous position they occupy in two provinces, feel the need for separation, we submit that a racial minority, such as is the Anglo-Indian community, one which occupies a peculiarly disadvantageous position in India, deserves similar consideration and so do all other minority communities'.[167] Gidney presented the stark alternatives of leaving behind a prospering 'Anglo-Indian community ... as proud standard bearers of the Great British nation and its connection with India', and offering 'her offspring' for 'annihilation ... as her sacrifice on the altar of India's political expediency'—'Great Britain's bankrupt legacy to this country'.[168] As Wallace astutely reflected, approaching Cripps along these emotive lines, Gidney was 'doomed to disappointment ... Cripps could give him no hopes, no assurances, no promises; the Anglo-Indian just did not enter into his scheme of things ... Gidney was accustomed to dealing with British Conservatives and Liberals, he understood them, their sympathies and ways, but a British socialist was something totally different, and socialism Gidney abhorred.'[169] 'A general sigh of relief went up, not only from certain Anglo-Indians, when it was found the negotiations between ... Cripps, Congress and the Muslim League had failed. One speaker said in public [that] it was providential.'[170] Gidney understood it to be only a temporary reprieve. Wallace describes Gidney as

> fighting a rearguard action ... It would seem that he intended making another journey to England. I think he felt momentarily defeated ... [Gidney] was losing his grip on things—the tragic end of a trusted lieutenant ... Disappointment in ... [others he had elevated,] troubles over McCluskiegunge, a mass meeting in Calcutta that for once he failed to control, the strain of work, the pessimism following his interview with ... Cripps, all these were taking their toll. They say in

Sanskrit that worry consumes more than does the funeral flame. In his last letter to me Gidney wrote: 'I shall spend all my life working for an ungenerous and ungrateful community. But let me not complain, for after all, I feel that God is helping me. My health has certainly given me cause for grave concern, and I feel the daily increasing burden of my responsibility is fast bending me. Anyhow, I would rather bust than rust and ... so I still have my hand on the communal plough till I am called to my ever rest.'[171]

That moment came on the morning of 5 May 1942 at the age of sixty-eight, just twenty-three days after Cripps's departure. Gidney's last broadcast to the community was described as the 'last S.O.S. of despair' from 'a man who [had] never before admitted defeat'.[172] Frank Anthony—the man who would succeed Gidney—was, at the time, a relatively unknown lawyer and 'elected President of the local branch' of the Association in his home town of Jubbulpore, which, being a major railway junction, had 'a large-ish Anglo-Indian community'.[173]

The fortunes of war

The service of Anglo-Indians and the closely intertwined and overlapping Anglo-Burman group during the Second World War is a subject so vast that it really deserves its own book. That work would have to cover the role of the men and women of these communities in manning the railways, nursing stations, telegraph offices and wireless telephone exchanges right up to the last moments of the Japanese advance; the even more harrowing story of the overland trek to India on which so many died; the targeted and cruel internment of many among the mixed who did not manage to escape; and the return of individual fighting men not only with the regular British forces, but with small commando-style American OSS units. These disproportionately recruited from the mixed to take advantage of their familiarity with Burma and the complexions of those with a chance of successfully passing as Asians or Burmese in order to avoid detection behind enemy lines. In the meantime, an excellent summary covering much of their wartime record is set forth in an article by Mains, who was posted to Rangoon as assistant military governor in an early phase of the war, and who later recounted his dramatic escape back to India in March 1942. Mains reflects that amid wholesale desertion by other railway staff, the trains which were used to ferry military forces back and forth almost up to the front line of fighting could not have been kept going without their Anglo-Indian and Anglo-Burman drivers and firemen. Mains asserts that, in spite of supposed restrictions, even in peacetime Anglo-Indians who were not 'of a very dark complexion' managed to enlist, and that 'a sizeable number were commissioned into the Indian Army either as British or Emergency Commissioned Officers' once war broke out.[174]

The Second World War generally meant new and enlarged opportunities, with the prospect of close to full employment for Anglo-Indians, who once again volunteered enthusiastically for service in British, Commonwealth and Indian Army regiments, in nursing, auxiliary and support units. Rather than attempting to capture the full range of Anglo-Indians' wartime service, we must confine ourselves here to a few salient issues, many similar to those the community had faced in the First World War. Despite racial and colour discrimination impacting upon recruitment and promotion prospects, and creating moments of individual alienation, for the vast majority military service reinforced and amplified empire loyalism, monarchism, and persisting patriotic identification with Britishness. Anthony's *Review* castigated

> this fetish of wanting to join 'Royal' instead of 'Indian' Corps. Many misguided lads prefer to join the R.A.F. [Royal Air Force] as private[s], than to get a commission in the I.A.F. [Indian Air Force.] Very often, the parents pander to the foolish notion that there is greater prestige attaching to a unit with the prefix 'Royal' than to an 'Indian' Corps.[175]

The manpower requirements of wartime recruitment meant that many were openly or tacitly accepted into branches of military service which had been barred to them on grounds of colour and race in peacetime. However, it was still often necessary for individuals to engage in passing in order to enter more prestigious and better-paid services, and yet again some travelled to Britain to do so. Lamenting that 'the credit of all their achievements' would be 'lost ... to the European community',[176] Anthony estimated that 'between three and five thousand members of the Community are serving with the R.A.F. in England'.[177] They included Flight Lieutenant Dyson

(Abbott's grandson), who set a 'record for the largest numbers of aeroplanes shot down in a single aerial combat ... 6 Italian planes in 15 minutes in the Middle East ... [and Flight Lieutenant] Daniell [*sic*], the son of a former member of the Governing Body, [who] won the D.F.M. [Distinguished Flying Medal], as a Flight Sergeant and then the D.F.C. [Distinguished Flying Cross] as a pilot officer'.[178]

In India the RAF was keen to recruit Anglo-Indians but only for technical support roles. During the first two months of 1943 alone, thirty-five Anglo-Indians and Domiciled Europeans signed up, including eleven flight mechanics, nine wireless operators and miscellaneous other technical support staff such as fitters, welders and electricians.[179] When, in December 1942, two brothers from Calcutta, R. A. and I. H. Wells, who believed they had enlisted for training as pilots and aircrew, having been 'medically examined according to R.A.F. standards and [been] found fit',[180] reported to the RAF base at Kankinara as instructed by the 'Technical Recruiting Officer Calcutta', they discovered they were ineligible as non-Europeans.[181] As Air Headquarters India instructed by postgram: 'if the Wells brothers are European then they are eligible ... for aircrew duties ... If you have any doubt as to whether they are Anglo-Indian or not ask them if they are subject to the National Service Act. If they are then they are Europeans. From your letter however the impression is given that the Wells brothers are Anglo-Indians.'[182]

In practice this must have operated as a colour test, in which if a Domiciled European or fair-complexioned Anglo-Indian had shown up, they would have been cleared for flight training. Variable outcomes on this basis led to repeated disappointments for Anglo-Indians who had successfully passed through one stage of the process but then learned that they would only be trained for technical ground-crew roles. The authorities were willing to allow these individuals to be discharged, in order to prevent the growing discontent from hampering further RAF recruitment of Anglo-Indians in India. Yet even in this climate Anglo-Indians recruited to the IAF sought transfer to the RAF. Anthony tried to persuade Anglo-Indians to prioritise the 'officer cadre of the I.A.F ... [as] perhaps the finest of all openings for our lads', noting in November 1943 'that in the last batch of sixteen I.A.F. officers sent to England six were Anglo-Indians'.[183] Nearly a year later his president-in-chief's page in the *Review* led with 'JOIN THE I.A.F.', emphasising that this 'still comparatively very small' branch of service would keep growing and that 'the lads who secure commissions now ... [would] have the prospect of permanency, more than the officers of any other corps or unit'.[184] However, Anthony also warned Anglo-Indians that they could not enrol as 'Indian Other Ranks' and expect to be granted the British pay scales they enjoyed in the AF(I) or in British units. In practice he worked to improve Anglo-Indian pay and conditions in every branch of service, whether Indian or British. Anthony consistently argued for an equalisation of their position to British standards wherever possible, and used his new platform in the Assembly to berate his European colleagues over

> differential [pay] scales. Europeans were given certain scales. Indian King's Commissioned Officers were given a different scale. The European K.C.O. got a different and higher scale. What was the result? Because of the different emoluments Anglo-Indians were encouraged to make false declarations. I gave ... scores of instances to the military authorities. One brother because he was not prepared to deny his parentage ... got the scales of the Indian K.C.O. The other the renegade, the cheat and the liar, because he made a false declaration, was getting the higher scales ... This is all part of your ... insidious policy of preventing a person who has the courage of his conviction, from achieving a position commensurate with his ability and thereby encouraging renegadism in my community.[185]

Anthony claimed to have

> protested over and over again to the military authorities that their recruiting officers deliberately encouraged and even compelled Anglo-Indians to register themselves as Europeans. I cited case after case. When a boy would go to a recruiting officer and say 'I am an Anglo-Indian' the recruiting officer would say 'Go back. Think over it and come back tomorrow and enrol yourself as a European.' He went back and the next day he was recruited as a European.[186]

Only aged thirty-four upon his nomination to the Central Legislative Assembly, Anthony was told, 'You look like a boy!' by the six-foot-three Scottish Viceroy, Lord Linlithgow, at their first meeting.[187] Nonetheless Linlithgow invited him to serve on his wartime 'National Defence Council'.[188] Here Anthony faced off against the

Commander-in-Chief, Archibald Wavell, who would later replace Linlithgow as Viceroy. Anthony confessed that the two had 'never got on well together'.[189] He believed that 'Wavell had a chip on his shoulder' because he had risen 'from the ranks',[190] thereby inverting the usual dismissive comment Britons so often made about Anglo-Indians 'having chips on their shoulders' and suffering from 'inferiority complexes'.[191] As he had done in the Assembly, Anthony kept hammering at the point of the discriminatory pay scales between British and Indian officers, which was no doubt music to the ears of the Council's other Indian members, despite their being 'Maharajahs' and hand-picked 'political leaders'.[192] He used this wider issue as a wedge to highlight the incentivisation of passing:

> I said ... 'General Wavell, I don't think you know the full truth ... I will give you at least six examples, one Anglo-Indian, the browner type, who's got a commission as a British officer, in the role of a renegade, getting twice as much as his fairer brother, who refused to be a renegade.' ... And overnight, because Linlithgow supported me, the discrimination was done away with. The salaries were equated ... I used to criticise Wavell quite a lot. And ... his wife. She ... acted, fortunately only temporarily ... as the head of the ... WACs, Women's Auxiliary Corps [India] ... Now 80% of those women were Anglo-Indians. There were barely 15% of British people. But ... we had ... second Lieutenants, but all the upper ranks were only British. So I raised that ... and I criticised her ... Lady Wavell had a chip on her shoulder like her husband. I said 'Why do you do it?' She said 'Why do I do it?' I said 'Yes, why do you do it? Some of these Anglo-Indian women can eat the heads off your British women. They were maids ... in their own country, they've married some British officers and come out here, you've made them Captains and Majors, but you won't allow the Anglo-Indians to be more than Lieutenants.' So there again Linlithgow helped and a large percentage of Anglo-Indian women were put in. Of course ... with independence the Anglo-Indians ... came right to the top ... About ... eight years after independence, the head of the nursing service ... [with the] rank of Brigadier was always an Anglo-Indian, because the Anglo-Indians had almost monopolised the nursing services.[193]

The British 'decision ... to disband the W.A.C.(I)' upon the war's conclusion came as a 'direct blow' to Anglo-Indian women, especially given assurances that Anthony had received from 'Indian leaders ...

that they would welcome the permanent retention of a nucleus of this Corps, provided European control and consequent racial discrimination ... [were] done away with'.[194] A similarly petty postwar decision came in a letter from the Commander-in-Chief 'stating that Anglo Indians could not be given special rations represent[ing] ... an attitude which ... [Anthony felt that] even Indian leaders would not have taken up'.[195] Although he might have been overlooked in any event, perhaps this personal enmity with the Wavells played a role in Anthony's not being invited to the Simla Conference of 1945. Anthony responded to this bitter blow with a lengthy, panic-stricken and desperately pleading telegram to London, in which he asserted that 'Indian leaders [had] already granted [the] community [a] separate seat in the central cabinet' through their endorsement of the Sapru Report, and emphasising Anglo-Indians' gargantuan contribution to the war effort out of all proportion to the size of the community.[196] Anthony also blamed Wavell for having 'ignored' a Congress proposal that he be given a place in the Interim Government, in his first letter to Wavell's successor, the final Viceroy, Lord Louis Mountbatten.[197] Wavell's diary reveals that he repeatedly considered including an Anglo-Indian in his Council in 1946,[198] but decided to appoint 'a Parsee, Sir N. P. Engineer' instead.[199] Wavell later concluded that 'perhaps Engineer was a mistake. If Anthony had been suitable it would have been better to include an Anglo-Indian.'[200]

Diverging allegiances

In January 1938, Subhas Chandra Bose returned from a two-month vacation in Austria, to take up his position as president-elect of the Congress. From the radical hard-socialist wing of the party, he advocated use of force to expel the British from India, thus putting him at immediate loggerheads with Gandhi's non-violent *ahimsa* ideals and non-cooperationist *satyagraha* methods. The secular Nehru was only pragmatically aligned with his mentor's religiously inspired notions, having flirted with the possibility of violent revolution. Yet although their socialisms overlapped, Bose posed a direct political threat to Nehru, and as Bose became increasingly authoritarian, Nehru developed a growing respect for democratic ideals and ultimately concluded that a transfer of the apparatus of state machinery was desirable if this could be achieved constitutionally. Bose's election thus caused a deep split within the Congress, which was only resolved when he was forced out of the leadership in April 1939. On the preceding 5 February, at Congress's Bengal Provincial Conference, Bose

> expressed jubilation ... that for the first time ... the members of the Anglo-Indian community are interesting themselves in the Congress movement [and] enrolling themselves as Congress members ... British imperialism in India rest[s] ... on [the] unstinted support it receive[s] ... from the ... Anglo-Indians, the Gurkhas, the Punjabis and ... the Sikhs ... [Sikhs are] no longer regarded [as] safe for the maintenance of ... British imperialism ... The Nepalese were no longer to be lulled into ignoring India's demand. Similar was the growing attitude of the Anglo-Indian community.[201]

Given the actual state of affairs at this moment, this could only have been a cynical attempt at political persuasion, if it was not pure wish-fulfilment. Yet Bose was certainly making the best propaganda use of the speaker who had preceded him, an Anglo-Indian provincial leader from the Punjab named Cecil Edward Gibbon, who had joined the Congress Party and addressed the gathering in a khadi sherwani, or homespun Indian frock coat, to say 'that the Anglo-Indian community was now being convinced that its interests lay with the progress of Mother India rather than with that of England ... [and] asked for toleration of the slowness of the progress of the Congress movement among the Anglo-Indian community ... [asserting his belief] that if not to-day but by tomorrow they would be in the first line of defence in safeguarding India's interest by becoming the rank and file of the Congress'.[202]

A month later, according to Kalsoom Hanif and Muhammad Iqbal Chawla, 'Gibbon addressed a public meeting ... where he asked communists to join the Congress in large numbers' to remould it 'on more human lines' and turn it into an 'innovative body determined to protect the complete freedom of our Motherland purged of spiritualism'.[203] Given that he would also 'demand freedom for propagation of religion' as a Congress-nominated member of the Constituent Assembly tasked with drawing up a constitution for independent India after the war,[204] this may have been a merely tactical move, but such flexibility in supporting communist entryism would most likely have endeared Gibbon to Bose. His address to yet another meeting at Simla in November 1946, arguing 'that the education of the Anglo-Indian youths should be on purely nationalist lines', might lead us to assume that his future in the Congress was certain.[205] However, Gibbon happened to have been introduced to Jinnah by Gidney as early as 1935, and by May 1946 Gibbon had decided that the best interests of his Anglo-Indian constituents in the Punjab would be for the province to remain undivided and go to Pakistan, thereby creating an immediate rupture with both the Congress and Anthony's All-India Anglo-Indian Association, a story we shall return to in the next chapter.

After his term as Congress president, Bose would also take a series of similarly dramatic steps. With the onset of the Second World War in Europe, he was arrested, released and then kept under surveillance by the British for organising protests in Calcutta. Escaping via Afghanistan, he arrived in Moscow and sought Soviet support for an anti-British uprising. Disappointed by the Russian response, Bose next travelled to Berlin, where the Nazis allowed him to set up his first Indian Legion from captured Indian prisoners of war. Incidentally, at least one Anglo-Indian, a former signaller for the Telegraphs Department in Madras who had been sent to work in Iraq and who became 'a confidential clerk to the Resident Director' of the Anglo-Persian Oil Company, became 'an admirer of Nazism', after learning to speak 'German fluently', developing friendships with Germans overseas, and making trips to Germany until early 1938.[206] Back in India, he fell under the gaze of colonial intelligence for allegedly hosting 'radio-parties in his house, where local Germans and other foreigners used to collect to hear the Berlin Broadcasts' and have 'discussions ... [in which] he posed as an authority on any subject connected with Germany and expressed pro-Nazi views'.[207] Whether Bose was attracted to anything in the Nazi ideology beyond its model of totalitarian leadership is open to debate, but by 1943 he had come to the conclusion that Germany would not take sufficient practical steps to advance his aims, and he was permitted to depart by U-boat to rendezvous with a Japanese submarine in order to solicit Japanese support for the creation of a more effective Indian National Army (INA).

Again recruiting from Indian prisoners of war, the Japanese sought to control and limit the INA in order to ensure that it would further their own purposes. Nonetheless, it went on to play a significant fighting role against the British and Indian armies in Southeast Asia, Burma and eastern India. Although the British tried their best to keep the INA and the scale of its recruitment secret, the *Statesman*'s editor Ian Stephens recalls one British acquaintance of his 'known for his Indian friendships', who, at a Calcutta evening party in 1943, 'made the ill-received remark that if a Japanese plane parachuted Subhas on to the Maidan next morning, 90% of the city's Bengali inhabitants would rush forth to join him'.[208] The story of the INA has a remarkable intersection with Anglo-India through another of the Stracey brothers, Captain Cyril John Stracey, who was able to rise to the rank of colonel by becoming a 'senior staff officer in the INA'.[209] Gidney had not lived long enough to hear of this, which was just as well. For, as Wallace commented in his sympathetic but not uncritical biography, given Gidney's 'mendicancy and obsequiousness at times' in expressing 'Anglo-Indian loyalty to the British ... a Col. Stracey in the I.N.A. was beyond his imagination'.[210] There is an added irony, given that Gidney had personally nominated his elder brother Ralph 'for the Lawrence D'Souza I.C.S. scholarship in 1930' and celebrated his successful admission two years later.[211] In 1945–6 their police superintendent brother, Eric, was posted to Bengal to interrogate the 'INA prisoners who had been recaptured in Burma and to that extent I found myself in an opposite camp, as it were, to my brother because he had joined the Army' and gone over to the INA.[212] This took place at

> a main interrogation centre at Jhikargacha, a river village some 70 miles north of Calcutta ... [which] had been requisitioned and turned into a POW camp with barbed-wire enclosures for about 5,000 prisoners. There were a few pukka buildings ... [for] the officers ... The rest of the camp, including a battalion of the Burma Rifles for guard duties and a large commissariat made do in huts, bashas or tents ... Most of the INA prisoners had already passed through forward interrogation centres (FICs) behind the battle line and were awaiting a decision on their fate ... The OC [Officer Commanding] had hardly finished greeting me on the first day when he asked: 'Are you the brother of Colonel Stracey of the INA?' I was not as surprised as I might have been for I had already got hint, from a broadcast of his from Saigon, that my brother ... had joined Bose's INA. For an

Anglo-Indian to have done so was unique and I soon had a number of officers around me to make my acquaintance and find out what sort of family had produced this. I was, of course, immediately in good standing with the INA officers of the camp ...[213]

Challenged by an interviewer on this 'irony in your family's history', Eric understatedly commented that 'it was a very interesting state, of course'[214]—especially seeing, as their elder brother Ralph reflected, that

> my mother was one of those who practically worshipped the British Royal family and had many souvenirs of their photographs ... in her album. My brother [Cyril] went into the Indian Army by competition to Dehra Dun where the Indian Military Academy was, and then joined the First 14th Punjab Regiment. They were posted in Malay when the Jap[anese][215] ... swooped down on them and they found that the backing from the British Regiments and the Australian Regiments was just not there ... Anyway, he was taken a prisoner by the Jap[anese] ... and after some months he joined the Indian National Army ... He reached the rank of Adjutant General, Colonel in that Army.[216]

According to Stracey's own retrospective account, upon being captured in what was then Malaya,

> along with me there was a British officer ... and we were taken to Alor Setar town where immediately the Japanese officers in charge ... decided that the Indian element of this little group ... should be separated from the British ... And in that process I also was put on one side along with the British officer. And my orderly said 'Oh, but no, my Sahib is an Indian'. The Japanese had probably looked at my face and ... colour and thought I was British. Well this Japanese officer decided to leave me with the Indians ... and then I met a co-officer of mine, Capt. Mohan Sing ... and I said 'I'm glad to see you. What has happened?' He said 'Well I was also captured ... and now, as you have referred to the flag of the Indian National Congress fluttering over this building I will tell you a moment later what all this is about.' ... [He] then explained ... that a group of Indians under the leadership of an old revolutionary ... [Rash Behari] Bose [had] ... come down to the headquarters of the victorious general ... [Yamashita] and ... proposed to him that he should found an Indian National Army alongside the Japanese Army to fight the British and eventually make them leave India.[217]

Stracey claimed that he did not actually sign up to this first incarnation of the INA until November 1942 once they were in Singapore, but his British interrogators believed he had already defected by August.[218] By the war's end Stracey was 'Second in Command' to Major-General Zaman Kiani, whom Bose had put in charge of all INA 'troops in Singapore'.[219] However, after landing in Singapore, Allied military authorities prioritised apprehending Stracey, who recalled

> a young British Major and a young Indian Lieutenant ... [arriving and] ask[ing] who were all the officers in the camp ... [General] Kiani said 'Well speak to Colonel Stracey and he will give you the names of the officers.' And when he reached my name which was about third or fourth on the list ... this young Major stopped writing and I said 'Don't you want to know who these others are?' and he said 'Oh yes, we'll get the list alright'. And actually they were looking for me. And that afternoon a group of three officers from the Counter Intelligence ... all Colonels ... a Britisher ... an Australian and ... an American, they ... called my name out and I responded. Then they said 'Will you please get a blanket roll and come with us?' And I said 'Oh?' and they said 'Yes, we want you to come with us to our Headquarters'. I said 'Well, I must go and report to my Senior Officer.' ... General Kian[i] ... hadn't much to say about it. I think he felt himself rather helpless ... General Alagapin and Colonel Khasli who were living with me in the adjoining house ... were all in tears ... wondering what was to be my fate ... I was placed in a cell [in Pearl's Hill Gaol] without any clothing and no blanket ... wondering why I had been picked out, and of course I realized why, because I was an Anglo-Indian and they didn't expect an Anglo-Indian to do what I had done ...[220]

Peter Fay similarly concluded that 'what must have puzzled and eventually infuriated his captors' was that Stracey, whom they believed to be the 'chief' among those responsible for 'torture in the interrogation of suspects' and allied prisoners during his time running 'the Adjutant-General's branch at Singapore INA Headquarters', was of 'fair complexion and excellent connections (one brother with the forest service, another with the police, a third in the ICS)'.[221] The eldest 'brother [who had] successfully entered ... the Imperial Forest Service in 1928' is the only one we have not yet encountered.[222] While conceding his 'thorough ideological conversion', they accused Stracey of having defected 'from motives of greed, ambition and pleasure-seeking'.[223] Stracey would later claim that he had wrestled with the question where his ultimate allegiance should lie with a view to posterity and the postcolonial future of his fellow Anglo-Indians:

> My own feelings were awfully confused. I think that I belonged to the more conservative type of Indian officer who felt that you suddenly can't make this big change in dealing with your erst-while enemy ... And ... I tried to solicit the opinions of these junior Indian officers and N.C.O.s ... A number of them were as confused as myself, but one or two were prepared to go along heartily with Mohan Singh ... [and after] the Japanese moved us ... and finally we and two other Anglo-Indian officers and one or two Anglo-Indian N.C.O.s were taken to Singapore ... in November 1942 ... into a camp where there were a number of Indian Army Transport drivers ... [working] for the Japanese Command ... to supply the huge Changi Camp ... This Indian officer who came from one of the state units, he knew me earlier and was awfully pleased to see me, and we were on first-name basis. He said 'Well now, Cyril, I think it is high time that you came and joined us'. I then consulted with my other two Anglo-Indian colleagues. One of them was orthodox and he said 'I'm not going to touch this at all'. The other one ... asked to be sent to his own Hyderabad Regiment which was also in Singapore in one of the camps ... [while] I asked them as to what role any Anglo-Indian is going to play in this new movement ... And I said that I think one of us should be in the I.N.A. 'Times have changed and we have a duty to perform, if not in the distant future, about any significant participation in the actual struggle in India then at least among the Indian prisoners of war because they need officers with a sane and sober view to see that everything went well and that we also can one day say that we have played our part along with our Indian comrades for whatever India is aspiring for.'[224]

At Stracey's last meeting with Bose on the morning of 15 August 1945, before the radio announcement of Japan's surrender, Bose commissioned him to erect a 'memorial to the fallen heroes of the INA'.[225] Bose asked whether this could be done 'before the British make a landing'. Stracey replied, 'Certainly, Sir,' with a salute and a 'Jai Hind', before marching 'off to build [it] in record time'.[226] However, upon arriving in Singapore, Mountbatten, then Supreme Allied Commander South-East Asia, promptly ordered its demolition. Bose's dramatic death, around which rumours and conspiracy theories have never ceased, in an overloaded bomber aircraft which crashed in Japanese-occupied Taiwan, provided a convenient means for Nehru and the Congress leaders to co-opt the story of the INA without facing its full implications for their own entirely contrary approach. Condemning the INA trials was more straightforward than contending with the triumphant return from exile of a military hero who had aimed to lead the nation. Relying on the revulsion towards the INA they believed to be widespread within the Indian Army, the British hoped that convicting and executing INA officers as traitors would establish and anchor their desired narrative. As Stracey recalls, this strategy backfired spectacularly under the pressure of wider public opinion:

> This was the big trial of officers ... captured in Burma ... before the eastern part of the War was over. These officers were ... defended by a panel of eminent Indian lawyers headed by Vallabhbhai Patel who was a great lawyer in Bombay. Well, it was fortunate that this trial happened because the whole story of the INA came out ...
>
> [Before we were] lodged in the Red Fort ... [in Delhi for] interrogations ... Mahatma Gandhi, Mr. Nehru, Sardar Patel, Maulana Azad, Asaf Ali and others had all visited us. And on one very early occasion Mr. Nehru put his arm around me and he said 'Well you know I have heard all about you but you can go home one day and tell your people that if you lose your job in the Indian Army you shall get one back when we are independent for I shall take you into the Indian Foreign Service.' ... There was a settlement between Mahatma Gandhi and the Viceroy, and the British ... [were persuaded that] it was foolish to continue these trials ... So they ... start[ed] releasing us ... [I was] released in April 1946 and ... was [then] able to ... go home and to meet my mother in Bangalore whom I had not seen for five years.[227]

What passed at this emotionally charged meeting between a stereotypically arch-royalist Anglo-Indian mother and her Indian nationalist revolutionary son, just reprieved from execution for treason against the King-Emperor, can only be imagined. With the vast majority of Anglo-Indians patriotically supporting Britain's imperial war effort, Stracey's actions and choices would have been surprising, even horrifying, to the sensibilities of a great many of his fellow Anglo-Indians. Yet presumably Stracey left some impact on the Indian nationalist perspective towards Anglo-Indians. Ralph details how

Nehru lived up to his promise, with a fascinating account of his brother's subsequent career:

> my brother was at least a free man but without any money because he was out of the Indian Army and didn't even get his prisoner of war pay. Later he became the Secretary of the Indian National Army Committee in Delhi and persuaded Nehru and Patel to grant something like thirty Lakhs of rupees … to the ex-Indian Army personnel who had joined the INA. He then was sent on assignment to Abyssinia … [in] the Foreign Service and has been posted in many countries … He was Consul General at San Francisco; a Counsellor at the Indian Embassy at New York … chargé d'affaires at the Indian Embassy in Paris, [spent] four years at Bonn, and his last appointment before retiring this year [1973] was as Indian Ambassador to Finland.[228]

5

THE END OF ANGLO-INDIA?

The hats we wear

When Paul Scott's fictional English public school-educated and almost wholly anglicised Harry Coomar finds himself invisible and unnoticed by his British school friend, now a British Army officer, in a chance encounter at a cricket match, he spends an evening with some Indian friends drinking heavily to forget his sense of hurt. His transformation (or 'reversion') into Hari Kumar, a 'good Indian', is symbolised by the destruction of his topi: 'The topee was a joke to them ... They said only Anglo-Indians and Government toadies and old-fashioned sahibs wore topees. So we burned mine.'[1] The topi was the symbolic antithesis of the white khadi pointed sidecap or 'Gandhi cap' popularised among Indian nationalists during the non-cooperation movement of 1920–2. Topi-wearing also serves as a leitmotif for the Anglo-Indians in *Bhowani Junction*, with the stereotypical Anglo-Indian railwayman Patrick wearing 'his topi all day and most of the night, to show he was not an Indian'.[2] Patrick expresses dismay after encountering Victoria without her topi in the midday sun. He greets her response that she never wears one, with exasperation that she 'will get all brown!', to which she retorts, 'It isn't sunburn that makes us brown, is it?'[3] A similar scene takes place in *Queenie*, where the young child representing Merle Oberon is scolded for ignoring repeated instructions to put on her topi, made to repeat a rote-learned answer that the sun will darken her skin, and reminded that only 'natives go hatless in the sun'.[4]

Colonial Britons had long been fastidious topi-wearers; every man was expected to don one once their ship passed through the Suez Canal, and a tradition developed of casting them into the sea at this point on the homeward journey. Bishop Lesslie Newbigin of the Church of South India perceptively noted that the topi was 'the white tribe's fetish. And if you didn't wear a topee then you were not part of the tribe', you were 'a cad ... [who] had gone native'.[5] Yet the practical exigencies of the Second World War and the experience of desert warfare in North Africa led to a dramatic U-turn: 'One day it was a military offence to go out without a topee and the next day it was a military offence to go out with one. And so then all the rest of us ... with great relief threw away our topees. But the Anglo-Indians stuck to them because you see their identity is bound up with the topee.'[6] Jinnah's wearing of a topi as late as the Simla Conference of 1945, rather than the fur qaraqul (or karakul) he was persuaded to adopt to appeal to Muslim crowds, could be read as signalling not only his own sartorially anglophile tastes, but his desire to appeal to a British audience. Frank Anthony would similarly pose in a three-piece suit, topi in hand, for a portrait on the cover of his emotively titled pamphlet *Will Britain Tarnish Her Honour?* (1943). Such seemingly small choices remained deeply symbolic in an era of rising sartorial nationalism, amid attacks on Europeans and fellow Indians in the streets for wearing topis and European-style suits and ties during the Quit India movement of 1942.

Nissen recounts how 'walking down Chowringhee I had my topee taken off, and jumped upon, and smashed ... I had my tie taken off and thrown on the ground ... [and] all around the boundary wall of my house ... [in] big letters ... [they daubed] Quit India, Quit India'.[7] In 'WHY QUIT INDIA?' an Anglo-Indian regional member of the Legislative Assembly (MLA) condemned the targeting of anyone wearing 'trousers ... a coat or a neck tie or a topi or frock ... for maltreatment in any outburst of anti-British feelings', arguing that, as 'many ... Bengalis, Beharis, Punjabis, Marwaris etc. ... [also adopt] European fashion', 'dress' could provide 'no test' of nationalism.[8] In a letter to the *Statesman*, Abdul Haji recounted how recent disturbances, [and] hooliganism … was characterized by the absurd notion that every person who wore a topee or a necktie was a British Imperialist. I, a Punjabi … was on that unpropitious day in European dress. An emotional mob relieved me of my topee by setting fire to it. I was then coerced into taking off my necktie and pulling my shirt over my trousers … [while] an English friend who had recently come out to India but … wore no topee or necktie, was allowed to pass peacefully. The national movement has degenerated into mob violence. Indian and Chinese establishments … were damaged by rioters … Dress is no criterion of a person's national spirit, and I am certain many Anglo-Indians were abused and insulted because of their European dress, while Col. C. J. Stracey, an Anglo-Indian in the I.N.A. is … facing trial.[9]

The tables were turning on the 'British authorities … [who had previously] clamp[ed] down on Gandhi cap-wearers by dismissing them from government jobs, fining them and at times physically beating them'.[10] Anglo-Indians were particularly vulnerable as representative stand-ins for British oppressors. At the beginning of 1947 the *Review* pushed back forcefully against the common Indian charge that Anglo-Indians were

> living unnatural lives and aping the European. Nothing is further from the truth. We Anglo-Indians have a mother-tongue that the first Anglo-Indian to be created in India had, and the same would apply to our religion, our dress and our customs. Our culture is therefore traditional and not an aped culture. The accusation would apply more to those of other Indian Communities who vie with each other in dressing in European fashion and speaking in English. It is they who are living unnatural lives and aping the European, not we … Whenever Anglo-Indians are goaded by … such remarks this paragraph will help them to give a suitable retort. We can maintain our traditional culture and yet be as good Indians as those of other communities.[11]

This was essential to Anthony's communal nationalist formula—Anglo-Indian by community, Indian by nationality—as he sought to reassure his flock that the maintenance of their sartorial, cultural, religious and linguistic freedoms was entirely compatible with their acceptance of Indian nationality and citizenship and wholehearted embrace of India as their home. Anthony's uphill task of winning over his constituents to this vision was not aided by calls from Shri B. Das in 1949 in the Constituent Assembly, tasked with drawing up the Indian constitution, for 'anybody' wearing 'foreign dress' or, at the very least, anybody 'in the employment of the State' to 'be debarred from doing it ... by legislation'—unthinkable and outrageous demands to most Anglo-Indians at the time.[12] However, in the decades that followed, some Anglo-Indians, particularly women, found it necessary to make cultural accommodations in the workplace by, for example, switching from frocks and skirts to saris. During those same years, however, there were repeated waves of Anglo-Indian emigration. Although dress was but one of the emotive issues contributing to this 'exodus', with material concerns for the future of their children in education and employment weighing more heavily in most cases, pressures to sartorially and linguistically Indianise themselves prompted cultural resistance to any abandonment of their existing outlook, orientation and identity.

Communal nationalism

As early as 1934 Henry Gidney had sought to dissuade Anglo-Indians from emigrating to Britain with the message that 'you are sons and daughters of India. When you say you are proceeding Home you are really saying you are going away from home. Your prosperity depends on how you treat your fellow Indians. Think that you are Indians first and Anglo-Indians afterwards.'[13] Elected as president-in-chief in the wake of Gidney's death in late 1942, Anthony gave a 'maiden speech' in December that went much further, triggering a firestorm. From Lahore, Edward Few, MLA in Punjab (1937–45) and president of the Punjab branch, accused Anthony of adopting a pro-Indian or pro-Congress position in a letter he circulated to other branches.[14] Accusing Few of 'a gross misrepresentation', the Governing Body denied Anthony's new approach was 'pro-this or pro-that but only pro-Anglo-Indian—the policy of enlisting maximum help from and friendship of all communities, Indian and European'.[15] At the next meeting Few insisted 'that the policy of the Association should be pro-Government and pro-British', and only withdrew his motion on Anthony's assurance 'that his policy was certainly not "pro-Congress" or "pro-Muslim League"', for any such 'alignment would be unwise and incorrect at this juncture', and 'that we as a Community must naturally support the Government', as they were doing through 'the great part the Community … [was] playing in the war effort'.[16] Anthony subsequently characterised Few as having 'moved a vote of no confidence against me for postulating that we are Indians. He didn't want the community to be referred to as Indians.'[17]

At the Association's AGM, Anthony emphasised the unexpectedly 'hopeless situation with which we were confronted when Cripps came to this country'. 'If those proposals had been accepted we would have been caught of[f] both legs', facing economic 'extinction'.[18] The year 1943 had begun with his whistle-stop tour of twenty-one Association branches across South India, Bengal and Bihar in just over a month, with speeches everywhere he went.[19] At Bangalore, Anthony presented 'the future for Anglo-Indians as grim of prospect', complaining that 'Bangalore could and should be one of the main bulwarks of Anglo-India' but for so many preferring 'to stay without the Association and criticise those who are elected to office'.[20] The *Daily Post* blamed the slow 'awakening to reality' on internal 'quarrel[s] … personal and petty jealousies … rivalries … prejudices … [and] complexes of colour, pay and pension grade'.[21] Declaring that 'the community cannot be too often or too severely provoked', it 'welcomed' Anthony's 'provoking agency', insisting that 'his frankness and outspokenness [were] generally appreciated'.[22] Told by critics 'outside the fold of the Association' that he was 'preaching defeatism', Anthony described himself as 'a stern realist', stressing the need to 'act in a spirit of the most intense realism'.[23] Faced with widespread intransigence among the older generation, Anthony redirected much of his energy towards the young and persuadable. The *Review*'s March editorial heralded the dawn of 'MILITANT YOUNG ANGLO-INDIA'.[24]

> In welcoming Mr. Anthony to … Bandikui … Mr. Atkins, the young and ardently enthusiastic [Branch] President … referred to the part which 'militant young Anglo-India' is now playing … In this phrase he struck a chord which was touched upon by Mr. Anthony in addressing the meeting. Militant young Anglo-India is now on the march. Our younger standard bearers are infusing a new spirit and new energy into the Association. Their enthusiasm and zeal are inspir-

ing ... Young men ... are awakening increasingly to the needs of Anglo-Indians ... in the immediate future ... [and] harnessing a new spirit to Anglo-Indian communa[l] affairs ... The young women ... are lagging behind ... But we feel sure that militant Anglo-India will attract increasingly into its fold the younger women ... to occupy an honoured place in the future India ... We want real and enthusiastic workers. Young Anglo-Indian men and women[,] we have a proud history as a community. We have our culture and heritage to preserve. You can help us build for ourselves a substantial place in the future India.[25]

In a pamphlet directed towards a British audience, Anthony described himself 'as a liberal and a nationalist' disillusioned by communalism having 'become more intense than ever before'.[26] He described the concept 'of a common nationality' with every citizen being 'judged on merit alone, irrespective of caste or creed ... [as] still a distant ideal', given that 'most, if not all, of the leaders, however idealistic their professions', were still 'ardent and incurable communalists'.[27] Ethno-religious 'intolerance' stalked the land, threatening Anglo-Indians with 'the sectarian claims of larger communal bodies, which might seek to overrun us at any time'.[28] Testifying before the Sapru Conciliation Committee of 1944–5, he courted an influential body of Indian nationalist opinion, separated from, but in close sympathy with, the aims of the Congress Party. His rejection of the Muslim League's demand for partition or any 'Balkanising of India' was prompted by fears that the difficulties of 'the minorities would be as acute, perhaps much more acute, in both Pakistan and Hindustan', and would result in 'the probability, if not the certainty, of war between Hindustan and Pakistan and ... the propagation of narrow and fanatical economic and political ideologies'.[29] Anthony won over Sapru's Committee sufficiently for them to sympathetically conclude 'that the Anglo-Indian Community must ... elect to be treated under the future Constitution as an integral part of the Indian Community and if they do so, they must receive adequate protection in all matters affecting their position, e.g. representation in the Legislature, the Executive and the Services, etc.'[30]

Stanley Henry Prater, Bombay MLA and president of the Bombay branch, believed this 'very accommodating' approach could provide a window of 'five years' for 'the Anglo-Indian Community to prepare itself for the new India that was in the making'.[31] Invited to address the 'mainly' Anglo-Indian 'staff of the Barnes High School, Deolali,' and other 'members of the community' gathered to create a new branch in March 1946, Prater 'urged that Anglo-Indians should associate themselves more with Indians and things Indian, rather than continue to adopt a British outlook', declaring 'it imperative for the Community to throw in its lot with the Indians'.[32] In another 'lightning tour of Bengal … [and] South India' ahead of the provincial elections in January, Anthony had sought to establish a united front among the community's MLAs.[33] He 'exhorted the Community to vote for the All-India representatives', including the 'Anglo[-]Indian United Group', pledged 'to work not only as a team but within the policy of the All India Association', which went on to win convincingly in all four of the Anglo-Indian separate electorates in Bengal.[34] 'In Madras, the two Association representatives, Messrs Fowler and Fernandez, beat by an overwhelming majority the two candidates put up by the South India Association'. There were similar results in Bombay, where Prater was unopposed, and 'Punjab, [where] Mr. Manuel … defeated Mr. Few'.[35] Anthony's slate candidates were also 'returned unopposed' in the United Provinces, Central Provinces and Bihar.[36]

While the pro-British faction was caught off guard, the *Review* crowed at this 'cent per cent success'.[37] Nonetheless, the surprise political decapitation of leaders like Few did not mean that the sentiments they represented had been vanquished. At no stage on the difficult road ahead would it prove easy for Anthony to bring all or most of his community with him. In the midst of Britain's precipitous and blood-stained retreat from empire, through the chaos and violence of Partition, and for some time thereafter, a great many Anglo-Indians remained diametrically opposed or highly resistant to Anthony's prescription. For the most part they saw being Anglo-Indian as antithetical to being Indian, because they equated culture with citizenship—as indeed many Indian nationalists did. Accordingly, they were adamant that they were not Indians, in any sense. Some of these, especially after emigrating, responded by accusing Anthony of being an Indian Christian posing as an Anglo-Indian. Self-identifying 'Domiciled Europeans' were further alienated by Anthony's moves to collapse their designation entirely into the Anglo-Indian category. In common with a considerable Anglo-Indian faction, they remained implacably conservative in their identity, having been unwilling to go even so far as Gidney had tried to take them. The Second World War had brought the alignment between the bulk of the community and the imperial state to its zenith. The speed of the changes that followed in its wake left many in a state of denial. In his 1947 New Year message, Anthony described how

> the political developments of the past years have come as a shock to some Anglo-Indians ... [who] could never envisage a Government of India for Indians and by Indians. When this burst on to the political scene as a reality, some ... who have not only not identified themselves with the interests of the Country but had remained aloof from their own Community, were caught up in a psychological convulsion ... [becoming] panic-stricken and ... [feeling] they were going to be engulfed immediately in some kind of debacle. Counsels of ... despair have been fairly prevalent: an appreciable number talk vaguely of emigration: *some have already left but I also know that several have already returned. There is no bed of roses or Utopia awaiting anyone in any country.*[38]

Naturally many individuals were apolitical, while others failed to notice the momentous changes taking place around them. Just two months prior to independence, the community's MLA in the United Provinces described

> a section of opinion that believed that somehow and in some way Britain would continue as the ruling power here ... Lulled by this false hope, they were content to remain indifferent and apathetic ... For these people ... there would be a rude awakening ... Their fate would be worse than that of the escapists who were quitting because these people still could not read the 'signs of the times'. .... [Anglo-Indians had] long enjoyed a protected but mistaken existence ... For this ... in a large measure ... Britain was to blame ... [As the] community was the *child* and the *creation* of the British, it was the duty of Britain as a good parent to make adequate provision for the[m] ... before she handed over the reins of government. However, Britain had even failed the Community in this, and they were now faced with the realisation that Britain could not and would not help them ... a grievous and unpardonable act of ingratitude for all the loyal services which Britain had exacted and expected from the Community, during the many cris[es] ... through which she had passed ...[39]

Roy Nissen recalls how the moment of independence almost passed him by:

> I didn't like the idea, of course, of India being taken over by the Indian ... because after all, one has to reluctantly admit that ... my lot ... did hang onto the coat-tails of the British ... and so we were ... treated as part of the British Raj ... I saw the Indian point of view ... this was their country ... but it came quite as a shock I must say ... Right up to ... August 47 ... my lot ... never ... really realised ... how far this business had advanced about handing over India, independence ... and I remember ... cycling to the office every morning ... past the high court, and right on top of the tower ... was the union jack, and ... on that [morning of] 16th of August 1947 [I was] cycling along and I saw the Indian flag up there and really it gave me quite a shock and that was really the first time I really realised that the British were out.[40]

There was thus a curious combination of apathy and anxiety, complacency and panic, everyday living for the moment and deep existential dread concerning the future. Perhaps some found solace in refusing to believe in or acknowledge the direction which events appeared to be taking. Those who had given the matter any thought probably hoped that an incoming Indian government would remain under British influence or supervision, at least at a higher level, under some kind of Dominion status. Yet even the politically engaged and well-informed found it difficult to anticipate the dramatic changes that were to come with independence, or the decisiveness of the rupture.

'Britain's betrayal'

In the midst of far weightier concerns, Anglo-Indians were hardly thought of in the run-up to the disastrously hasty British 'transfer of power'. During the Simla Conference from which Anthony had been excluded, a pivotal general election was held in Britain, in which a large Labour majority government was swept to power, reshaping the prospects and timing of Indian independence entirely. After this, Anthony travelled to London to lobby the incoming Labour Secretary of State for India, Lord Pethick-Lawrence, who cabled General Wavell to report that he had given him 'no undertakings or assurances' but felt that, in spite of Anglo-Indians presumably not qualifying in numerical terms under the Cripps plan, 'they have some right to be heard in regard to the nature of the constitution-making body'.[41] However, on their 'educational problem[s]' Pethick-Lawrence recognised that Britain 'clearly could not include any specific safeguards ... in an Indian-made constitution'.[42] Anthony probably shared the perception that Cripps, who had rejoined the Labour Party in time to enter the cabinet, was particularly insensitive and perhaps even coldly hostile towards those who had supported British rule. The reciprocal side of that relationship, the outmoded concepts that animated men of Gidney's generation in particular, of honour, duty, loyalty, shared history and service on behalf of the empire, moved him not one whit. Perhaps such expressions further alienated him. This was the man to whom Attlee again turned to lead a group of three cabinet ministers to India in March 1946.

Displaying a better understanding of Cripps than his predecessor, Anthony's memorandum to the Cabinet Mission sought to assure them that, despite having been seen as 'the "Standard Bearers" of British Imperialism in India' and 'regarded with distrust and even hostility', Anglo-Indians had now 'proved themselves ready to take their place in the front rank of Indian Nationalism'.[43] To bolster his numerical case for Anglo-Indian 'representation in a Constituent Assembly', Anthony began by condemning the 'financial advantages' which incentivised 'renegadism' by 'so-called Domiciled Europeans' and demanding the complete elimination of 'the term ... from Government usage'.[44] Anthony 'told Cripps ... "Give me one seat. Let me state my special case."'[45] However, Cripps remained unmoved, as Anthony unhappily recalled:

> Cripps ... knew nothing about us, and he said 'But how can I give you representation in the Constituent Assembly?' I said 'Why? We've made a tremendous contribution to this country. You made us standard-bearers of British imperialism ... Politically we're the best hated community in India. And ... we may be 200,000 people but [—]' But, he says 'Our Constituent Assembly will be based on one seat for one million people. How can I give you 500% weightage?' I said 'You can't deal with this in a legal, in an ultra legalistic, statistical kind of way'. But he didn't understand.[46]

Anthony criticised this approach as 'numerical democracy', contending that given 'the present communal divisions in India' it was necessary to give 'weightage' to prevent 'the squeezing out of the smaller minorities and what little chance they may have to secure a rightful place'.[47] Through a detailed analysis of the census data, Anthony's memorandum sought to expose the full extent of passing in support of his earlier contention to the British government that the community's 'real strength' was 'approximately half a million'.[48] It also echoed the two resolutions of the 1942 Calcutta conference which Gidney had enthusiastically taken up—'to request His Majesty's Government for a grant of £10,000,000 to enable us to endow and stabilize Anglo-Indian education' and for 'a grant of about 500,000 acres of land' on which 'to settle thousands of Anglo-Indian ex-soldiers'.[49] Perhaps these were politically or financially unrealistic positions. Yet in Anthony's estimation, Cripps's implacable indifference was responsible for the Mission's failure to support any measure whatsoever for the Anglo-Indians.

Anthony emerged from his meeting with the Mission at Viceroy's House on 10 April 1946 to face a pack of reporters, immaculately dressed in a three-piece pin-striped greyish suit, holding his white topi in one hand and a cigarette in the other. He gave a press conference to 'representatives of numerous newspapers, such as the London Times, the Daily Mail, Reuters, the Associated Press, the United Press, the Statesman, the Bombay Times and the Hindustan Times'.[50] His statement reiterated 'the main points of the memorandum',[51] presumably excluding its 'Origin and History' chapter covering 1678 to the present, which was not limited to Lord Valentia, the Haitian Revolution, prominent personages like Ricketts and Skinner, 'the Mutiny', and both world wars.[52] Nonetheless, the Statesman sympathetically reported: 'It is understood that the memorandum … began by outlining the history of the Anglo-Indian community, which is half a million strong.'[53] Their correspondent emphasised that Anglo-Indians were now 'a nationalist community that had no sectarian leanings', who 'felt … that the best interest of the country would be served by political unity with as strong a centre as possible', and desired that 'plebiscite[s]' should be held in 'the areas concerned' 'before any decision was taken on a division of India'.[54] However, it also quoted Anthony's assurances that 'we shall give to the future administration, whether Congress or Muslim League, the same loyalty and steadfastness that we have exhibited in the past'.[55]

The *Hindustan Times*, edited by Gandhi's son and evidently gratified by Anthony's pleas 'for a strong Centre', commended Anglo-Indians' 'able spokesman' for informing the 'Mission that the community had completely entered the nationalist fold and would be content with such safeguards as it could obtain from its countrymen on grounds of reason and justice'.[56] Noting that Indian Christians had come round to the nationalist position earlier, the newspaper judged that

> the awakening of patriotism among Anglo-Indians has been more recent, but they, too, have nearly fallen into line. The difficulties of this small community are many ... [In] its origin, it was an alien and almost hostile element, but through the pressure of circumstances and wise leadership it has come to feel that it should throw in its lot with the people of India ... [In] their reply to the questionnaire of the Sapru Committee, [Anthony's Association] bitterly complained of the false position in which the Anglo-Indians had been placed through wrong education and step-motherly patronage.[57]

The Mission's failure to secure an agreement once again held out a glimmer of hope of reprieve to Anthony, who returned to London to make a final appeal to the British Government and Parliament:

> I went to the U.K. in '45, I met Attlee and his Cabinet, but there was no rapport. And I met Churchill and ... he placed Rab Butler at my disposal ... and we used to meet every day in the House of Commons over lunch, and a beer or whisky, but the Conservatives were not in power ... [Had] Churchill ... [still been in office] I don't know whether they would have agreed to hand over.[58]

Churchill was evidently still more sympathetic to the Anglo-Indian case, as he was also more supportive of Jinnah and the case for Pakistan. This most likely combined his imperialist desire to hold on to India longer or to offer some less genuine form of self-government, with a residual emotional feeling for those to whom, as loyalists, he felt Britain owed a greater obligation. In the face of an insuperable Labour majority, Churchill's attempts to influence the nature and timing of the British withdrawal were now reduced to warnings that Britain should vindicate national and imperial honour in the process.

Accordingly, as Anthony explained: 'Churchill did his best to help' and Conservatives raised the matter from the opposition benches, but to no avail.[59] Momentarily defeated, Anthony despairingly told a colleague: 'Well, this is the end of the Community.'[60]

Turning to Congress

Feeling let down by the British, Anthony was surprised to receive a much more sympathetic hearing from the Congress high command. Anthony's first meeting was with Gandhi on 10 June 1946 at 'the "Bhangi" (Sweeper) Colony'.[61] Back in 1944, Prater had concluded that presenting the Anglo-Indian case to both Gandhi and Jinnah before the much-anticipated meeting between the two was the Association's 'most important and urgent task'.[62] Prater's good sense in having visited Gandhi within the first month of his release[63] may have helped to pave the way for Anthony. Gandhi gave Anthony 'a long and patient hearing',[64] telling him, 'We have been in jail, but we've been following your [work.]'[65] 'We've read a lot about you, and you seem to have brought your community, where they were almost anti-Indian, you have made them feel that they're Indians.'[66] Greater willingness on Gandhi's part to reconsider his longstanding refusal to recognise Anglo-Indians politically and constitutionally was born of an acknowledgement of Anthony's project to reorient Anglo-Indian identity towards Indian nationalism. Anthony reflected that the Congress leaders recognised this as 'a revolution in our thinking',[67] recalling Gandhi's frank message 'that but for the policies I had pursued during the past 4 years, there would have been little hope of the Anglo-Indian Community receiving any consideration from the leaders of Indian opinion. Gandhiji asked me why the Community wanted recognition as a separate entity: it was an Indian community and Christian, and he felt that it could take its place as part of the Indian Christian Community.'[68] Noting that 'hostile members in the Central Legislature' had previously challenged Gidney on this same point, Anthony explained the differences between the 1935 constitutional definition of an Anglo-Indian and that of an Indian Christian 'in the Indian Succession Act of 1925 ... as a native of India of unmixed Asiatic descent who professed any form of the Christian religion'.[69]

Gidney had sought to downplay the racial question and to portray Anglo-Indians as just another rights-seeking Indian minority. However, since the Sapru Committee, Anthony had increasingly emphasised Anglo-Indians' uniqueness as a racial-linguistic minority in order to distance them from the growing Muslim separatism and militancy, widely blamed upon colonial 'divide and rule' policies. The implication was that concessions to Anglo-Indians could be treated as an exception predicated on their distinct status and particular position, and need not, therefore, be admitted as universally applicable to other larger minorities. Presenting his case to Gandhi, Anthony again dwelt upon Anglo-Indian historical exceptionalism as 'the only real racial-cum-linguistic minority in India. Over a period of 300 years we had evolved into a distinctive, homogen[e]ous entity with our own way of life, our culture and our language, English. I pointed out that the Anglo-Indians would regard any de-recognition of our position as a distinctive minority as a blow at our very existence, which could not be acceptable to the Community.'[70] Given Gandhi's long-stated opposition to racial distinctions and frequent disparagement of history, the arguments themselves may have done less to make Anthony's case than his face-to-face expression of determination and emotive conviction. Yet if Gandhi perceived any value in co-opting Anglo-Indians as a token of enlightened Congress policy towards the minorities, Anthony's closing argument held the best chance of conveying the degree to which any Anglo-Indian leader conceding recognition of their community would be undercutting their own base of support, and probably rendering their own position untenable.

Anthony describes how Gandhi finally turned to the question '"How many seats do you want?" So ... being a lawyer I pitched it at a ceiling, I said "Gandhiji, give me three seats". He said "alright"'[71]— 'I will back you for three seats'.[72] Whether or not he let it show, Anthony must have been momentarily overwhelmed; he had finally been given the chance to make his case to the constitution-making body. Given their various acrimonious exchanges, with Gandhi refusing to recognise Gidney in his representative capacity and Gidney charging that the Mahatma's political non-violence was either naive or disingenuous, Gandhi's subsequent embrace of Anthony towards the end of empire was all the more striking. The very next day Anthony met Nehru, apprehensive that the 'unflattering references to the arrogance of the Anglo-Indians and their overbearing attitude towards other Indian communities' in Nehru's autobiography did not augur well.[73] In his book Nehru had recalled how

> in railway trains compartments were reserved for Europeans ... however crowded the train might be ... I was filled with resentment against the alien rulers of my country who misbehaved in this manner, and whenever an Indian hit back I was glad. Not infrequently one of my cousins ... became personally involved ... One ... loved to pick a quarrel with an Englishman, or more frequently with Eurasians, who, perhaps to show off their oneness with the ruling race, were often even more offensive ... Such quarrels took place especially during railway journeys ... I had no feeling whatever ... against individual Englishmen. I had English governesses and occasionally I saw English friends of my father's visiting him. In my heart I rather admired the English.[74]

Nehru himself had had mixed experiences with Anglo-Indians. During his childhood his sartorially Westernised father, Motilal, a wealthy Allahabad lawyer of Kashmiri Brahmin descent, employed one as a 'housekeeper'.[75] Despite the growing and ardent nationalism that characterised his mature years, Nehru remained, of all the Indian leaders, the most culturally anglicised. English was spoken in his childhood home and, when he went to study in England at fifteen, his father corresponded with him in English. Six years of the best education that money and merit could provide in England led Indian contemporaries in later life to judge Nehru 'too much a gentleman, and worse, an English gentleman'.[76] Of his time in England he recalled, 'I had imbibed most of the prejudices of Harrow and Cambridge and in my likes and dislikes I was perhaps more an Englishman than an Indian.'[77] In seeking to discover India, as the title of one of his extremely learned books termed it, his approach was that of the gentleman scholar-intellectual—the scientist and the socialist. This was not out of keeping with the milieu of the British intelligentsia and the trend of postwar politics in Britain. While Gandhi reinvented himself as an apparently authentic but in fact deeply syncretic incarnation of the quintessential Hindu holy man, a Tolstoyan avatar of

India's labouring peasantry, Nehru remained detached and techno-cratic, seeking to uplift the rural masses materially with a mentality somewhere in-between the most well-meaning of colonial British officials and the radical state-planners of the Soviet Union.

Nehru himself reflected upon his ineradicable cultural hybridity when he stated, 'I have become a queer mixture of East and West, out of place everywhere, at home nowhere ... I am a stranger in the West. I cannot be of it. But in my own country also, sometimes, I have an exile's feeling.'[78] It might be expected that an individual so culturally hybridised would be proximate to a people who embodied a similarly mixed experience and background. At the same time Nehru's elite status, in terms of both caste and the markers and men-tality of upper-class British society, also placed him in a position where he might just as easily look down upon Anglo-Indians in both Indian and British terms. Nonetheless, Nehru had put out feelers to Anglo-Indian leaders as early as 1929,[79] and corresponded with Cedric Dover in the 1930s.[80] The Reverend Thomas Cashmore recalled Nehru approaching him on the subject, 'because he wasn't aware too much of the anglo-Indian [sic] problem and wanted to know about it, so we had lunch together and discussed it'.[81]

Anthony was thus supremely fortunate to encounter an enlight-ened Indian leader who was culturally open-minded enough to hear and respond to the Anglo-Indian case sympathetically. Though long considered a political and economic radical and potential revolution-ary actor by the British, Nehru remained socially patrician, substan-tially anglicised and ultimately amenable to a peaceable and consen-sual transfer of the machinery of the colonial state into Indian hands by constitutional means. He was also wedded to a secular and civic nationalist vision for India into which Anglo-Indians could fit, with the possibility if not probability that they might come to symbolise the successful integration of one numerically small, model minority, to set against the lasting stain of Partition upon India's pluralistic promise. When the two did finally meet, Anthony 'found Nehru very charming'.[82] Characteristically, 'Nehru was not concerned with details', and in any case Anthony was given less time than he had had with Gandhi to present his case.[83] Nehru asked questions which Anthony regarded as 'not duly pertinent to the constitutional or political position' of Anglo-Indians, such as 'whether his relative's children were Anglo-Indians'.[84] Having fortunately overlapped with the Oxford- and LSE-educated Braj Kumar Nehru while qualifying as a barrister at the Inner Temple, Anthony 'mentioned that I knew him well and although he had married a European woman, under the definition of the term "Anglo-Indian" the children would not be Anglo-Indians: I said that biologically they might be … but not legally since the definition postulated European descent in the male line.'[85]

Next came a more detail-oriented and political conversation with 'Sardar' Vallabhbhai Patel, who, unlike Gandhi, Nehru and Anthony, had attended the Middle rather than the Inner Temple. Patel was regarded as the principal figure on the right wing of the Congress. Back in 1930 J. S. Turner had alluded to an 'Indian public gentleman', stating that 'India will not rest content until she has every Anglo-Indian woman a domestic servant'.[86] If there was any truth to the attribution to Patel of a similarly expressed 'wish to see every Anglo-Indian carrying a beggar's bowl' by one Anglo-Indian interviewee, this clearly did not augur well.[87] Despite Anthony's practising lawyer's habit of attempting to get the measure of an individual through a brief visual inspection, he found it hard to penetrate Patel's 'heavy-lidded, half-closed eyes and sphinx-like manner'.[88] Yet Patel heard Anthony out at length, without interruption, at first offering only 'a few non-committal, monosyllabic grunts', and leaving Anthony wondering 'how much he had taken in'.[89] To Anthony's surprise, Patel then put 'a series of staccato questions which no other leader had asked', aimed at getting straight to the nitty-gritty of machine politics 'within the shortest possible time'.[90] Patel wished to know how many seats Anthony wanted in the Constituent Assembly, and how many Provincial Assembly seats would be needed to return each representative to the Constituent Assembly. Only in Bengal were the community's four seats sufficient to support their hopes of getting even a single member onto the constitution-making body. Their other eight seats were scattered in such a way as to be of no help.

Patel, however, could make some use of these votes, and asked, 'How many of these representatives … would vote according to' Anthony's direction?[91] India's 'Iron Man … was a little incredulous that ... [Anthony] could command the vote of every Anglo-Indian in every Legislature', but Anthony reassured Patel 'that this was a fact'.[92] On Anthony's 'assurance of their voting solidly' according to his instructions 'in support of non-Anglo-Indian Congress candidates in States where no Anglo-Indian representative could be returned', Patel agreed 'to recommend 3 seats' and 'ensure' that Congress votes in the necessary provinces would be cast to return the three Anglo-Indians.[93] As all four lawyer-politicians undoubtedly knew, in itself this would not guarantee that Anthony could obtain his desired concessions in the new constitution. Anthony could no more than any other Anglo-Indian predict what the result of his further efforts might be. His role might well have been planned to show the inclusivity of the Constituent Assembly before being required to give up any hope of special provisions to safeguard his group. After all, this is what happened to all the other minorities apart from the Dalits and Adivasis. Nonetheless it was a highly magnanimous and conciliatory gesture. Anthony was able to live up to his side of the bargain with Patel because candidates backing Anthony's Association had made a clean sweep in 'the recent Provincial Assembly elections'.[94]

At an extraordinary general meeting on 22 June, 'the *elected* representatives of almost every Province' passed the Delhi Resolution endorsing Anthony's policy for the community.[95] H. O. Fowler, MLA, characterised it as a choice between 'liv[ing] ... on in a fool's paradise' or acknowledging 'our past folly and set[ing] our house in order'; 'exist[ing] as aliens in our homeland ... [giving] our loyalty to a land we ... shall never see or pledg[ing] ... our whole-hearted support to the land of our birth'; 'treat[ing] our Indian brothers with a mixture of disdain and toleration or stretch[ing] out the hand of friendship and co-operation'; and either continuing 'to be the guardians of imperialism for a few crumbs from the Master's table or throw[ing] our weight definitely on the side of Indian nationalism'.[96] When the 'resolution passed', Fowler felt it 'came, no doubt, as an unpleasant shock to many, but the time and occasion demanded no mincing of words but plain, blunt speaking ... Let us take our rightful place ... remembering that India would want us only if we want India.'[97]

Following his meetings with Gandhi and Patel, Anthony exchanged lengthy letters with each. Gandhi endorsed the recommendations of the Sapru Committee. According to Anthony, both men assured him that Jinnah was responsible for blocking their attempt to secure a place for him in the Interim Government, as Jinnah would apparently only consent to Sikh and Christian representatives.[98] If so, there may have been something slightly disingenuous in this, as, according to Wavell—no friend to Anthony—Nehru had only 'pressed for ... the inclusion of Ant[h]ony as Anglo-Indian representative' as part of his demand for an additional minority seat.[99] Bringing the size of the council up to fifteen was clearly a tactical move to strengthen Congress's hand against Jinnah. Understanding that this 'would increase the suspicion of the Muslim League and make their joining more difficult', Wavell rejected any enlargement but was prepared to 'consider' Anglo-Indian representation on the existing fourteen-member Council.[100]

At the same meeting of 22 August 1946, Wavell agreed to Nehru's six Congress members and 'three Minority representatives[:] Baldev Singh (Sikh), Matthai (Christian), and Bhabha (Parsee)'.[101] Presumably, therefore, the Congress high command only wanted Anthony if he was an additional, apparently neutral minority representative on whom they now felt they could rely, and not as a substitute for representatives of the much larger Indian Christian community or the similarly small Parsi minority. This did not necessarily mean that the Congress valued these other minorities more highly, for 'the National leaders [had] recognised' Anthony's 'Association as being the sole authoritative spokesman of the Community throughout India', whereas, when they conceded seats on the Constituent Assembly to the Indian Christians, Congress leaders 'ignored the only two organisations' claiming to represent them—'the Indian Christian Association' and 'the Catholic Union of India',[102] presumably in favour of individuals who were more pliable and amenable to Congress influence or control. In what the Madras branch described as 'a poor compensation' for Anthony's 'failure to get into the Interim Government',[103] Nehru appointed Anthony in late 1946 'as one of the principal delegates', led by his sister Vijaya Lakshmi Pandit, 'to represent India at the United Nations' for the first time.[104] That the other delegates included Sir Maharaj Singh (subsequently Governor of Bombay, 1948–52), Justice M. C. Changla of the Bombay High

Court and Nawab Ali Yavar Jung Bahadur, then a minister 'of the Hyderabad State Government',[105] indicates a combination of co-opting talent while seeking to secure the future allegiance of Princely India to the Union. Anthony made the best use of this by presenting it to his constituents as 'a unique tribute to the Community' and the first opportunity for an Anglo-Indian to have 'the privilege of representing his country in what is the Parliament of the world'.[106]

By November 1947 the *Review* was contrasting Cripps's refusal to grant Anglo-Indians even 'one seat in the Constituent Assembly' with the magnanimity of Congress, who, although owing 'us nothing[,] have given us a great deal'.[107] When the time came, 'the British Bania forgot all his pledges', including repeated and 'solemn' undertakings 'that no settlement would be reached in India until the position of the minorities was first guaranteed'.[108] They had agreed to transfer power 'without worrying if ... [the] Anglo-Indians, Sikhs, Indian Christians, [and] Scheduled Castes would be fairly treated or destroyed'.[109] Anthony stated that he 'never became *friendly* with' Gandhi, 'but with Nehru ... because I met him in the Constituent Assembly ... [as] one of the eight members of the ... Steering Committee ... [I] got very friendly with him'.[110] Anthony would later wax nostalgic about the moment of independence itself, when he and his two colleagues 'had a front seat ... There was this tremendous feeling of pride and thanksgiving ... The atmosphere was ... you couldn't capture it. And we were party to it, because we were given a place of pride. But uh, only thing is, we Anglo-Indians went in European dress, we wore dress suits.'[111] His interviewer laughed: 'You must have been the only people there almost in dress suits', to which Anthony replied, 'Naturally!'[112] The rest of the hall was a sea of homespun white khadi and Gandhi caps.

Anthony, who was at this point thirty-eight, nearly two decades Nehru's junior, fondly recalled hugging him immediately following the soaring rhetoric of his famous 'Tryst with Destiny' speech. Anthony was expansive in remembering the quality of Nehru's 'tremendous' prose—'It was a beautiful speech, a moving speech'.[113] These fond recollections are hardly surprising. Yet it should be borne in mind that Anthony had sound political reasons for subsequently emphasising his good relations with the Congress leaders. A corrective to his rather glowing account can be found in their reaction to a letter of 1948 from Anthony to a correspondent in England, Colonel Douglas M. Reid. A former 'Commandant of the Madras Guards', Reid was credited in the *Review* for 'his ardent enthusiasm' in having 'done so much to help Anglo-Indians',[114] and taking a 'special interest' in the Andamans colonisation scheme.[115] In 1946 Reid wrote to Anthony to 'most heartily congratulate you on getting three seats in the Constituent Assembly' 'and gladly accept' 'to join your London Committee'.[116] Two years later Anthony claimed to 'have been approached to accept the Governorship of Madras', explaining that he had declined, feeling it essential to remain 'in Delhi to guide the destinies of the community at this critical period'.[117] Quite willing to avail himself as home minister of the vestiges of the Raj's security state, Patel had been forwarded this intercepted letter by the Intelligence Bureau, and wrote to Nehru to state: 'This is perhaps due to a false sense of self-importance on the part of Anthony', to which Nehru tersely replied, 'About Frank Anthony, no one has ever thought of him as the Governor of Madras.'[118] Nonetheless, two questions in the Legislative Assembly in February 1947 reflect the shifting perceptions of Anglo-Indians months before independence and the effect of support from the Congress high command.

When Seth Sukhdev complained that some government departments were still employing Anglo-Indians on 'a minimum of Rs. 55 per mensem irrespective of the lower scale of pay attached to the post held', which was 'resented by ... [their] Indian colleagues', and asked why 'this difference in wages based on racial grounds' was not to be abolished, Patel, speaking on behalf of government, defended the Anglo-Indian position.[119] Perhaps already anticipating the use to which he might put the AF(I), Patel unconsciously echoed Gidney by justifying this communal (or racial) minimum wage as 'a special allowance on account of their liability to serve in the Indian Auxiliary Force'.[120] Anthony found Patel to possess a 'supreme sense of realism. He was nothing if he was not practical ... He recognised that idealism is a good thing, but realities inescapable.'[121]

A subsequent question by Maharajkumar Dr. Sir Vijaya Ananda highlighted 'the assault by a batch of about 200 British soldiers and officers on the Anglo-Indian men and women at Jhansi on the refusal of the Anglo-Indian girls to dance with the British soldiers and officers during Christmas week 1946'.[122] Sardar Mangal Singh raised the issue again a week later, asking the government to confirm or deny the account given in the *Hindustan Times*. Several others interjected, including Mr. Manu Subedar, who asked if the government were 'fully alive to the very strong feeling in this country with regard to the honour of Indian women, so far as soldiers are concerned'.[123] Anthony's own sources had characterised the incident as 'a premeditated and organised attack by British troops on the Institute. Armed with rifles, bayonets and knives these troops molested our women and injured some of our men. Wanton destruction to property was indulged in and damage to the extent of about Rs. 15,000/-was committed.'[124] Anthony immediately raised the matter with Patel, as well as 'Sardar Baldev Singh, the Defence member, and Pandit Pant, the Premier of the U.P.'[125] In March Mr. Ahmed E. H. Jaffer tabled another question in the Assembly, asking whether it was true 'that 200 armed British service personnel raided the Railway Institute at Jhansi, when the Anglo-Indians were celebrating Christmas and assaulted some Anglo-Indians and set fire to furniture and canopies in the ball room'.[126] Government admitted damages estimated at Rs. 10,745 and issued a statement recounting how the Railway Institute was 'normally out of bounds to BORs [British Other Ranks]', but said that some orders had been issued giving permission to attend a boxing tournament on another date and this had created confusion, leading to four men of the Wiltshire Regiment arriving 'under the misapprehension that they were allowed to attend the function taking place there', who, on being refused entry, 'became truculent' and, managing to find another means of entry, precipitated an incident of manhandling and other 'actual scuffles'.[127]

Two days later they returned as part of a larger group of around '50 or 60' British soldiers, who 'rushed in and started breaking up the furniture, etc., and … the Christmas decorations caught fire', after which they fled, and soon afterwards 'an armed patrol of one NCO and 13 BORs' arrived, who 'had a salutary effect on the Anglo-Indian element … some of whom had shown signs of violence'.[128] The statement, which had doubtless filtered through from the military inquiry set up within the British Army to judge its own men, displays curious understatements and inversions. Indeed, at the time Subedar contended that the court had put 'the aggression on the Anglo-Indians, whereas the aggression was entirely on the other side'.[129] The statement had further stressed that the men had been unarmed, that no casualties had been admitted to hospital and that no 'women were molested'.[130] Anthony alleged that 'British officials and the officers of the court … [had] tried to cover up the tracks of the miscreants'— this and the question whether women had been assaulted were entirely refuted by Mr. G. S. Bhalja.[131] We may conjecture that the British soldiers had felt a proprietorial right of access to Anglo-Indian women, and that the Anglo-Indian women's refusal to dance with those men who had slipped into the Institute after being refused entry instigated an escalating conflict.

This was not entirely unlike other commonplace wartime incidents in which, for example, American servicemen stationed in the UK and Australia became involved in fights, which were often connected with women, alcohol consumption, and mutual resentments between groups. However, in this case there was a racialised as well as gendered dimension to the assumed privilege of the men of the more emphatically superordinate group. In the debate triggered in the Legislative Assembly, Anglo-Indian womanhood came to clearly symbolise Indian womanhood, in the stereotypical sense that women are often taken to embody the honour and virtue of a group and a nation. Viewing the episode through this frame had the incidental effect of identifying Anglo-Indians not with the British colonisers, but with the aggrieved colonised subject. All the same, men and women dancing and drinking together at a Christmas party was atypical of the gender interactions of other Indian communities, and would probably, in other circumstances, have been a subject of criticism of Anglo-Indian women's supposed morality and virtue by Hindu nationalists. Yet issues of Anglo-Indians' dress and social mores became irrelevant to the sense that Indian women had suffered assault and insult by British colonial soldiers. In a strange way, this episode had transformed the Anglo-Indian woman into an Indian woman without the demand for her to don a sari.

The end of empire

The determined policy of Attlee's government to quit India on the shortest possible timescale and regardless of the costs, as Stanley

Wolpert argued, led to the unwise choice of a Viceroy even more determined to accelerate that process, to the shock and horror of many Indian and British contemporaries.[132] Like the Cabinet Mission, Mountbatten earnestly wished to help the Congress leaders to come to a settlement with Jinnah that would avoid Partition. However, upending earlier interpretations, Ayesha Jalal has argued that in key respects Mountbatten became a tool of Nehru, and that 'in the end game, Congress not the Viceroy was calling the shots ... It was Congress that insisted on partition ... [and] Jinnah who was against partition.'[133] In this reading, Jinnah used the demand for a maximalist Pakistan to try to extort a power-sharing agreement at the centre, while Nehru and Patel were so opposed to conceding 'parity', at a weakened federal centre that they preferred partition. A strong federal centre under firm Congress control was the only way for Nehru to fulfil his own ambitions for a centrally planned economy. Although Nehru had 'suggested a transfer of power by June 1947 to the existing central government, leaving the whole question of Pakistan and the partition of Bengal and Punjab until later', dangling the prospect of India remaining within the Commonwealth as bait,[134] Mountbatten alone must bear responsibility for his disastrous decision to bring forward the date of independence by almost a year.

While Mountbatten frequently attempted to bounce the various parties into quick decisions by placing them under the pressure of artificial time constraints, the only plausible defence for this reckless rescheduling was his predecessor's warning to Attlee's government. Wavell had concluded that, in the context of their military drawdown in India, if put to the test the remnant of the colonial state would no longer be able to control the situation. As well as reflecting real apprehensions for a complete breakdown of law and order, Wavell's warnings appear to have constituted a tacit plea to have his position militarily reinforced—something which the new prime minister had no intention of doing, and which contributed to Attlee's decision to replace Wavell. Wolpert was too charitable in his conclusion that 'Attlee was wise enough to realize what a dreadful mistake he had made in relying on Mountbatten's inept judgement to accelerate his cabinet's timetable for withdrawing Britain's martial shield from South Asia'.[135] For it was Attlee who was ultimately responsible for determining the pace and scale of British military demobilisation and withdrawal. Aware that their election had been heavily supported by British troops hoping for accelerated demobilisation, Attlee's government prioritised the maintenance of deployments in occupied Germany, Greece and Mandate Palestine. A detailed reading of the British cabinet papers suggests that even senior cabinet colleagues had been hesitant to adopt this course, and that it was Attlee's unobtrusive but ruthlessly effective hand that forced through the central policy framework, over the waverers and the repeated objections of his foreign secretary, Ernest Bevin, who felt that more time and resources should be committed if circumstances required them or if they might ensure a better final outcome.

However, Attlee's policy was that there would be no delay in handing over by June 1948, regardless of the pace of progress or developments on the ground; but, what was worse, that British armed forces should effect a staged withdrawal as quickly as possible and that those still present should not intervene to defend Indian lives and property. British officials were instructed to protect only the few remaining Britons, leaving their erstwhile colonial subjects to their fate in the ensuing bloodbath. These decisions, so often ignored because they can be presented as a fixed contextual background, by implication the practically inevitable consequences of Britain's depleted postwar condition, when they were in fact questions of political priority, were more determinative than many of the intricate negotiations overseen by Mountbatten between the Congress leaders and Jinnah. Attlee's biographer emphasises that although he 'did more to oversee the transition of the British Empire into the British Commonwealth' than any other Briton, his approach had 'never [been] intended as a repudiation of its whole history'.[136] Attlee wanted to move beyond the 'stigma of racism and self-aggrandisement' and incidents like the Jameson Raid of 1895–6, which he believed had besmirched the work of many high-minded colonial administrators.[137] He held to the view, expressed by one of Scott's characters in the *Raj Quartet*, that 'the promise of self-government that the British had always held out for some distant future … [was] an] unwritten contract [which] had to be fulfilled'.[138]

As John Bew puts it, Attlee 'hoped, above all, to salvage something honourable from the morass'.[139] If independence could be presented in this guise, and, even better, if Indian leaders could be brought around to accepting membership in the Commonwealth as well, then Attlee would be well pleased. However, any and all of these objectives were to be subordinated to effecting a British withdrawal in the shortest possible time, which would also serve to minimise the appearance of British responsibility for ongoing violence and potential societal collapse or civil war. Sir Cyril Radcliffe, the British barrister tasked with finalising the border between India and Pakistan, on account of the presumed impartiality of a man who had never before travelled east of Paris, was barred from announcing where precisely the line would fall until after the formal handover. Nehru had been opposed to any retention of British soldiers beyond the formal date of independence. Intertwined with the policy straitjacket imposed by Attlee's government and Mountbatten's decision that independence and partition should formally coincide, this meant that British forces would not be available when they were most needed to oversee the process in Punjab and Bengal and along the new frontier. In the event the Punjab Boundary Force, composed of Indian and Pakistani units led by Major General Thomas Wynford Rees, was so inadequate to the task that it was disbanded less than two months after having been established.

In the context of the chaos of Partition, there was presumably a horrified recognition by Patel and Nehru that the one saving grace of the calamitous process by which they achieved India's independence was that they had, at a constitutional level at least, peacefully taken over the remaining infrastructure of the state. They avoided a wider and more costly civil war, and they escaped the price of temporary statelessness which a revolutionary or violent seizure of power would most likely have entailed. Indian members of the Indian Civil Service (ICS), whom they had suspected as former agents of British imperial rule, were now essential to them. They had looked into the chasm of what complete lawlessness would entail and could have brought about on an even more unfathomably tragic scale. Pragmatism dictated that they must deploy those tools which they had immediately to hand. Patel even requested the re-embodiment of the AF(I), as Anthony recalls:

> Sardar Patel ... took a fancy to me ... and he said: 'Mr. Anthony would you agree ... to re-embody the Auxiliary Force.' ... In Delhi

... at that time, we would have been about a thousand ... I said 'For God's sake ... please don't do that ... Let us work in an unofficial capacity, but you shouldn't embody us, then we'll start shooting Hindus and Muslims', because ... the Hindus ... [and] Sikhs were reacting, they were killing Muslims in Delhi. Most of the Muslims were ... slaughtering Hindus ... sending them out slaughtered in the street. So we would have had to maintain order, and we would have done it. So that's why I said 'no, please don't, please don't', then they were able to get some Gurkha units ... My wife and I used to drive about, nobody touched us ... But that was a terrible time ... Human memory being what it is, we forgot, we lived through one of the ... greatest traumas in history. How many millions each way? Ten, twenty million altogether involved. I don't know how many—one million or two million people killed.[140]

Judged by the consequences of his decisions—unspeakable horrors that continue to haunt those who lived through them—Mountbatten merited Churchill's castigating words by overseeing a 'shameful flight, by a premature, hurried scuttle'.[141] But judged solely by the limited set of priorities which Attlee had set him, Mountbatten may have been thought by the Labour leader to have made the best of a bad job, by effecting a formal transfer of power in a suitably ceremonious fashion while appearing to minimise British responsibility for the ongoing and still mounting carnage. The Mountbattens exuded charisma, played their parts fantastically for the world's cameras, and managed to generate personal intimacy and genuine friendship with many of those they met. Anthony was no more immune to their personal charms than most of his contemporaries, as indicated by his fond recollection of their first meeting:

I wrote to Mountbatten, I said 'I'd like to meet Your Excellency.' And he gave me a date, [7 April,[142] and] I went there. And to my ultra-pleasant surprise ... who should open the door but Mountbatten to greet me ... and take me to my seat ... No Viceroy ever did that before ... and they did it naturally. It was not a cultivated artificiality. They were like that ... Not because ... he was aristocratic ... other aristocrats ... were not as easy to get on with. But ... the Mountbattens ... were really down to earth ...

... I got very friendly with the[m] ... They were very charming people, and ... easy to get along with, very likeable. And they blunted the ... anti-British feeling ... In spite of Gandhi's non-violent movement there was tremendous violence in different parts of the country ... rails being uprooted ... violent action of one sort or another against the British, and ... it would [have] taken over that complexion but for Gandhi. And also for the Mountbattens.[143]

Edwina befriended Anthony's wife while they worked together visiting refugee camps. Anthony noted how this glamorous and uninhibited power couple cut through stuffy precedents, stripped away many of the arcane rituals of empire, broke down racial barriers, and went freely among the people. Anthony echoes other accounts that blame the colonial British memsahibs for much of this, but he also reveals how Edwina's puncturing of the racial norms of colonial society caused even some Anglo-Indian women consternation:

A lot of the British who came out ... were known as ... [sahibs], gentlemen, and even those who came from the lower middle classes, tut, they were assimilated to that kind of ... behaviour ... Some of them married lower middle class women. But ... it's the women really, as I told Edwina Mountbatten, when they first came out ... She asked me ... to tea, [on 21 April,[144] and] I said 'Oh well, I wonder how many there'll be', there was nobody else, only myself ... for over an hour. And ... she told me ... 'You know ... both the British and the Anglo-Indian women have a lot of inhibitions ... The English women more so. They got shocked ... at the things I do. The ease with which I mix with Indians of all levels ... The Anglo-Indians too ...['] She was the head of the nursing service ... She landed at Karachi ... She said ... 'The ... Superintendent was an Anglo-Indian ... she took me around, [and] I started shaking hands with everybody, including the Class Four staff.' So she said 'I could see her, she was a fair Anglo-Indian—[but her] colour was rising, and she said "Your Excellency, you don't do that. You don't shake hands with the Class Four ..."' [Edwina] said 'Why?' '"No, Your Excellency, you don't shake hands with Class Four staff."' [Edwina] said, 'Well I do, I'll do it again.'[145]

Having embraced Indian nationalism and aligned himself with the Congress, Anthony was clearly not unbiased, deflecting any share of responsibility from the Congress leaders and Mountbatten onto Jinnah. Anthony's narrative began with Jinnah's Direct Action Day of 16 August 1946:

the hatred was really started by Jinnah, there's no doubt about it. The Muslim religion ... in its own way, can be extremely fanatical ... And he played on that … religious fanaticism. The 80% of illiterate people … the killings in Calcutta … [were] something indescribable. There we had the largest number of Anglo-Indians, about 30,000, but … Anglo-Indians were not touched … My Anglo-Indian Association saved thousands of Hindus. Went into the Muslim localities … gave them … food, and … brought some of them out … but nobody touched them …[146]

In Anthony's view, having been 'born in hatred … [and] still living in hatred', the Muslim League was responsible for an inevitable cycle of violence.[147] Grilled by an interviewer on the role of Mountbatten's decision to bring 'forward Independence' in letting 'loose the blood-bath of Partition',[148] Anthony responded:

people blamed … [Mountbatten] for pushing things fast, but … the Muslim position became extreme under Jinnah. And … you would have had these continuing riots—a … bloodbath … had to come, sooner or later. Once you got that [Royal Indian Navy] Mutiny [in February 1946] … then the British knew they couldn't depend on the armed forces. They had to go. And sooner or later independence was bound to come. And … my own feeling is that Mountbatten helped the transfer … to be set in a … friendly British milieu. He was made the first Governor-General of India, and the British left without any anti-British feeling. Otherwise … they might well have been slaugh-tered, and we would have been slaughtered with them …[149]

Anthony's assessment that an imperial withdrawal amid wide-spread anti-British violence would have redounded upon Anglo-Indians was obviously shared by British military experts, who had, at least, thought to include them in the evacuation contemplated in Wavell's 'Breakdown Plan' of 1945–7.[150] However, colonial British authorities avoided this by abdicating their responsibility to prevent growing communal violence. As well as relying on the by now ques-tionable loyalty and impartiality of the Indian Army, the Raj had always depended for its existence upon a degree of ostentatious mili-tary display, which often amounted to mere bluff combined with exemplary shows of force. After India had been denuded of British troops, the willpower to play this game came to an end. A failed attempt to impose martial law or to cow a hostile crowd engaged in communal killings could have removed the last semblance of state control and invited the anti-European massacre which had haunted the colonial British imagination since 1857. Instead, anti-British and anti-imperial sentiment subsided as communal hatred mounted.

Once again dress in general, and hats in particular, including the Sikh turban, functioned as markers of the religious communal tribes who were targeting one another. This point was later satirised in Saadat Hasan Manto's fictionalised account of switching between Hindu and Muslim (Rumi) caps to pass safely through different neighbourhoods: 'Previously religion used to be in one's heart, now it's in caps ... Politics too operates through these caps. Long live caps!'[151] In Punjab, the most inflamed site of partition, a pro-Pakistan Anglo-Indian leader declared it to be a matter of police record that 'dastardly attacks by members of the Sikh community [had been carried out] on innocent, undefended and disinterested Anglo-Indian women'.[152] Anglo-Indian railwaymen also drove and manned a great proportion of the trains which limped into stations full of dead bodies. Tony Mains argued that 'few, if any, refugee or other trains could have been run across the disturbed Indo-Pakistan border' without them.[153] Some Anglo-Indians brought risks upon themselves by sheltering members of other communities. However, more often than not, Anglo-Indians as a group were ignored. While picking up his wife near old Delhi, Anthony witnessed

> a horse ... drinking from a trough ... [with the tonga driver] hanging out ... [with] his throat cut from ear to ear. I said 'My God'. Then, about 800 yards down there's ... Willingdon Hospital ... And ... I saw some policemen there ... And I drove in, and ... said 'Look here, there's a person lying with his throat cut' ... There was masses of dead bodies, masses, mostly Hindus ... Then I picked my wife up, coming back we saw three or four corpses on the road, and ... in those days we had, we still have at the Gidney Club ... a dance on a Sunday. And the Anglo-Indian girls [were] riding along on cycles. So I stopped someone and said 'Where the hell do you think you're going?! They're killing ...' 'But nobody'll touch us.' And nobody touched them. You see. And they went to the club, and they danced themselves silly ... then we went to the club too.[154]

Dorothy McMenamin has addressed this 'curious exclusion of Anglo-Indians from the mass slaughter during the Partition of India'.[155] Nonetheless, knowledge of what was happening and existential fears that the violence might spread were traumatic enough for any minority insecure about its own future under the new regimes of postcolonial states. In his 1949 AGM speech, in the gendered language of the time, Anthony sought to dampen what were obviously very real anxieties: 'Too many of our people have developed the mentality of fearful old women ... During the September killings in Delhi, panic-stricken, backboneless, so called Anglo-Indian men came to me saying, "When is the Anglo-Indians' turn coming when our women's throats [will] be cut?["]'[156]

Swimming against the tide

In the climate of fear and violence created by Partition, and without the need any longer to placate the Muslims as the largest minority, Sikhs and other smaller minorities had come under enormous pressure in the Constituent Assembly and from Patel in the Minorities Committee to voluntarily surrender their colonial-era protections. Rochana Bajpai's *Debating Difference* (2011) has sought to recast this process in broad analytical terms, highlighting shifts in political rhetoric and downplaying the significance of the personal in politics and of Partition.[157] Yet what Bajpai does not explain was how and why Anglo-Indians almost uniquely bucked this general curtailment of minority group rights. It was all the more striking because Anglo-Indians were, on average, materially in advance of most of the Indian population and far ahead in school-level literacy. Anthony was therefore asking, as Gidney had done in London over a decade before, for positive discrimination (or 'affirmative action') for a minority with a better standard of living than the great majority of the Indian people. Again, he argued that it was necessary as a transitional measure to prevent their wholesale economic dislocation, promising that his community could be an asset to the new India.

Given the managerial deficit at the top levels of colonial and railway administration created by the British departure and the loss of many railway workers and officers to Pakistan, this was perhaps not so inconvenient to India's new leaders as it might once have seemed. Anthony could also make an argument similar to the one Gidney had made at the Round Table Conference in 1931:

I would request my Indian colleagues to ask themselves seriously and without prejudice if we, the Anglo-Indians, have not been nation-builders in India in the true sense. We have built and worked India's communications. We have shed our blood in defence of India. We have been active and law-abiding citizens. Innumerable units of local self-government have benefitted by the work of thousands of obscure Anglo-Indians ... Is it not worth India's while to preserve the integrity of such a body of citizens in her midst? We could be crushed out of existence easily enough. But in so crushing us, would not India lose something which it would be well worth her while to preserve? Let me repeat: the key-note of our nature is loyalty and that loyalty is to India no less than to Britain. We are so small in numbers that the posts which we occupy in the public service form a merely infinitesimal percentage of the total number ... available. India would gain nothing by expropriating us. On the contrary, she would lose what I think I am justified in describing as a most valuable element in the Indian politic. That is our claim on India.[158]

Rhetorically repurposing service to the Raj as service to the new India posed a greater challenge for Anglo-Indians than for Indian officers of the Army or the ICS or even the so-called martial races who supplied India's fighting soldiers. Yet as Gidney had earlier suggested, the small numbers of the Anglo-Indian group meant that the price for India's leaders was low. It is easier to retain people in their current positions without political cost than to displace some to make space for others. Anthony could also emulate Gidney by presenting his case as a transitional and temporary one, thereby making it more palatable to members of the Constituent Assembly. He later recalled how 'it took me four years of ... continuous battling. Because I had tremendous opposition ... even from the ruling Congress Party. Because they hadn't forgotten our role ... How we'd helped the British ... to rule India.'[159] In his 1949 AGM speech, Anthony described it as 'a period of the most intense and the most acute anxiety. Political currents moved and changed, very often from week to week, in a radical way. No one was able to say for a period of even two months precisely how the constitution would take shape, particularly with regard to the [minority] provisions.'[160] For the first two years, relatively generous provisions had been hammered out

> in a spirit of accommodation, tolerance and magnanimity ... guaranteeing our political representation, our quotas in the services and our education ... [and were] embodied in a very satisfactory form in the draft constitution. Then, currents again began to change rapidly and

radically, and leaders of certain minority communities felt that per-haps they would get more by pursuing the pre-independence tactics ... This resurgence of militant communalism gave rise to a tremen-dous back wash of antipathy ... There was a growing feeling, which no one could resist, in the Constituent Assembly that ... safeguards for the minorities would only feed the kind of communalism which led to the Muslim League's militant politics and vivisection of the country. There was a bitter revulsion of feeling against minority claims, as a result of the sabre-rattling on the part of the leaders of a particular community. That was, perhaps, the most critical period for us. I knew that it had been virtually decided that minority safeguards would be withdrawn, but with the consent of the minorities' repre-sentatives ... I felt that our particular safeguards could not survive. *If the Christians surrendered their reservations ... if the other members wished to withdraw the reservations ...* [for] *Muslims,* [and] *if the majority were determined not to give the Sikhs any reservation, then I did not see how a microscopic minority, which a few months ago were regarded as anti-Indian ... alone could survive in the matter of reservations ...* It was recognised that the scheduled castes, being socially and economically backward, had to get some concession, but those considerations did not apply to the Anglo-Indian community ... [who] it was often argued ... [were] the most economically advanced community, in the country.[161]

Right up to the last moment Anthony's colleagues challenged him: 'Do you think they will give you these safeguards in the final constitu-tion? They will bluff you to the end and just when the Constitution is to be adopted they will be withdrawn.'[162] Anthony described the critical moment when

the Minorities Committee, presided over by Sardar Patel ... rejected my [proposals], I argued for two days, they said 'no'. The Sikhs wanted separate representation, the Muslims. They rejected them all. Then I came last, and ... they said 'no, we're not going to give you anything'. Then I met Sardar Patel at night. I said 'well, what can I do in the Constituent Assembly, I may as well resign. I can't be party to the effacing of my community.' And then, the old man, when he came the next morning, he said something, which was not correct. He said 'I've given an assurance to Mr. Anthony that we are going to consider their case'.[163]

From this point on, as Anthony explained,

with the support of the Sardar ... [and] the Prime Minister, [I was able] to have the Anglo-Indian reservation accepted ... Although ...

numerous influential Congressmen tabled amendments seeking either completely to withdraw ... [them] or to whittle them down very considerably ... on the 16th June ... a red-letter day for the Anglo-Indian community ... section 297 guaranteeing our quotas and section 298 which I regard as an even more important provision guaranteeing our educational grants, were passed in their original form, and last month, in July, our two remaining provisions [in articles 293 and 295] were adopted ... [giving] power to the President ... and to the Governors ... to nominate representatives of the Anglo-Indian community, either to the Lower House in the Centre or to the Provincial Legislatures ...[164]

To his own surprise, Anthony also secured a continuation of Gidney's 1935 Act employment reservations for ten years, with a phased reduction 'as nearly as possibly' by ten per cent every two years.[165] He later reflected that the 'special chapter on the Anglo-Indian community in the Constitution [was] something unique ... We are the only community, as a community, to have ... representation in Parliament, in certain legislatures, by nomination. And I've continued to be there since '42.'[166] Anthony had 'faced the storm ... weathered it and ... emerged on the crest of the wave, riding triumphantly'.[167] He could once again contrast Congress's magnanimity with British 'betrayal', thereby contributing to his evolving construction of a historical master narrative capable of assisting in a profound psychological decoupling from Britain and cementing a radical reformulation of Anglo-Indian identity towards Indian nationalism.

However, Anthony found that the concessions he had won were initially insufficient to persuade most Anglo-Indians that they could now feel safe and secure in the new India; while his increasingly resentful rhetoric towards the British only served to further alienate a large swathe of 'unreconstructed' Anglo-Indians. In a way that confirmed the degree to which Anthony's top-down prescription for identity reformulation remained a 'hard sell', many would-be émigrés emphasised their Britishness or Britain-orientated identities, while pan-Eurasianist socialist movements also re-emerged, as much in response to the perceived threat of regional and linguistic sub-nationalisms as to Indian or Hindi nationalism. The strain of colonisation rhetoric continued, with fresh proposals for the creation of a new mixed-race nation or collective settlement overseas, to be dubbed Anglo-India, Britasia or Eurasia. We will conclude with short summaries of the continuing appeal of overseas colonisation and attempts to maintain a British status in India, followed by longer discussions of the fate of Anglo-Indians residing in or opting for Pakistan, and the exodus of a considerable proportion of Anglo-Indians from South Asia.

The 'Britasian' League and pan-Eurasianist socialists

Addressing the opponents of the Delhi Resolution of 22 June 1946, H. O. Fowler stated that

> those who cannot live on in India as people of this country would be helping the community by packing their bags and leaving … Those who still dream of colonisation are … seeking a doubtful and cowardly retreat out of a difficult situation … [and] indulging in wishful thinking, building their castles in the air; for mass colonisation is a gigantic venture, beset with obstacles that are practically insurmountable.[168]

Nonetheless, shortly before independence a new body calling itself the Britasian League was founded under the leadership of Captain G. Ambler, which attempted to renew the earlier abortive post-First World War scheme to colonise the Andaman Islands.[169] Ralph Stracey later stated that 'they didn't call themselves Anglo-Indians but Brit-Asians', which he judged 'a truer name for the Anglo-Indians than what we have'.[170] Brent Otto's observation that Ambler obtained the backing of the 'Progressive Loyalist Association of Mussoorie'[171] supports the obvious conclusion that 'Britasian' was intended to signal a more traditional British-aligned empire loyalism, in contrast to Anthony's efforts to radically reorient Anglo-Indian identity. However, the new designation also had the potential to encompass a broader collectivity across Asia, embracing Eurasians from other British colonial territories such as Malaya and Hong Kong, although not mixed-race peoples from other European empires, such as the Dutch East Indies. This observation is supported by enquiries in 1949 by Charles Campagnac, the leader of the Anglo-Burman Union, to the British embassy in Rangoon as to 'whether the Government of India would consider taking a number of Anglo-Burmans in their proposed settlement in the Andaman Islands'.[172]

Ambler's League presumably considered the Andaman Islands as a better homeland for the group than landlocked McCluskiegunge, as their location would have appeared more compatible with greater autonomy within an Indian federation, or potential independence and ongoing affiliation to Britain and the Crown, if India opted to secede from the Commonwealth. In December 1946 Ralph co-signed a letter addressed to the British Chief Commissioner of the Andaman Islands as well as Patel at the Home Ministry, to enquire about the feasibility and success of Ambler's project.[173] Its other signatories included members of Anthony's Association, all four of the community's Bengal MLAs, the president of the Anglo-Indian Federation, and the secretary of the Anglo-Indian Civic Union.[174] Given the prominence of these Bengal bigwigs, Anthony felt constrained to express his own opposition in uncharacteristically measured language. However, back in March he had criticised 'the renegade element … obsessed with ideas of escaping anywhere, whether it be to South Africa, Australia or even lesser known places'.[175] Anthony was accordingly relieved when the British Commissioner's reply sought to kill the proposals by painting Anglo-Indian colonisation prospects in the Andamans in as gloomy a light as possible. With his officially stated opposition to emigration or renewed attempts at colonisation overseas, Anthony was widely rumoured to have been secretly offered various alternatives by the British but to have misguidedly turned them down.

In 1947, Wallace observed that 'in British Dominions (the Anglo-Indian seldom sees beyond them) colour and race prejudice are too rife to offer a welcome home to any large number of our people'.[176] Yet by November, the *Review* was frantically denouncing 'some unbalanced people [who] have talked of Brazil, a country about which the Community knows nothing … which every now and then throws a Coup d'etat, and where the language is a foreign one'.[177] Otto has explored a pan-mixed-race movement called 'Mestizoism', led by Colonel Georges L. Fleury, who in the autumn of 1946 advocated emigration en masse to Brazil, citing the prevalence of racial mixing there, and the wide spectrum of colour and race, alongside 'its tropical climate, Catholic Christian majority and the apparent absence [of] colour prejudice'.[178] However, the British ambassador to Brazil was keen to quash the idea, observing that Brazil did have a colour bar and that the policy of their government was to promote immigration that would '"whiten" the stock'.[179] Pan-Eurasianist socialists inspired by Dover and Wallace continued to look further afield than the Andamans for a possible site for their proposed nation of Eurasia.

In 1956 R. G. Chatelier, the 'Founder and Leader' of the 'Eurasian Collectivist Party', apparently established in 1947, headquartered in Bangalore, and somewhat implausibly claiming to have additional branches in Burma, Ceylon, Indonesia, Malaya and Thailand, wrote to the British prime minister seeking his help in co-sponsoring a ten-year plan with India, Pakistan and Australia 'for the establishment of a separate state or national homeland of its own in British [formerly German] New Guinea'.[180] Chatelier complained of the 'balkanising of India into Linguistic States', and the 'farce' of constitutional safe-guards which he argued had failed to protect Anglo-Indians from the overwhelming pressure on their 'language, culture, customs and religion ... [from] these 16 states which ... [were] now in the process of formation'.[181] Citing the 'thousands of our people ... fleeing to the United Kingdom, their Fatherland', Chatelier presented the alterna-tives in equally stark and apocalyptic terms as a choice between 'emancipation' and 'annihilation'.[182] A British civil servant tersely noted that it was not a matter which 'Eden would consider appropri-ate to raise with' Nehru.[183]

Registration as British

Those hoping to migrate to Britain itself or its neo-British settler society offshoots, including Australia, were presumably happy to seek to merge themselves into nations they perceived to be culturally, religiously and racially proximate. However, most who wished to follow this course lacked the documentary or financial means to do so, while others who were professionally better placed may not have wanted to abandon lucrative careers to take on more lowly or ques-tionable employment in a new country, where their existing qualifica-tions were unlikely to be recognised. Seeking to hedge their bets, and retain the option of future emigration upon retirement, or in the event of a dramatic deterioration in conditions for Anglo-Indians, many registered themselves as British under section 12(6) of the British Nationality Act of 1948, while continuing to live and work in India. This would have been entirely sensible but for the fact that the new Indian administration had no intention of allowing dual citizenship. The *Review* had repeatedly warned its readers of 'the serious consequences involved by members of the Community registering under this act ... [as those] who are accepted will lose their Indian citizenship ... [and] without doubt, be expelled from any employment they are holding under Government'.[184] Anthony labelled the Act 'pernicious',[185] comparing it to earlier structural incentives for Anglo-Indians to pass as European, and returning to the multiple statuses issue raised by Gidney's 1925 London deputation:

> I have over and over again explained that the British Nationality Act was never intended for the Anglo-Indians, but the Anglo-Indian has, for one reason or another, and it is understandable, never understood that he was never a British national. At one time, according to Lord Birkenhead, for the purpose of nationality we were statutory Indians, for the purpose of education we were European British subjects, for the purpose of military service we were something else. As a result of this confused status some Anglo-Indians felt that they were not British subjects but British nationals ... Some of them think as Anglo-Indians, they can continue to get employment in this country if they register under the ... Act, and, if trouble starts, that Britain will send all her planes to evacuate them ... It is long overdue that we recognise ... even at this late stage ... [that] we have always had one nationality—Indian Nationality. We have been, still are and will continue to be Anglo-Indians by community. The fact that we are Indian nationals does not mean an abatement by one iota of everything that you [and I] hold dear as an Anglo-Indian ... That is a matter which I want every Anglo-Indian to realise ... because people still put themselves down as British. The result will be that ... you will never get employment under the Indian Government ... and if any Government authority comes to know of it you will be kicked out ...[186]

This issue would continue to pose problems for Anthony well into the next decade, when he was still denouncing such registrations as 'renegadism',[187] repurposing the same emotive term he had used before independence for those who passed as Europeans.[188] Eliding effect with intent, George P. V. Miller similarly argued that with the British Nationality Act 'the British authorities are doing a gross piece of injustice by driving a wedge into the community and creating a canker which would be difficult to remedy ... undoing all that is now being done to bring about a camaraderie between the Anglo-Indians and the other communities in the land ... likely to revive the fast-ebbing suspicion and hostility'.[189]

In 1955 the *Review* highlighted one case in which an Anglo-Indian in the employ of the Government of India, 'under the impression that as an Anglo-Indian, and an Indian citizen, he was entitled to opportunities of advancement open to all other Indian citizens', had been promoted to become 'the Head of one of the most important departments of the Government, where vital information and secret codes are specially dealt with', only for the government to subsequently discover when he retired 'that he had already surrendered his Indian citizenship and had acquired U.K. citizenship while still in employment'.[190] Such conduct, stated the *Review*, had 'understandably ... shocked' and 'outraged the conscience of the Government', but, what was worse, 'this kind of criminal renegadism ... [had] disastrous repercussions on the rest of the Community', threatening their future employment 'in this key department'.[191] Nonetheless, Anthony succeeded in securing an amendment to the Indian Citizenship Act of 1955 enabling 'Anglo-Indians who had acquired U.K. citizenship between Independence and the 26th of January, 1950 ... to retain their Indian citizenship'.[192]

Anglo-Pakistanis?

In early 1947, just as Anthony's embrace of Indian nationalism and efforts to come to terms with Congress appeared to be bearing fruit, a key front-rank figure in his own Association was beginning to tack in the opposite direction. We previously encountered Cecil Gibbon in a khadi sherwani alongside Subhas Chandra Bose as the most ardent of Congress supporters, in stark contrast to Anthony's continuing insistence that 'neither dress nor language form any precondition of patriotism, that we yield ... to no one in our love for this country ... Equally, we intend to cling and cling tenaciously to our form of dress, to English which is our mother tongue and to everything which we ... hold dear as representing our way of life.'[193] As Edward Few had lost his seat in 1945 and died two years later,[194] Gibbon was by now the community's MLA for the Punjab. He was also a prominent member of Anthony's Governing Body and, alongside Prater and Anthony himself, one of the initial three Anglo-Indian members of the Constituent Assembly. Presumably still a member of the Congress, or at least known for his earlier dramatic visual demonstration of commitment to the nationalist cause, Anthony considered Gibbon as 'invaluable for the purpose of canvassing and securing support from all sections of the House'.[195] However, this uniquely flexible individual was about to undergo another remarkable transformation.

In February, Gibbon and his branch hosted Anthony in Lahore,[196] receiving thanks in the *Review* along with congratulations on his re-election to the Punjab Legislative Assembly and recent appointment as 'Parliamentary Private Secretary' to the province's Unionist Party premier, Sir Malik Khizar Hayat Tiwana.[197] However, Anthony's editorial in the same issue suggested that storm clouds were already gathering:

> We do appreciate the difficulties of our representatives in the Muslim majority provinces but there is the dangerous tendency for them … being invested continuously by a Muslim majority, to become obsessed by a purely parochial point of view … The real danger … is that under pressure from persons unable to look at the interests … and in fact the existence of the Community, as a whole, our representatives in Bengal and the Punjab may be stampeded into policies which will lay the Community open to the charge of being political time-servers … [and] can be characterised as political apostasy, and cheap opportunism, the repercussions [of which] will operate against … [and] may jeopardise the future of the [whole] Community not only in their Provinces but throughout India.[198]

While clearly increasingly aligned with Congress, Anthony still claimed not to be 'anti-Muslim League'.[199] Unexpectedly delayed in Karachi on his way back from the United Nations in New York towards the end of 1946, Anthony 'reiterated that it was the policy of the Association … to maintain an attitude of equal friendship between the Congress and the Muslim League', to the local Anglo-Indian leadership there.[200] It was not his intention 'to take sides in … party disputes between these two groups', and although his 'declared … support for a United India and a strong Centre … was obviously against Muslim League policy', it had been 'subscribed to … as being in the best interests of the country' and not out of 'anti-Muslim League or pro-Congress' sentiment or political affiliation.[201] 'Anthony advised … [them] that co-operation with' either party in the interests of the community or the nation did not mean 'joining with that party' or becoming 'subservient to it'.[202] Following the Association's AGM of 5–7 April 1947 in Delhi, which Gibbon attended as usual, Anthony met with Jinnah and sought assurances that the Muslim League would 'recognise the existing position of the Community as not only a communal but a political entity', provide 'adequate political representation [i]n the Legislatures', and continue 'our educational grants' and 'the reservation of necessary quotas in the services', to which no immediate reply was forthcoming.[203] By the first week of June, Gibbon was ready to make a dramatic press statement, declaring that

> the bitterly resented, political directive and interference in provincial affairs by the Governing Body … has given rise to the demand by an overwhelming majority of Anglo-Indians domiciled in the Punjab, Sind, N-WF Province and Baluchistan for the immediate dis-establishment of the All-India … Association in these provinces, and for the formation of a new organization which would be free to pursue policies in keeping with the wishes of the community in a free and democratic state … In response … I am announcing the formation of the Anglo-Indian Association of Pakistan with its headquarters at Lahore, and Provincial Councils at Karachi, Quetta and Peshawar.[204]

Essentially this amounted to the secession of these branches and their legal reconstitution into a new body. Evidently, it had become apparent to Gibbon that most of his flock would fall on the Pakistani side of the new border, and that their interests lay in coming to their own accommodation with the Muslim League. That month's issue of the *Review* gave voice to Anthony's scepticism 'that a completely independent Muslim state' could be 'viable' or 'economically self-sufficient', 'especially if the Punjab and Bengal … [were] divided'.[205] Even if this came to pass, Anthony insisted, the All-India Association with all its 'strength and resources … organisation … national and international contacts' would remain the 'only' body capable of defending the interests of Anglo-Indians in Pakistan.[206] Anthony was not alone in supposing that addresses to the Indian government to intervene on their behalf would remain effective 'in the same way that Hindus ... [in] Pakistan will best be protected by the Congress and the Muslims who fall into Hindustan will best be protected by the Muslim League'.[207] Failing this, his All-India Association would aim to operate 'at an international level', 'co-operate with the Muslim League there and also, if necessary, fight in order to secure what we regard as the well-being of the Anglo-Indians who will fall into those areas'.[208] Such thinking was a measure of the more widespread failure to anticipate the extent of the population exchanges, violence and ethnic cleansing that were to follow Partition. A month later, galvanised by 'the fantastic gyrations of some [Anglo-Indians] wanting to become Anglo-Pakistanis and a frantic zeal, acquired overnight, to wave the Star and Crescent',[209] Anthony was still trying to make the case that with

> only about 5,000 Anglo-Indians in the Punjab, 2,000 in Sind and another 2,000 in Eastern Bengal ... Anglo-Indians in Pakistan will have to look to their brothers across the borders for the continuance of their communal existence. By cutting themselves off ... they can only deprive themselves of the support and the resources of the Community and of the All-India Association ... The home of the Community is identified with the Presidency towns of Bombay, Calcutta and Madras and other centres all of which are in the Indian Union. The few Anglo-Indians who will be isolated in Pakistan will have to decide whether they will ... become some new species known as Anglo-Pakistanis or whether they will join themselves to the present body, where the cohesion and integrity of the Community will be the guarantee of their interests and their way of life for the future.[210]

This followed on from another unhappy precedent, in the earlier rupture between the community in India and the ethnic Anglo-Indians and their Anglo-Burman cousins in Burma, who had all been constitutionally reclassified as Anglo-Burmans to better suit themselves to the demands of Burmese nationalism and rising anti-Indian sentiment, with the constitutional separation of Burma from India in 1935–7. Gibbon opted for a similar rebranding, adopting the term 'Anglo-Muslim' rather than 'Anglo-Pakistani' while addressing the Boundary Commission later in July.[211] Declaring his belief 'that the interests of my small community are well placed in the hands of the architects of Pakistan', Gibbon denied having 'changed sides', or even having ever 'taken sides to change sides', despite what he described as 'diabolical' attempts to coerce him and his community.[212] Gibbon pleaded for Anglo-Indians in the region to be considered 'as "another factor" in the case of Pakistan', by which he meant that to avoid splitting his community further, the whole of Punjab should go to Pakistan.[213] Proceeding to shape a locally inflected historical narrative constructed to situate the mixed as ideal citizens of the new Pakistani state, Gibbon asserted that it was

> a well known fact that the 'cream' of the Anglo-Indian community comes from the Punjab. Their origin dates back nearly to 200 years … to the days of the Afghans and the Mughals, mighty Muslim rulers in this land. Many of us … can even trace our descent to the Kings of Oudh … I am in fact an Anglo-Muslim. My great grandfather married a Muslim princess, and so by descent I am a European-cum-Muslim. Such is the case with practically 99% of the Anglo-Indians of the Punjab. They are the descendants of the Anglo-Muslim race.[214]

This imaginative construction is fascinating, although neither 'Anglo-Muslim' nor the more commonly ascribed term 'Anglo-Pakistani' became widely used as self-identifiers.[215] In the years after independence, individuals were more likely to default to just 'Anglo' or to acquiesce in Pakistani assumptions that they were British, European or 'Native' Christians, based upon perceptions of their complexion and socio-economic status. While many Anglo-Indians already residing in what was to become Pakistan were no doubt content to remain where they were, others chose to relocate to the new state, which was equally in need of experienced managerial staff in its newly reconstituted railways and armed forces. In December 1947 the *Review* reported on Anglo-Indians who had chosen to move to Pakistan in the belief that it 'would offer them some kind of haven', but who had 'already begun to regret their decision', and were writing to the Association's head office,

> or coming all the way to Delhi in order to beg the President-in-Chief to intervene with the Government to allow them to change their option. Some Anglo-Indians on the loco[motive] staff of the railways were ill-advised enough to opt for Pakistan. They now find that Pakistan has not enough jobs to offer them. On an average 47% of the loco staff in India was Muslim … [and] practically all opted for

Pakistan. It is not physically possible to squeeze in the personnel of 6 or more Indian railways into 1½ railways which have fallen to Pakistan. A large number of Muslims who have opted for Pakistan, but who cannot now be absorbed into the railways are returning and begging for their jobs back in India. It is not likely that the Railway authorities in India will allow Muslims to change their option. Non-Muslims have already been given … [that] opportunity … [including] several ill-advised Anglo-Indians … Anglo-Indian railwaymen in Eastern Pakistan are being deliberately discriminated against and superseded 'en masse' by Muslim juniors. A large number of Anglo-Indian Sergeants in the Calcutta Police … opted for Eastern Pakistan. When they arrived there they were informed that there was not a vacancy for even one of them. They were fortunate that the West Bengal Government was generous enough to allow them to resume their former appointments in the police department.[216]

Anthony's Association was not unbiased on this subject, as he would have preferred Anglo-Indians to migrate in the other direction, from Pakistan to India, to offset the exodus of Anglo-Indians leaving for Britain and Australia. However, in August 1949 the head office furnished a list of forty-three individual cases in which it had succeeded in assisting Anglo-Indians from various branches in employment and similar matters, sixteen of whom had opted either provisionally or finally for Pakistan.[217] Three were employees of the Posts and Telegraphs department, the rest worked for railways all over India, with the Pakistan returnee cases emanating from Association branches at Agra, Delhi, Gonda, Jubbulpore, Madras, Moradabad and Saharanpur. Non-Pakistan-returnee cases included a Mrs. Myra Sharkey, a member of the WAC(I) from Jubbulpore for whom the Association had secured a '50% disability pension'; Mrs. Olga D'Souza, a teacher at the East Indian Railway School, Mughal Sarai, who had had 'arrears of pay and allowance sanctioned'; the 'upgrading of pay' for school teachers at Oak Grove, Mussoorie; and the 'proposed closing down of [Barnes High] School [Deolali] and sale of [its] property averted'.[218]

By the 1950s the 'plight of ANGLO-INDIANS in East Pakistan' was attracting significant attention in Britain. Lord Waverley complained to the government that 'many Anglo-Indians attracted … after partition by a promise of work are now without work … [For] in practice the term Pakistani means Moslem and Anglo-Pakistanis are retrenched whenever a Moslem is trained to take his place.'[219] Lacking 'adequate records many are unable to claim U.K. citizenship and attempts to claim citizenship of the other Commonwealth countries usually fail. As a result they are regarded as Pakistan citizens', while the acquisition of Pakistani passports, which would also have allowed them to land in the UK, was capriciously biased against non-Muslims, requiring a declaration of intent to return 'to Pakistan' and costing 'hundreds of rupees'.[220] One British official unsympathetically responded: 'I was not aware that there was a large influx of Anglo-Indians into East Pakistan after partition'; if they lacked education and finances 'they would not be much of an asset to any other Commonwealth country'; and 'The crux of the matter is that this community do not find it easy to bow to the inevitable, i.e., to say they are Pakistani citizens and are proud of it'.[221]

At the time Anglo-Indians (or Anglo-Pakistanis) had the right to land in the UK on a Commonwealth passport, by which means they could subsequently obtain naturalisation like other South Asian migrants to Britain. However, the British authorities colluded with both the Indian and Pakistani governments to deter Anglo-Indians from doing so, unless they had relatives, places to live or prospects for immediate employment, worrying that otherwise they would become a burden upon the postwar welfare state. Some Anglo-Indians who registered themselves as British had managed to avail themselves of an 'Assisted Passage Scheme'; however, around six months later British officials noted that proposals were already 'afoot to restrict further the scope of that scheme in a way that would exclude all Anglo-Indians except those few who may have veritable and recent roots in this country'.[222] In Pakistan, 'Anglos' had been accorded no distinct constitutional recognition, coming to be seen under the broader category of Christians by a state that constructed Muslims as its core citizens. The same danger was latent in India in the Hindutva ideology—that Hindus, with the addition of Sikhs, Buddhists and Jains whose holy places were also in Mother India, would be seen as the only groups with a natural claim to the full exercise of Indian citizenship. However, Nehru's enlightened secular civic nationalism and the Congress's embrace of Anthony appeared to have negated that potential threat, at least at the high constitutional level.

Exodus

In March 1946, the *Review* had proclaimed:

> We are not concerned with renegades or escapists. The function of
> the Association is to work for the rightful place of those Anglo-Indians
> who cannot or will not leave India and rightfully regard it as their
> home. Some of the saner elements in the community, however, are
> also anxious. They are inclined to see and paint developments in lurid
> and highly imaginative colours. One cannot blame them, as they have
> no political experience or knowledge of constitutional law ...[223]

In 1949 Anthony railed against senior members of the Association
for feeding still widespread fears for the future. As he told his branch
presidents and their committees, 'a not inconsiderable amount of
anxiety' among Anglo-Indians was an undeniable reality, and this
'PSYCHOLOGICAL PROBLEM' was to be regarded 'AS EASILY
OUR FIRST AND GREATEST PROBLEM TODAY'.[224] He advised
them to instil a sense of confidence and 'attempt to analyse ... and to
evolve measures how best to allay that anxiety'.[225] 'Before
Independence', Anthony had been content to use what he called
'sledge-hammer methods', telling 'those who did not feel that they
were Indians ... [to] leave the country, that the sooner they got out
the better'.[226] Now he was convinced that the problem had become
more complicated psychologically, but in the main he blamed widespread ignorance of the constitutional 'guarantees' he had secured.[227]
A week after they had been confirmed, even members of Anthony's
own governing body in Delhi had apparently not learned of the fact.[228]
Anthony expressed himself stunned to have received a letter from a
school principal asking 'whether from next year [he] could ... expect
any grant from Government as the whole position had changed, with
the British going—no guarantees having been given by the British,
how could we expect from next year any grants for the schools?'[229]
Anthony replied by asking the man, '[D]on't you read the papers? You
don't get the Review, perhaps. [But] At least you [must have] read the
newspapers[?] ... Haven't you read there that Anglo-Indian education
has been guaranteed[?]'[230] Anthony told his branch presidents that

> removing anxiety as a result of ignorance ... is going to be a very
> difficult problem but it can be done, if you do not also join in this

chorus and say, 'We are going to get nothing.' We are getting a great deal ... more than we will get anywhere else. We are gregarious by instinct. When anybody begins to shout that we are not going to get anything, people listen ... and begin to feel that they are going to get nothing ... If you can stop this loose talk it will be a great thing. I get so terribly disappointed ... when I get among intelligent Anglo-Indians who talk in terms of defeatism ... Let us resolve that we will stop it ... [and] that anybody in office who talks in terms of defeatism will be expelled from office. Let us resolve that we will appoint only those who have got their heart in this country, who really feel that they have a place in this country.[231]

The first Chief Minister of Bombay had held out to Anthony the attractive prospect that 'if the Anglo-Indians would only pause and analyse conditions they would realise that they occupy a position of respect which should enable them to take their place as the Brahmins of the new India'.[232] It was an overly optimistic suggestion, but one which Anthony could put to good effect in his speech-making to combat what he termed 'stupid inhibitions and baseless fears'.[233] In late 1949 George Miller expressed alarm at the growing 'exodus of Anglo-Indians who have for several decades—nay generations—lived in India to England, Australia, Canada etc., [which] is causing anxiety to the community who have decided to identify themselves with Free India'.[234] Miller blamed actual or would-be émigrés for a torrent of

insidious propaganda, such as 'India is no place for Anglo-Indians and we will not be treated well', 'How can Anglo-Indians adapt themselves to Indian conditions', 'We are looked upon with suspicion' etc. ... Such statements, coming as they do from people well placed in life ... [who were] supposed leaders of the community, but the first to beat a retreat, are taken seriously by members of a gullible community ... The exodus of a certain section ... is inevitable ... a psychologically wobbly, half-hearted, unstable element who by their intransigence and affectations of superiority ... could not fit in with the new set-up. *Taken from a long range point of view it augurs well for the future of the community that it is drained, nay purged, of an element whose roots ... are not embedded in Indian soil* ... [who, as a result of] their education, social system and aloofness, fostered by the British ... look[ed] away from their country and community ... [The sooner they] quitted the country, bag and baggage, the better ... [Given] their refusal to re-orientate their outlook, change their complexes—superiority and inferiority ... [and] passing-off as an alien in the land of their birth ... used as they were to ... [British] spoon-feeding ... they feel that the line of least resistance should be taken by migration to 'fields afresh and pastures new' which, to their bitter experience, in most cases, has not been the Utopia they hoped for.[235]

Many of Anthony's own arguments against emigration were profoundly gendered, laying much of the blame on 'the Anglo-Indian woman, who refuses to argue with her husband, who just tells him that, "For the sake of the education of your children you must leave the country." The children may be 2 or 3 years old but his wife says to him, in season and out of season: For the sake of the children.'[236] He recounted the story of a gentleman from Bombay he had met while travelling who apparently told him, 'I do not want to leave the country—I am a dark man, I have a good job. Where am I to go? Where will I be accepted?'[237] Anthony agreed that it was indeed better for him to remain in India, to which he apparently replied: 'I will tell my wife, if it becomes necessary we shall have to get a divorce.'[238] Anthony claimed this 'tremendous battle' of continual 'badgering by ... wives and daughters' was going on in 'so many' Anglo-Indian homes, with wives asking, 'Who is your daughter going to marry?'[239] Anthony's answer was a confident assertion that Anglo-Indian young men would rise to greater heights in the new India, and that whereas a typical Anglo-Indian woman might now be 'married [to] a railway subordinate', her daughter would 'probably marry an Anglo-Indian officer'.[240] Another fear he sought to address was a rising tide of insults to Anglo-Indian women by Indian men in public, to which he could only respond:

When you go to England will your wife never be insulted? If your wife ... or your daughter is insulted—and after all, you get scallywags everywhere—is that any reason for bolting? When they were insulted by the British soldier, did you make that a grievance against the British nation ... What are these cowardly Anglo-Indians running away from? An imaginary fear that their women are going to be insulted and that they themselves will lose their jobs.[241]

Anthony also expressed his irritation at the constant stream of 'Anglo-Indian announcements over All India Radio wishing their friends and relatives goodbye as they are proceeding to the U.K. They even put it in the Statesman and other leading papers.'[242] He insisted that 'large numbers of Anglo-Indians' were in fact 'returning, some of them demure—they sneak about in different parts of the country ashamed to tell people of their experience'.[243] Stressing the colour prejudice in Britain and Australia, he commented:

> When they were leaving the country they thought they were doing something laudable ... but when they come back realising their mistake, realising that in England they were nothing but black men, that they were only Indians—at least here you are an Anglo-Indian—there nobody knows who an Anglo-Indian is ... You may wear the latest type of hat but the English butcher will say there goes an Indian gentleman ... He won't refer to you as anything else, and if the children are a little on the lighter side than their darker parents then those children will at one time or another repudiate their darker parents ... The other day two friends ... were over at my place, very dark people, who had been on a tour of Australia. He is a senior officer: he told me that he and his wife were never mistaken for Indians but were taken for Samoans. He seemed glad ... It is a peculiar psychology. Some persons may be mistaken for anything but if they are not regarded as Indian they feel it is a matter for great pride ... We are not entirely to blame. We are a mixture of east and west. We still have an unreasoning fear that something or other is going to happen ... [to us in India.] We still believe that if we go abroad we will be accepted by our kinsmen across the seas. It is a tragic thing ... We know this country, we understand it. Do we suffer from homesickness? ... How can you suffer from homesickness when you are living in your own homeland? When I go to England some of my colleagues meet me and say we are very happy in England. They keep on drumming it in. I ask them why they insist on asserting that they are happy ... Tears come to their eyes when they think of the duck shooting and other things that they have gone from ... gone to suffer life-long nostalgia.[244]

Given his goal of dissuading further emigration, Anthony's repeated assertions that Anglo-Indians were returning to India having had negative experiences overseas may well have been exaggerated. While asserting 'that the Indian High Commissioner in London is sending back destitute Anglo-Indians', Anthony acknowledged having 'lost quite a number of members as the result of this exodus'.[245] He took the emigration of former colleagues, which eventually included

Prater and V. N. Collins (Gibbon's replacement on the Constituent Assembly),[246] and other prominent 'representatives … leaders and presidents' of the Association, as 'a bitter disappointment', and even 'a grave and gross betrayal'.[247] Anthony emphasised that such people had 'given up lucrative appointments … [and] rushed to England only to find out that conditions are strange, foreign and unacceptable. As Anglo-Indians they are not known and have no place in a Britain which is becoming, increasingly, hard-pressed economically and faces a steadily mounting unemployment problem. Anglo-Indians who have acted in foolish haste are repenting at leisure.'[248]

For the most part we can perceive the number and significance of these disproportionately affluent and successful Anglo-Indians and self-identifying Domiciled Europeans mainly through Anthony's diatribes against them. This is like looking at a photographic negative. It should go without saying that the émigrés had their own divergent narratives, seasoned with plenty of criticisms of Anthony's ideas, approach and achievements. Yet these were hardly ever recorded at the time, and the sentiments on both sides have long since mellowed. The few interviews that were conducted at or near to the time give us a sense, apparently lost in later testimony,[249] of one key respect in which some émigrés were at one with Anthony. Even for those able to migrate to the UK, in the immediate aftermath of independence a deep well of resentment existed towards the British for letting the community as a whole down. For most, such feelings probably cooled over time, as Anthony's own anger towards the émigrés eventually did. Eugene Pierce was an emigrant to Britain who was still bitter when he was interviewed in the early 1970s, recounting how

> all the key positions in the country's arterial services were in the hands of loyal Anglo-Indians who, under British administration, formed the backbone of such services. This practically precluded any kind of organised industrial action in … these vital services … Though the Anglo-Indians were shamefully abandoned by the British on granting Independence … from the accounts received I understand there are to be seen in the back streets and chawls [tenements] of India's large cities pale-faced human 'ghosts' living in dire poverty … the vestiges of a white race, witnesses to the past presence of proud and powerful British rulers who made a hasty withdrawal leaving these their blood brothers and sisters to languish and die in the land

they and their ancestors served the British so well. Indeed the day of reckoning is at hand, and heavy will be the price that a degenerate, decadent Britain will ultimately have to pay for the betrayal of her own people both abroad and at home.[250]

Roy Nissen remained in India to continue his career for more than a decade after independence, before emigrating to Britain. Describing the poverty among some of the less fortunate Anglo-Indians, he lamented that the British did not find it in themselves to simply load the Anglo-Indian community onto a few naval vessels and bring them home with them.[251] Some sympathetic Britons, prompted by British consular officials and Christian clergy in India, ignored the position of Anthony's Association to champion the cause of many of the poorer Anglo-Indians who had never had the opportunity to emigrate. Towards the end of 1957, when a new British nationality bill was being debated in the British Parliament, Lord Ogmore turned to

the saddest case we have had to consider for a long time ... a large number of persons of ... Anglo-Indian descent ... living in conditions of the greatest possible hardship. When I was in Calcutta ... my wife and I went to see some of the places where these unfortunate people were living, in slums which are indescribably sordid ... in conditions of the greatest misery and hardship ... This is not the fault of the Indian Government ... There has been a vast influx of refugees from Pakistan, and the ... Calcutta Municipality have done all they can ... Even ... [during] the British Raj, Calcutta was a city which was by no means 'underfull', ... and it is now intensely overcrowded. Whole families of Eurasians are living in one or two rooms. I went ... accompanied by Mrs. Smedley, wife of the United Kingdom Deputy High Commissioner, who, with other European ladies, is doing a wonderful job in trying to look after these ... families. Mrs. Smedley had with her a number of forms, which ... she [often] filled in for them ... One difficulty is that many ... are unable to provide any proof that they are directly descended from United Kingdom citizens ... All they can say is, 'I believe my father or grandfather came from such-and-such a place in England.' This becomes a matter for the Secretary of State['s] ... discretion whether or not he is going to accept such evidence as these people can provide, and I hope that he will be very lenient ... There are funds out of which these people can get assisted passages, and if they feel that they can no longer fit into modern India they can, as so many have done before them, go to Australia, the United Kingdom or elsewhere ... They are cases of hardship in which we, as a country, have a special responsibility. Therefore I would ask the noble Earl to ... see what he can do to clear up the backlog ...[252]

Most British official sentiment, with notable exceptions, desired to transfer the responsibility for Anglo-Indians and their problems to the new nation-states, and to avoid any ongoing liabilities for their failure to integrate or succeed. Yet between the postcolonial states—initially three, eventually four, in what had been the expansive Anglo-India of the Indian Empire, extending from the North-West Frontier with Afghanistan to Burma—there were divergent outcomes for the mixed in terms of their constitutional status, their material and cultural well-being, and their physical safety. India was the nation which did the most to ease the profound psychological adjustment which Anthony saw it as the Association's primary role to effect following the constitutional concessions he had won. In India the interests of the nation, of Anthony, and of the consensus of official opinion in London coincided in opposing any mass exodus of Anglo-Indians. The policy which the British wished to pursue therefore seemed most reasonable in the Indian case, less so in the Pakistani, and ultimately untenable in Burma. Another official minute countered the views of Mr. Smedley, the Deputy High Commissioner, that Britain had ongoing 'moral obligations' to Anglo-Indians in India with the assertion that, whatever the praiseworthiness of such 'humanitarianism', 'legally they seem for the most part to be no concern of the U.K. Government', especially as 'the policy of the Government of India [was] that they should throw in their lot completely with India', and further British interference was 'surely likely to annoy the Government of India'.[253]

Noting that Smedley himself had acknowledged that 'many of these Anglo-Indians who turn up are likely to become a burden upon the National Assistance',[254] the Foreign Office official in London who penned the minute was clearly irked that

> our Office in Calcutta should have gone out of its way to show Lord Ogmore the bad conditions in which Anglo-Indians, who are no concern of the U.K., are living in Calcutta. Such a step is surely likely to lead to Opposition pressure upon the U.K. Government to '*do something*' about a question which we obviously can do nothing about.[255]

He suggested that Smedley be informed of the growing opposition to 'the influx of Coloured Workers ... flocking in from India and

Pakistan (who cannot be assimilated anywhere near so easily as the useful West Indians) and also to the correspondence where we have been urging the Government of India and Pakistan to tighten up their procedure for granting passports to people to come and settle here'.[256] As with other British consular officials in Calcutta and Rangoon, Smedley's arguments and actions in support of the group ran counter to policy emanating from London. That in the Indian case London's priorities dovetailed with those of Anthony and the Indian government was merely a convenient justification of a policy which they were just as eager to apply to Pakistan and Burma even in dramatically divergent circumstances. Another British source made the same point that South Asians had 'greater difficulty in fitting in than the coloured folk from the West Indies ... [and although the] position may be a little different with Anglo-Indians having different background & traditions from Hindus and Moslems ... the difficulty of ... absorbing them is still great'.[257]

Another confidential note on the Anglo-Indians and the closely intertwined 'Anglo-Burman' group was apparently more sympathetic in tone but, in practical terms, equally in line with the official view that Britain ought to wash its hands of such postcolonial liabilities:

> The position of these communities is tragic. They grew up in a certain milieu—the British Empire in Asia—which has disappeared practically overnight. They must inevitably adjust themselves to a new environment ... where they cannot expect to retain their old privileged position ... or they must uproot themselves entirely ... But I am certain ... that the majority ... will be far better off in the long run if they resign themselves to absorption into the general society of the country of their origin. They will no doubt have to face an extremely disagreeable few years ... Many of them will probably make matters worse for themselves by attempting to cling to their former habits.[258]

None of this—notwithstanding Anthony's own efforts to fully integrate the Anglo-Indian community within the new India—prevented waves of emigration to Britain and the predominantly Christian countries of the wider Anglosphere, especially the former 'White Dominions' of Australia, Canada and New Zealand. Thus the reformulated and reimagined Anglo-India of today lives on not only under its hitherto constitutionally recognised status in India, but also as the basis of a broader worldwide diaspora which seeks to periodically reconnect its various branches online and through triennial international reunions. The first of these was held in London in 1989 and the second in Toronto in 1992, although Australian cities, including Perth and Sydney, have long since become the most frequent venue, to which were added Kolkata in 2013 and Chennai in 2019.

EPILOGUE

Tragically fulfilling Anthony's prophecy before the Sapru Committee only a couple of years before, the Indo-Pakistani War of 1947–8 erupted almost immediately after the creation of the two new post-colonial states. The Princely State of Kashmir and Jammu had a Hindu ruler but a Muslim-majority population. The framework created by Mountbatten for pressuring such nominally self-governing states to elect to join one or other Dominion broke down spectacularly when Hari Singh, its last maharaja, attempted to maintain Kashmir and Jammu's independence, and Pakistani-state-sponsored tribal forces sought to force the issue by invading the state. Under pressure from the Kashmiri-descended Nehru, Singh belatedly signed a disputed accession to India in order to secure Indian military support. Anglo-Indians who had been trained during the Second World War went straight into action on behalf of their new nations, most of them for the Union of India.[1]

One of many Anglo-Indian pilots to serve in the first Indo-Pakistan conflict was Flight Lieutenant Clifford Mendoza, who had joined the Indian Air Force (IAF) in 1942 and gave his life in 1947. Again in 1965 Anglo-Indian pilots played a leading role. Denzil and Trevor Keelor were the first two brothers to receive the Vir Chakra for the same reason—shooting down F-86 Sabre fighters of the Pakistani Air Force (PAF). 'Wing Commander Trevor Keelor ... was the first IAF pilot to score an air kill in independent India.'[2] His brother Denzil, a future air marshal, then a squadron leader, oversaw the downing of another by his subsection leader, while 'he himself engaged another

Sabre jet and crippled it'.[3] Flight Lieutenant Alfred Cooke, another Anglo-Indian to be awarded a Vir Chakra for his service in the 1965 war, who retired to Australia in 1969, returned to gift his medal to his squadron in Ambala in 2015. In an interview with the *Indian Express* Cooke recounted how

> I was on a Combat Air Patrol near the East Pakistan border with the instruction that we were not to enter Pakistani airspace. We were told to engage Pakistani jets only if they ventured into our territory. I was diverted to the Kalaikunda air force station near Kharagpur in West Bengal which was under attack from the PAF. As I neared it, I saw black smoke rising and my blood boiled. I told my wingman, Flying Officer S C Mamgain, that we are going to get these b******s.[4]

Mamgain would also be awarded a Vir Chakra in the action. But Cooke took the lion's share of the glory, as Vishnu Som reported for NDTV:

> It's a story of the Indian Air Force which has perhaps not been told enough. It's the story of a rare hero. A man who in 1965 [with a single wingman] engaged not one, but four Pakistani Sabre Fighters. He's back in India now, he lives in Australia, but Flight Lieutenant Alfred Cooke is a legend for what he did and that dogfight which he flew over the skies of Kalaikunda goes down as one of the greatest dogfights in the Indian Subcontinent.[5]

In the interview that followed, Cooke recounted the melee, some of it at tree-top height. The Pakistani Sabres flew very low to avoid him, diving down, decelerating and accelerating. As Cooke doggedly pursued one, rushing headlong towards the foliage below at 'around 400 knots', he got the enemy in his gunsight, but failed to realise that his 'wingtip was hitting the scrub', small bushes only a few feet from the ground:

> I was so close that when I hit him and stopped firing his aircraft exploded and I could not avoid flying through the fireball, and ... I felt that, not exactly the impact, but the heat made my aircraft sort-of [jolt], like when you hit a little air-pocket, and I was ... just about 50 feet off the ground at that stage.

He had not a moment to savour the kill, as another aircraft was pursuing him. He pulled up, turning hard right, to engage his next opponent. Cooke described the relentless pace as the greater manoeuvrability and tighter turning circle of the Sabres allowed them to get on the inside of him and repeatedly out-turn him as they crossed and crisscrossed one another in 'a classic scissors' pattern. Cooke pulled up very steeply, making the most of the 10,000 pounds of thrust and faster rate of acceleration of his Hawker Hunter Rolls-Royce Avon engine, escaping from his opponent's line of fire and forcing him to lose speed. The Sabre dived down again to build up its flying speed, Cooke then got behind and followed him, but again the two repeated their crossing turns. Suddenly seeing his opponent's increased angle of dive and steep banking away from him, he said, 'Uh-oh, somebody has warned him, so that person has to be behind me.' Having run out of high-explosive ammunition, Cooke could only use limited bursts of what remained, carefully restraining his firing until he was in a good position and had the Sabre clearly in his gunsights. He knew he was hitting his opponent and expected 'him to explode, but nothing happened'. Then pieces started flying off the aircraft immediately in front of him, but Cooke had to break away and pull up at about eighty yards distant to avoid a collision, whereupon he saw the third Sabre over his right shoulder coming at him from behind. Within a couple of reversals he managed to get behind this new opponent and 'was on *his* tail', following close behind him in a vertical dive, and again wondering why he was not hitting him. Distracted by this thought, Cooke

> suddenly ... realised that the ground was coming up pretty fast, and with my finger still on the trigger I pulled back on the joystick and unfortunately I expended whatever ammunition I had left ... because on the Hunter we only have about five seconds firing time, and you are firing at a hundred rounds per second. So I expended my ammunition while pulling up from the dive, and I almost hit the ground, and I was *very, very shaken* at that stage.[6]

Momentarily recovering his composure and 'equilibrium', Cooke warned Mamgain, to '"break port" ... break port means do a hard evasive turn to the left', and the enemy plane 'started doing loops and acrobatics to try and shake [me off]'.

> I was fiddling with my gun-selector switch, hoping that I'd have at least one or maybe two bullets left, so I fiddled with the switches, got it back ... got into position, had a shot, but only the camera worked ... He obviously realised that it's his lucky day ... [but] pieces were

flying off the aircraft so ... the enemy are supposed to have given credit for that one. I don't know.[7]

However, when the IAF arrived above Karachi, and the PAF took to the skies to defend it, one of their Sabres was piloted by Flight Lieutenant Mervyn Leslie Middlecoat, the fourth child of Percy Middlecoat, an Anglo-Indian railway officer from Lahore.

> In the dogfight that followed, Mervyn shot down two enemy aircrafts, a feat for which he came to be known as the 'Defender of Karachi'. He was then deployed at Mushaf Air Base, Lahore, where he was given the command of Squadron 9. During the three-week war, he kept his squadron's spirits high with the firm conviction of a commander who leads from the front ... perform[ing] ... an impressive series of seventeen 'Air Sorties' and three 'Photo Reconnaissance' missions. At the end of the war, he was awarded the ... 'Sitara-e-Jurat' [Star of Courage] for his bravery and professional leadership.[8]

By the time another conflict broke out in 1971, now Wing Commander Middlecoat was one of six pilots to be selected for a daring mission devised by

> the PAF high command ... to take out the Indian Air Force's radar capability by attacking the heavily defended Jamnagar airbase ... [While] strafing aircrafts of the Indian Air Force at the base, they were set upon by IAF MiGs. Forced to abort the mission, Mervyn narrowly avoided two incoming missiles by lowering his altitude and increasing his speed. But when his aircraft was near the Gulf of Kutch, a third missile hit him. According to Flight Lieutenant Bharat Bhosan Soni, the pilot who shot him down, Mervyn managed to eject from the aircraft and fell into the sea below. Soni radioed for a rescue team, but by the time they got there ... [he] was nowhere to be found and was declared 'Missing in Action'.[9]

Treated as a martyr by the Islamic Republic of Pakistan, Middlecoat 'was awarded the Sitara-e-Jurat for the second time',[10] and in 2017 the PAF named 'a park in Islamabad E9, Middlecoat *Shaheed* Park'.[11] On the other side, Anthony professed his belief that Anglo-Indians' impressive military contributions to the new India had entirely melted away any lingering resentment and prejudice towards them. This was an excessively optimistic or politically driven assertion perhaps, but directionally true in respect of the trend among a large swathe of educated and elite opinion at the time, as confirmed by the reflections of Indian businessman Raj Chatterjee: 'I'm glad to say that since independence the one community that has … come out and really shown itself … [in] the three wars we've had … [shown] the really good stuff they're made of … are the Anglo-Indians.'[12] Anthony celebrated how the community had proved itself in

> our wars with Pakistan … [when] Anglo-Indians … shone in their patriotism. You take the '65 war … or before that, take the Kashmir campaign … in '47, '48. Now, they would have captured Srinagar but for the Anglo-Indians. They sent in their Pathans. Then we sent in our Air Force. And in that Air Force 50% of the awards for gallantry, Vir Chakra, were won by Anglo-Indian fighter pilots. You see it was … the Air Force—an elite corps—but a decisive corps, that the Anglo-Indians dominate. Today you've got an Anglo-Indian, [Air Chief Marshal Denis Anthony] La Fontaine, [as] Chief of the Air Force …[13] [and Admiral Ronald Lynsdale] Pereira … was the head of the Navy about four years ago.[14] The second line in the Navy was all Anglo-Indian, all the officers.[15]

The record itself was no overstatement. During and immediately following the first Indo-Pakistan War of 1947–8 alone, Vir Chakras had been conferred on Flight Lieutenants Aloysius William Barrette (died in service 1948), Michael Patrick Owen Blake, Leslie Richard Dickinson Blunt (later Group Captain), Gerald Bertram Cabral, and Anthony Suares (later Wing Commander); Flying Officers George Douglas Clarke (later Wing Commander), Dennis Osman Barty, Desmond Pushong, and Geoffrey Charles Wilks; and Squadron Leaders Kenneth Merals David and Ezra D'Sylva Masillamani; as well as the Maha Vir Chakra on Flight Lieutenant Sidney Basil Noronha.

This was strong evidence for Anthony's promise to Anglo-Indians that independence would bring them new opportunities by removing the formal and informal racialised constraints that the colonial state had placed upon their aspirations. However, as in earlier periods, the achievements of exceptional Anglo-Indians could never be the measure of the economic well-being of the community as a whole. In spite of a temporary and phased continuation of reserved employment in some of these areas, the colonial-era association of Anglo-Indians with the railways, posts and telegraphs, and customs departments did not long survive formal decolonisation. The involvement of the group's women with the nursing service was more enduring, although their proportional predominance declined dramatically in the post-independence decades. As Lionel Caplan has argued in *Children of Colonialism: Anglo-Indians in a Postcolonial World*, Anglo-Indian women generally fared better in adjusting to fast-changing employment markets, finding work in new fields such as travel and tourism, retail sales, and telecommunications. Anthony's efforts in founding the Frank Anthony Public Schools and defending the already existing anglophone educational institutions of the community from the colonial period constituted a major focus of his political, legal, constitutional and economic strategy to secure the future of the new Anglo-India in a new India. These were largely successful and meant that, apart from its military heroes, the Anglo-Indian community in India would be increasingly known and often fondly remembered for its English-language educators.

NOTES

INTRODUCTION

1. M. Solly, 'Why the controversy over a black actress playing Anne Boleyn is unnecessary and harmful: Long before Jodie Turner-Smith's miniseries came under criticism, British Indian actress Merle Oberon portrayed the Tudor queen' (3 June 2021), https://www.smithsonianmag.com/smart-news/who-was-first-woman-color-bring-anne-boleyns-story-screen-180977882/.
2. C. Higham and R. Moseley, *Princess Merle: The Romantic Life of Merle Oberon* (New York, 1983), p. 59.
3. Ibid., p. 58.
4. S. Broughton, *Brando's Bride* (Cardigan, 2019), p. 32.
5. D. O'Flaherty, 'The Trouble with Merle: A Study Guide', A Film Australia National Interest Program, p. 2, https://www.nfsa.gov.au/collection/curated/trouble-merle.
6. A. Korda (director), *The Private Life of Don Juan*, film, London Film Productions (UK, 30 November 1934), c.27:43–59.
7. E. Woo, 'Foreword', in D. Groves, *Anna May Wong's Lucky Shoes: 1939 Australia through the Eyes of an Art Deco Diva* (Ames IA, 2011), p. 5.
8. *The Age*, cited in ibid., p. 8.
9. *Loving v. Virginia*, 388 U.S. 1 (1967).
10. *Northern Territory Times*, cited in Groves, *Anna May Wong's Lucky Shoes*, p. 8.
11. Ibid.
12. Ibid.
13. *Sydney Morning Herald*, cited in ibid.
14. C. Dover, *Half-Caste* (London, 1937), p. 15.
15. Groves, *Anna May Wong's Lucky Shoes*, p. 19.
16. N. Coward, *The Lyrics of Noël Coward: With an Introduction by Noël Coward Himself* (Bloomsbury, 1965; reprint, 2012), p. 107.
17. Ibid.

18. Ibid., p. 108.

19. J. Bright-Holmes (ed.), *Like It Was: The Diaries of Malcolm Muggeridge* (New York, 1981), p. 102.

20. Higham and Moseley, *Princess Merle*, pp. 12–13. My emphasis.

21. Ibid., p. 13.

22. Ibid., p. 12.

23. Ibid., p. 18.

24. Ibid.

25. Ibid., p. 45.

26. Ibid., p. 97.

27. Ibid.

28. Broughton, *Brando's Bride*, p. 32.

29. L. Ashford, *Whisper of the Moon Moth* (Seattle WA, 2017), p. 170.

30. Ibid.

31. Ibid., pp. 170–1.

32. Higham and Moseley, *Princess Merle*, pp. 56–7.

33. Ibid., p. 101.

34. Ibid., p. 100.

35. Ibid., p. 101.

36. M. Delofski (director), *The Trouble with Merle*, documentary film, Australian Broadcasting Corporation et al. (Australia, 13 June 2002).

37. Ashford, *Whisper*, pp. 314–15.

38. Higham and Moseley, *Princess Merle*, p. 46.

39. Ibid., p. 10.

40. Ibid.

41. Ibid.

42. O'Flaherty, 'The Trouble with Merle', p. 2.

43. Higham and Moseley, *Princess Merle*, p. 11.

44. Ibid.

45. O'Flaherty, 'The Trouble with Merle', p. 2.

46. F. Anthony, *Britain's Betrayal in India: The Story of the Anglo-Indian Community* (New Delhi, 1969), p. 160.

47. B. Nichols, *Verdict on India* (New York, 1944), p. 225.

48. N. Jog, *Judge or Judas?* (Bombay, 1945), pp. 194–5.

49. Nichols, *Verdict*, p. 223.

50. Jog, *Judge or Judas?*, p. 197.

51. *The Collected Works of Mahatma Gandhi* (1931–2), vol. 48, p. 259.

52. Original theatrical trailer of *Bhowani Junction* (1956), reproduced as a 'Home Video Trailer from Warner Home Video', https://www.imdb.com/video/vi750387481/?ref_=tt_vi_i_1.

53. Ibid.

54. Ibid.

55. J. Masters, *Bhowani Junction* (New York, 1954), p. 92.

56. Ibid., p. 11.

57. Ibid., p. 210.

58. Ibid., p. 89.

59. B. Leadon, 'The Future of Anglo-Indians', *AIR* (December 1940), p. 22, republished in *Colonization Observer* (April 1941), p. 4.

60. R. Pearson, *Eastern Interlude: A Social History of the European Community in Calcutta* (Calcutta, 1954), p. 229, cited in A. Blunt, *Domicile and Diaspora: Anglo-Indian Women and the Spatial Politics of Home* (Malden MA, 2005), p. 130.

61. Blunt, *Domicile and Diaspora*, p. 130.

62. T. Royle, *The Last Days of the Raj* (London, 1989), p. 38.

63. Cited in ibid.

64. Ibid.

65. NAUK, FO/643/140, C. H. Campagnac, M.B.E., Barrister-at-Law, President [Anglo-Burman Union], Rangoon, 'Most Confidential: A Note on the Present Position of the Anglo-Burman Community' (4 September 1947), signed note (11 May), p. 20.

66. BL, OIOC, MSS Eur T29 (see also R29/1–6), Transcript of interview with Irene Edwards [née Green] (1972–4), pp. 6/10–6/11.

67. M. Bose, *The Magic of Indian Cricket: Cricket and Society in India* (rev. edn, Abingdon, 2006), p. 99.

68. Bright-Holmes, *Like it Was*, p. 102.

69. Masters, *Bhowani Junction*, pp. 27–8.

70. Ibid.

71. Ibid.

72. Ibid.

73. Ibid., p. 4.

74. F. Marshall (director), *Congo*, film, The Kennedy/Marshall Company (United States, 9 June 1995), 26:20–7.

75. G. Cukor (director), *Bhowani Junction*, film, Metro-Goldwyn-Mayer (United States, 1 May 1956), 55:23–34.

76. H. Mitra (ed.), *The Govt. of India Act 1919: Rules Thereunder and Govt. Reports, 1920* (Calcutta, 1921), 'Provincial Council Rules', schedule II: Qualification of Electors, p. 214.

77. 1935 Government of India Act, ch. 42, article 26-(1), p. 308. Europeans were similarly defined but it was specified that they were not natives of India.

78. Dixona, 'The Top Classic Horror Actors' (8 April 2011), https://www.imdb.com/list/ls000791185/.

79. S. Mizutani, *The Meaning of White: Race, Class, and the 'Domiciled Community' in British India 1858–1930* (Oxford, 2011), p. 72; cf. U. Charlton-Stevens, 'Anglo-Indians in Colonial India: Historical Demography, Categorization, and Identity', in P. Aspinall and Z. Rocha (eds.), *The Palgrave International Handbook of Mixed Racial and Ethnic Classification* (Cham, 2020).

80. *Census of India* (1911), part 2, ch. 4, subsidiary table 6: 'Statistics of Europeans and Anglo-Indians', p. 146.

81. Ibid., pp. 139–40.

82. Hansard, HC Debates, 2 August 1922, vol. 157, col. 1511.

83. G. Morton-Jack, *Army of Empire: The Untold Story of the Indian Army in World War I* (ebook, 2018), ch. 11.

84. C. Allen (ed.), *Plain Tales from the Raj* (London, 1975), pp. 57–8.

85. G. D'Cruz, 'Christopher Hawes in Conversation with Glenn D'Cruz', *IJAIS* 3:1 (1998), p. 1, http://www.international-journal-of-anglo-indian-studies.org/.

86. Ibid., p. 2.

87. Ibid.

88. Ibid.

89. Ibid.

90. Ibid., p. 3.

91. Dispatch from 'Court of Directors to the President of Madras ... 1687', cited in E. Hedin, 'The Anglo-Indian Community', *American Journal of Sociology* 40:2 (September 1934), pp. 166–7.

92. U. Charlton-Stevens, *Anglo-Indians and Minority Politics in South Asia: Race, Boundary Making and Communal Nationalism* (London, 2017/2018), pp. 243–8.

93. U. Charlton-Stevens, 'The End of Greater Anglo-India: Partitioned Anglo Identities in Burma and Pakistan', in R. Andrews and M. Simi Raj (eds.), *Anglo-Indian Identity in India and the Diaspora* (Cham, 2021).

1. FORGING A 'MIXED-RACE' COMMUNITY IN INDIA

1. C. Hawes, 'Eurasians in British India, 1773–1833: The Making of a Reluctant Community', PhD dissertation, Department of History, School of Oriental and African Studies, University of London (1993).

2. C. Hawes, *Poor Relations: The Making of a Eurasian Community in British India, 1773–1833* (Richmond, 1996), p. 85.

3. D. Chew, 'Book Review: Anglo-Indians and Minority Politics in South Asia: Race, Boundary Making and Communal Nationalism', *IJAIS* 18:1 (2018), pp. 37–8, http://www.international-journal-of-anglo-indian-studies.org/.

4. M. Paranjape, '"East Indian" Cosmopolitanism: *The Fakeer of Jungheera* and the Birth of Indian Modernity', Interventions, *International Journal of Postcolonial Studies* 13:4 (2011), p. 565, https://doi.org/10.1080/1369801X.2011.628119.

5. R. Chaudhuri, 'The Politics of Naming: Derozio in Two Formative Moments of Literary and Political Discourse, Calcutta, 1825–31', *Modern Asian Studies* 44:4 (2010), p. 880.

6. Compare Paranjape '"East Indian" Cosmopolitanism', p. 556, with S. Choudhuri, 'Introduction', in E. Madge, *Henry Derozio: The Eurasian Poet and Reformer* (Calcutta, 1905; reprint, 1982), pp. iv, viii.

7. 'The East-Indians', Asiatic Intelligence—Calcutta, *Asiatic Journal and Monthly Register for British and Foreign India, China, and Australia* (London), NS, 5 (May 1831), p. 16.

8. Mrs. Postans, 'Native Indian Society', *The Albion, or, British, Colonial and Foreign Weekly Gazette* (New York, 18 November 1843), p. 564.

9. R. Kipling, 'Kidnapped', in *Plain Tales from the Hills* (North Falmouth MA, 1899), p. 135.

10. S. Neill, *A History of Christianity in India: The Beginnings to AD 1707* (Cambridge, 1984), pp. 371–2.

11. Ibid., p. 371.

12. Ibid.

13. Cited in ibid., p. 372.

14. Ibid.

15. Equivalent to eight or nine shillings or approximately five rupees.

16. Dispatch from 'Court of Directors to the President of Madras … 1687', cited in E. Hedin, 'The Anglo-Indian Community', *American Journal of Sociology* 40:2 (1934), pp. 166–7.

17. G. D'Cruz, *Midnight's Orphans: Anglo-Indians in Post/colonial Literature* (Bern, 2006), p. 46.

18. W. Dalrymple, *White Mughals: Love and Betrayal in Eighteenth-Century India* (London, 2002), p. 30.

19. Cited in ibid., p. 382.

20. Ibid., p. 62.

21. See R. Copleston quotation in E. Chatterton, *Anglo-Indian and Eurasian Origins* (Westminster, 1937), p. 5.

22. D. McMenamin, 'Anglo-Indian Lives in Pakistan through the Lens of Oral Histories', PhD thesis, University of Otago, New Zealand (2019), p. 249.

23. J. Brown, 'Preface', in U. Charlton-Stevens, *Anglo-Indians and Minority Politics* (London, 2017/2018), p. ix.

24. D. Ghosh, *Sex and the Family in Colonial India: The Making of Empire* (Cambridge, 2006), p. 18.

25. R. Andrews, '"Did You Know Your Great-Grandmother Was an Indian Princess?": Early Anglo-Indian Arrivals in New Zealand', in S. Bandyopadhyay and J. Buckingham (eds.), *Indians and the Antipodes: Networks, Boundaries and Circulation* (New Delhi, 2019).

26. W. Dalrymple, *Forgotten Masters: Indian Painting for the East India Company* (New Delhi, 2019), p. 14.

27. G. D'Cruz, 'Christopher Hawes in Conversation with Glenn D'Cruz', *IJAIS* 3:1 (1998), p. 1, http://www.international-journal-of-anglo-indian-studies.org/.

28. Ghosh, *Sex and the Family*, p. 237.

29. Ibid., pp. 237–8.

30. V. Falkland, *Chow-Chow: Being Selections from a Journal Kept in India, Egypt, and Syria*, vol. 1 (London, 1857), p. 23.

31. Ibid., p. 25.

32. Ibid., pp. 23–4.

33. *Second Report from the Select Committee on the Affairs of the East India Company; Together with an Appendix of Documents, and Index* (London, 1830), p. 45.

34. Ibid.

35. P. de Silva, *Colonial Self-fashioning in British India c.1785–1845: Visualising Identity and Difference* (Newcastle, 2018), p. 34.

36. Dalrymple, *Forgotten Masters*, p. 14.

37. T. Edwards, 'Art. VI: The Eurasian Movement of 1829–30', *Calcutta Review* 76:151 (January 1883), p. 111.

38. Ghosh, *Sex and the Family*, p. 225.

39. Dalrymple, *White Mughals*, pp. 67–8.

40. Ibid.

41. Ibid., p. 62.

42. Ibid.

43. Ibid., pp. xvi–xvii, 62.

44. J. Cotton, 'Art. III: Kitty Kirkpatrick', *Calcutta Review* 108:216 (April 1899), pp. 239–40.

45. De Silva, *Colonial Self-fashioning*, p. 6.

46. Ibid.

47. Women's inner apartments of a large house.

48. Dalrymple, *White Mughals*, pp. 343–4.

49. Ibid., p. xvii.

50. Ibid., p. xix. Original emphasis removed.

51. Cotton, 'Kitty Kirkpatrick', p. 236.

52. Cited in ibid., p. 245.

53. Ibid., p. 247.

54. Ibid., p. 245.

55. Cited in ibid., p. 247.

56. *AIR* (February 1931), p. 11.

57. Ibid.

58. Ibid.

59. M. Fisher, *The Inordinately Strange Life of Dyce Sombre: Victorian Anglo-Indian MP and Chancery 'Lunatic'* (London, 2010), pp. 1, 3, 7.

60. Ibid., p. 1.

61. Ibid., pp. 1, 3.

62. Ibid.

63. Hansard, HC Debates, 16 February 1842, vol. 60, cols. 623–4 and 27 August 1841, vol. 59, col. 451, https://api.parliament.uk/historic-hansard/commons/1842/feb/16/corn-laws-ministerial-plan-adjourned and https://api.parliament.uk/historic-hansard/commons/1841/aug/27/address-in-answer-to-the-speech.

64. Cited in Edwards, 'The Eurasian Movement', p. 129.

65. E. Roberts, *Scenes and Characteristics of Hindostan, with Sketches of Anglo-Indian Society*, vol. 3 (London, 1835), pp. 96–8.

66. J. Stocqueler, *Hand-Book of India, Guide to the Stranger and the Traveller, and a Companion to the Resident* (London, 1844), p. 49.

67. J. Stocqueler, 'The Crime of Colour', ch. 6, *Patriotic Fund Journal* 1:7 (27 January 1855), p. 117.

68. O. Snell, *Anglo-Indians and Their Future* (Bombay, 1944), pp. 11–12.

69. Cited in *Report of Proceedings Connected with the East Indians' Petition to Parliament, Read at a Public Meeting Held at the Town Hall, Calcutta March 28, 1831; with an Appendix* (Calcutta, 1831), p. 82; also cited in Edwards, 'The Eurasian Movement', p. 110.

70. H. Stark, *Hostages to India, or, The Life-Story of the Anglo-Indian Race* (Calcutta, 1926), p. 60.

71. Ibid.; Stark's original source is cited in V. Anderson, *Race and Power in British India: Anglo-Indians, Class and Identity in the Nineteenth Century* (London, 2014) as BL, 'IOR/B/113, John Turing Nominated as a Cadet for Madras—Refused', Court Minute Book, 19 April 1791'; a photograph of the relevant extract was posted along with William Turing's 1782 will (IOR/L/AG/34/29/186, p. 47) in M. Makepeace, 'The Turings of India' (4 May 2017) on the British Library's *Untold Lives* blog, https://blogs.bl.uk/untoldlives/2017/05/the-turings-of-india.html.

72. Hansard, HC Debates, 4 May 1830, vol. 24, col. 378, https://api.parliament.uk/historic-hansard/commons/1830/may/04/petition-of-indo-britons.

73. 'Injudicious Nature of the Policy of the Honourable East India Company, as Exemplified in the Condition of the Indo-Britons', *Alexander's East India and Colonial and Commercial Journal* (London), 1 (April 1831), pp. 462–3.

74. 'Speech by Mr. Kenneth E. Wallace at the Ministers' Association on 9th March, 1931', *AIR* (March 1931), p. 25.

75. Anderson, *Race and Power*, p. 20.

76. A. Upjohn, 'Art. II: Map of Calcutta, 1792–3', *Calcutta Review* 18 (July–December 1852), p. 284.

77. G. Valentia, *Voyages and Travels in India, Ceylon, the Red Sea, Abyssinia and Egypt in the Years 1802, 1803, 1805, and 1806*, vol. 1 (London, 1809), pp. 241–2.

78. Cited in W. Sykes, 'On the Population and Mortality of Calcutta', *Journal of the Statistical Society of London* 8:1 (March 1845), p. 50.

79. Ibid.

80. *The Legislative Assembly Debates: Official Report*, vol. 4, First Session of the Sixth Legislative Assembly, 15 March to 30 March 1946 (Delhi, 1947), 25 March 1946, p. 2870.

81. D'Cruz, 'Christopher Hawes', pp. 2–3.

82. John Wade, *The Extraordinary Black Book: An Exposition of the United Church of England and Ireland; Civil List and Crown Revenues; Incomes, Privileges, and Power, of the Aristocracy; Privy Council, Diplomatic, and Consular Establishments; Law and Judicial Administration; Representation and Prospects of Reform under the New Ministry; Profits, Influence, and Monopoly of the Bank of England and East-India Company; Debt and Funding System; Salaries, Fees, and Emoluments in Courts of Justice, Public Offices, and Colonies; Lists of Pluralists, Placemen, Pensioners, and Sinecurists: The Whole Corrected from the Latest Official*

Returns, and Presenting a Complete View of the Expenditure, Patronage, Influence, and Abuses of the Government, in Church, State, Law and Representation (London, 1831), pp. 364–6.

83. 'Injudicious Nature' (1831), pp. 465–6.

84. Report from the Select Committee of the House of Lords Appointed to Inquire into the Present State of the Affairs of the East India Company, and into the Trade between Great Britain, the East Indies and China; with the Minutes of Evidence Taken before the Committee (London, 1830), p. 45.

85. Ibid., p. 27.

86. J. Fraser (ed.), Military Memoir of Lieut.-Col. James Skinner, C.B. (London, 1851), pp. 159–60.

87. Y. Park and R. Rajan (eds.), The Postcolonial Jane Austen (London, 2000), p. 174.

88. Cited in Report of Proceedings Connected with the East Indians' Petition to Parliament (1831), p. 91, and, with minor differences in transcription, in T. Edwards, Henry Derozio, the Eurasian: Poet, Teacher and Journalist (Calcutta, 1884), p. 236; also transcribed in abbreviated third-person form in Hansard, HC Debates, 4 May 1830, vol. 24, cols. 379–80, https://api.parliament.uk/historic-hansard/commons/1830/may/04/petition-of-indo-britons.

89. F. Anthony, Britain's Betrayal in India: The Story of the Anglo-Indian Community (New Delhi, 1969), p. 30.

90. Roberts, Scenes and Characteristics, vol. 2, p. 188.

91. Ibid., pp. 190–2.

92. Ibid., p. 193.

93. Edwards, 'The Eurasian Movement', p. 103.

94. BL, P/4089, Report of the Pauperism Committee (Calcutta, 1892), appendix I, Statistics Sub-committee evidence, pp. xv–xvi.

95. Dalrymple, White Mughals, pp. 144–5.

96. Upjohn, 'Map of Calcutta', p. 283.

97. D'Cruz, 'Christopher Hawes'.

98. Report from the Select Committee of the House of Lords Appointed to Inquire into the Present State of the Affairs of the East India Company (1830), p. 195.

99. Second Report from the Select Committee on the Affairs of the East India Company (1830), p. 47.

100. Ibid., pp. 36, 42.

101. Cited in Report Connected with the East Indians' Petition (1831), p. 79; also cited in Edwards, 'The Eurasian Movement', p. 108.

102. Index of 'Commons Sitting of 4 May 1830, series 2, vol. 24', https://api.parliament.uk/historic-hansard/sittings/1830/may/04.

103. Cited in Report Connected with the East Indians' Petition (1831), p. 81; also cited in Edwards, 'The Eurasian Movement', p. 109.

104. 'The East-Indians', p. 15.

105. Ibid.

106. Ibid., pp. 15–16.

107. Ibid.

108. Ibid.

109. Stark, *Hostages*, p. 66.

110. Edwards, 'The Eurasian Movement', p. 114.

111. K. Ballhatchet, *Race, Sex and Class under the Raj: Imperial Attitudes and Policies and Their Critics, 1793–1905* (London, 1980), p. 102.

112. Ibid., pp. 102–3.

113. Ibid., pp. 108–9.

114. Ibid., p. 110.

115. Ibid., p. 108.

116. Ibid.

117. BL, MSS Eur F531, 'Memorandum C/IND/MADRAS 2.f.1, 'SPG'.

118. Ibid., 'Surveyors'.

119. Stocqueler, *Hand-Book*, pp. 46–7.

120. Anon. ('V. G. Clarke'), *The Fortunes of the Anglo-Indian Race: Considered Retrospectively and Prospectively by One of Fifty Years Knowledge and Experience* (2nd edn, Madras, 1878), p. 14.

121. *Report of the Pauperism Committee* (1892), p. 6.

122. Ibid.

123. D'Cruz, 'Christopher Hawes'.

124. Stocqueler, 'Crime of Colour', ch. 2, *Patriotic Fund Journal* 1:5 (13 January 1855), p. 77.

125. Ibid., ch. 4, *Patriotic Fund Journal* 1:6 (20 January 1855), p. 98.

126. Ibid.

127. Ibid.

128. Ibid., p. 100.

129. Ibid., ch. 6, *Patriotic Fund Journal* 1:7 (27 January 1855), p. 120.

130. Ibid., p. 119.

131. Ibid., p. 121 and Stocqueler, 'Crime of Colour', ch. 7, *Patriotic Fund Journal* 1:8 (3 February 1855), p. 129.

132. Ibid., ch. 7, p. 129.

133. Ibid.

134. Ibid.

135. Ibid.

136. Ibid.

137. *Calcutta Review* 7 (January–June 1847), p. 217.

138. *Report of the Commissioners Appointed to Inquire into the Sanitary State of the Army in India; with Abstract of Evidence, and of Reports Received from Indian Military Stations* (London, 1864), p. 33.

139. Ibid.

140. Dr. Chambers, *Anglo-Indian Prospects in India: Read at a Meeting of the Board of Direction of the Anglo-Indian Association* (Calcutta, 1879), p. 12.

141. T. Royle, *The Last Days of the Raj* (London, 1989), pp. 28, 39.

142. I. Stephens, *Monsoon Morning* (London, 1966), pp. 27–8.

143. W. Burchett, *Trek Back from Burma* (Allahabad, 1944), p. 273.

144. Cited in H. Vickers, *Vivien Leigh* (London, 1988), p. 7.

145. L. Chater, 'Armenian: Something Vivien Leigh and Her Cousin Xan Fielding a British Spy Had in Common', *Chater Genealogy* blog (12 August 2015), http://chater-genealogy.blogspot.com/2015/08/armenian-something-vivien-leigh-and-her_12.html.

146. R. Kipling, 'Kidnapped', in *Plain Tales* (1899), pp. 134–5.

147. Ibid.

148. A. de Courcy, *The Fishing Fleet: Husband-Hunting in the Raj* (London, 2012), p. 174.

149. Ibid., p. 175.

150. Ibid.

151. Ibid.

152. Ibid., pp. 175–6.

153. Ibid., p. 176.

154. Ibid.

155. Ibid.

156. Ibid., p. 177.

157. Ibid., p. 181.

158. Ibid., pp. 181–3.

159. Ibid., p. 182.

160. Ibid., pp. 181–3.

161. E. Thurston, *Castes and Tribes of Southern India*, vol. 2: C to J (Madras, 1909), p. 232.

162. Ibid., pp. 232–3.

163. Ibid., p. 238.

164. Ibid., pp. 237–8.

165. Cited in A. Ganachari, '"White Man's Embarrassment": European Vagrancy in 19th Century Bombay', *Economic and Political Weekly* 37:25 (22–28 June 2002), p. 2480.

166. H. Skipton, *Our Reproach in India* (Oxford, 1912), pp. 12–15.

167. Cited in Ganachari, '"White Man's Embarrassment"', p. 2479.

168. Cited in ibid., pp. 2478–9. Original emphasis removed.

169. Ibid., p. 2478.

170. Anthony, *Britain's Betrayal*, pp. 78–9.

171. R. Maher, 'The Anglo-Indian Position in India', *AIR* (May 1939), p. 12.

172. *Report of the Pauperism Committee* (1892), appendix I, Statistics Sub-committee evidence, pp. xiv–xv.

173. Ibid., p. 8.

174. *Indian Round Table Conference (Third Session) (17th November 1932—24th December 1932)* (London, 1933), p. 176.

175. S. Brendish, 'George (William) Brendish and the Indian Mutiny of 1857', *IJAIS* 7:1 (2003), http://www.international-journal-of-anglo-indian-studies.org/.

176. W. Madge, cited in 'Anglo-Indian Regiment', *Statesman* (12 July 1912).

177. NAI, Political Department, Political Branch (Confidential), 1908, file no. 42, nos. 1–4, 'Proposal for the Enrolment of a Special Police Reserve Composed Mainly of Europeans and Eurasians', p. 14.

178. NAUK, WO/32/6889, handwritten note on file: 'on 5983', signed '29–12–86 Wolseley'.

179. 'Proposal for the Enrolment of a Special Police Reserve' (1908), pp. 13–14.

180. Ibid., p. 2.

181. BL, OIOC, MSS Eur F111/158, (from the Viceroy) nos. 6, 29c, and 38a, pp. 21, 130d, and 178a.

182. BL, OIOC, MSS Eur F111/159, (from the Viceroy) no. 7, p. 35.

183. Ibid., no. 18, p. 79.

184. H. Roseboom and C. Dover, 'The Eurasian Community as a Eugenic Problem', in *A Decade of Progress in Eugenics: Scientific Papers of the Third International Congress of Eugenics Held at American Museum of Natural History New York, August 21–23, 1932* (Baltimore, 1934), p. 92.

185. Curzon of Kedleston, *Speeches by Lord Curzon of Kedleston, Viceroy and Governor-General of India: 1898–1901* (Calcutta, 1901), 'Anglo-Indian Association, 23rd March, 1900', p. 262, and Curzon of Kedleston, *Lord Curzon in India: Being a Selection from His Speeches as Viceroy and Governor-General of India: 1898–1905*, ed. Thomas Raleigh (London, 1906), pp. 372–3.

186. C. Wolmar, *Railways and the Raj: How the Age of Steam Transformed India* (London, 2017), ch. 13.

187. *Speeches by Lord Curzon*, pp. 258–9, and *Lord Curzon in India*, pp. 368–9.

2. A NEW ANGLO-INDIA

1. R. Chaudhuri, 'The Politics of Naming: Derozio in Two Formative Moments of Literary and Political Discourse, Calcutta, 1825–31', *Modern Asian Studies* 44:4 (2010), p. 880.

2. BL, F/4/1115, Extract of Fort St. George Military Correspondence (30 November 1827), folio 12839, no. 39, pp. 333–4.

3. Ibid., pp. 339.

4. Ibid., pp. 347–8.

5. Ibid. (28 December 1827), folio 13834, no. 192, pp. 352, 354.

6. Ibid. (30 November 1827), folio 12839, no. 39, p. 346.

7. Ibid. (28 December 1827), folio 13834, no. 192, pp. 353–4.

8. Ibid., p. 355.

9. BL, F/4/1259, Extract Bombay Revenue Consultations (8 July 1829), no. 119, 'Resolutions Passed at a Convened Meeting of East Indians Held at Bombay on Saturday the 30th May 1829', Resolution 10, p. 21.

10. Letter signed 'A. H.', *Calcutta Journal* (6 November 1821), cited in Chaudhuri, 'The Politics of Naming', p. 880.

11. T. Edwards, 'Art. VI: The Eurasian Movement of 1829–30', *Calcutta Review* 76:151 (January 1883), p. 106.

12. BL, F/4/1115, Extract of Fort St. George Military Corr. (30 November 1827), folio 12839, no. 39, p. 346.

13. Hansard, HC Debates, 19 July 1915, vol. 73, cols. 1275–76, https://api.parliament.uk/historic-hansard/commons/1915/jul/19/government-of-india-bill-lords.

14. Cited in E. Buettner, *Empire Families: Britons and Late Imperial India* (Oxford, 2004), p. 12.

15. Ibid.

16. I. Stephens, *Monsoon Morning* (London, 1966), p. 146.

17. Ibid., p. 28.

18. Ibid.

19. Ibid., p. 114.

20. Buettner, *Empire Families*, p. 74.

21. Cited in C. Allen (ed.), *Plain Tales from the Raj* (London, 1975), p. 180.

22. *Kutcha Butcha Half Baked Bread*, BBC Radio 4 FM (18 August 1997).

23. Irene Edwards (née Green), cited in Allen, *Plain Tales*, p. 180.

24. Buettner, *Empire Families*, p. 74.

25. Ibid., pp. 74, 94.

26. *AIR* (June 1928), p. 2.

27. BL, OIOC, MSS Eur R189, Roy Edward King Nissen interviewed in 1989 on four cassettes covering 1905–60.

28. Ibid.

29. Ibid.

30. Ibid.

31. 'Speech by Mr. Kenneth E. Wallace', *AIR* (March 1931), p. 26.

32. Ibid.

33. G. Morton-Jack, *Army of Empire: The Untold Story of the Indian Army in World War I* (ebook, 2018), ch. 11.

34. W. Madge, cited in 'Anglo-Indian Regiment', *Statesman* (12 July 1912).

35. *Abstract of the Proceedings of the Council of the Governor General of India, Assembled for the Purpose of Making Laws and Regulations*, vol. 52, April 1913 to March 1914 (Calcutta, 1914), 9 September 1913, p. 1.

36. Viceroy (Chelmsford) to J. Abbott, p. 6, NAI, Legislative Department, Assembly Council Branch, Progs., no. 85 (February 1921), part B.

37. C. Robbie, *The Anglo-Indian Force* (Allahabad, 1919), p. 6.

38. Cited in B. Nanda, *Gandhi: Pan-Islamism, Imperialism, and Nationalism in India* (New York, 1989), ch. 8.

39. A. Besant, 'To Arms', cited in document no. 148, Government Fortnightly Report, 18 May 1918, Demi-official from L. Davidson, Acting Chief Secretary to the Government of Madras, to S. Highnell, Secretary to the Government of India,

Home Department (18 May 1918), cited in M. Venkatarangaiya (ed.), *The Freedom Struggle in Andhra Pradesh (Andhra)*, vol. 2: *1906–1920 A.D.* (Andhra, 1969), p. 475.

40. Robbie, *Anglo-Indian Force*, p. 41.
41. Ibid., p. 6.
42. Ibid., pp. 36–9.
43. Ibid., pp. 6–7.
44. F. Anthony, *Britain's Betrayal in India: The Story of the Anglo-Indian Community* (New Delhi, 1969), pp. 128–9.
45. 'Col. Gidney's Speech at the Minorities Sub-committee at St. James's Palace on the 31st December, 1930', *AIR* (February 1931), p. 5.
46. *Joint Committee on Indian Constitutional Reform (Session 1932–3)*, vol. IIC: *Minutes of Evidence Given before the Joint Committee on Indian Constitutional Reform* (London, 1934), q. 16,521, p. 2015.
47. Robbie, *Anglo-Indian Force*, p. 56.
48. Ibid., pp. 14–16.
49. Ibid., p. 38.
50. Ibid., p. 29.
51. Not to be confused with the First Australian Imperial Force or more general references to Indian Army forces collectively.
52. Robbie, *Anglo-Indian Force*, p. 8.
53. Ibid., pp. 38, 8.
54. Ibid., p. 8.
55. Ibid.
56. Ibid., p. 39.
57. Cited in Morton-Jack, *Army of Empire*, ch. 11.
58. Ibid., ch. 2.
59. Robbie, *Anglo-Indian Force*, p. 38.
60. Ibid., p. 37.
61. Ibid., p. 19.
62. Ibid., p. 38.
63. Ibid., p. 61. My emphasis.
64. Ibid. My emphasis.
65. Ibid., pp. 39–40. My emphasis; original emphasis in caps.
66. A. Blunt, *Domicile and Diaspora: Anglo-Indian Women and the Spatial Politics of Home* (Malden MA, 2005), p. 46.
67. Cited in Robbie, *Anglo-Indian Force*, pp. 64–6.
68. Morton-Jack, *Army of Empire*, ch. 24.
69. Ibid., ch. 21.
70. Ibid.
71. Ibid., ch. 3.
72. NAUK, CAB/37/159/42, Lieutenant H. S. D. McNeal, 'Report on the Siege of Kut-El-Amara' (5 December 1915—29 April 1916), p. 4.
73. Robbie, *Anglo-Indian Force*, p. 11.

74. Ibid.

75. Cited in ibid., p. 65.

76. Ibid., p. 29.

77. Ibid., p. 37.

78. *AIR* (October 1932), p. 23.

79. Ibid.

80. Ibid., p. 24.

81. Robbie, *Anglo-Indian Force*, p. 37.

82. Ibid., p. 38.

83. See L. Ingels, *Anglo-Indian Amalgamation: The Pressing Need of the Community* (Calcutta, 1918).

84. 'Lord Lloyd's Speech', *AIR* (January 1936), pp. 12–13.

85. Robbie, *Anglo-Indian Force*, p. 38.

86. *Joint Committee on Indian Constitutional Reform (Session 1932–3)* (1934), p. 2015.

87. P. Scott, *The Raj Quartet*, vol. 1: *The Jewel in the Crown* (Chicago, 1998), p. 98.

88. Buettner, *Empire Families*, p. 103.

89. *Pioneer Mail and Indian Weekly News* (Allahabad, 25 May 1923), p. 9.

90. Robbie, *Anglo-Indian Force*, p. 37.

91. M. Rashiduzzaman, 'The Central Legislature in British India: 1921 to 1947', PhD thesis, Durham University (1964), pp. 201–2, http://etheses.dur.ac.uk/8122/.

92. Curzon of Kedleston, *Lord Curzon in India: Being a Selection from His Speeches as Viceroy and Governor-General of India: 1898–1905*, ed. Thomas Raleigh (London, 1906), 'Seventh Budget Speech (Legislative Council at Calcutta), March 29, 1905', p. 162.

93. *Abstract of the Proceedings of the Council of the Governor General of India, Laws and Regulations*, vol. 56, April 1917 to March 1918 (Delhi, 1918), 27 February 1918, pp. 601, 613.

94. Ibid., pp. 612–13.

95. *Proceedings of the Council*, vol. 56 (1918), 27 February 1918, p. 613.

96. Ibid.

97. *Legislative Assembly Debates*, First Session (1921), 10 March 1921, p. 844.

98. Ibid.

99. *Proceedings of the Council*, vol. 56 (1918), 27 February 1918, p. 613.

100. K. Wallace, *Life of Sir Henry Gidney* (Calcutta, 1947), p. 256.

101. *The Legislative Assembly Debates (Official Report)*, First Session of the Legislative Assembly, 1921 (Simla, 1921), 10 March 1921, pp. 875–6.

102. Ibid., pp. 876–7.

103. Ibid., p. 877.

104. Ibid.

105. *Pioneer Mail* (30 March 1923), p. 36.

106. Ibid.

107. Anthony, *Britain's Betrayal*, pp. 120–1.

108. Ibid., p. 120.

109. 'Colonel Gidney's Letter to the "Statesman"' (Simla, 31 August), *AIR* (September 1929), p. 6.

110. *AIR* (September 1929), p. 6.

111. Anthony, *Britain's Betrayal*, pp. 120–1.

112. Cited in ibid.

113. *AIR* (June 1931), pp. 34–5.

114. Anthony, *Britain's Betrayal*, p. 385.

115. L. Hopkins, 'Anglo-Indian Psychology and Policy', *AIR* (November 1943), p. 16. Original emphasis in bold face.

116. McNeelance, 'This Land Is Ours', *AIR* (October 1944), pp. 7–8.

117. Ibid., p. 7.

118. F. W. Corbett, 'Anglo-Indians and the Future', *AIR* (April 1944), pp. 17, 33.

119. Cited in Buettner, *Empire Families*, p. 104.

120. Corbett, 'Anglo-Indians', p. 33.

121. Ibid.

122. A. Rush, *Bonds of Empire: West Indians and Britishness from Victoria to Decolonization* (Oxford, 2011).

123. Ibid., p. 99.

124. Ibid.

125. Cited in ibid., pp. 97–8.

126. Ibid., p. 98.

127. G. Miller, 'Mr. Fowler's Clarion Call for Community's Readjustment', *AIR* (September 1944), p. 19.

128. *AIR* (April 1930), p. 15.

129. G. Mackay, *Serious Reflections and Other Contributions* (Bombay, 1881), p. 95.

130. Buettner, *Empire Families*, ch. 2: '"Not Quite Pukka": Schooling in India and the Acquisition of Racial Status'; ch. 3: 'Separation and the Discourse of Family Sacrifice'; and ch. 4: 'Sent Home to School: British Education, Status, and Returns Overseas'.

131. E. Sen, *Testament of India* (London, 1939), p. 69.

132. *AIR* (July–August 1943), p. 6.

133. Cited in ibid.

134. *AIR* (January 1931), p. 11.

135. *AIR* (November 1929), p. 9.

136. W. Crawshaw, 'Member of Council U.P. of Agra and Oudh, Representing the Anglo Indian and Domiciled European Community, "Gulistan", Lucknow', to the Private Secretary to the Viceroy, Simla (30 September 1920), p. 3, NAI, Legislative Department, Assembly and Council Branch, Progs., no. 86 (February 1921), part B.

137. *AIR* (November 1930), p. 11.

138. Anthony, *Britain's Betrayal*, p. 99.

139. *AIR* (May 1929), p. 5.

140. *AIR* (November 1931), p. 8.

141. *AIR* (June 1928), p. 2.
142. Ibid.
143. *Anglo-Indian Citizen* (June 1928), cited in ibid., p. 9.
144. *AIR* (June 1928), p. 9.
145. Anthony, *Britain's Betrayal*, p. 117.
146. *The Queenslander* (Brisbane, Australia), 'Surgeon's "Bag" of 53 Tigers: Ambidexterity and Shooting Help Him to Operate' (2 January 1936), p. 4, http://nla.gov.au/nla.news-article23379997; see also *Evening Post* (Wellington, New Zealand), 'Hunting Surgeon: Record of Tigers Shot', CXXI:24 (29 January 1936), p. 10, https://paperspast.natlib.govt.nz/newspapers/EP19360129.2.50.
147. H. Hobbs, *Extracts from My Diary* (8 November 1934), pp. 1–2.
148. Honorary Secretary, Anglo-Indian and Domiciled European Association, U.P., to the Home Member, Government of India Head Quarters, Simla (28 August 1922), NAI, Legislative Department, Assembly and Council Branch, Progs., no. 8 (November 1922).
149. C. Walsh, *The Agra Double Murder: A Crime of Passion from the Raj* (London, 1929; reprint, New Delhi, 2017), p. 5.
150. Ibid., pp. 5–7.
151. Anthony, *Britain's Betrayal*, pp. 90–1.
152. NAI, Legislative Department, Assembly and Council Branch, February 1923, Progs., no. 5, Deposit, 'Communiqué from Simla' of 'members of the Executive Committee' of 'the Simla–Delhi Branch', cited in Abbott to the editor, *Indian Daily Telegraph*, p. 6.
153. Ibid.
154. 'Sequel to the Filose Case: Col. Gidney's Application Rejected; Allahabad 17th February', *Pioneer Mail* (Allahabad, 23 February 1923), p. 37.
155. Cited in ibid.
156. *AIR* (September 1932), p. 10.
157. H. Stark, *The Call of the Blood, or, Anglo-Indians and the Sepoy Mutiny* (Rangoon, 1932), front matter.
158. Anthony, *Britain's Betrayal*, p. 168.
159. *AIR* (March 1929), dustjacket. Original in caps.
160. *AIR* (November 1931), p. 8.
161. Hansard, HL Debates, 17 December 1934, vol. 95, col. 493, https://api.parliament.uk/historic-hansard/lords/1934/dec/17/indian-constitutional-reform.
162. *The Legislative Assembly Debates: Official Report*, vol. 3, 13–30 March 1933, 5th Session (Simla, 1933), 30 March 1933, p. 2863.
163. *AIR* (May 1930), p. 35.
164. *AIR* (June 1928), p. 10.
165. *AIR* (October 1930), p. 5.
166. Ibid., p. 9.
167. H. Gidney, Simla, to M. Ismail, Diwan of Mysore (copy) (29 September 1934),

p. 2, NAI, Mysore Residency Department, Bangalore Branch, Progs., no. 26 (5-c) (1932), part B.

168. Hansard, HL Debates, 17 December 1934, vol. 95, col. 494, https://api.parliament.uk/historic-hansard/lords/1934/dec/17/indian-constitutional-reform.

169. *Graham v. Henry Gidney*, original civil, before Ameer Ali J., *Calcutta Series*, vol. 60 (9, 10, 13, 14, 28 February 1933), pp. 957–960, www.scconline.com.

170. Ibid.

171. Ibid.

172. Ibid.

173. Ibid.

174. Ibid.

175. Ibid.

176. Ibid., p. 960.

177. Ibid., pp. 961–2.

178. Ibid., p. 969.

179. BL, OIOC, P/W/588, *Memorandum Relative to the Deputation of the Anglo-Indian and Domiciled European Community of India and Burma to the Right Honorable the Secretary of State for India* (30 July 1925).

180. Ibid.

181. Ibid.

182. Ibid.

183. *AIR* (November 1929), p. 9.

184. *Pioneer Mail* (18 May 1923), p. 25.

185. 'Col. Gidney's Speech', *AIR* (February 1931), pp. 5–6.

186. Cited in ibid., p. 6.

187. *AIR* (November 1929), p. 6.

188. 'Position of Anglo-Indians: Mr. Sastri's Advice', Delhi, 21 March, in *Pioneer Mail* (30 March 1923), p. 36.

189. 'Col. Gidney's Speech', *AIR* (February 1931), p. 6.

190. 'Speech Delivered at the Plenary Session on 19th November 1930', *AIR* (April 1931), p. 13.

191. *Morning Post* (22 November 1930); *AIR* (January 1931), p. 9.

192. *The Times* (22 November 1930); *AIR* (January 1931), p. 9.

193. *Daily Telegraph* (19 November 1930); *AIR* (January 1931), p. 9.

194. *Morning Post* (22 November 1930); *AIR* (January 1931), p. 9.

195. *Daily Mail* (19 November 1930); *AIR* (January 1931), p. 9.

196. Ibid.

197. J. Masters, *Bhowani Junction* (New York, 1954), p. 226.

198. *AIR* (March 1930), p. 7.

199. *Young India* (14 May 1931), in *The Collected Works of Mahatma Gandhi*, vol. 52, pp. 98–9.

200. *Manchester Guardian* (9 October 1931), p. 4.

201. B. Ambedkar (Minorities Committee, Eighth Sitting, 1 October 1931), in

V. Moon and H. Narke (eds.), *Dr. Babasaheb Ambedkar: Writings and Speeches*, vol. 2 (New Delhi, 1979; 2nd edn, 2014), p. 655.

202. M. Gandhi (Minorities Committee, Ninth Sitting, 8 October 1931), in Moon and Narke, *Ambedkar*, p. 660.

203. Ambedkar (Minorities Committee, Ninth Sitting, 8 October 1931), in Moon and Narke, *Ambedkar*, pp. 661–2.

204. Ambedkar (Plenary Session, Eighth Sitting, 19 January 1931), in Moon and Narke, *Ambedkar*, p. 598.

205. *Manchester Guardian* (14 November 1931), p. 14.

206. H. Gidney, 'Problem of the Minorities in India, with Special Reference to the Anglo-Indian Community', address at a meeting of the Empire Parliamentary Association, at the Rooms of the Association, Westminster Hall (5 February 1931), in *AIR* (May 1931), p. 8.

207. Ibid., p. 11.

208. Ibid., p. 9.

209. H. Gidney and Ambedkar (Committee of the Whole Conference, 16 December 1930; Sub-committee no. 3: Minorities, Fifth Sitting, 14 January 1931 and Sixth Sitting, 16 January 1931), in Moon and Narke, *Ambedkar*, vol. 2 (2014), pp. 511, 535, 540.

210. Gidney and Ambedkar (Sub-committee no. 6: Franchise, Second Sitting, 22 December 1930), in Moon and Narke, *Ambedkar*, p. 564.

211. Ambedkar (Minorities Committee, Eighth Sitting, 1 October 1931), in Moon and Narke, *Ambedkar*, p. 655.

212. Gidney, in Moon and Narke, *Ambedkar*, p. 656.

213. Gandhi, in Moon and Narke, *Ambedkar*, p. 659.

214. Ibid., pp. 658–9.

215. *Manchester Guardian* (9 October 1931), p. 4.

216. Ibid.

217. Ibid.

218. Ibid.

219. Ibid.

220. *Manchester Guardian* (14 November 1931), p. 14.

221. Ibid.

222. Ibid.

223. *Legislative Assembly*, 30 March 1933, pp. 2859, 2863.

224. *Manchester Guardian* (14 November 1931), p. 14.

225. *Manchester Guardian* (9 October 1931), p. 4.

226. *The Collected Works of Mahatma Gandhi* (1931–2), vol. 48, p. 259.

227. C. Campagnac, *The Autobiography of a Wanderer in England and Burma: The Memoirs of a Former Mayor of Rangoon*, ed. S. Campagnac-Carney (Raleigh NC, 2011), p. 156.

3. CONTESTING ANGLO-INDIA

1. *AIR* (March 1930), p. 8.
2. Ibid.
3. Ibid.
4. *AIR* (November 1930), p. 5.
5. Ibid., p. 17.
6. Ibid.
7. Ibid.
8. *AIR* (November 1930), p. 17.
9. 'Working Committee: Summary of Proceedings: Delhi, August 27, 1930', *The Indian National Congress, 1930–34: Being the Resolutions Passed by the Congress, the All India Congress Committee and the Working Committee during the Period between Jan. 1930 to Sep. 1934 …* (Allahabad, 1934), p. 50.
10. *AIR* (November 1930), p. 5.
11. *AIR* (August 1932), pp. 17–19.
12. K. Wallace, 'The Anglo-Indian Community', *Capital* (8 December 1932); *AIR* (January 1933), p. 21.
13. *AIR* (August 1930), p. 7.
14. *The Leader* (29 June 1932), p. 24.
15. NAI, Home Department, Establishment Branch, Progs., no. 389 (1932), part I, serial nos. 1–7: 'Representations from the Anglo-Indian and Domiciled European Association, All-India and Burma, Regarding the Employment of Anglo-Indians, in the Public Services', serial no. 5—Office Memorandum from the Railway Department, no. 1399-E.G. (13 February 1933), Government of India letter (September 1928), serial nos. 3–5, C. Trivedi (20 March 1933), para. 3, p. 4.
16. Ibid., serial no. 6—O. M. from Railway Department, no. 1399-E.G. (23 March 1933), M. Hallett (13 April 1933), p. 4.
17. 'Sir H. Gidney's Statement', *Federated India* (13 July 1932); *AIR* (August 1932), p. 24.
18. *AIR* (August 1930), p. 7.
19. Ibid.
20. *Daily Gazette* (25 July 1932); *AIR* (August 1932), p. 24.
21. Ibid.
22. Ibid.
23. K. Reddy, *Class, Colonialism and Nationalism: Madras Presidency, 1928–1939* (New Delhi, 2002), pp. 97–8.
24. 'Extracts from an Indian's Letters', *AIR* (Christmas 1930), pp. 11–12.
25. 'Speech by Mr. Kenneth E. Wallace', *AIR* (March 1931), pp. 25–6.
26. *AIR* (January 1931), p. 6.
27. Ibid.
28. 'Note Submitted to the Round Table Conference by Col. Gidney on the Definition of a "European" and a "European British Subject" as Expressed by the Legal Sub-committee of the Council of the European Association', in ibid., p. 21.

29. Ibid.

30. *AIR* (September 1932), pp. 16–17.

31. K. Wallace, Vice President, Bengal Provincial Branch, to Secretary, European Association, Calcutta, in *AIR* (May 1939), p. 13.

32. Ibid.

33. Ibid.

34. Reply of the Secretary, Calcutta Branch of the European Association, in ibid., p. 13.

35. *AIR* (January 1931), p. 5.

36. Ibid., pp. 14, 26, 32.

37. Ibid., pp. 5–6.

38. S. A. Nollen, *Boris Karloff: A Gentleman's Life* (Baltimore, 1999), pp. 17–18.

39. Ibid., pp. 17–18, 20.

40. S. Morgan, *Bombay Anna: The Real Story and Remarkable Adventures of the King and I Governess* (Berkeley, 2008), p. 1.

41. Ibid., pp. 22–3.

42. Nollen, *Boris Karloff*, p. 19.

43. Ibid.

44. Ibid.

45. Ibid., p. 20.

46. Ibid.

47. Ibid., p. 21.

48. Ibid., p. 20.

49. Ibid., p. 67.

50. P. Coats, *The China Consuls: British Consular Officers, 1843–1943* (Oxford, 1988), pp. 429–30.

51. Nollen, *Boris Karloff*, p. 21.

52. Ibid., p. 66.

53. P. Underwood, *Karloff: The Life of Boris Karloff* (Grass Valley CA, 1972), p. 21.

54. Coats, The China Consuls, p. 429.

55. Nollen, *Boris Karloff*, p. 66.

56. *Bombay Legislative Council Debates: Official Report*, vol. 37 (Bombay, 1922), 20 February 1922, p. 543.

57. Ibid., p. 548.

58. Ibid.

59. NAUK, CO/123/276/86, B. Honduras 34397, Asst Medical Officer (19 September 1913), p. 244.

60. Ibid.

61. BL, OIOC, MSS Eur T14 (see also R14/1–2), Interview with Marjorie Cashmore (1972–4), p. 4/1.

62. NAI, Punjab State Agency, 1922, 'Return of Europeans, Eurasians and other nationalities', Faridkot State and Sirmoor State.

63. Ibid., Bahawalpur State.

64. S. Bradley, *An American Girl in India: A Novel* (London, 1911), p. 198.

65. NAI, Punjab State Agency, 1922, Kapurthala State.

66. Mrs. Irene Edwards by marriage—for the sake of consistency, her unmarried name Green will be used throughout.

67. BL, OIOC, MSS Eur T29, Interview with Irene Edwards, pp. 12–13.

68. Ibid., p. 1.

69. Ibid., pp. 1, 3.

70. Ibid., p. 5.

71. Ibid., pp. 3–4.

72. Ibid., p. 1.

73. Ibid., p. 2.

74. Ibid., pp. 9, 11–13.

75. Ibid., p. 13.

76. Ibid.

77. Ibid., pp. 2/2–2/3.

78. *Bombay Legislative Council*, vol. 22 (1928), 21 February 1928, p. 112.

79. Ibid., p. 113.

80. Ibid.

81. Ibid., p. 112.

82. BL, OIOC, MSS Eur T29, Interview with Irene Edwards, p. 2/9.

83. Ibid., pp. 1–2, 2/12—2/13.

84. *AIR* (October 1932), p. 11.

85. BL, OIOC, MSS Eur T29, Interview with Irene Edwards, p. 3/2.

86. Ibid., p. 4/1.

87. Ibid., p. 3/11.

88. Ibid., p. 2/7.

89. Ibid., p. 3/1.

90. See, in order of original publication, Adela Quested (at least initially) in E. M. Forster, *A Passage to India* (reprint, London, 1979), Anne Torel in S. Maugham, 'The Door of Opportunity', in *Collected Short Stories*, vol. 2 (London, 2002), Daphne Manners in Paul Scott, *Jewel in the Crown* (London, 1998), and Grace Collins in J. Sweeney, *Elephant Moon* (Worcestershire, 2012).

91. See especially W. Burchett, *Trek Back from Burma* (Allahabad, 1944), pp. 274–5.

92. BL, OIOC, MSS Eur R189, Interview with Roy Nissen.

93. P. Scott, *The Alien Sky* (St. Albans, 1953), pp. 106–7.

94. Ibid.

95. Ibid.

96. Ibid., pp. 110–12.

97. N. Slate, *Colored Cosmopolitanism: The Shared Struggle for Freedom in the United States and India* (Cambridge MA, 2012), and *The Prism of Race: W. E. B. Du Bois, Langston Hughes, Paul Robeson and the Colored World of Cedric Dover* (New York, 2014).

98. See Slate, *Colored Cosmopolitanism*, pp. 84–5.

99. Letter from Cedric Dover to Jawaharlal Nehru, February 1938, W. Du Bois Papers (MS 312), Special Collections and University Archives, University of Massachusetts

Amherst Libraries, http://credo.library.umass.edu/view/full/mums312-b085-i092.

100. Cited in *AIR* (August 1939), p. 18. Original emphasis removed.

101. C. Dover, *Half-Caste* (London, 1937), p. 131.

102. Ibid., p. 139.

103. Ibid., p. 87.

104. Cited in *AIR* (August 1939), p. 18.

105. Ibid.

106. Ibid.

107. E. Sen, *Testament of India* (London, 1939), pp. 280–1.

108. Ibid., p. 69.

109. *AIR* (August 1939), p. 18.

110. K. Wallace, *Brave New Anglo-India, in a Brave New India, in a Brave New World* (Calcutta, 1935), p. 49.

111. 'Extracts', *AIR* (Christmas 1930), p. 11.

112. Ibid., p. 12.

113. Ibid.

114. Ibid.

115. Ibid.

116. Ibid., pp. 11–12.

117. Wallace, *Brave New Anglo-India*, pp. 45–8.

118. *AIR* (May 1947), p. 3.

119. K. Wallace, Letter to the editor, *AIR* (May 1936), p. 35.

120. Ibid.

121. Ibid.

122. H. Ellis, *The Task of Social Hygiene* (Boston MA, 1912), p. 401.

123. Ibid.

124. Cited in G. Griffith, *Socialism and Superior Brains: The Political Thought of George Bernard Shaw* (London, 1993), p. 57.

125. Cited in ibid.

126. E. Morselli, 'Ethnic Psychology and the Science of Eugenics', in *Problems in Eugenics: Papers Communicated to the First International Eugenics Congress Held at the University of London, July 24th to 30th, 1912* (London, 1912), pp. 61–2.

127. C. Davenport, 'Marriage Laws and Customs', in *Problems in Eugenics*, pp. 151–4.

128. Ibid., p. 154.

129. Ibid., pp. 154–5.

130. C. Dover, *Cimmerii?, or, Eurasians and their Future* (Calcutta, 1929), p. 57.

131. Ibid., pp. 49–50.

132. Cited in Slate, *Colored Cosmopolitanism*, p. 83.

133. *Singapore Free Press and Mercantile Advisor* (24 March 1930), p. 20.

134. H. Roseboom and C. Dover, 'The Eurasian Community as a Eugenic Problem', in *A Decade of Progress in Eugenics: Scientific Papers of the Third International Congress*

of Eugenics Held at American Museum of Natural History New York, August 21–23, 1932 (Baltimore, 1934), pp. 87–94.

135. Ibid., pp. 87, 92.

136. Ibid., pp. 93–4.

137. Ibid., p. 90.

138. Ibid., p. 92.

139. Ibid., p. 90.

140. G. K. Chesterton, *Eugenics and Other Evils* (London, 1922), p. 97.

141. Cited in G. D'Cruz, *Midnight's Orphans: Anglo-Indians in Post/colonial Literature* (Bern, 2006), p. 125.

142. C. Dover, 'The Eurasian Problem and Its Solution', in S. Sinha (ed.), *The Hindustan Review* 54:306 (January 1930), p. 147.

143. Cited as 'Memoirs of the Bernice P. Bishop Museum, XI, no. 1, Honolulu, 1929' in ibid.

144. Slate, *Colored Cosmopolitanism*, pp. 83–4.

145. D'Cruz, *Midnight's Orphans*, p. 125.

146. Dover, *Half-Caste*, p. 112.

147. Ibid., pp. 21–2.

148. C. Dover, 'Population Control in India', *Eugenics Review* 26:4 (January 1935), p. 285.

149. D'Cruz, *Midnight's Orphans*, p. 123.

150. Dover, *Half-Caste*, pp. 103, 109.

151. Ibid., p. 22.

152. Ibid., pp. 108–12.

153. Ibid.

154. Ibid.

155. Ibid., pp. 90–1.

156. Ibid., p. 93.

157. Ibid., p. 95.

158. Cited in ibid., p. 94.

159. Ibid., pp. 20–1.

160. Ibid., pp. 27–8.

161. 'Extracts', *AIR* (Christmas 1930), p. 13.

162. M. Wilson, *The Domiciled European and Anglo-Indian Race of India* (Bombay and Bangalore, 1928), p. 14.

163. Ibid.

164. Ibid.

165. Ibid., pp. 32–3.

166. H. Gidney, 'Preface' (3 February 1928), in ibid., p. i.

167. Ibid., pp. i–ii.

168. BL, OIOC, MSS Eur R189, Interview with Nissen.

169. Ibid.

170. Ibid.

171. I. Stephens, *Monsoon Morning* (London, 1966), p. 145.

172. T. Royle, *The Last Days of the Raj* (London, 1989), p. 25.

173. Ibid., pp. 28, 39.

174. T. Mains, 'The Anglo-Indian Community Services in World War II before, during and after', *Journal of the Society for Army Historical Research* 74:298 (Summer 1996), p. 122.

175. Royle, *Last Days*, p. 38.

176. BI, OIOC, MSS Eur T29, Interview with Irene Edwards, pp. 2–3, 4/3.

177. Ibid., pp. 5–6.

178. H. Gidney to Adjutant General, Army Headquarters, Simla (26 April 1926), in *AIR* (May 1929), pp. 33–4.

179. A. Blunt, *Domicile and Diaspora: Anglo-Indian Women and the Spatial Politics of Home* (Malden MA, 2005), pp. 67–8.

180. Ibid., p. 67.

181. Hopkins, 'Anglo-Indian Psychology', p. 18.

182. Ibid.

183. Ibid., p. 16.

184. B. Nichols, *Verdict on India* (New York, 1944), p. 224.

185. Evans, 'Women and Cosmetics', *AIR* (April 1944), p. 26.

186. Anthony, *Britain's Betrayal*, p. 7.

187. F. W. Corbett, 'Anglo-Indians and the Future', *AIR* (April 1944), p. 9.

188. Ibid.

189. Ibid.

190. *AIR* (August 1930), pp. 29–30.

191. J. Turner, 'Pride of Nationality', *AIR* (May 1930), p. 19.

192. Ibid.

193. Ibid.

194. Corbett, 'Anglo-Indians', p. 9.

195. McNeelance, 'This Land Is Ours', *AIR* (October 1944), pp. 7–8.

196. *The Legislative Assembly Debates: Official Report*, vol. 1, 21 January to 11 February 1946 (Delhi, 1947), 4 February 1946, pp. 448–9.

197. Turner, 'Pride', p. 19.

198. Ibid.

199. Ibid., pp. 19–20.

200. T. Marshall, *A Flag Worth Dying For: The Power and Politics of National Symbols* (New York, 2016), p. 5.

201. Turner, 'Pride', p. 20.

202. Ibid.

203. Ibid.

204. Ibid.

205. *AIR* (July 1930), p. 30.

206. Ibid.

4. ANGLO-INDIA UNDER SIEGE

1. *Abstract of the Proceedings of the Council of the Governor General of India, Assembled for the Purpose of Making Laws and Regulations*, vol. 50, April 1911 to March 1912 (Calcutta, 1912), 28 February 1912, p. 282.

2. Ibid., pp. 270–1.

3. *The Legislative Assembly Debates (Official Report)*, 2nd Session, 1922 (Simla, 1922), 11 February 1922, p. 2372.

4. B. Nichols, *Verdict on India* (New York, 1944), p. 225.

5. P. Mason, 'Introduction', in C. Allen (ed.), *Plain Tales from the Raj* (London, 1975), p. 16.

6. T. Mains, 'The Anglo-Indian Community Services in World War II before, during and after', *Journal of the Society for Army Historical Research* 74:298 (Summer 1996), p. 124.

7. University of Cambridge, Centre of South Asian Studies, Archive, Audio, Interview no. 35, E. Stracey, https://www.s-asian.cam.ac.uk/archive/audio/collection/e-stracey/.

8. Ibid.

9. Ibid.

10. Ibid.

11. Ibid.

12. Ibid.

13. University of Cambridge, Centre of South Asian Studies, Archive, Audio, Interview no. 34, R. Stracey, available at https://www.s-asian.cam.ac.uk/archive/audio/collection/r-stracey/.

14. *AIR* (October 1932), p. 8.

15. Ibid.

16. Ibid.

17. Ibid.

18. Ibid.

19. University of Cambridge, Centre of South Asian Studies, Audio, Interview no. 34, R. Stracey.

20. *AIR* (October 1932), p. 8.

21. *AIR* (April 1933), p. 9.

22. University of Cambridge, Centre of South Asian Studies, Audio, Interview no. 34, R. Stracey.

23. M. Silvestri, *Policing 'Bengali Terrorism' in India and the World: Imperial Intelligence and Revolutionary Nationalism, 1905–1939* (ebook, 2019), p. 143.

24. Ibid., p. 86.

25. Ibid., p. 34.

26. Cited in C. Robbie, *The Anglo-Indian Force* (Allahabad, 1919), p. 37.

27. NAI, Political Department, Political Branch (Confidential), 1908, file no. 42, nos. 1–4, 'Proposal for the Enrolment of a Special Police Reserve Composed Mainly of Europeans and Eurasians'.

28. K. Wallace, 'Anglo-Indian Community', *Capital* (8 December 1932); *AIR* (January 1933), p. 19.

29. *AIR* (May 1933), p. 7.

30. NAI, Government of India, Army Department, General Staff Branch, file no. 13430-M.T.-3, Notes, Schools A, May 1930, Progs., nos. 2239–73, 'Admission of Anglo-Indian to the Prince of Wales' Royal Indian Military College, Dehra Dun, and Royal Military College, Sandhurst', 'Note by the Adjutant-General in India' (30 June 1925), p. 18.

31. *AIR* (May 1933), p. 7.

32. Wallace, 'Anglo-Indian Community', p. 19.

33. *AIR* (May 1933), p. 7.

34. BL, OIOC, MSS Eur R193/1, Frank Reginald Anthony interviewed by Gillian Wright (between November 1987 and January 1988).

35. 'Examination by the Royal Commission on Labour in India on a Memorandum Submitted by the Ajmer Provincial Branch of the A.-I. & D.E. Association, All-India Burma, on behalf of Anglo-Indian and Domiciled European Employees of the B.B. & C.I. Railway Metre Gauge on the 12th November, 1929', *AIR* (December 1929), pp. 34–5.

36. 'Memorandum Submitted by the Bombay Provincial Branch of the Anglo-Indian and Domiciled European Association, All-India and Burma, for the Consideration of the Chairman and Members of the Royal Commission on Labour in India', *AIR* (December 1929), p. 44.

37. *Servant of India* (Poona, 25 February 1937), p. 80.

38. *AIR* (May 1933), p. 7.

39. *Pioneer Mail* (18 May 1923), p. 25.

40. NAI, file no. 13430-M.T.-3, 'Note by the Adjutant-General' (1925), p. 18.

41. Ibid.

42. Ibid., Progs., no. 2268: Military Despatch from Secretary of State, no. 22 (2 December 1926), A. Skeen, Lieut.-General (17 January 1927), p. 34.

43. Ibid., Letter from the Secretary Military Department, India Office, no. M.-8912–24 (16 April 1925), Note by 'C. A. I[nnes]', pp. 16–17.

44. Ibid., Note by 'S. R. D[as]' (3 May 1926), p. 31.

45. *Pioneer Mail* (18 May 1923), p. 25.

46. NAI, file no. 13430-M.T.-3, note by E. Burdon (18 November 1922), p. 5.

47. Ibid., Note by 'W. M. H[ailey]' (29 November 1922), p. 6.

48. Ibid., Note by 'R[awlinson]' (2 December 1922), p. 6.

49. Ibid., Note by 'C. A. I[nnes]' (30 April 1926), pp. 29–30.

50. Ibid., Note by 'T. B. S[apru]' (27 November 1922), p. 6.

51. Ibid., Note by 'B. N. S[arma]' (29 November 1922).

52. Ibid.

53. Ibid., Burdon (18 November 1922), p. 5.

54. Ibid., Demi-official letter from Mr. E. Burdon, to Lieut. Colonel H. A. J. Gidney, no. 278-S (15 December 1922), p. 7.

55. Ibid., Burdon (21 March 1926), p. 23.

56. Ibid., 'War Office reply no. 61462-S.D.-3' (20 September 1921), cited in Telegram P., to Secretary of State for India, London, no. 193-S. (30 January 1926), p. 12 or 48. [Supplementary correspondence annexure with identical main document title repeated; confusingly, internal page numbers begin again at 1 while hand-annotated pagination continues from 37, therefore both are provided alternatively for the supplementary annexure.]

57. Ibid., [supplementary] Telegram P., from Secretary of State, no. 102 (12, received 13, January 1926), and no. 279 (27 January 1926), and no. 3054 (19, received 20, November 1925), pp. 11–12 or 47–8.

58. Ibid., Burdon (21 March 1926), p. 23.

59. Ibid.

60. Ibid., [supplementary] 'War Office reply no. 61462-S.D.-3' (20 September 1921), cited in Telegram P., to Secretary of State, no. 193-S. (30 January 1926), p. 12 or 48.

61. Ibid., [supplementary] Telegram P., to Secretary of State, no. 193-S. (30 January 1926).

62. Ibid., Burdon (21 March 1926), p. 23.

63. Ibid., Demi-official letter from Lieut. Colonel H. A. J. Gidney to Mr. E. Burdon, no. 1228–1 (20 December 1922), p. 7.

64. *AIR* (June 1924), cited in ibid., [supplementary] Enclosure A., p. 5 or 41.

65. Ibid., [supplementary] Letter from War Office, London, to Under Secretary of State for India, Military Department, India Office, London, no. 100s Candidates—6623 (S D.-3-a) (8 February), p. 2 or 38.

66. Ibid., Burdon (21 March 1926), p. 23.

67. Ibid., [supplementary] Telegram P., from Secretary of State, no. 102 (12, received 13, January 1926), p. 11 or 47.

68. Ibid., Note by 'W. R. B[irdwood] (22 March 1926), p. 24.

69. Ibid., Note by 'J. C[rerar]' (1 May 1926), p. 30.

70. H. Gidney to G. Tottenham, Army Department, Government of India (28 March 1933), in *AIR* (May 1933), p. 23.

71. Mains, 'The Anglo-Indian Community Services in World War II', p. 123.

72. F. Anthony to the Commander-in-Chief (16 February 1946), *AIR* (March 1946), p. 5.

73. Ibid., p. 6.

74. Ibid.

75. Aga Khan, *The Memoirs of Aga Khan: World Enough and Time* (New York, 1945), p. 130.

76. D. Gilmartin, 'Migration and Modernity: The State, the Punjabi Village, and the Settling of the Canal Colonies', in I. Talbot and S. Thandi (eds.), *People on the Move: Punjabi Colonial, and Post-colonial Migration* (Karachi, 2004), p. 5.

77. Ibid., p. 4.

78. G. Morton-Jack, *Army of Empire: The Untold Story of the Indian Army in World War I* (ebook, 2018), ch. 25.

79. Cited in J. Cell, *Hailey: A Study in British Imperialism* (New York, 1992), pp. 28–9.

80. Cited in *AIR* (September 1933), p. 3.

81. Robbie, *Anglo-Indian Force*, p. 36.

82. University of Cambridge, Centre of South Asian Studies, Audio, Interview no. 34, R. Stracey.

83. K. Lahiri-Dutt, *In Search of a Homeland: Anglo-Indians and McCluskiegunge* (Calcutta, 1990).

84. Talbot and Thandi, *People on the Move*, pp. 9, 17.

85. F. Devji, 'ThinkFest Conversations 12: Are Gandhi and Jinnah Still Relevant?', *ThinkFest Pakistan* livestream (30 July 2020), 25:38–29:25, https://www.youtube.com/watch?v=KtA4ZByiW5A&t.

86. Ibid.

87. BL, OIOC, W/2388, D. White, 'Introduction', in S. Lee (ed.), *Eurasian and Anglo-Indian Association: Guide to the Eurasian and Anglo-Indian Villages Proposed to Be Established in the Province of Mysore* (Madras, 1882), p. 3.

88. BL, OIOC, F/4/1259, Extract Bombay Revenue Consultations (8 July 1829), 'From Mr. Henshaw, and Other Indo Britons, no. 118 to Sir John Malcolm, Governor General of Bombay, 16th June 1829', para. 2.

89. Anon. ('V. G. Clarke'), *The Fortunes of the Anglo-Indian Race: Considered Retrospectively and Prospectively by One of Fifty Years Knowledge and Experience* (2nd edn, Madras, 1878), pp. 18–19.

90. BL, OIOC, W/2388, Lee, *Guide*, introduction, p. 4.

91. Ibid., p. 5.

92. Ibid., ch. III: Address of the Mysore Branch to H.H. the Maharajah of Mysore, p. 6.

93. Ibid., ch. IV: His Highness the Maharajah's Reply, p. 7.

94. *AIR* (June 1930), p. 11.

95. BL, OIOC, W/2388, Lee, *Guide*, introduction, p. 4.

96. *Colonization Observer* (March–April 1939), p. 44.

97. *Colonization Observer* (September 1934), p. 1.

98. E. McGowan to the editor, *Colonization Observer* (February 1934), pp. 6–7.

99. T. D. A., 'A Survey of India in the Future and the Position of the Community as Settlers', *AIR* (Christmas 1931), pp. 31–2, 34.

100. Ibid., p. 31. My emphasis.

101. J. Turner, 'The Apathy of the Anglo-Indian to His Community', Address at Moghalserai (22 February 1930), *AIR* (March 1930), p. 14.

102. Ibid., p. 13.

103. T. D. A., 'A Survey', pp. 31–2.

104. Ibid., p. 32.

105. Ibid., pp. 32–3.

106. Ibid., p. 33.

107. Ibid.
108. Ibid., pp. 32–3.
109. Ibid., p. 33.
110. Ibid., pp. 31–2.
111. Ibid., p. 32.
112. Ibid., pp. 31–3.
113. J. Moore, 'Utopia via "Eurasia"', *AIR* (Christmas 1934), pp. 35–6.
114. Ibid., p. 35.
115. Ibid., pp. 35, 37.
116. Ibid., p. 35.
117. Ibid.
118. Ibid.
119. Ibid.
120. Ibid.
121. 'The Triumph of Jewry's National Home: Palestine: The Promised Land', *John Bull* (n.d.), in *Colonization Observer* (October 1934), p. 3.
122. 'The Camp of Gurs: Camp of Horror for German Jews; Aged People Left to Die in Prison Provided by Vichy', *Bengal Weekly* (n.d.), in *Colonization Observer* (July 1941), pp. 22–3.
123. Ibid., p. 23. Original emphasis in bold face.
124. E. Hay-Ellis, 'The Germany Which I Knew', *AIR* (June 1943), pp. 12–14, and E. de la Croix, 'Nazi Marriage', *AIR* (May 1944), pp. 10–11.
125. S. Perry, 'Anglo-Indian Emigration', *AIR* (November 1943), p. 19.
126. 'The Triumph', *Colonization Observer* (October 1934), p. 3.
127. Ibid.
128. Ibid.
129. *Colonization Observer* (September 1934), p. 1.
130. E. Gyealy et al., Letter to the editor (10 September 1934), *Colonization Observer* (October 1934), p. 8.
131. J. Hutton, *Census of India, 1931*, vol. I: India, part I: Report (Delhi, 1933), ch. 12: 'Caste, Tribe and Race', p. 426.
132. *Colonization Observer* (October 1934), p. 2.
133. J. Locke, *Second Treatise of Government* (1690), ch. 5, sections 26–7.
134. 'Sense', 'Anglo-Indians and Industry', *AIR* (May 1934), p. 11.
135. N. Jog, *Judge or Judas?* (Bombay, 1945), p. 192.
136. Ibid., p. 195.
137. University of Cambridge, Centre of South Asian Studies, Audio, Interview no. 34, R. Stracey.
138. *AIR* (November 1932), p. 34.
139. H. Hobbs, *Extracts from My Diary* (8 November 1934), p. 2.
140. K. Wallace, *Life of Sir Henry Gidney* (Calcutta, 1947), p. 245.
141. B. Leadon, 'Future of Anglo-Indians', *AIR* (December 1940), pp. 22–3, republished in *Colonization Observer* (April 1941), pp. 3, 5.

142. J. Brachio, Letter to the editor (9 October 1943), *AIR* (November 1943), p. 22.

143. Perry, 'Anglo-Indian Emigration', p. 19.

144. Ibid.

145. Ibid.

146. Ibid.

147. *Legislative Assembly Debates*, 30 March 1933, p. 2867.

148. Ibid., pp. 2867–9.

149. Hansard, HL Debates, 18 July 1935, vol. 98, col. 578, https://api.parliament.uk/historic-hansard/lords/1935/jul/18/government-of-india-bill.

150. 'Mr. Churchill under Fire', *Manchester Guardian* (26 October 1933), p. 4.

151. Hansard, HC Debates, 4 April 1935, vol. 300, cols. 560–2, https://api.parliament.uk/historic-hansard/commons/1935/apr/04/clause-231-application-of-preceding.

152. Ibid.

153. Ibid.

154. Ibid.

155. Ibid.

156. Ibid.

157. Ibid., col. 553.

158. *AIR* (November 1930), p. 11.

159. H. Gidney, 'Presidential Speech' at the AGM (1 December 1939), *AIR* (January 1940), p. 6.

160. J. Schneer, *Ministers at War: Winston Churchill and His War Cabinet* (New York, 2015), ch. 9.

161. Ibid., ch. 10.

162. Wallace, *Gidney*, ch. 13. Original caps removed.

163. Ibid., pp. 242–3.

164. Ibid., p. 245.

165. Ibid., pp. 244–5.

166. Ibid., p. 243.

167. Cited in ibid.

168. Cited in ibid.

169. Ibid., p. 244.

170. Ibid.

171. Ibid., pp. 244, 257.

172. Brachio, 'Letter' (9 October 1943), p. 22.

173. BL, OIOC, MSS Eur R193/1, Interview with Anthony.

174. Mains, 'The Anglo-Indian Community Services in World War II', p. 122.

175. *AIR* (January 1944), p. 2.

176. Ibid.

177. *AIR* (September 1944), p. 14.

178. Ibid.

179. NAI, Air Forces in India, file no. 4006/9/ON-G4B, vol. 2, Air Headquarters,

India, subject: 'Personnel Enlisted into RAFVR: Anglo-Indians—Europeans', date of opening, January 1943, 'Anglo Indian and Domiciled Europeans Reporting at this Station for Ground Duties in the R.A.F.', ITC/2314/2/P3, from I.A.F. Initial Training Centre to Air Headquarters, India (18 March 1943).

180. Ibid., no. RAF/35, from Deputy Technical Recruiting Officer EA, Lucknow, to Officer Commanding, no. 313, M.U. Kankinara, B & A Railway, 24 Parganas (19 December 1942).

181. Ibid., 313MU/S.1215/1/P.3, from O.C. no. 313, Maintenance Unit, Kankinara, to Headquarters, 22nd Group (15 March 1943).

182. Ibid., postgram from Air HQ, India, to 313 Maintenance Unit (24 March 1943).

183. *AIR* (November 1943), p. 10.

184. *AIR* (September 1944), p. 14. Original emphasis in bold face.

185. *Legislative Assembly Debates*, vol. 4, 15 March to 30 March 1946 (Delhi, 1947), 25 March 1946, p. 2871.

186. Ibid., pp. 2870–1, also cited in F. Anthony, *Britain's Betrayal in India: The Story of the Anglo-Indian Community* (New Delhi, 1969), p. 171.

187. BL, OIOC, MSS Eur R193/1, Anthony interviewed.

188. BL, OIOC, L/PJ/7/7880, Anthony to Secretary of State (1945), p. 1.

189. BL, OIOC, MSS Eur R193/1, Anthony interviewed.

190. Ibid.

191. BL, OIOC, MSS Eur R189, Nissen interviewed.

192. BL, OIOC, MSS Eur R193/1, Anthony interviewed.

193. Ibid.

194. Ibid.

195. Ibid.

196. BL, OIOC, L/PJ/7/7880, Telegram from F. Anthony, New Delhi, to the Secretary of State for India, London, CD202/VWK1246/H (received 5 July 1945), pp. 1–4, 6–8.

197. F. Anthony to the Viceroy (Mountbatten), *AIR* (May 1947), p. 4.

198. On 3 May, 14 June and 22 August; see P. Moon (ed.), *Wavell: The Viceroy's Journal* (London, 1973), pp. 256, 293, 337.

199. Ibid., p. 293. Original emphasis removed.

200. 'A Retrospect: Summary of Cabinet Mission's Work (March–June 1946)', in ibid., p. 313.

201. N. Mitra (ed.), *The Indian Annual Register*, vol. 1 (Calcutta, January–June 1939), The Bengal Provincial Political Conference, 36th Session (Jalpaiguri, 4–5 February 1939), p. 420.

202. Ibid.

203. K. Hanif and M. Chawla, 'State, Religion and Religious Minorities in Pakistan: Remembering the Participation of Christians in Punjab Legislative Assembly 1947–55', *Pakistan Social Sciences Review* 4:2 (June 2020), p. 845.

204. Mitra, *Indian Annual Register*, vol. 2 (July–December 1946), Indian Constituent Assembly, pp. 320, 342.

205. Ibid., Chronicle of Events, p. 44.

206. Kerala State Archives, 614/40, Confidential B. no. 1022, no. D. Dis. 614/40/C.S. (31 December 1940), Subject: 'Movements and Activities: W. E. Goudie alias Bean, an Anglo-Indian', Confidential Section, Government of Travancore, Secret 'Note on W. E. Goudie (an Anglo-Indian) alias Bean'.

207. Ibid.

208. I. Stephens, *Monsoon Morning* (London, 1966), p. 148.

209. K. Noles, '"Waging War against the King": Recruitment and Motivation of the Indian National Army, 1942–1945', The British Empire at War Research Group, *Research Papers*, no. 6 (2014), p. 21.

210. Wallace, *Gidney*, p. 232.

211. *AIR* (October 1932), p. 8.

212. University of Cambridge, Centre of South Asian Studies, Archive, Audio, Interview no. 35, E. Stracey, https://www.s-asian.cam.ac.uk/archive/audio/collection/e-stracey/.

213. E. Stracey, *Odd Man In: My Years in the Indian Police* (New Delhi, 1981), pp. 34–6.

214. University of Cambridge, Centre of South Asian Studies, Audio, Interview no. 35, E. Stracey.

215. Original source uses the then commonplace but pejorative term 'Japs'.

216. University of Cambridge, Centre of South Asian Studies, Audio, Interview no. 34, R. Stracey.

217. University of Cambridge, Centre of South Asian Studies, Archive, Audio, Interview no. 36, C. Stracey, https://www.s-asian.cam.ac.uk/archive/audio/collection/c-stracey/.

218. Interrogation of Captain C. J. Stracey, Selected papers of CSDIC(I), BL, MSS Eur F275/15, cited in Noles, '"Waging War against the King"', p. 21.

219. University of Cambridge, Centre of South Asian Studies, Audio, Interview no. 34, C. Stracey.

220. Ibid.

221. P. Fay, *The Forgotten Army: India's Armed Struggle for Independence 1942–1945* (Ann Arbor MI, 1995), pp. 104–5.

222. *AIR* (October 1932), p. 8.

223. 'Interrogation', cited in Noles, '"Waging War against the King"', p. 21.

224. University of Cambridge, Centre of South Asian Studies, Audio, Interview no. 34, C. Stracey.

225. S. Bose, *His Majesty's Opponent: Subhas Chandra Bose and India's Struggle against Empire* (Cambridge MA, 2011), p. 299.

226. Ibid.

227. University of Cambridge, Centre of South Asian Studies, Audio, Interview no. 34, C. Stracey.

228. Ibid., Interview no. 34, R. Stracey.

5. THE END OF ANGLO-INDIA?

1. P. Scott, *The Raj Quartet*, vol. 2: *The Day of the Scorpion* (Chicago, 1998), p. 255.

2. J. Masters, *Bhowani Junction* (New York, 1954), p. 85.

3. Ibid., pp. 13–14.

4. M. Korda, *Queenie* (New York, 1985), pp. 25–6.

5. University of Cambridge, Centre of South Asian Studies, Archive, Audio, Interview no. 61, J. Newbigin, https://www.s-asian.cam.ac.uk/archive/audio/collection/j-e-l-newbigin/.

6. Ibid.

7. BL, OIOC, MSS Eur R189, Nissen interviewed.

8. M. Moris, 'Why Quit India?', *AIR* (September 1946), p. 14.

9. Cited in ibid., p. 15.

10. E. Tarlo, *Clothing Matters: Dress and Identity in India* (London, 1996), p. 84.

11. *AIR* (December 1946—January 1947), p. 21.

12. *Constituent Assembly of India Debates (Proceedings)*, vol. 11, Thursday, 17 November 1949, pp. 31–2.

13. Cited in G. Miller, 'Anglo-Indian "Exodus" Causing Anxiety: Insidious Propaganda Condemned', *AIR* (October–November 1949), p. 6.

14. 'Minutes of the Governing Body Meeting' (11 February 1943), item 10: 'Mr. Few's Letter, Dated 21st December, 1942', *AIR* (March 1943), p. 18.

15. Ibid.

16. 'Minutes of the Meeting of the Governing Body' (5 March 1943), item 1: 'Confirmation of Minutes', *AIR* (March 1943), p. 19.

17. *The Anglo-Indians*, documentary film, produced by Central Independent Television for Channel 4 (United Kingdom, 1986).

18. F. Anthony, AGM 'Address', *AIR* (May 1943), p. 16. Original emphasis removed.

19. *AIR* (February 1943), pp. 15–18.

20. 'Anglo-India', *Daily Post* (5 February 1943); *AIR* (March 1943), p. 13. Original emphasis removed.

21. Ibid.

22. Ibid. Original emphasis removed.

23. Anthony, AGM 'Address', *AIR* (May 1943), p. 15. Original emphasis removed.

24. *AIR* (March 1943), p. 3. Original emphasis in bold face.

25. Ibid.

26. F. Anthony, *Will Britain Tarnish Her Honour? Being a Brief Review of the History, Present Position and Needs of the Anglo-Indian Community in India and of Britain's Solemn Obligations to the Community* (New Delhi, 1943), p. 35.

27. Ibid.

28. Ibid.

29. Cited in T. Sapru et al., *Constitutional Proposals of the Sapru Committee* (Bombay, 1945), ch. VII: Minorities and Fundamental Rights, para. 357, p. 250.

30. Ibid., p. 251.

31. *AIR* (December 1946—January 1947), p. 20.

32. Ibid.

33. *AIR* (March 1946), p. 18D. Original emphasis removed.

34. Ibid. Original emphasis removed.

35. Ibid. Original emphasis removed.

36. Ibid. Original emphasis removed.

37. Ibid. Original emphasis removed.

38. *AIR* (December 1946—January 1947), p. 6. Original emphasis in bold face.

39. *AIR* (June 1947), p. 20.

40. BL, OIOC, MSS Eur R189, Nissen interviewed.

41. BL, OIOC, L/PO/10/22, Private and Secret Weekly Letters between the Secretary of State for India and the Viceroy (printed), no. 78, Secretary of State for India to the Viceroy (8 November 1945), item 6, pp. 323–4.

42. Ibid., p. 324.

43. F. Anthony, *Memorandum of the Anglo-Indian and Domiciled European Community to the Cabinet Mission* (New Delhi, 10 April 1946), p. 5; *AIR* (March 1946), p. 18A.

44. Anthony, *Memorandum*, pp. 1, 5; *AIR* (March 1946), p. 18A. Original emphasis removed.

45. BL, OIOC, MSS Eur R193/1, Anthony interviewed.

46. Ibid.

47. Anthony, *Memorandum*, p. 8; *AIR* (March 1946), p. 18A.

48. BL, OIOC, L/PJ/7/7880, Telegram from F. Anthony, New Delhi, to the Secretary of State for India, London, CD202/VWK1246/H (received 5 July 1945), p. 3. Original in caps.

49. Anthony, *Memorandum*, pp. 7–8; *AIR* (March 1946), p. 18A.

50. *AIR* (March 1946), p. 18B.

51. Ibid.

52. Anthony, *Memorandum*, pp. 2–4; *AIR* (March 1946), p. 18A. Original emphasis removed.

53. 'Anglo-Indians Enter Nationalist Fold: Community Seeks No Privileges, Says Memorandum', *The Statesman* (New Delhi, 11 April 1946); *AIR* (March 1946), p. 18B.

54. Ibid.

55. Cited in ibid.

56. 'Patriotic Minorities', *Hindustan Times* (12 April 1946); *AIR* (March 1946), p. 18C.

57. Ibid.

58. BL, OIOC, MSS Eur R193/1, Anthony interviewed.

59. *The Anglo-Indians* (1986), film.

60. Ibid.

61. F. Anthony, *Britain's Betrayal in India: The Story of the Anglo-Indian Community* (New Delhi, 1969), p. 181.

62. *AIR* (October 1944), p. 4.

63. On 30 May, as recorded in the *Indian Annual Register* (January–June 1944), vol. 1, p. 57.

64. Anthony, *Britain's Betrayal*, p. 181.

65. *The Anglo-Indians* (1986), film.

66. BL, OIOC, MSS Eur R193/1, Anthony interviewed.

67. *The Anglo-Indians* (1986), film.

68. Anthony, *Britain's Betrayal*, p. 181.

69. Ibid., pp. 181–2.

70. Ibid., p. 181.

71. BL, OIOC, MSS Eur R193/1, Anthony interviewed.

72. *The Anglo-Indians* (1986), film.

73. Anthony, *Britain's Betrayal*, p. 182.

74. J. Nehru, *An Autobiography* (1936; reprint, New Delhi, 1982), p. 6.

75. J. Brown, *Nehru: A Political Life* (New Haven CT, 2003), p. 35.

76. Ibid., p. 37.

77. *The Times* (London, 20 May 1922).

78. Nehru, *Autobiography*, p. 596.

79. *AIR* (September 1929), pp. 5–6.

80. See N. Slate, *Colored Cosmopolitanism: The Shared Struggle for Freedom in the United States and India* (Cambridge MA, 2012), pp. 84–5, and Letter from Cedric Dover to Jawaharlal Nehru, February 1938, http://credo.library.umass.edu/view/full/mums312-b085-i092.

81. BL, OIOC, MSS Eur T13 (see also R13/1–5), Interview with the Reverend Thomas Herbert Cashmore (1972–4), p. 4/1.

82. Anthony, *Britain's Betrayal*, p. 182.

83. Ibid.

84. Ibid.

85. Ibid.

86. J. Turner, 'The Apathy of the Anglo-Indian to His Community', *AIR* (March 1930), p. 14.

87. BL, OIOC, MSS Eur T52 (see also R52/1–4), Transcript of interview with Eugene A. H. Pierce, prefaced by 'Mr. Pierce's Statement: Position of Anglo-Indians within British Raj' (1973).

88. Anthony, *Britain's Betrayal*, p. 183.

89. Ibid.

90. Ibid.

91. Ibid.

92. Ibid.

93. Ibid.

94. *AIR* (March 1946), p. 18D.

95. H. Fowler, 'The Delhi Resolution', *AIR* (December 1946—January 1947), p. 27.

96. Ibid.

97. Ibid.

98. Anthony, *Britain's Betrayal*, p. 185.

99. P. Moon (ed.), *Wavell: The Viceroy's Journal* (London, 1973), p. 337.

100. Ibid.

101. Ibid.

102. *AIR* (December 1946—January 1947), pp. 3–4.

103. Ibid., p. 33.

104. Ibid., p. 22.

105. Ibid.

106. Ibid.

107. *AIR* (November 1947), p. 2. Original emphasis removed.

108. Ibid. Original emphasis removed.

109. Ibid. Original emphasis removed.

110. BL, OIOC, MSS Eur R193/1, Anthony interviewed.

111. Ibid.

112. Ibid.

113. Ibid.

114. *AIR* (September 1946), p. 7.

115. S. Perry, 'Anglo-Indian Emigration', *AIR* (November 1943), p. 19.

116. D. Reid to F. Anthony, *AIR* (September 1946), p. 7.

117. NAI, 'Frank Anthony intercepted letter', digitised document, file no. 2/242 (1948).

118. Ibid.

119. *The Legislative Assembly Debates: Official Report*, vol. 1, 3 February to 18 February 1947 (Delhi, 1947), 6 February 1947, p. 191.

120. Ibid., p. 192.

121. F. Anthony, 'Sardar Patel and the Minorities', in R. Kumar, *Life and Work of Sardar Vallabhbhai Patel* (New Delhi, 1991), p. 5.

122. *Legislative Assembly Debates*, vol. 1, 6 February 1947, p. 192.

123. Ibid., 14 February 1947, p. 609.

124. *AIR* (February 1947), pp. 6–7.

125. Ibid., p. 7.

126. *The Legislative Assembly Debates: Official Report*, vol. 4, 10 March to 24 March 1947 (Delhi, 1947), 12 March 1947, p. 1733.

127. Ibid., p. 1734.

128. Ibid.

129. Ibid., p. 1736.

130. Ibid., p. 1734.

131. Ibid.

132. S. Wolpert, *Shameful Flight: The Last Years of the British Empire in India* (2006).

133. A. Jalal, *The Sole Spokesman* (Cambridge, 1994), p. 262.

134. Ibid., p. 269.

135. Wolpert, *Shameful Flight*, p. 188.

136. J. Bew, *Clement Attlee: The Man Who Made Modern Britain* (New York, 2017), p. 45.

137. Ibid.

138. Ibid.

139. Ibid.

140. BL, OIOC, MSS Eur R193/1, Anthony interviewed.

141. Hansard, HC Debates, 6 March 1947, vol. 434, col. 678, https://api.parliament.uk/historic-hansard/commons/1947/mar/06/india-government-policy.

142. *AIR* (May 1947), p. 4.

143. BL, OIOC, MSS Eur R193/1, Anthony interviewed.

144. *AIR* (May 1947), p. 4.

145. BL, OIOC, MSS Eur R193/1, Anthony interviewed.

146. Ibid.

147. Ibid.

148. Ibid.

149. Ibid.

150. NAUK, CAB/195/4, C.M. 55(46), 'India: Constitutional Problem', Cabinet minutes in note form (5 June 1946), p. 230.

151. A. Jalal, *The Pity of Partition: Manto's Life, Times, and Work across the India–Pakistan Divide* (Princeton NJ, 2013), p. 126.

152. C. Gibbon, cited in M. Sadullah, *The Partition of the Punjab 1947: A Compilation of Official Documents*, vol. II (Lahore, 1983), p. 238.

153. T. Mains, 'The Anglo-Indian Community Services in World War II before, during and after', *Journal of the Society for Army Historical Research* 74:298 (Summer 1996), p. 127.

154. BL, OIOC, MSS Eur R193/1, Anthony interviewed.

155. D. McMenamin, 'The Curious Exclusion of Anglo-Indians from the Mass Slaughter during the Partition of India', *IJAIS* 9:1 (2006), http://www.international-journal-of-anglo-indian-studies.org/.

156. F. Anthony, AGM 'Presidential Address', *AIR* (December 1949), p. 18. Original emphasis removed.

157. R. Bajpai, *Debating Difference: Group Rights and Liberal Democracy in India* (Oxford, 2011).

158. 'Col. Gidney's Speech at the Minorities Sub-committee', *AIR* (February 1931), p. 6.

159. BL, OIOC, MSS Eur R193/1, Anthony interviewed.

160. Anthony, 'Presidential Address', *AIR* (December 1949), p. 14.

161. Ibid., pp. 14–15. Original emphasis in bold face.

162. Cited in ibid., p. 18.

163. BL, OIOC, MSS Eur R193/1, Anthony interviewed.

164. Anthony, 'Presidential Address', *AIR* (December 1949), p. 15.

165. *The Constitution of India* (1st edn, 1950), article 335, article 336 (1).

166. BL, OIOC, MSS Eur R193/1, Anthony interviewed.

167. Anthony, 'Presidential Address', *AIR* (December 1949), p. 15.

168. Fowler, 'The Delhi Resolution', p. 27.

169. G. Wilks et al. to N. Patterson, Chief Commissioner, Andaman Islands (18 December 1946), *AIR* (June 1947), p. 11.

170. University of Cambridge, Centre of South Asian Studies, Audio, Interview no. 34, R. Stracey.

171. B. Otto, 'Anglo-Indians in the Tumultuous Years: Community, Nationality, Identity and Migration, 1939–1955', Master of Arts thesis in International History, London School of Economics, University of London (2010), p. 46.

172. NAUK, FO/643/140, Confidential, Minutes: 'Record of Meeting between H.E. and Deputation of the Anglo-Burman Union in H.E.'s Office on Monday 7th March, 1949', p. 30.

173. Wilks to Patterson (18 December 1946), *AIR* (June 1947), pp. 11–12.

174. Ibid., p. 12.

175. *AIR* (March 1946), p. 3.

176. K. Wallace, *Life of Sir Henry Gidney* (Calcutta, 1947), p. 245.

177. *AIR* (November 1947), p. 2.

178. Otto, 'Anglo-Indians in the Tumultuous Years', p. 51.

179. BL, OIOC, L/PJ/7/10647, D. St. Clair Gainer, British Ambassador to Brazil, to Sir William Croft, India Office (30 October 1946), cited in ibid., pp. 45–6.

180. NAUK, DO/35/6163, R. G. Chatelier, 'Founder and Leader, Eurasian Collectivist Party', 'Head Quarters: 30/B Cubbon Road, Bangalore-1, (Mysore State), South India', to Sir Anthony Eden, Prime Minister, 10 Downing Street, London (16 June 1956), pp. 1–2.

181. Ibid., p. 2.

182. Ibid., pp. 1–2.

183. Ibid., 'Draft 3rd person note', GEN T/26, U.K.H.C., New Delhi, copy to M.S.46, CRO, Downing Street (3 July 1956), handwritten, para. 2.

184. *AIR* (September 1949), p. 2.

185. Anthony, 'Presidential Address', *AIR* (December 1949), p. 17.

186. Ibid. Original emphasis removed.

187. *AIR* (September 1955), p. 18. Original emphasis removed.

188. *Legislative Assembly Debates*, vol. 4, 25 March 1946, p. 2870.

189. G. Miller, 'Anglo-Indian "Exodus" Causing Anxiety: Insidious Propaganda Condemned', *AIR* (October–November 1949), p. 7. Original emphasis removed.

190. *AIR* (September 1955), pp. 1, 18.

191. Ibid. Original emphasis removed.

192. *AIR* (December 1955), p. 1.

193. F. Anthony, AGM 'Presidential Address', *AIR* (May 1947), p. 8. Original emphasis removed.

194. *AIR* (May 1947), p. 5.

195. *AIR* (February 1947), p. 4.

196. 'Mr. Anthony Visualises Strife and Bloodshed', *Civil and Military Gazette* (15 February 1947); *AIR* (March 1947), pp. 9–10.

197. *AIR* (March 1947), p. 13.

198. Ibid., p. 7.

199. Ibid.

200. *AIR* (December 1946—January 1947), p. 9.

201. Ibid.

202. Ibid.

203. *AIR* (May 1947), p. 5.

204. 'Gibbon Forms Anglo-Indian Association of Pakistan', *Dawn* (7 June 1947), p. 5.

205. *AIR* (June 1947), p. 4.

206. Ibid.

207. Ibid.

208. Ibid.

209. *AIR* (July 1947), p. 4.

210. Ibid., pp. 4–5. Original emphasis removed.

211. Cited in Sadullah, *Partition of the Punjab*, p. 236.

212. Cited in ibid., pp. 235–6.

213. Cited in ibid., p. 239.

214. Cited in ibid., p. 236.

215. D. McMenamin, 'Anglo-Indian Lives in Pakistan through the Lens of Oral Histories', PhD thesis, University of Otago, New Zealand (2019), pp. 16, 160.

216. *AIR* (December 1947), p. 5.

217. *AIR* (August 1949), pp. 6–8.

218. Ibid.

219. NAUK, DO/35/6163, 'The Plight of Anglo-Indians in East Pakistan and Elsewhere', note by A. Ross (7 January 1953), 'Mr. Gibson', pp. 1–2. Original draft quotation, handwritten annotations or amendments have been removed.

220. Ibid.

221. Ibid., p. 2.

222. Ibid., item 8 (14 June 1954), p. 9.

223. *AIR* (March 1946), p. 3.

224. Anthony, 'Presidential Address', *AIR* (December 1949), p. 15.

225. Ibid.

226. Ibid.

227. Ibid., p. 16.

228. Ibid.

229. Ibid.

230. Ibid.

231. Ibid., pp. 18, 21. Original emphasis removed.

232. *AIR* (September 1949), p. 10. Original emphasis removed.

233. Ibid.

234. Miller, 'Anglo-Indian "Exodus"', *AIR* (October–November 1949), p. 6. Original emphasis removed.

235. Ibid., pp. 6–7. Original emphasis in bold face.

236. Anthony, 'Presidential Address', *AIR* (December 1949), p. 16. Original emphasis removed.

237. Cited in ibid., p. 18.

238. Cited in ibid.

239. Ibid. Original emphasis removed.

240. Ibid. Original emphasis removed.

241. Ibid., p. 21. Original emphasis removed.

242. Ibid., p. 19.

243. Ibid.

244. Ibid., pp. 19–21. Original emphasis removed.

245. Ibid., pp. 18, 20. Original emphasis removed.

246. B. O'Brien, chief guest, book launch of M. Simi Raj and R. Andrews (eds.), *Anglo-Indian Identity: Past and Present in India and the Diaspora*, Centre for Memory Studies, Indian Institute of Technology Madras, livestreamed on 25 August 2021, 9.30 a.m. IST.

247. Anthony, 'Presidential Address', *AIR* (December 1949), p. 17. Original emphasis removed.

248. *AIR* (September 1949), p. 10. Original emphasis removed.

249. See R. Almeida, *Britain's Anglo-Indians: The Invisibility of Assimilation* (Washington DC, 2017).

250. BL, OIOC, MSS Eur T52, Interview with Pierce.

251. BL, OIOC, MSS Eur R189, Nissen interviewed.

252. Hansard, HL Debates, 16 December 1957, vol. 206, cols. 1189–91, https://api. parliament.uk/historic-hansard/lords/1957/dec/16/british-nationality-bill-hl.

253. NAUK, DO/35/6163, item 22: 'Mr. Gibson' (31 January 1958). Original handwritten amendments included.

254. Ibid.

255. Ibid.

256. Ibid.

257. NAUK, DO/35/6163, Draft no. 309 in NAT 154/64/1, 'Confidential': J. Gibson to H. Smedley, UK High Commission, New Delhi (signed 10 February 1958), p. 3. Original draft quotation without handwritten annotations or amendments added.

258. NAUK, FO/643/140, British Embassy, Rangoon, file no. 4405/49, Anglo-Burmans, Minutes, note by P. Murray (12 May 1949), pp. 20–1.

EPILOGUE

1. A Dominion until the Constitution of India of 1949–50, which created the Republic of India.

2. S. Philip, 'History lesson for Pakistan's military: IAF's Keelor brothers shot down PAF jets in 1965: Denzil, Trevor Keelor shot down Pakistan's Sabre jets in 1965. They were honoured with Vir Chakra, first time two brothers received the award

for the same reason', *The Print* (29 July 2019, 5.49 p.m. IST), https://theprint.in/defence/history-lesson-for-pakistans-military-iafs-keelor-brothers-shot-down-paf-jets-in-1965/269463/.

3. Ibid.

4. M. Chhina, 'A 1965 Vir Chakra fighter pilot returns home from Australia: My Vir Chakra belongs to my squadron, I was only doing my job, says Flt Lt Alfred Tyrone Cooke who took on three Pak Sabres over Kalaikunda', *Indian Express* (Ambala, updated 8 September 2015), https://indianexpress.com/article/india/india-others/a-1965-vir-chakra-fighter-pilot-returns-home-from-australia/.

5. Accompanying (second full-length) video in V. Som, '4 Pak fighter jets, but an Indian Air Force hero won the day', NDTV (14 September 2015), https://www.ndtv.com/india-news/4-pak-fighter-jets-but-an-indian-air-force-hero-won-the-day-1217303.

6. Ibid.

7. Ibid.

8. M. Azam, 'Presenting "Neglected Christian Children of Indus" to a Hero' (22 August 2018), https://michelleazam.wordpress.com/2018/08/22/presenting-neglected-christian-children-of-indus-to-a-hero/.

9. Ibid.

10. Ibid.

11. A. Mairaj, *Neglected Christian Children of Indus: True Bitter Stories Narrating How the Christian Children of Indus Are Alienated from Their Ancestors' Land and Society*, trans. M. A. Mairaj (Karachi, 2018), p. 99.

12. BL, OIOC, MSS Eur T15 (see also R15/1–4), Interview with Raj Chatterjee (1972–4), pp. 4–5.

13. Air Chief Marshal D. A. La Fontaine (1929–2011), Chief of the Indian Air Force (3 July 1985—31 July 1988).

14. Admiral R. L. Pereira, PVSM, AVSM (1923–1993), ninth Chief of Naval Staff (1 March 1979—28 February 1982).

15. BL, OIOC, MSS Eur R193/1, Anthony interviewed.

BIBLIOGRAPHY

PRIMARY SOURCES

1. Private Archive of the All-India Anglo-Indian Association, New Delhi.

AIR: *The Anglo-Indian Review*; briefly *The Anglo-Indian Review and Railway Union Journal* between October 1930 and July 1931, and shortened to *The Review* after 1948 (monthly journal of the All-India Anglo-Indian Association, published in Calcutta and later Delhi, c.1900s to the present; however, pre-1929 issues may be found only sporadically in other British and South Asian archives).

2. Private Collection of the DeRozario Family, McCluskieganj, Jharkhand.

Colonization Observer (monthly journal of the Colonization Society of India, selected issues, 1934–41): 1934 (April, July, September, October); 1937 (August, November); 1938 (August, November, December); 1939 (February, March–April); 1940 (April); 1941 (January, April).
Hobbs, H., *Extracts from My Diary* [pamphlet] (8 November 1934).
McCluskie, E., *The Dawn of a New Era* [pamphlet] (rev. edn, 1 July 1934), included as a supplement to *Colonization Observer* (July 1934).

3. University of Cambridge, Centre of South Asian Studies, Archive.

Audio, Interview no. 61, J. E. L. Newbigin, https://www.s-asian.cam. ac.uk/archive/audio/collection/j-e-l-newbigin/.
Audio, Interview no. 35, E. Stracey, https://www.s-asian.cam.ac.uk/ archive/audio/collection/e-stracey/.
Audio, Interview no. 34, R. Stracey, https://www.s-asian.cam.ac.uk/ archive/audio/collection/r-stracey/.
Audio, Interview no. 36, C. Stracey, https://www.s-asian.cam.ac.uk/ archive/audio/collection/c-stracey/.

Interview, Bishop Newbigin, 1978 (created digitally 12 August 2009), https://sms.cam.ac.uk/media/654746.

4. National Archive of India (NAI), New Delhi.

Air Forces in India, Air Headquarters:.
File no. 4006/9/ON-G4B, vol. 2 (January 1943).
Central Board of Revenue, Customs Establishments Branch:.
Progs., nos. 165-CE (1935).
Progs., nos. 28-CE (1936).
Progs., nos. 502-Admn (CE), Part A (1937).
Central India Agency, Finance Branch:.
Progs., no. 146-C (1934).
Digitised (NAI online):.
'Frank Anthony intercepted letter', digitised document, file no. 2/242 (1948).
Finance Department:.
Progs., nos. 80–1 (February 1885).
Finance Department, Regulation Branch, II:.
Progs., nos. 2 (1)—R11 (1929).
Progs., nos. 5 (XVI)—R11 (1929).
Foreign and Political Department, Establishment Branch:.
Progs., no. 241 (1931).
Progs., no. 128 (1932).
Foreign and Political Department, External Branch:.
Progs., nos. 103-X (1930).
Government of India, Army Department, General Staff Branch:.
Progs., nos. 2239–73 (May 1930).
Home Department, Education Branch:.
Unnumbered file relating to scholarships.
Home Department, Establishment Branch:.
Progs., no. 21 (July 1908).
Progs., no. 27, deposit (February 1918).
Progs., nos. 357–8, Part A (February 1920).
Progs., no. 389 (1923).
Progs., nos. 11–5 (1929).
Progs., no. 266 (1929).
Progs., nos. 16–2 (1932).
Progs., no. 192 (1932).
Progs., no. 389, Part I (1932).
Progs., no. 528 (1932).
(R), Progs., nos. 5/13/47 (1947).
Home Department, Police Branch:.

Progs., nos. 11/XI (1931).

Legislative Department, Assembly Council:.

(Speeches), Progs., no. 85, Part B (February 1921).

Legislative Department, Council General:.

Progs., nos. 255 (1)-CG (1928).

Malwa Agency, Finance Branch:.

Progs., nos. 170-C (1934).

Political Department, Political Branch:.

(Confidential), Progs. 42, nos. 1–4 (1908).

Private Secretary to the Viceroy, Honours Branch:.

(Secret), Progs., nos. 18 (13)-H (1946).

Punjab State Agency, General Branch:.

Unnumbered file (1922).

Railways Department, Establishment Branch:.

1059-EG-2027, Part B (1933).

E-35CM-126, Part B (August 1935).

Reforms Department, Franchise Branch:.

Progs., nos. 156-R (1933).

Progs., nos. 41-F (1935).

5. National Archives, United Kingdom (NAUK).

Cabinet Papers (non-exhaustive list of the most relevant):.

CAB/24/116, CP 2230, Cabinet: Circulated by the Secretary of State for India (2 December 1920), enclosing *Proposals of the Government of India for a New Constitution for Burma* (London, 1920).

CAB/24/158, CP 58 (23), Cabinet: Legislature in India to Remove Racial Distinctions in Criminal Procedure (January 1923).

CAB/24/224, CP 272 (31), Cabinet: Government Policy at the Indian Round Table Conference (11 November 1931).

CAB/24/232, CP 266 (32), Cabinet: Communal Decision (July 1932).

CAB/24/278, CP 187 (38), Cabinet: India, Defence Questions (29 July 1938), enclosing *Committee of Imperial Defence, Chiefs of Staff Sub-committee, The Defence of India: Report* (July 1938).

CAB/37/159/42, Lieutenant H. S. D. McNeal, 'Report on the Siege of Kut-El-Amara' (5 December 1915 to 29 April 1916).

CAB/66/23/40, WP (42) 160, War Cabinet: Evacuation of Indians from Burma (11 April 1942).

CAB/66/26/13, WP (42) 283, War Cabinet: Report on Mission to India (6 July 1942).

CAB/66/65/40, WP (45) 290, War Cabinet: White Paper on Burma Policy (8 May 1945).

BIBLIOGRAPHY

CAB/67/5/23, WP (G) (40) 73, War Cabinet: Congress and the War: Memorandum by the Secretary of State for India (11 March 1940).

CAB/67/8/1, WP (G) (40) 201, War Cabinet: India and the War (27 July 1940).

CAB/67/9/69, WP (G) (41) 69, War Cabinet: India and the War (16 July 1941).

CAB/68/9/47, WP (R) (42) 47, War Cabinet: Report for the Month of September 1942, for the Dominions, India, Burma and the Colonies and Mandated Territories (26 October 1942).

CAB/128/7, CM (46) 55th Conclusions: Confidential Annex (5 June 1946, 10 a.m.).

CAB/129/154, CP (70) 122, Cabinet: Sale of Arms to South Africa (31 December 1970) [see Section IV: Citizenship and Immigration Aspects, pp. 18–20, and Annex. 4, pp. 1–5].

CAB/195/4, CM 55 (46), India: Constitutional Problem, in note form (5 June 1946).

Dominions Office; Commonwealth Office; and Commonwealth Relations Office, etc.:.

CO/123/276/86, General: B[ritish] Honduras 34397, Assistant Medical Officer (19 September 1913).

CO/968/142/3, Defence and General, Miscellaneous, file no. 14516/49/5: Demobilisation, Malaya, Eurasian Volunteers (1946).

DO/35/6163, General Dept, file no. GEN T/26: The Plight of Anglo-Indians in East Pakistan and Elsewhere (file begins 4 January 1954).

DO/196/76, South Asia Dept, file no. SEA 44/5/2: The Position of Anglo-Indians (file begins 5 July 1960).

Department of Education:

ED/54/72, O.400/341–70: Further Education and Training Scheme, General (1947–8).

Foreign Office; and Foreign and Commonwealth Office:.

FCO/15/56, Foreign Office, South-East Asia Dept, file no. DB 3/4: Burma, Political Affairs (bilateral), UK, Anglo-Burmese in Burma (1967).

FO/369/4421, K Consular Dept, Burma, KG 17945/1: Possibility of Resettling Anglo Burmans in N[orth] Borneo (1950).

FO/369/4904, K Consular Dept, Burma, KG 791/6: Welfare of the Anglo-Burman Community in Burma (1953).

FO/369/5223, Foreign Office (Consular Dept), Burma, file no. KG 1791/2: Richard George Gyi, request for an assisted passage; and subsequent related files (1955).

FO/371/69480, F, Burma, F 309/309/79: Anglo-Burmans and Anglo-Indians Wishing to Leave for Permanent Settlement in Australia (1948).

FO/371/83206, F, South-East Asia Dept, Burma, FB 1601/1: Regarding the Nationality, and Passage to the UK, of Carlyle Seppings; and subsequent related files (1950). ´

FO/371/111998, D, South-East Asia Dept, Burma, DB 1482/1: Far Eastern War Damage Schemes (1954).

FO/371/123374, D, South-East Asia Dept, Burma, DB 1821/1: Copy of a letter to Sir R. Scott, Singapore … [and] copies of notes on Anglo-Burmans and the Problems of Claimants to British Nationality in Burma (1956).

FO/643/52, Governor's Secretary's Office, no. 1M2/GS44 (confidential): Reconstruction, Evacuation, Anglo-Burmans and Other Evacuees (1944).

FO/643/140, British Embassy, Rangoon, file no. 4405/49: Anglo-Burmans (1949).

FO/916/786, KW 59/22: Welfare of Eurasians in the Far East, general questions (1943).

War Office; and Admiralty Papers:

ADM/1/8690/208: 'Admiralty. 208/25: Ex N.4620/25: Anglo-Indians (Eurasians): Entry into R[oyal] N[avy]: Genl. Service' (1925).

WO/32/6889: '27.Gen. no. 8550: Enlistment of Eurasians into British Regiments' (1886–95).

WO/361/2227: Prisoners of War, Far East, General Information, Locally Enlisted Eurasians (1945).

6. Kerala State Archives, Trivandrum.

614/40, Confidential B, no. 1022, no. D, Dis. 614/40/CS (31 December 1940): 'Movements and Activities: W. E. Goudie alias Bean, an Anglo-Indian', Confidential Section, Government of Travancore, Secret 'Note on W. E. Goudie (an Anglo-Indian) alias Bean'.

7. State Archives of West Bengal, Kolkata.

Political Confidential, file no. M-25, serial no. 1–2.
Political Confidential, file no. 314/1909, serial no. 1–10.
Political Confidential, file no. 42, serial no. 1–4.

8. Official Papers Reading Room, Bodleian Library, Oxford: British Parliamentary Papers.

Hansard

Report on Indian Constitutional Reforms (London, 1918).
Reports of the Indian Round Table Conferences:.
First Session (London, 1931).
Second Session (London, 1932).

Third Session (London, 1933).

Reports of the Joint Committee on Indian Constitutional Reform:

Volume IIA: Minutes of Evidence Given before the Joint Committee on Indian Constitutional Reform (London, 1934).

Volume IIC: Minutes of Evidence Given before the Joint Committee on Indian Constitutional Reform (London, 1934).

Reports of the Select Committee on Colonization and Settlement:.

First Report—Third Report (London, 1858), Fourth Report (London, 1859).

9. *Indian Institute Library, Bodleian Library, Oxford.*

Bombay Legislative Council Debates (1920s).

Census of India (1891, 1901, 1911, 1921, 1931, 1941).

(Central) Legislative Assembly Debates (1920–35).

Proceedings of the Council of the Governor General of India (1909–19).

Waterfield, H., *Memorandum on the Census of British India 1871–72* (London, 1875).

IND Bengal.K.2: *General Report of Public Instruction for Bengal, for 1875–76* (Government of Bengal, Calcutta, 1876).

IND B.2: 'India in 1926–27: A Statement Prepared for Presentation to Parliament in Accordance with the Requirements of the 26th Section of the Government of India Act' (Government of India, Calcutta, 1928).

IND Bengal.K.3: Quinquennial Reviews of Education in Bengal (Government of Bengal, Calcutta, five reports from 1902 to 1922).

IND 75.E.41: *Royal Commission on Public Services in India*, vol. I: *Report* (London, 1917).

Pamphlets (loose and bound), 8287 c50 and 08023 aaa46:

Chambers, Dr., *Anglo-Indian Prospects in India: Read at a Meeting of the Board of Direction of the Anglo-Indian Association* (Calcutta, 1879).

Chatterton, E. D. D., *Anglo-Indian and Eurasian Origins* (Westminster, 1937).

Ingels, L., *Anglo-Indian Amalgamation: The Pressing Need of the Community* (Calcutta, 1918).

Sutherland, D., *The Grievances of the East Indian Community: A Paper to Be Read before the East India Association* (London, 1880).

10. *Oriental and India Office Collections, British Library, London (BL, OIOC).*

Anglo-Indian Journal (monthly journal of the Eurasian and Anglo-Indian Association of Western India, published in Bombay, 1897–1901).

F/4/1259: Extract Bombay Revenue Consultations.

F/4/1115: Extract of Fort St George Military Correspondence.

F/4/1408/55600: 'Minute by the Honble the Governor [Sir John Malcolm], dated 30th November 1830'.

L/PJ/7/7880: Telegram from F. Anthony, New Delhi, to the Secretary of State for India, London, CD202/VWK1246/H (received 5 July 1945).

L/PJ/7/10647: D. St. Clair Gainer, British Ambassador to Brazil, to Sir William Croft, India Office, 30 October 1946.

L/PO/10/22: Letters between the Viceroy, Viscount Wavell, and the Secretary of State for India, Lord Pethick-Lawrence.

MSS Eur D703/42: Birkenhead Collection, Deputations received by Lord Birkenhead at the India Office (Anglo-Indians, Trades Union Congress, Labour Party), *Proceedings at a Deputation from the Anglo-Indian Community to the Secretary of State for India, 30 July 1925*.

MSS Eur E238/55A (III), pp. 619–32: Reading Collection, 'Memorandum Submitted to the Joint Select Committee on Indian Constitutional Reform by Lt. Col. Sir Henry Gidney'.

MSS Eur F77/106: Simon Collection, 'Memorandum Submitted on Behalf of the Anglo-Indian and Domiciled European Community of India for the Consideration of the Chairman and Members of the Indian Statutory Commission, from Lt Col. Sir Henry Gidney, 25 June 1928'; letter from Hon. Mr. H. G. Haig, Secretary to the Government of India, to Gidney, 11 September 1928.

MSS Eur F84/64: Elgin Papers, Letters between the Viceroy and the Secretary of State for India.

MSS Eur F111/158–61: Curzon Papers, Letters between the Viceroy and the Secretary of State for India.

MSS Eur F531: Papers of Christopher J. Hawes, 1950–2004, writer and historian.

MSS Eur R189: Roy Edward King Nissen, b. 1905, interviewed in 1989 on four cassettes covering 1905–60.

MSS Eur R193/1, Frank Reginald Anthony interviewed by Gillian Wright (between November 1987 and January 1988).

MSS Eur T13 (see also R13/1–5), Interview with the Reverend Thomas Herbert Cashmore (1972–4).

MSS Eur T14 (see also R14/1–2), Interview with Marjorie Cashmore (1972–4).

MSS Eur T15 (see also R15/1–4), Interview with Raj Chatterjee (1972–4).

MSS Eur T29 (see also R29/1–6), Transcript of interview with Irene Edwards [née Green] (1972–4).

MSS Eur T52 (see also R52/1–4), Transcript of interview with Eugene

BIBLIOGRAPHY

A. H. Pierce, prefaced by 'Mr. Pierce's Statement: Position of Anglo-Indians within British Raj' (1973).

8285/g/43: *Report of the Calcutta Domiciled Community Enquiries Committee, 1918–1919* (Calcutta, 1920).

V/6: Viceregal correspondence with Secretary of State for India.

V/9: [Indian Central] *Legislative Assembly Debates* (1920–47).

V/27/720/28: F. D'Souza, Government of India, Railway Department (Railway Board): *Review of the Working of the Rules and Orders Relating to the Representation of Minority Communities in the Services of the State-Managed Railways* (New Delhi, 1940).

V/27/861/1: *Report on the Existing Schools for Europeans and Eurasians through-out India* (Calcutta, 1873).

W/2388: Eurasian and Anglo-Indian Association, Mysore Branch (Bangalore), *Guide to the Eurasian and Anglo-Indian Villages, Proposed to Be Established in the Province of Mysore*, ed. S. Lee (Madras, 1882).

P/W/588 (see also MSS Eur D/925): *Memorandum Relative to the Deputation of the Anglo-Indian and Domiciled Community of India and Burma to the Rt Hon. the Secretary of State for India, 30 July 1925*.

P/4089: *Report of the Pauperism Committee* (Calcutta, 1892).

11. Special Collections and University Archives, University of Massachusetts Amherst Libraries.

W. E. B. Du Bois Papers (MS 312), Letter from Cedric Dover to Jawaharlal Nehru, February 1938, http://credo.library.umass.edu/view/full/mums312-b085-i092.

NEWSPAPERS

Dawn (Karachi).
Manchester Guardian (Manchester).
Pioneer Mail and Indian Weekly News (Allahabad).
Servant of India (Poona).
Statesman and Friend of India or *The Statesman* (Calcutta).
The Times of London (London).

FILMS, TELEVISION AND RADIO

The Anglo-Indians, documentary film, produced by Central Independent Television for Channel 4 (UK, 1986).

Cukor, G. (director), *Bhowani Junction*, film, Metro-Goldwyn-Mayer (United States, 1 May 1956).

Delofski, M. (director), *The Trouble with Merle*, documentary film, Australian Broadcasting Corporation et al. (Australia, 13 June 2002).

BIBLIOGRAPHY

Korda, A. (director), *The Private Life of Don Juan*, film, London Film Productions (UK, 30 November 1934).

Kutcha Butcha Half Baked Bread, BBC Radio 4 FM (18 August 1997).

Marshall, F. (director), *Congo*, film, The Kennedy–Marshall Company (US, 9 June 1995).

Original theatrical trailer of *Bhowani Junction* (1956), reproduced as a 'Home Video Trailer from Warner Home Video', https://www.imdb.com/video/vi750387481/?ref_=tt_vi_i_1.

LEGAL CASES

Graham v. Henry Gidney, original civil, before Ameer Ali J., *Calcutta Series*, vol. 60 (9, 10, 13, 14 & 28 February 1933), pp. 957–60, www.scconline.com.

PUBLISHED SOURCES

Abbott, B., 'Captain John Harold (Arnold) Abbott (b. 10th January, 1863, d. 28th June, 1945)', Genealogy.com, http://familytreemaker.genealogy.com/users/a/b/b/Warren-B-Abbott/WEBSITE-0001/UHP-0075.html.

———, 'Quartermaster Sergeant William Lumsden Abbott (b. 26th July, 1828, d. 25th August, 1880)', Genealogy.com, http://familytreemaker.genealogy.com/users/a/b/b/Warren-B-Abbott/WEBSITE-0001/UHP-0241.html.

Aga Khan, *The Memoirs of Aga Khan: World Enough and Time* (New York, 1945).

Almeida, R., and K. Cassity (eds.), *Curtain Call: Anglo-Indian Reflections* (New Jersey, 2015).

Ambedkar, B. R., *Annihilation of Caste* (London, 1936).

Anglo-Indian Association, *The Ilbert Bill: A Collection of Letters, Speeches, Memorials, Articles, &c., Stating the Objections to the Bill* (London, c.1883).

Anglo-Indian Christian Union, *Fifth Report of the Anglo-Indian Christian Union for Promoting the Spiritual Interests of Europeans and Other English-Speaking People in India, 1875* (Edinburgh, 1876).

Anglo-India, Social, Moral and Political; Being a Collection of Papers from the Asiatic Journal, 3 vols. (London, 1838).

Anon., 'The East-Indians', *Asiatic Journal and Monthly Register for British and Foreign India, China, and Australia* (London), NS, 5 (May 1831).

Anon. [handwritten annotation 'V. G. Clarke'], *The Fortunes of the Anglo-Indian Race: Considered Retrospectively and Prospectively by One of Fifty Years Knowledge and Experience* (2nd edn, Madras, 1878).

Anon., 'Injudicious Nature of the Policy of the Honourable East India

Company, as Exemplified in the Condition of the Indo-Britons', *Alexander's East India and Colonial and Commercial Journal* 1 (April 1831).

Anthony, F., *Britain's Betrayal in India: The Story of the Anglo-Indian Community* (New Delhi, 1969).

————, 'Sardar Patel and the Minorities', in R. Kumar, *Life and Work of Sardar Vallabhbhai Patel* (New Delhi, 1991).

————, *Will Britain Tarnish Her Honour? Being a Brief Review of the History, Present Position and Needs of the Anglo-Indian Community in India and of Britain's Solemn Obligations to the Community* (New Delhi, 1943).

Ashford, L, J., *Whisper of the Moon Moth* (Seattle WA, 2017).

Aung San, 'Address Delivered at a Meeting of the Anglo-Burman Council, at the City Hall, Rangoon' (8 December 1946), http://www.aungsan. com/Anglo_Burmans.htm.

Bradley, S., *An American Girl in India: A Novel* (London, 1911).

Bright-Holmes, J. (ed.), *Like It Was: The Diaries of Malcolm Muggeridge* (New York, 1981).

British Medical Journal, 'Front Matter', 2:4171 (14 December 1940).

Burchett, W., *Trek Back from Burma* (Allahabad, 1944).

Butler, K., *The Secret Vindaloo: Tell Me What You Eat and I'll Tell You Who You Are* (Auckland, 2014).

Calcutta Review, vol. 7 (Calcutta, January–June 1847), vol. 18 (Calcutta, July–December 1852), vol. 24 (Calcutta, January–June, 1855), vol. 28 (Calcutta, January–June 1857), and vol. 69 (Calcutta, October 1879).

Campagnac C., *The Autobiography of a Wanderer in England and Burma: The Memoirs of a Former Mayor of Rangoon*, ed. S. Campagnac-Carney (Raleigh NC, 2010).

Campagnac-Carney, S., *Burma: Memories of WWII* (Raleigh, 2014).

Campbell, D., and A. H. Bartley, 'Indian Medical Department', *British Medical Journal* 1:4175 (11 January 1941).

Chesterton, G. K., *Eugenics and Other Evils* (London, 1922).

The Constitution of India (1st edn, 1950).

Cotton, J., 'Art. III: Kitty Kirkpatrick', *Calcutta Review*, 108:216 (April 1899).

Craik, D. M. M., *The Half-Caste: An Old Governess's Tale* (reprint, Memphis, 2012).

Cross, J., *Secret Daughter: A Mixed-Race Daughter and the Mother Who Gave Her Away* (New York, 2006).

Curzon of Kudleston, *Lord Curzon in India: Being a Selection from His Speeches as Viceroy and Governor-General of India: 1898–1905*, ed. Thomas Raleigh (London, 1906).

————, *Speeches by Lord Curzon of Kedleston, Viceroy and Governor-General of India: 1898–1901* (Calcutta, 1901).

Dady, D. S., *Scattered Seeds: The Diaspora of the Anglo-Indians* (New Delhi, 2007).

Daily News (London, 4 November 1857).

Davenport, C., 'Marriage Laws and Customs', in *Problems in Eugenics: Papers Communicated to the First International Eugenics Congress Held at the University of London, July 24th to 30th, 1912* (London, 1912).

Deefholts, M. (ed.), *Haunting India: A Collection of Short Fiction, Poetry, Travel Tales, and Memoirs* (New Jersey, 2003).

Deefholts, M., and G. Deefholts (eds.), *The Way We Were: Anglo-Indian Chronicles* (New Jersey, 2006).

Deefholts, M., and S. Deefholts (eds.), *Women of Anglo-India: Tales and Memoirs* (New Jersey, 2010).

Deefholts, M., and S. W. Staub (eds.), *Voices on the Verandah: An Anthology of Anglo-Indian Prose and Poetry* (New Jersey, 2004).

De Silva, P., *Colonial Self-fashioning in British India c.1785–1845: Visualising Identity and Difference* (Newcastle, 2018).

Dover, C., *American Negro Art* (London, 1960).

———, *Brown Phoenix* (London, 1950).

———, *Cimmerii?, or, Eurasians and Their Future* (Calcutta, 1929).

———, 'Eugenic Legislation in India', *Quarterly Review* (January 1935).

———, 'The Eurasian Problem and Its Solution', in S. Sinha (ed.), *The Hindustan Review* 54:306 (January 1930).

———, *Half-Caste* (London, 1937).

———, *Hell in the Sunshine* (London, 1943).

———, *Know This of Race* (London, 1939).

———, 'Population Control in India', *Eugenics Review* 26:4 (1935), pp. 283–5.

D'Souza, T., *The Silence beyond the Pain: Waiting for Answers* (CreateSpace [online], 2013).

Dunlop, R., *Behind Japanese Lines: With the OSS in Burma* (Chicago, 1979).

Eden, Emily, *Letters from India*, vol. II, ed. Eleanor Eden (London, 1872), http://digital.library.upenn.edu/women/eden/letters/letters.html.

Edwards, T., 'Art. VI: The Eurasian Movement of 1829–30', *Calcutta Review* 76:151 (January 1883).

———, *Henry Derozio, the Eurasian: Poet, Teacher, and Journalist* (Calcutta, 1884).

Ellis, H., *The Task of Social Hygiene* (Boston MA, 1912).

Evening Post (Wellington, NZ), 'Hunting Surgeon: Record of Tigers Shot', 121:24 (29 January 1936), 10, http://paperspast.natlib.govt.nz/cgi-bin/paperspast?a=d&cl=search&d=EP19360129.2.50&srpos=1&e=———10——1———2hunting+surgeon———.

BIBLIOGRAPHY

Falkland, V., *Chow-Chow; Being Selections from a Journal Kept in India, Egypt, and Syria*, vol. 1 (London, 1857).

Forbes-Mitchell, W., *The Gospel of Regeneration of the Anglo-Indian and Eurasian Poor* (Calcutta, 1900).

Forster, E. M., *A Passage to India* (London, 1979).

Fraser, J. (ed.), *Military Memoir of Lieut.-Col. James Skinner, C.B.* (London, 1851).

Ganachari, A., '"White Man's Embarrassment": European Vagrancy in 19th Century Bombay', *Economic and Political Weekly* 37:25 (22–28 June 2002).

Gandhi, M. K., *The Collected Works of Mahatma Gandhi*, 98 vols. (ebook; 1st edn, Delhi, 1958–63).

Gidney, H., 'Indian Medical Department', *British Medical Journal* 2:4171 (14 December 1940), p. 850.

Humperdinck, E., and K. Wright, *Engelbert: What's in a Name? My Autobiography* (London, 2004).

Indian National Congress, *Indian National Congress: 1930–34: Being the Resolutions Passed by the Congress, the All India Congress Committee and the Working Committee during the Period between Jan. 1930 to Sep. 1934 ...* (Allahabad, 1934).

Jog, N., *Judge or Judas?* (Bombay, 1945).

Kipling, R., *Plain Tales from the Hills* (North Falmouth MA, 1899).

Korda, M., *Charmed Lives: A Family Romance* (New York, 1979).

——, *Queenie* (New York, 1985).

Laurie, W. F. B., *Sketches of Some Distinguished Anglo-Indians: With an Account of Anglo-Indian Periodical Literature* (New Delhi, 1887).

Law-Yone, W., *Golden Parasol: A Daughter's Memoir of Burma* (London, 2010).

Locke, J., *Second Treatise of Government* (1690).

Lok Sabha Secretariat, *Constituent Assembly of India Debates (CAD)*, 12 vols. (Delhi, 1946–1950; reprint, 1999), http://164.100.47.132/lssnew/cadebatefiles/cadebates.html.

Lumb, L. (ed.), *More Voices on the Verandah* (New Jersey, 2012).

Lumb, L., and D. van Veldhuizen (eds.), *The Way We Are: An Anglo-Indian Mosaic* (New Jersey, 2008).

Lyons, E. M., *Bitter Sweet Truth: Recollections of an Anglo Indian Born during the Last Year of the British Raj* (New Delhi, 2001).

Mackay, G., *Serious Reflections and Other Contributions* (Bombay, 1881).

Maher, R., *These Are the Anglo-Indians* (Calcutta, 1962).

Mains, T., 'The Anglo-Indian Community Services in World War II before, during and after', *Journal of the Society for Army Historical Research* 74:298 (Summer 1996).

Mansergh, N., et al. (eds.), *The Transfer of Power, 1942–7*, vol. I: *The Cripps Mission, January–April 1942* (London, 1970).

————, vol. II: *'Quit India', 30 April—21 September 1942* (London, 1971).

————, vol. III: *Reassertion of Authority, 21 September 1942—12 June 1943* (London, 1971).

————, vol. IV: *The Bengal Famine and the New Viceroyalty, 15 June 1943—31 August 1944* (London, 1973).

————, vol. V: *The Simla Conference, 1 September 1944—28 July 1945* (London, 1974).

————, vol. VI: *The Post-war Phase: New Moves by the Labour Government, 1 August 1945—22 March 1946* (London, 1974).

————, vol. VII: *The Cabinet Mission, 23 March—29 June 1946* (London, 1977).

————, vol. VIII: *The Interim Government, 3 July—1 November 1946* (London, 1979).

————, vol. IX: *The Fixing of a Time Limit, 4 November 1946—22 March 1947* (London, 1980).

————, vol. X: *The Mountbatten Viceroyalty, Formulation of a Plan, 22 March—30 May 1947* (London, 1981).

————, vol. XI: *The Mountbatten Viceroyalty, Announcement and Reception of the 3 June Plan, 31 May—7 July 1947* (London, 1982).

————, vol. XII: *The Mountbatten Viceroyalty, Princes, Partition, and Independence, 8 July—15 August 1947* (London, 1983).

Mason, P., *Skinner of Skinner's Horse: A Fictional Portrait* (London, 1979).

Masters, J., *Bhowani Junction* (New York, 1954).

Maugham, S., 'The Door of Opportunity', in *Collected Short Stories*, vol. 2 (London, 2002).

Merchant, I., *Cotton Mary* (New Delhi, 2000).

Mitchell, D., *Tea, Love and War: Searching for English Roots in Assam* (Leicester, 2012).

Mitra, H. (ed.), *The Govt. of India Act 1919: Rules Thereunder and Govt. Reports, 1920* (Calcutta, 1921).

Mitra, N. (ed.), *The Indian Annual Register*, vol. 1 (Calcutta, January–June 1939), The Bengal Provincial Political Conference, 36th Session (Jalpaiguri, 4–5 February 1939).

Montagu, E. S., *An Indian Diary*, ed. V. Montagu (London, 1930).

Moon, P. (ed.), *Wavell: The Viceroy's Journal* (London, 1973).

Moon, V., and H. Narke (eds.), *Dr. Babasaheb Ambedkar: Writings and Speeches*, vol. 2 (New Delhi, 1979; 2nd edn, 2014).

Moreno, H. W. B., *Anglo-Indian Education: An Open Letter to All Educational Authorities* (Calcutta, 1920).

————, *Anglo-Indians and the Housing Problem* (Calcutta, 1917).

BIBLIOGRAPHY

————, *The Call to Arms for Anglo-Indians* (Calcutta, 1916).

————, *Freemasonry Revealed! Being a Series of Short Stories of Anglo-Indian Life Concerning Masons and Masonry* (Calcutta, 1907).

Morselli, E., 'Ethnic Psychology and the Science of Eugenics', in *Problems in Eugenics: Papers Communicated to the First International Eugenics Congress Held at the University of London, July 24th to 30th, 1912* (London, 1912).

Moss, P., *Bye-Bye Blackbird: An Anglo-Indian Memoir* (Lincoln NE, 2004).

Nehru, J., *An Autobiography* (1936; reprint, New Delhi, 1982).

Nehru, J., and M. Khosla (ed.), *Letters for a Nation: From Jawaharlal Nehru to His Chief Ministers 1947–1963* (Gurgaon, 2014).

Nevil-Chambers, H., *Usury, and Its Relations to Anglo-Indian Poverty* (Calcutta, 1913).

Nichols, B., *Verdict on India* (New York, 1944).

'Officers of the Civil Division of the Said Most Excellent Order' of the British Empire, 'India', *Second Supplement to the London Gazette of Tuesday, the 7th of January, 1919* (London, 8 January 1919), p. 461, https://www.thegazette.co.uk/London/issue/31114/supplement/461.

Oman, J. C., *The Education of Eurasians and of Europeans Domiciled in India* (Agra, 1877).

Postans, Mrs., 'Native Indian Society', *The Albion, or, British, Colonial and Foreign Weekly Gazette* (New York, 18 November 1843).

Proceedings of the Sub-committee, Public Service Commission: Salt Department, Northern India, part I (Calcutta, 1887).

Pyke, J., *The Tea Planter's Son: An Anglo-Indian Life* (Gurgaon, 2014).

The Queenslander (Brisbane), 'Surgeon's "Bag" of 53 Tigers: Ambidexterity and Shooting Help Him to Operate' (2 January 1936), p. 4, http://nla.gov.au/nla.news-article23379997.

Report from the Select Committee of the House of Lords Appointed to Inquire into the Present State of the Affairs of the East India Company, and into the Trade between Great Britain, the East Indies and China; with the Minutes of Evidence Taken before the Committee (London, 1830).

Report of the Commissioners Appointed to Inquire into the Sanitary State of the Army in India; with Abstract of Evidence, and of Reports Received from Indian Military Stations (London, 1864).

Report of Proceedings Connected with the East Indians' Petition to Parliament, Read at a Public Meeting Held at the Town Hall, Calcutta, March 28, 1831: with an Appendix (Calcutta, 1831).

Reynolds, H., *The Anglo-Indian Manifesto* (Lahore, 1946).

Richard, C., *My Life, My Way* (London, 2008).

————, *Which One's Cliff* (London, 1977).

Robbie, C., *The Anglo-Indian Force* (Allahabad, 1919).

Roberts, E., *Scenes and Characteristics of Hindostan with Sketches of Anglo-Indian Society*, vol. 2 (London, 1837), vol. 3 (London, 1835).

Rodriguez, H., *Helen of Burma: The Autobiography of a Wartime Nurse* (London, 1983).

Roseboom, H., and C. Dover, 'The Eurasian Community as a Eugenic Problem', in *A Decade of Progress in Eugenics: Scientific Papers of the Third International Congress of Eugenics Held at American Museum of Natural History New York, August 21–23, 1932* (Baltimore, 1934).

Royal Society, 'List of Fellows of the Royal Society 1660–2007: A Complete Listing of All Fellows and Foreign Members since the Foundation of the Society', 2007, Royal Society: Library and Information Services, http://royalsociety.org/uploadedFiles/Royal_Society_Content/about-us/fellowship/Fellows1660–2007.pdfc.

Sadleir, H. W. M., *Inter-provincial Board for Anglo-Indian and European Education Report: Commission Appointed by the Board for the Purpose of Carrying Out a Survey of Anglo-Indian Education in India with a View to Its Post-war Reconstruction* (1946).

Sadullah, M., *The Partition of the Punjab 1947: A Compilation of Official Documents*, vol. II (Lahore, 1983).

Sapru, T., et al., *Constitutional Proposals of the Sapru Committee* (Bombay, 1945).

Scott, P., *The Alien Sky* (St. Albans, 1953).

———, *The Raj Quartet*, vol. 1: *The Jewel in the Crown* (Chicago, 1998).

———, *The Raj Quartet*, vol. 2: *The Day of the Scorpion* (Chicago, 1998).

———, *The Raj Quartet*, vol. 3: *The Towers of Silence* (Chicago, 1998).

———, *The Raj Quartet*, vol. 4: *A Division of the Spoils* (Chicago, 1998).

———, *Staying On* (London, 1977).

Sealy, A., *The Trotter-Nama* (New York, 1988).

Second Report from the Select Committee on the Affairs of the East India Company; together with an Appendix of Documents, and Index (London, 1830).

Sen, I., *Testament of India* (London, 1939).

Shepard, E., *A Marooned People: The Anglo-Indian Community* (Westminster, 1930).

Singapore Free Press and Mercantile Advisor (24 March 1930).

Skipton, H. P. K., *Our Reproach in India* (Oxford, 1912).

Snell, O., *Anglo-Indians and Their Future* (Bombay, 1944).

Staines, J. R., *Country Born: One Man's Life in India* (London, 1986).

Stark, H. A., *The Call of the Blood, or, Anglo-Indians and the Sepoy Mutiny* (Rangoon, 1932).

———, *Hostages to India, or, The Life-Story of the Anglo-Indian Race* (Calcutta, 1926).

————, *John Ricketts and His Times: Being a Narrative Account of Anglo-Indian Affairs during the Eventful Years from 1791 to 1835* (Calcutta, 1934).

Stark, H. A., and E. Madge, *East Indian Worthies, Being Memoirs of Distinguished Indo-Europeans* (Calcutta, 1892).

Stephen, I., *Monsoon Morning* (London, 1966).

Stocqueler, J. H., 'The Crime of Colour', *Patriotic Fund Journal* (1855).

————, *Hand-Book of India, Guide to the Stranger and the Traveller, and a Companion to the Resident* (London, 1884).

Stracey, E., *Odd Man In: My Years in the Indian Police* (New Delhi, 1981).

Sweeney, J., *Elephant Moon* (Worcestershire, 2012).

Sykes, W., 'On the Population and Mortality of Calcutta', *Journal of the Statistical Society of London* 8:1 (March 1845).

Thurston, E., *Castes and Tribes of Southern India*, vol. 2: C to J (Madras, 1909).

————, *Madras Government Museum: Bulletin*, vol. II, no. 2: *Anthropology: Eurasians of Madras and Malabar; Notes on Tattooing; Malagasy-Nias-Dravidians; Toda Petition* (Madras, 1898).

'A Traveller', *The Widow of Calcutta; The Half-Caste Daughter; and Other Sketches*, vols. I–II (London, 1841).

Upjohn, A., 'Art. II: Map of Calcutta, 1792–3', *Calcutta Review* 18 (July–December 1852).

Valentia, G., *Voyages and Travels in India, Ceylon, the Red Sea, Abyssinia and Egypt in the Years 1802, 1803, 1805, and 1806*, vol. 1 (London, 1809).

Wade, John, *The Extraordinary Black Book: An Exposition of the United Church of England and Ireland; Civil List and Crown Revenues; Incomes, Privileges, and Power, of the Aristocracy; Privy Council, Diplomatic, and Consular Establishments; Law and Judicial Administration; Representation and Prospects of Reform under the New Ministry; Profits, Influence, and Monopoly of the Bank of England and East-India Company; Debt and Funding System; Salaries, Fees, and Emoluments in Courts of Justice, Public Offices, and Colonies; Lists of Pluralists, Placemen, Pensioners, and Sinecurists: The Whole Corrected from the Latest Official Returns, and Presenting a Complete View of the Expenditure, Patronage, Influence, and Abuses of the Government, in Church, State, Law and Representation* (London, 1831).

Wallace, K. E., *Brave New Anglo-India, in a Brave New India, in a Brave New World* (Calcutta, 1935).

————, *Life of Sir Henry Gidney* (Calcutta, 1947).

Walsh, C., *The Agra Double Murder: A Crime of Passion from the Raj* (London, 1929; reprint, New Delhi, 2017).

Whitworth, G. C., *An Anglo-Indian Dictionary: A Glossary of Indian Terms Used in English and of Such or Other Non-Indian Terms as Have Certain Special Meanings in India* (London, 1885).

BIBLIOGRAPHY

Wilson, M., *The Domiciled European and Anglo-Indian Race of India* (Bombay and Bangalore, 1928).

Woolley, P. W., *Some Problems of the Domiciled Community* (Calcutta, 1912).

Yule, H., and A. C. Burnell, *Hobson-Jobson: Being a Glossary of Anglo-Indian Colloquial Words and Phrases and of Kindred Terms; Etymological, Historical, Geographical, and Discursive* (London, 1886).

UNPUBLISHED DISSERTATIONS

Hawes, C. J., 'Eurasians in British India, 1773–1833: The Making of a Reluctant Community', PhD thesis, Department of History, School of Oriental and African Studies, University of London (1993).

McCabe, J., 'Kalimpong Kids: The Lives and Labours of Anglo-Indian Adolescents Resettled in New Zealand between 1908 and 1938', PhD thesis, University of Otago, Dunedin (2014).

McMenamin, D., 'Anglo-Indian Lives in Pakistan through the Lens of Oral Histories', PhD thesis, University of Otago, Dunedin (2018).

Mizutani, S., 'The British in India and Their Domiciled Brethren: Race and Class in the Colonial Context, 1858–1930', DPhil thesis, University of Oxford (2004).

Otto, B., 'Anglo-Indians in the Tumultuous Years: Community, Nationality, Identity and Migration, 1939–1955', Master of Arts in International History, London School of Economics, University of London (2010).

Rashiduzzaman, M., 'The Central Legislature in British India: 1921 to 1947', PhD thesis, Durham University (1964), http://etheses.dur.ac.uk/8122/.

SECONDARY SOURCES

Abel, E., *The Anglo-Indian Community: Survival in India* (Delhi, 1988).

Allen, C. (ed.), *Plain Tales from the Raj* (London, 1975).

Almeida, R., *Britain's Anglo-Indians: The Invisibility of Assimilation* (Washington DC, 2017).

Anderson, B., *Imagined Communities: Reflections on the Origin and Spread of Nationalism* (London, 1983).

Anderson, V., *Race and Power in British India: Anglo-Indians, Class and Identity in the Nineteenth Century* (London, 2014).

Andrews, R., *Anglo-Indian Residential Care Homes: Accounts from Kolkata and Melbourne* (Aotearoa, 2011).

———, 'Anglo-Indian Reunions: Secular Pilgrimages?', *South Asian Diaspora* (2012), pp. 1–15.

———, 'Book Review: Lines of the Nation: Indian Railway Workers, Bureaucracy, and the Intimate Historical Self', *International Journal of*

Anglo-Indian Studies 11:1 (2011), http://www.international-journal-of-anglo-indian-studies.org/.

———, 'Christianity as an Indian Religion: The Anglo-Indian Experience', *Journal of Contemporary Religion* 25:2 (2010), pp. 173–88.

———, *Christmas in Calcutta: Anglo-Indian Stories and Essays* (New Delhi, 2014).

———, 'Quitting India: The Anglo-Indian Culture of Migration', *Sites*, NS, 4:2 (2007), pp. 32–56.

Arditti, R., 'Skills Project: Oral History', *International Journal of Anglo-Indian Studies* 6:1 (2001), http://www.international-journal-of-anglo-indian-studies.org/.

Arnold, D., 'European Orphans and Vagrants in India in the Nineteenth Century', *Journal of Imperial and Commonwealth History* 7 (1978), pp. 104–27.

The Australian Anglo Indian Association, *A West Australian Tapestry of Anglo-Indian Memories: From Both Sides Now* (Greenwood WA, 2004).

Azam, M., 'Presenting "Neglected Christian Children of Indus" to a Hero' (22 August 2018), https://michelleazam.wordpress.com/2018/08/22/presenting-neglected-christian-children-of-indus-to-a-hero/.

Bagley, C., *The Dutch Plural Society: A Comparative Study in Race Relations* (Oxford, 1973).

Bajpai, R., *Debating Difference: Group Rights and Liberal Democracy in India* (Oxford, 2011).

Ballhatchet, K., *Race, Sex and Class under the Raj: Imperial Attitudes and Policies and Their Critics, 1793–1905* (London, 1980).

Banerjee, M., 'The Trial of Derozio, or the Scandal of Reason', *Social Scientist* 37:7–8 (July–August 2009), pp. 60–88.

Barr, P., *The Dust in the Balance: British Women in India, 1905–1945* (London, 1989).

Bayer, J. M., *A Sociolinguistic Investigation of the English Spoken by the Anglo-Indians in Mysore City* (Mysore, 1986).

Bear, L. G., 'Miscegenations of Modernity: Constructing European Respectability and Race in the Indian Railway Colony', *Women's History Review* 3:4 (1994), pp. 531–48.

Bew, J., *Clement Attlee: The Man Who Made Modern Britain* (New York, 2017).

Bey, A., *That Eurasian* (London 1895; reprint, 2011).

Bhabha, H. K., *The Location of Culture* (London, 2004).

Bhattacharya, D. K., 'The Anglo-Indians in Bombay: An Introduction to Their Socio-economic and Cultural Life', *Race and Class* 10 (1968), pp. 163–72.

Bidwell, S., *Swords for Hire: European Mercenaries in Eighteenth-Century India* (London, 1971).

BIBLIOGRAPHY

Blackford, S., 'I Call Australia Home', *International Journal of Anglo-Indian Studies* 6:1 (2001), http://www.international-journal-of-anglo-indian-studies.org/.

Blunt, A., *Domicile and Diaspora: Anglo-Indian Women and the Spatial Politics of Home* (Malden MA, 2005).

————, 'Geographies of Diaspora and Mixed Descent: Anglo-Indians in India and Britain', *International Journal of Population Geography* 9 (2003), pp. 281–94.

————, 'Imperial Geographies of Home: British Domesticity in India, 1886–1925', *Transactions of the Institute of British Geographers*, NS, 24:4 (1999), pp. 421–40.

————, '"Land of Our Mothers": Home, Identity, and Nationality for Anglo-Indians in British India, 1919–1947', *History Workshop Journal* 54 (2002), pp. 49–72.

————, 'Postcolonial Migrations: Anglo-Indians in "White Australia"', *International Journal of Anglo-Indian Studies* 5:2 (2000), http://www.international-journal-of-anglo-indian-studies.org/.

Blunt, A., and R. Dowling, *Home* (New York, 2006).

Bose, M., *The Magic of Indian Cricket: Cricket and Society in India* (rev. edn, Abingdon, 2006).

————, *Raj, Secrets, Revolutions: A Life of Subhas Chandra Bose* (London, 2004).

Bose, S., *His Majesty's Opponent: Subhas Chandra Bose and India's Struggle against Empire* (Cambridge MA, 2011).

Boucher, E., *Empire's Children: Child Emigration, Welfare, and the Decline of the British World, 1869–1967* (Cambridge, 2014).

Brendish, S., 'George (William) Brendish and the Indian Mutiny of 1857', *International Journal of Anglo-Indian Studies* 7:1 (2003), http://www.international-journal-of-anglo-indian-studies.org/.

Broughton, S., *Brando's Bride* (Cardigan, 2019).

Brown, J. M., *Gandhi: Prisoner of Hope* (New Haven, 1989).

————, *Global South Asians: Introducing the Modern Diaspora* (Cambridge, 2006).

————, 'Imperial Facade: Some Constraints upon and Contradictions in the British Position in India, 1919–35', *Transactions of the Royal Historical Society*, 5th series, 26 (1976), pp. 35–52.

————(ed.), *Mahatma Gandhi: The Essential Writings* (Oxford, 2008).

————, *Nehru: A Political Life* (New Haven, 2003).

Brown, P., *Anglo-Indian Food and Customs* (New Delhi, 1998).

Brown, W., *Anglo-Indian Race Preservation Course* (Raleigh NC, 2010).

————, *Neighbourhood: A Collection of Three Anglo-Indian Short Stories* (London, 2016).

————, *The Secret Race: Anglo-Indians* (Raleigh NC, 2010).

Buckland, Charles Edward, *Dictionary of Indian Biography* (New York, 1906).

Buettner, E., *Empire Families: Britons and Late Imperial India* (Oxford, 2004).

————, 'Problematic Spaces, Problematic Races: Defining "Europeans" in Late Colonial India', *Women's History Review* 9:2 (2000), pp. 277–98.

Burnett, D., 'A History of the Anglo-Burmese Community', *International Journal of Anglo-Indian Studies* 7:1 (2003), http://www.international-journal-of-anglo-indian-studies.org/.

Caplan, L., *Children of Colonialism: Anglo-Indians in a Postcolonial World* (New York, 2001).

————, 'Colonial and Contemporary Transnationalisms: Traversing Anglo-Indian Boundaries of the Mind', *International Journal of Anglo-Indian Studies* 3 (1998), http://www.international-journal-of-anglo-indian-studies.org/.

————, 'Creole World, Purist Rhetoric: Anglo-Indian Cultural Debates in Colonial and Contemporary Madras', *Journal of the Royal Anthropological Institute* 1:4 (December 1995), pp. 743–62.

————, 'Iconographies of Anglo-Indian Women: Gender Constructs and Contrasts in a Changing Society', *Modern Asian Studies* 34:4 (2000), pp. 863–92.

————, '"Life Is Only Abroad, Not Here": The Culture of Emigration among Anglo–Indians in Madras', *Immigrants and Minorities* 14:1 (1995), pp. 26–46.

Capua, M., *Vivien Leigh: A Biography* (Jefferson, 2003).

Carton, A., 'Beyond "Cotton Mary": Anglo-Indian Categories and Reclaiming the Diverse Past', *International Journal of Anglo-Indian Studies* 5:1 (2000), http://www.international-journal-of-anglo-indian-studies.org/.

————, *Mixed-Race and Modernity in Colonial India: Changing Concepts of Hybridity across Empires* (New York, 2012).

Cassity, K., 'Emerging from Shadows: The "Unhomed" Anglo-Indian of 36 Chowringhee Lane', *International Journal of Anglo-Indian Studies* 6:2 (2001), http://www.international-journal-of-anglo-indian-studies.org/.

————, 'Home Is Where the Food Is: Recurrent Motifs in Anglo-Indian Self-representation', *International Journal of Anglo-Indian Studies* 11:1 (2011), http://www.international-journal-of-anglo-indian-studies.org/.

————, 'Identity in Motion: Bhowani Junction Reconsidered', *International Journal of Anglo-Indian Studies* 4:1 (1999), http://www.international-journal-of-anglo-indian-studies.org/.

————, '"There Are No Soldiers Anymore": The Persistence of Anglo-Indian Stereotypes in Bow Barracks Forever', *International Journal of*

Anglo-Indian Studies 10:1 (2010), http://www.international-journal-of-anglo-indian-studies.org/.

Cell, J., *Hailey: A Study in British Imperialism* (New York, 1992).

Charlton-Stevens, U., *Anglo-Indians and Minority Politics in South Asia: Race, Boundary Making and Communal Nationalism* (London, 2017).

———, 'Anglo-Indians in Colonial India: Historical Demography, Categorization, and Identity', in P. J. Aspinall and Z. L. Rocha (eds.), *The Palgrave International Handbook of Mixed Racial and Ethnic Classification* (Cham, 2020).

———, 'The End of Greater Anglo-India: Partitioned Anglo Identities in Burma and Pakistan', in R. Andrews and M. Simi Raj (eds.), *Anglo-Indian Identity in India and the Diaspora* (Cham, 2021).

———, 'The Professional Lives of Anglo-Indian Working Women in the Twilight of Empire', *International Journal of Anglo-Indian Studies* 16:2 (2016), http://international-journal-of-anglo-indian-studies.org/index.php/IJAIS.

Chater, L., 'Armenian: Something Vivien Leigh and Her Cousin Xan Fielding a British Spy Had in Common', *Chater Genealogy* blog (Wednesday, 12 August 2015), http://chater-genealogy.blogspot.com/2015/08/armenian-something-vivien-leigh-and-her_12.html.

Chatterji, J., *The Spoils of Partition: Bengal and India, 1947–1967* (Cambridge, 2007).

Chaudhuri, R., 'The Politics of Naming: Derozio in Two Formative Moments of Literary and Political Discourse, Calcutta, 1825–31', *Modern Asian Studies* 44:4 (2010), pp. 857–85.

Chew, D., 'Book Review: Anglo-Indians and Minority Politics in South Asia: Race, Boundary Making and Communal Nationalism', *International Journal of Anglo-Indian Studies* 18:1 (2018), http://www.international-journal-of-anglo-indian-studies.org/.

Chhina, M. A. S., 'A 1965 Vir Chakra fighter pilot returns home from Australia: My Vir Chakra belongs to my squadron, I was only doing my job, says Flt Lt Alfred Tyrone Cooke who took on three Pak Sabres over Kalaikunda', *Indian Express* (Ambala, updated 8 September 2015), https://indianexpress.com/article/india/india-others/a-1965-vir-chakra-fighter-pilot-returns-home-from-australia/.

Coates, P. D., *The China Consuls: British Consular Officers, 1843-1943* (Oxford, 1988).

Coelho, G. M., 'Anglo-Indian: A Nativized Variety of Indian English', *Language in Society* 26:4 (December 1997), pp. 561–89.

Cohn, B., *Colonialism and Its Forms of Knowledge: The British in India* (Princeton, 1996).

BIBLIOGRAPHY

Colquhoun, S., 'A Research Note: Adaptation and General Well-Being of Anglo-Indian Immigrants in Australia', *International Journal of Anglo-Indian Studies* 2:1 (1997), http://www.international-journal-of-anglo-indian-studies.org/.

Cressey, P. F., 'The Anglo-Indians: A Disorganized Marginal Group', *Social Forces* 14:2 (December 1935), pp. 263–8.

Dalrymple, W., *White Mughals: Love and Betrayal in Eighteenth-Century India* (London, 2002).

Darwin, J., *Britain and Decolonisation* (Hampshire, 1988).

———, *Unfinished Empire: The Global Expansion of Britain* (London, 2012).

D'Costa, A., 'Anglo-Indian Nostalgia: Longing for India as Homeland', presented to the Second Annual Rhizomes: Re-visioning Boundaries Conference of the School of Languages and Comparative Cultural Studies, University of Queensland, Brisbane, February 2006.

D'Cruz, G., 'Christopher Hawes in Conversation with Glenn D'Cruz', *International Journal of Anglo-Indian Studies* 3:1 (1998), http://www.international-journal-of-anglo-indian-studies.org/.

———, *Midnight's Orphans: Anglo-Indians in Post/colonial Literature* (Bern, 2006).

———, '"Mixed Feelings": A Review of The Jadu House: Intimate Histories of Anglo-India', *International Journal of Anglo-Indian Studies* 5:1 (2000), http://www.international-journal-of-anglo-indian-studies.org/.

———, 'My Two Left Feet: The Problem of Anglo-Indian Stereotypes in Post-independence Indo-English Fiction', *Journal of Commonwealth Literature* 38:2 (2003), pp. 105–23.

———, 'Racial Science, Social Science and the Anglo-Indian', *International Journal of Anglo-Indian Studies* 2:1 (1997), http://www.international-journal-of-anglo-indian-studies.org/.

———, 'Review: Last Dance at Dum Dum', *International Journal of Anglo-Indian Studies* 4:1 (1999), http://www.international-journal-of-anglo-indian-studies.org/.

De Courcy, A., *The Fishing Fleet: Husband-Hunting in the Raj* (London, 2012).

Deefholts, M., 'Book Review: Anglo-Indians: Vanishing Remnants of a Bygone Era', *International Journal of Anglo-Indian Studies* 7:1 (2003), http://www.international-journal-of-anglo-indian-studies.org/.

———, 'Who Are the Anglo-Indians?', *International Journal of Anglo-Indian Studies* 8:1 (2005), http://www.international-journal-of-anglo-indian-studies.org/.

Devji, F., *The Impossible Indian: Gandhi and the Temptation of Violence* (Cambridge MA, 2012).

———, *Muslim Zion: Pakistan as a Political Idea* (Cambridge MA, 2013).

———, 'ThinkFest Conversations 12: Are Gandhi and Jinnah Still

Relevant?', *ThinkFest Pakistan* livestream (30 July 2020), https://www.youtube.com/watch?v=KtA4ZByiW5A&t.

Dhavle, S., 'Anglo Indians and Economic Activity', *International Journal of Anglo-Indian Studies* 10:2 (2010), http://www.international-journal-of-anglo-indian-studies.org/.

Dixona, 'The Top Classic Horror Actors' (8 April 2011), https://www.imdb.com/list/ls000791185/.

Doctor, V., 2007, 'How Amul Became Utterly Butterly Delicious and Salty', *Economic Times*, http://articles.economictimes.indiatimes.com/2007–07–21/news/27671277_1_butter-milk-dairy-operations.

Doshi, I., 'Food and Language as Markers of Identity: The Anglo Indian Community's Survival since Partition (Part I)', *International Journal of Anglo-Indian Studies* 11:1 (2011), http://www.international-journal-of-anglo-indian-studies.org/.

———, 'Food and Language as Markers of Identity: The Anglo Indian Community's Survival since Partition (Part II)', *International Journal of Anglo-Indian Studies* 11:2 (2011), http://www.international-journal-of-anglo-indian-studies.org/.

D'Souza, A. A., *Anglo-Indian Education: A Study of Its Origins and Growth in Bengal up to 1960* (New Delhi, 1976).

D'Souza, B. (ed.), *150 Years of Indian Railways: The National Anglo-Indian Railway Convention, 18th to 19th January 2003, Chennai, India* (National Forum of Anglo-Indian Associations, Chennai).

Edwards, A., *Vivien Leigh: A Biography* (London, 1977).

Faassen, M., 'Imposed Identities: A Comparative Analysis of the Formation of the Anglo-Indian and Coloured Identities', *International Journal of Anglo-Indian Studies* 8:1 (2005), http://www.international-journal-of-anglo-indian-studies.org/.

Farmer, B. H., *Agricultural Colonization in India since Independence* (London, 1974).

Fay, P. W., *The Forgotten Army: India's Armed Struggle for Independence 1942–1945* (Ann Arbor, 1993).

Fernandez, S., 'How Can Contextual Theologies Assist Anglo-Indian Women in Understanding and Articulating Their Religious Experiences?', *International Journal of Anglo-Indian Studies* 10:1 (2010), http://www.international-journal-of-anglo-indian-studies.org/.

Fischer-Tiné, H., '"White Women Degrading Themselves to the Lowest Depths": European Networks of Prostitution and Colonial Anxieties in British India and Ceylon ca. 1880–1914', *Indian Economic and Social History Review* 40 (2003), pp. 163–90.

Fisher, M., *The Inordinately Strange Life of Dyce Sombre: Victorian Anglo-Indian MP and Chancery 'Lunatic'* (London, 2010).

Fleming, L., (ed.), *Last Children of the Raj: British Childhoods in India*, vol. I: *1919–1939* (London, 2004).

——, *Last Children of the Raj: British Childhoods in India*, vol. II: *1939–1950* (London, 2004).

Fontaine, D. L., 'Personal Reflections: A Statement by an Indian Anglo-Indian', *International Journal of Anglo-Indian Studies* 12:1 (2012), http://www.international-journal-of-anglo-indian-studies.org/.

Foster, A., 'George Thomas: The Rajah from Tipperary', *International Journal of Anglo-Indian Studies* 7:1 (2003), http://www.international-journal-of-anglo-indian-studies.org/.

——, 'Thomas Legge, Irish Adventurer Turned Fakir', *International Journal of Anglo-Indian Studies* 7:2 (2004), http://www.international-journal-of-anglo-indian-studies.org/.

Frick, G. D., M. K. Steinbach, R. Dwyer, and J. Phalkey (eds.), *Key Concepts in Modern Indian Studies* (New York, 2015).

Furness, J., 'The Forms and Functions of Hybridity in Allan Sealy's The Trotter-Nama', *International Journal of Anglo-Indian Studies* 12:1 (2012), http://www.international-journal-of-anglo-indian-studies.org/.

Gaikwad, V. R., *The Anglo-Indians: A Study in the Problems and Processes Involved in Emotional and Cultural Integration* (London, 1967).

Ganachari, A., '"White Man's Embarrassment": European Vagrancy in 19th Century Bombay', *Economic and Political Weekly* 37:25 (22–28 June 2002), pp. 2477–86.

Gardner, F., *Life and Legacy of Col. William Linnaeus Gardner* (Mumbai, 2009).

Gater, D., *A Season with Vivien Leigh: The Life and Art of an Actress* (Delhi, 2007).

Ghosh, D., *Sex and the Family in Colonial India: The Making of Empire* (Cambridge, 2006).

Gifford-Pritchard, S., *An Anglo-Indian Childhood* (Bloomington IN, 2005).

Gilbert, A., 'Book Review: One Hell of a Life', *International Journal of Anglo-Indian Studies* 6:2 (2001), http://www.international-journal-of-anglo-indian-studies.org/.

——, 'A Comparison of Anglo-Indian and Australian Earnings by Qualifications, Industry and Occupation', *International Journal of Anglo-Indian Studies* 1:1 (1996), http://www.international-journal-of-anglo-indian-studies.org/.

Gilmour, D., *The British in India: Three Centuries of Ambition and Experience* (London, 2018).

Gist, N., and R. Wright, *Marginality and Identity: Anglo-Indians as a Racially-Mixed Minority in India* (Leiden, 1973).

Griffith, G., *Socialism and Superior Brains: The Political Thought of George Bernard Shaw* (London, 1993).

Grimshaw, A. D., 'The Anglo-Indian Community: The Integration of a Marginal Group', *Journal of Asian Studies* 18:2 (February 1959), pp. 227–40.

Groves, D., *Anna May Wong's Lucky Shoes: 1939 Australia through the Eyes of an Art Deco Diva* (Ames IA, 2011).

The Guardian, 'Anglo-Indians wounded by Cotton Mary portrayal' (10 March 2000), http://www.theguardian.com/world/2000/mar/10/lukeharding.

Gupta, S. K., *Marriage among the Anglo-Indians* (Lucknow, 1968).

Hanif, K., and M. Chawla, 'State, Religion and Religious Minorities in Pakistan: Remembering the Participation of Christians in Punjab Legislative Assembly 1947–55', *Pakistan Social Sciences Review* 4:2 (June 2020).

Haslam, M., 'Queenie: Smudging the Distinctions between Black and White', *International Journal of Anglo-Indian Studies* 4:1 (1999), http://www.international-journal-of-anglo-indian-studies.org/.

Hawes, C., *Poor Relations: The Making of a Eurasian Community in British India, 1773–1833* (Richmond, 1996).

Hedin, E. L., 'The Anglo-Indian Community', *American Journal of Sociology* 40:2 (September 1934), pp. 165–79.

Henriques, F., *Children of Caliban: Miscegenation* (London, 1974).

Higham, C., and R. Moseley, *Princess Merle: The Romantic Life of Merle Oberon* (New York, 1983).

Hutchins, F. G., *Spontaneous Revolution: The Quit India Movement* (Delhi, 1971).

Hutchinson, M., *Great Conservatives* (Ghent, 2004).

Ifekwunigwe, J. O., *Mixed Race Studies: A Reader* (London, 2004).

The Information Office of the University of Sussex, [obituary:] 'Professor Fernando Henriques', *The Bulletin* (15 June 1976).

Jalal, A., *The Pity of Partition: Manto's Life, Times, and Work across the India–Pakistan Divide* (Princeton, 2013).

———, *The Sole Spokesman* (Cambridge, 1994).

James, S. P., 'The Anglo-Indians: "Home in Australia and the Dilemma of Identity"', *International Journal of Anglo-Indian Studies* 8:1 (2005), http://www.international-journal-of-anglo-indian-studies.org/.

———, 'Anglo-Indians: The Dilemma of Identity', *International Journal of Anglo-Indian Studies* 7:1 (2003), http://www.international-journal-of-anglo-indian-studies.org/.

———, 'The Anglo-Indians: Transcolonial Migrants and the Dilemma of Identity', *International Journal of Anglo-Indian Studies* 7:2 (2004), http://www.international-journal-of-anglo-indian-studies.org/.

————, 'The Origins of the Anglo-Indians', *International Journal of Anglo-Indian Studies* 10:2 (2010), http://www.international-journal-of-anglo-indian-studies.org/.

Jarnagin, L., *Portuguese and Luso-Asian Legacies in Southeast Asia, 1511–2011*, vol. 2: *Culture and Identity in the Luso-Asian World: Tenacities and Plasticities* (Singapore, 2012).

Jeffreys, M., 'Where Do Coloureds Come From?', *Drum*, nos. 102–6 and 108 (1959).

Jha, V. K., *McCluskieganj* (New York, 2015).

Kennedy, R., 'Racial Passing', *Ohio State Law Journal* 6:1145 (2001), pp. 1–28.

Kerr, I. J., *Engines of Change: The Railroads That Made India* (Westport CT, 2007).

Khan, Y., *The Raj at War: A People's History of India's Second World War* (London, 2015).

Lahiri-Dutt, K., *In Search of a Homeland: Anglo-Indians and McCluskiegunge* (Calcutta, 1990).

Lambton, A. K. S., 'Major-General Sir John Malcolm (1769–1833) and "The History of Persia"', *Iran* 33 (British Institute of Persian Studies, 1995), pp. 97–109.

Lasky, J, Jr., and P. Silver, *Love Scene: The Story of Laurence Olivier and Vivien Leigh* (London, 1978).

Lee, C., *Viceroys: The Creation of the British* (London, 2018).

Lewin, E., 'Anglo-Indian Women: Identity Issues', *International Journal of Anglo-Indian Studies* 1:2 (1996), http://www.international-journal-of-anglo-indian-studies.org/.

Lobo, A., 'Anglo-Indian Schools and Anglo-Indian Educational Disadvantage (Part I)', *International Journal of Anglo-Indian Studies* 1:1 (1996), http://www.international-journal-of-anglo-indian-studies.org/.

————, 'Anglo-Indian Schools and Anglo-Indian Educational Disadvantage (Part II)', *International Journal of Anglo-Indian Studies* 1:2 (1996), http://www.international-journal-of-anglo-indian-studies.org/.

————, 'The Feel Good Factor of the New Ethnicity Anglo-Indians of Kerala and Meghalaya', *International Journal of Anglo-Indian Studies* 2:1 (1997), http://www.international-journal-of-anglo-indian-studies.org/.

Lump, L., 'Book Notes', *International Journal of Anglo-Indian Studies* 8:1 (2005), http://www.international-journal-of-anglo-indian-studies.org/.

————, 'Cyber Links Help Anglo-Indians to Preserve Culture', *International Journal of Anglo-Indian Studies* 4:2 (1999), http://www.international-journal-of-anglo-indian-studies.org/.

————, 'Virtual Verandah: How the Internet Has Brought Anglo-Indians

Together', *International Journal of Anglo-Indian Studies* 7:2 (2004), http://www.international-journal-of-anglo-indian-studies.org/.

Lyons, E. M., 'Anglo-Indians at the End of the 20th Century', *International Journal of Anglo-Indian Studies* 3:2 (1998), http://www.international-journal-of-anglo-indian-studies.org/.

———, 'Book Review: Unwanted! Memories of a Priest's Daughter', *International Journal of Anglo-Indian Studies* 2:2 (1997), http://www.international-journal-of-anglo-indian-studies.org/.

———, 'A Note on Some Famous Anglo-Indian Families', *International Journal of Anglo-Indian Studies* 4:2 (1999), http://www.international-journal-of-anglo-indian-studies.org/.

———, 'The Place of Fiction in Anglo-Indian Writings', *International Journal of Anglo-Indian Studies* 5:2 (2000), http://www.international-journal-of-anglo-indian-studies.org/.

———, 'The Two Great Anglo-Indians', *International Journal of Anglo-Indian Studies* 5:2 (2000), http://www.international-journal-of-anglo-indian-studies.org/.

Madge, E. W., *Henry Derozio: The Eurasian Poet and Reformer* (3rd edn, Calcutta, 1982).

Mairaj, A., *Neglected Christian Children of Indus: True Bitter Stories Narrating How the Christian Children of Indus Are Alienated from Their Ancestors' Land and Society* (Karachi, 2018).

Makepeace, M., 'The Turings of India' (4 May 2017), British Library *Untold Lives* blog, https://blogs.bl.uk/untoldlives/2017/05/the-turings-of-india.html.

Malcolm, J., *Malcolm: Soldier, Diplomat, Ideologue of British India; The Life of Sir John Malcolm (1769–1833)* (Edinburgh, 2014).

Mallampalli, C., *Race, Religion and Law in Colonial India: Trials of an Interracial Family* (Cambridge, 2011).

Marshall, P. J., 'The Whites of British India, 1780–1830: A Failed Colonial Society?', *International History Review* 12:1 (February 1990), pp. 26–44.

Marshall, T., *A Flag Worth Dying For: The Power and Politics of National Symbols* (New York, 2016).

Matteo, S. K., *The Last Anglo-Indians: The Story of a Middle-Class Anglo-Indian Family in India; A Biographical Account of Events from the 1880s to 1950s* (ebook, 2015).

McMenamin, D., 'The Curious Exclusion of Anglo-Indians from Mass Slaughter during the Partition of India', *International Journal of Anglo-Indian Studies* 9:1 (2006), http://www.international-journal-of-anglo-indian-studies.org/.

———, 'Fallacies and Realities of the Anglo-Indian Stereotype: Verification through "Our" Primary Source, Namely Raj Days to Downunder; Voices from Anglo India to New Zealand, and to Some Extent CTR Chronicles', *International Journal of Anglo-Indian Studies* 11:2 (2011), http://www.international-journal-of-anglo-indian-studies.org/.

————, 'Identifying Domiciled Europeans in Colonial India: Poor Whites or Privileged Community?', *New Zealand Journal of Asian Studies* 3:1 (June 2001), pp. 106–27.

————, *Raj Days to Downunder: Voices from Anglo-India to New Zealand* (Chennai, 2012).

————, 'The Roots of Anglo-Indian Cultural Practices and Attitudes', *International Journal of Anglo-Indian Studies* 11:2 (2011), http://www.international-journal-of-anglo-indian-studies.org/.

Mijares, L., 'The Fetishism of the Original: Anglo-Indian History and Literature in I. Allan Sealy's The Trotter-Nama', *International Journal of Anglo-Indian Studies* 12:1 (2012), http://www.international-journal-of-anglo-indian-studies.org/.

————, '"You Are an Anglo-Indian?" Eurasians and Hybridity and Cosmopolitanism in Salman Rushdie's Midnight's Children', *Journal of Commonwealth Literature* 38 (2003), pp. 125–45.

Miller, G., 'Reviews of Tiger Dreams', *International Journal of Anglo-Indian Studies* 7:1 (2003), http://www.international-journal-of-anglo-indian-studies.org/.

Millet, A., 'They Stayed Back (Part I)', *International Journal of Anglo-Indian Studies* 10:2 (2010), http://www.international-journal-of-anglo-indian-studies.org/.

————, 'They Stayed Back (Part II)', *International Journal of Anglo-Indian Studies* 11:1 (2011), http://www.international-journal-of-anglo-indian-studies.org/.

Mills, M. M., 'Poor Relations: A Critical Note', *International Journal of Anglo-Indian Studies* 3:1 (1998), http://www.international-journal-of-anglo-indian-studies.org/.

Mills, M. S., 'The Anglo-Indians: A Christian Community of India', *International Journal of Anglo-Indian Studies* 3:2 (1998), http://www.international-journal-of-anglo-indian-studies.org/.

————, 'Burma, 1942 and the Anglo-Indian and Anglo-Burmese Community', *International Journal of Anglo-Indian Studies* 4:2 (1999), http://www.international-journal-of-anglo-indian-studies.org/.

————, 'Some Comments on Stereotypes of the Anglo-Indians (Part I)', *International Journal of Anglo-Indian Studies* 1:1 (1996), http://www.international journal-of-anglo-indian-studies.org/.

————, 'Some Comments on Stereotypes of the Anglo-Indians (Part II)', *International Journal of Anglo-Indian Studies* 1:2 (1996).

BIBLIOGRAPHY

Mizutani, S., 'Historicising Whiteness: From the Case of Late Colonial India', *ACRAWSA e-journal* 2:1 (2006), http://www.acrawsa.org.au/files/ejournalfiles/85SatoshiMizutani.pdf.

———, 'Hybridity and History: A Critical Reflection on Homi K. Bhabha's Post-historical Thoughts', *Ab Imperio: Studies of New Imperial History and Nationalism in the Post-Soviet Space* 4 (2013), pp. 27–48.

———, 'Loyalty, Parity, and Social Control: The Competing Visions on the Creation of a "Eurasian" Military Regiment in Late British India', *International Journal of Anglo-Indian Studies* 10:1 (2010), http://www.international-journal-of-anglo-indian-studies.org/.

———, *The Meaning of White: Race, Class, and the 'Domiciled Community' in British India 1858–1930* (Oxford, 2011).

———, 'Rethinking Inclusion and Exclusion: The Question of Mixed-Race Presence in Late Colonial India', *University of Sussex Journal of Contemporary History*, no. 5 (December 2002).

Moore, G. J., *Anglo-Indians: The Best of Both Worlds* (2nd edn, Melbourne, 2009).

———, *The Anglo-Indian Vision* (Melbourne, 1986).

———, 'A Brief History of the Anglo-Indians', *International Journal of Anglo-Indian Studies* 1:1 (1996), http://www.international-journal-of-anglo-indian-studies.org/.

———, *From India with Love: The Story of the Sellers Family* (Melbourne, 2006).

———, *The Lotus and the Rose: An Anglo-Indian Story* (Melbourne, 1986).

Moore, G., and P. McGready, 'The 6th International Anglo-Indian Reunion 2004: A Blast from the Past?', *International Journal of Anglo-Indian Studies* 7:2 (2004), http://www.international-journal-of-anglo-indian-studies.org/.

Moore, P., 'An Ordinary Bloke', *International Journal of Anglo-Indian Studies* 11:1 (2011), http://www.international-journal-of-anglo-indian-studies.org/.

Moore, R. J., *Churchill, Cripps and India, 1939–45* (Oxford, 1979).

Morgan, S., *Bombay Anna: The Real Story and Remarkable Adventures of the King and I Governess* (Berkeley, 2008).

Morley, S., *The Other Side of the Moon: The Life of David Niven* (New York, 1985).

Morton-Jack, G., *Army of Empire: The Untold Story of the Indian Army in World War I* (ebook, 2018).

Must See India, 'Abbott Mount, Uttaranchal', Roam Space Travel Solutions, 2011, http://www.mustseeindia.com/Abbott-Mount.

Muthiah, S., and H. MacLure, *The Anglo-Indians: A 500 Year History* (New Delhi, 2013).

BIBLIOGRAPHY

Naidis, M., 'British Attitudes toward the Anglo-Indians', *South Atlantic Quarterly* 62:3 (Summer 1963), pp. 407–22.

Nanda, B., *Gandhi: Pan-Islamism, Imperialism, and Nationalism in India* (New York, 1989).

Neill, S., *A History of Christianity in India: The Beginnings to AD 1707* (Cambridge, 1984).

Noles, K., '"Waging War against the King": Recruitment and Motivation of the Indian National Army, 1942–1945', The British Empire at War Research Group, *Research Papers*, no. 6 (2014).

Nollen, S. A., *Boris Karloff: A Gentleman's Life* (Baltimore, 1999).

O'Brien, B., chief guest at book launch of M. Simi Raj and R. Andrews (eds.), *Anglo-Indian Identity: Past and Present in India and the Diaspora*, Centre for Memory Studies, Indian Institute of Technology, Madras, livestreamed on 25 August 2021, 9:30 a.m. IST.

O'Brien, E., *The Anglo-Indian Way: Celebrating the Lives of the Anglo-Indians of India* (New Delhi, 2013).

O'Connor, G., *Darlings of the Gods: One Year in the Lives of Laurence Olivier and Vivien Leigh* (London, 1984).

O'Flaherty, D., 'The Trouble with Merle: A Study Guide', A Film Australia National Interest Program, https://www.nfsa.gov.au/collection/curated/trouble-merle.

Olumide, J., *Raiding the Gene Pool: The Social Construction of Mixed Race* (London, 2002).

Otter, R., 'Colourful Thoughts', *International Journal of Anglo-Indian Studies* 10:2 (2010), http://www.international-journal-of-anglo-indian-studies.org/.

———, 'The Future of Anglo-Indians', *International Journal of Anglo-Indian Studies* 9:1 (2006), http://www.international-journal-of-anglo-indian-studies.org/.

———, 'Unfair Attitudes', *International Journal of Anglo-Indian Studies* 8:1 (2005), http://www.international-journal-of-anglo-indian-studies.org/.

Otto, B., 'Book Review: Blunt, Alison. Domicile and Diaspora: Anglo-Indian Women and the Spatial Politics of Home', *International Journal of Anglo-Indian Studies* 11:2 (2011), http://www.international-journal-of-anglo-indian-studies.org/.

Paranjape, M., '"East Indian" Cosmopolitanism: The Fakeer of Jungheera and the Birth of Indian Modernity', Interventions, *International Journal of Postcolonial Studies* 13:4 (2011), https://doi.org/10.1080/13698 01X.2011.628119.

Park, Y., and R. S. Rajan (eds.), *The Postcolonial Jane Austen* (London, 2000).

Pearse, H. W., *The Hearseys: Five Generations of an Anglo-Indian Family* (Edinburgh, 1905).

Peppin, B., *Black and White: The 'Anglo-Indian' Identity in Recent English Fiction* (Milton Keynes, 2012).

————, 'A Critique of Allan Sealy's "The Trotternama"', *International Journal of Anglo-Indian Studies* 12:1 (2012), http://www.international-journal-of-anglo-indian-studies.org/.

Philip, S. A., 'History lesson for Pakistan's military: IAF's Keelor brothers shot down PAF jets in 1965: Denzil, Trevor Keelor shot down Pakistan's Sabre jets in 1965. They were honoured with Vir Chakra, first time two brothers received the award for the same reason', *The Print* (29 July 2019, 5:49 p.m. IST), https://theprint.in/defence/history-lesson-for-pakistans-military-iafs-keelor-brothers-shot-down-paf-jets-in-1965/269463/.

Pieterse, N. J., *Globalization and Culture: Global Mélange* (2nd edn, New York, 2009).

Rao, N., 'Goans and Anglo Indians: An Essay', *International Journal of Anglo-Indian Studies* 7:2 (2004), http://www.international-journal-of-anglo-indian-studies.org/.

Reddy, K. V., *Class, Colonialism and Nationalism: Madras Presidency, 1928–1939* (New Delhi, 2002).

Roychowdhury, L., *The Jadu House: Intimate Histories of Anglo-India* (New York, 2000).

Royle, T., *The Last Days of the Raj* (London, 1989).

Rush, A., *Bonds of Empire: West Indians and Britishness from Victoria to Decolonization* (Oxford, 2011).

Sanyal, T. K., *Anglo-Indians of Kolkata: A Study of Their Social Alienation* (Kolkata, 2007).

Schneer, J., *Ministers at War: Winston Churchill and His War Cabinet* (New York, 2015).

Sen, I., 'Devoted Wife–Sensuous Bibi: Colonial Constructions of the Indian Woman, 1860–1900', *Indian Journal of Gender Studies* 8 (2001), pp. 1–22.

————, *Woman and Empire: Representations in the Writings of British India, 1858–1900* (New Delhi, 2002).

Sen, S., *Anglo-Indian Woman in Transition: Pride, Prejudice and Predicament* (Singapore, 2017).

Shivan, C., 'Anglo-Indian Women: Yesterday, Today, Tomorrow', *International Journal of Anglo-Indian Studies* 10:1 (2010), http://www.international-journal-of-anglo-indian-studies.org/.

————, 'Dislocating the Dislocated: Imperial Constructs in Maud Diver's "Candles in the Wind"', *International Journal of Anglo-Indian Studies* 9:1 (2006), http://www.international-journal-of-anglo-indian-studies.org/.

Silvestri, M., *Policing 'Bengali Terrorism' in India and the World: Imperial Intelligence and Revolutionary Nationalism, 1905–1939* (ebook, 2019).

Slate, N., *Colored Cosmopolitanism: The Shared Struggle for Freedom in the United States and India* (Cambridge MA, 2012).

——, *The Prism of Race: W. E. B. Du Bois, Langston Hughes, Paul Robeson, and the Colored World of Cedric Dover* (New York, 2014).

Solly, M., 'Why the controversy over a black actress playing Anne Boleyn is unnecessary and harmful: Long before Jodie Turner-Smith's miniseries came under criticism, British Indian actress Merle Oberon portrayed the Tudor queen' (3 June 2021), https://www.smithsonianmag.com/smart-news/who-was-first-woman-color-bring-anne-boleyns-story-screen-180977882/.

Som, V., '4 Pak fighter jets, but an Indian Air Force hero won the day', NDTV (14 September 2015), https://www.ndtv.com/india-news/4-pak-fighter-jets-but-an-indian-air-force-hero-won-the-day-1217303.

Spurling, H., *Paul Scott: A Life* (London, 1990).

St. Clair-Butler, K., *Ishq and Other Essays* (Chennai, 2019).

Stevenage, P, H., *A Railway Family in India: Five Generations of the Stevenages* (British Association of Cemeteries in South Asia, London, 2001).

Stoler, A. L., *Carnal Knowledge and Imperial Power: Race and the Intimate in Colonial Rule* (Berkeley, 2002).

Swinden, P., *Paul Scott: Images of India* (New York, 1980).

Talbot, I., and S. Thandi (eds.), *People on the Move: Punjabi Colonial and Post-colonial Migration* (Karachi, 2004).

Tarlo, E., *Clothing Matters: Dress and Identity in India* (London, 1996).

Taylor, J. G., *The Social World of Batavia: European and Eurasian in Dutch Asia* (Madison WI, 1983).

Teng, E., *Eurasian: Mixed Identities in the United States, China, and Hong Kong, 1842–1943* (Berkeley, 2013).

Tindall, G., 'Book Review: Poor Relations: The Making of a Eurasian Community in British India 1773–1833', *International Journal of Anglo-Indian Studies* 2:2 (1997), http://www.international-journal-of-anglo-indian-studies.org/.

Turner, S., *Cliff Richard: The Biography* (Oxford, 1993).

Underwood, P., *Karloff: The Life of Boris Karloff* (Grass Valley CA, 1972).

Varma, L. B., *Anglo Indians: A Historical Study of Anglo Indian Community in 19th Century in India* (New Delhi, 1979).

Venkatarangaiya, M. (ed.), *The Freedom Struggle in Andhra Pradesh (Andhra)*, vol. 2: *1906–1920 A.D.* (Andhra, 1969).

Vickers, H., *Vivien Leigh* (London, 1988).

Wade, P., 'Rethinking Mestizaje: Ideology and Lived Experience', *Journal of Latin American Studies* 37 (2005), pp. 239–57, http://dx.doi.org/10.1017/S0022216X05008990.

Wald, E., 'From Begums and Bibis to Abandoned Females and Idle Women:

Sexual Relationships, Venereal Disease and the Redefinition of Prostitution in Early Nineteenth-Century India', *Indian Economic and Social History Review* 46:1 (2009), pp. 5–25.

Wald, G., *Crossing the Line: Racial Passing in Twentieth-Century U.S. Literature and Culture* (Durham NC, 2000).

Walker, A., *Vivien: The Life of Vivien Leigh* (London, 1994).

Watson, G., *Passing for White: A Study of Racial Assimilation in a South African School* (London, 1970).

Wertheim, W. F., 'The Indo-European Problem in Indonesia', *Pacific Affairs* 20:3 (September 1947), pp. 290–8.

White, B., *Anglo-Indian Delicacies: Vintage and Contemporary Cuisine from Colonial India* (Bangalore, 2007).

———, *The Anglo-Indian Festive Hamper: Cakes, Sweets, Puddings, Cookies, Homemade Wines and More …* (Bangalore, 2007).

———, *The Anglo-Indian Snack Box: Simple Snacks, Nibbles and Short Eats* (Bangalore, 2009).

———, *The Best of Anglo-Indian Cuisine: A Legacy* (Bangalore, 2004).

———, *A Collection of Anglo-Indian Roasts, Casseroles and Bakes* (Bangalore, 2005).

———, *Flavours of the Past: The Very Best of Classic Colonial Cuisine Featuring Railway Mutton Curry and Other Popular Delicacies* (Bangalore, 2006).

———, *Kolar Gold Fields: Down Memory Lane; Paeans to Lost Glory!!* (Milton Keynes, 2010).

Williams, B. R., 'Am I My Brother's Keeper?', *International Journal of Anglo-Indian Studies* 5:2 (2000), http://www.international-journal-of-anglo-indian-studies.org/.

———, 'Anglo-Indians in the UK and India Today: 1999', *International Journal of Anglo-Indian Studies* 4:2 (2000), http://www.international-journal-of-anglo-indian-studies.org/.

———, *Anglo-Indians: Vanishing Remnants of a Bygone Era; Anglo-Indians in India, North America and the UK in 2000* (New Jersey, 2002).

———, 'On Jamalpur: Anglo-Indian Railway Officers', *International Journal of Anglo-Indian Studies* 6:2 (2001), http://www.international-journal-of-anglo-indian-studies.org/.

———, 'Whither Anglo Indians?', *International Journal of Anglo-Indian Studies* 3:1 (1998), http://www.international-journal-of-anglo-indian-studies.org/.

Williams, G. H., *Life on the Color Line: The True Story of a White Boy Who Discovered He Was Black* (New York, 1995).

Wilson-deRoze, G. A., *Origins of the Anglo-Indian Community* (Kolkata, 2001).

BIBLIOGRAPHY

Wimmer, A., *Ethnic Boundary Making: Institutions, Power, Networks* (New York, 2013).

Wolmar, C., *Railways and the Raj: How the Age of Steam Transformed India* (London, 2017).

Wolpert, S., *Shameful Flight: The Last Years of the British Empire in India* (2006).

Wright, P., *Passport to Peking: A Very British Mission to Mao's China* (Oxford, 2010).

Wright, R. D., 'The Anglo-Indian Community's Fight for Cultural Identity', *International Journal of Anglo-Indian Studies* 2:2 (1997), http://www.international-journal-of-anglo-indian-studies.org/.

———, 'The Life and Times of Henry Louis Vivian Derozio: A Legend among Anglo-Indians (Installment Number 2)', *International Journal of Anglo-Indian Studies* 5:2 (2000), http://www.international-journal-of-anglo-indian-studies.org/.

———, 'The Loss of Community among Anglo-Indians in Indian Hill Stations: The Dehra Dun Case', *International Journal of Anglo-Indian Studies* 4:1 (1999), http://www.international-journal-of-anglo-indian-studies.org/.

———, 'Reinforcing Marginality through an Invisible Culture: The Anglo-Indian Community of India', *International Journal of Anglo-Indian Studies* 5:1 (2000), http://www.international-journal-of-anglo-indian-studies.org/.

———, 'The Shattering of Cultural Identity: The Anglo-Indian Community in Rural India', *International Journal of Anglo-Indian Studies* 2:1 (1997), http://www.international-journal-of-anglo-indian-studies.org/.

Wright, R. D., and E. D. Wright, 'An Anglo-Indian Enclave within an Indian Fortress: The Grant Govan Home', *International Journal of Anglo-Indian Studies* 3:1 (1998), http://www.international-journal-of-anglo-indian-studies.org/.

Wright, R. D., and S. W. Wright, 'The Anglo-Indian Community in Contemporary India', *eScholarShare@Drake* (1971), http://escholarshare.drake.edu/bitstream/handle/2092/237/Wright%23237.pdf?sequence=1.

Yadav, D., 'A Book Review of Colonial Cousins: A Surprising History of Connections between India and Australia', *International Journal of Anglo-Indian Studies* 10:2 (2010), http://www.international-journal-of-anglo-indian-studies.org/.

Young, R. J. C., *Colonial Desire: Hybridity in Theory, Culture and Race* (New York, 1995).

Younger, C., *Wicked Women of the Raj: European Women Who Broke Society's Rules and Married Indian Princes* (New Delhi, 2004).

INDEX

Note: Page numbers followed by "*n*" refer to notes

INDEX

INDEX

INDEX

INDEX